OTHER A

THE SCARECROW PRESS, INC.

1. *The A to Z of Buddhism* by Charles S. Prebish, 2001.
2. *The A to Z of Catholicism* by William J. Collinge, 2001.
3. *The A to Z of Hinduism* by Bruce M. Sullivan, 2001.
4. *The A to Z of Islam* by Ludwig W. Adamec, 2002.
5. *The A to Z of Slavery and Abolition* by Martin A. Klein, 2002.
6. *Terrorism: Assassins to Zealots* by Sean Kendall Anderson and Stephen Sloan, 2003.
7. *The A to Z of the Korean War* by Paul M. Edwards, 2005.
8. *The A to Z of the Cold War* by Joseph Smith and Simon Davis, 2005.
9. *The A to Z of the Vietnam War* by Edwin E. Moise, 2005.
10. *The A to Z of Science Fiction Literature* by Brian Stableford, 2005.
11. *The A to Z of the Holocaust* by Jack R. Fischel, 2005.
12. *The A to Z of Washington, D.C.* by Robert Benedetto, Jane Donovan, and Kathleen DuVall, 2005.
13. *The A to Z of Taoism* by Julian F. Pas, 2006.
14. *The A to Z of the Renaissance* by Charles G. Nauert, 2006.
15. *The A to Z of Shinto* by Stuart D. B. Picken, 2006.
16. *The A to Z of Byzantium* by John H. Rosser, 2006.
17. *The A to Z of the Civil War* by Terry L. Jones, 2006.
18. *The A to Z of the Friends (Quakers)* by Margery Post Abbott, Mary Ellen Chijioke, Pink Dandelion, and John William Oliver Jr., 2006.
19. *The A to Z of Feminism* by Janet K. Boles and Diane Long Hoeveler, 2006.
20. *The A to Z of New Religious Movements* by George D. Chryssides, 2006.
21. *The A to Z of Multinational Peacekeeping* by Terry M. Mays, 2006.
22. *The A to Z of Lutheranism* by Günther Gassmann with Duane H. Larson and Mark W. Oldenburg, 2007.
23. *The A to Z of the French Revolution* by Paul R. Hanson, 2007.
24. *The A to Z of the Persian Gulf War 1990–1991* by Clayton R. Newell, 2007.
25. *The A to Z of Revolutionary America* by Terry M. Mays, 2007.
26. *The A to Z of the Olympic Movement* by Bill Mallon with Ian Buchanan, 2007.

27. *The A to Z of the Discovery and Exploration of Australia* by Alan Day, 2009.
28. *The A to Z of the United Nations* by Jacques Fomerand, 2009.
29. *The A to Z of the "Dirty Wars"* by David Kohut, Olga Vilella, and Beatrice Julian, 2009.
30. *The A to Z of the Vikings* by Katherine Holman, 2009.
31. *The A to Z from the Great War to the Great Depression* by Neil A. Wynn, 2009.
32. *The A to Z of the Crusades* by Corliss K. Slack, 2009.
33. *The A to Z of New Age Movements* by Michael York, 2009.
34. *The A to Z of Unitarian Universalism* by Mark W. Harris, 2009.
35. *The A to Z of the Kurds* by Michael M. Gunter, 2009.
36. *The A to Z of Utopianism* by James M. Morris and Andrea L. Kross, 2009.
37. *The A to Z of the Civil War and Reconstruction* by William L. Richter, 2009.
38. *The A to Z of Jainism* by Kristi L. Wiley, 2009.
39. *The A to Z of the Inuit* by Pamela R. Stern, 2009.
40. *The A to Z of Early North America* by Cameron B. Wesson, 2009.
41. *The A to Z of the Enlightenment* by Harvey Chisick, 2009.
42. *The A to Z of Methodism* edited by Charles Yrigoyen Jr. and Susan E. Warrick, 2009.
43. *The A to Z of the Seventh-Day Adventists* by Gary Land, 2009.
44. *The A to Z of Sufism* by John Renard, 2009.
45. *The A to Z of Sikhism* by W. H. McLeod, 2009.
46. *The A to Z of Fantasy Literature* by Brian Stableford, 2009.
47. *The A to Z of the Discovery and Exploration of the Pacific Islands* by Max Quanchi and John Robson, 2009.
48. *The A to Z of Australian and New Zealand Cinema* by Albert Moran and Errol Vieth, 2009.
49. *The A to Z of African-American Television* by Kathleen Fearn-Banks, 2009.
50. *The A to Z of American Radio Soap Operas* by Jim Cox, 2009.
51. *The A to Z of the Old South* by William L. Richter, 2009.
52. *The A to Z of the Discovery and Exploration of the Northwest Passage* by Alan Day, 2009.
53. *The A to Z of the Druzes* by Samy S. Swayd, 2009.
54. *The A to Z of the Welfare State* by Bent Greve, 2009.

55. *The A to Z of the War of 1812* by Robert Malcomson, 2009.
56. *The A to Z of Feminist Philosophy* by Catherine Villanueva Gardner, 2009.
57. *The A to Z of the Early American Republic* by Richard Buel Jr., 2009.
58. *The A to Z of the Russo–Japanese War* by Rotem Kowner, 2009.
59. *The A to Z of Anglicanism* by Colin Buchanan, 2009.
60. *The A to Z of Scandinavian Literature and Theater* by Jan Sjåvik, 2009.
61. *The A to Z of the Peoples of the Southeast Asian Massif* by Jean Michaud, 2009.
62. *The A to Z of Judaism* by Norman Solomon, 2009.
63. *The A to Z of the Berbers (Imazighen)* by Hsain Ilahiane, 2009.
64. *The A to Z of British Radio* by Seán Street, 2009.
65. *The A to Z of The Salvation Army* edited by Major John G. Merritt, 2009.
66. *The A to Z of the Arab–Israeli Conflict* by P R Kumaraswamy, 2009.
67. *The A to Z of the Jacksonian Era and Manifest Destiny* by Terry Corps, 2009.
68. *The A to Z of Socialism* by Peter Lamb and James C. Docherty, 2009.
69. *The A to Z of Marxism* by David Walker and Daniel Gray, 2009.
70. *The A to Z of the Bahá'í Faith* by Hugh C. Adamson, 2009.
71. *The A to Z of Postmodernist Literature and Theater* by Fran Mason, 2009.
72. *The A to Z of Australian Radio and Television* by Albert Moran and Chris Keating, 2009.
73. *The A to Z of the Lesbian Liberation Movement: Still the Rage* by JoAnne Myers, 2009.

The A to Z of the Early American Republic

Richard Buel Jr.

The A to Z Guide Series, No. 57

The Scarecrow Press, Inc.
Lanham • Toronto • Plymouth, UK
2009

Published by Scarecrow Press, Inc.
A wholly owned subsidiary of
The Rowman & Littlefield Publishing Group, Inc.
4501 Forbes Boulevard, Suite 200, Lanham, Maryland 20706
http://www.scarecrowpress.com

Estover Road, Plymouth PL6 7PY, United Kingdom

British Library Cataloguing in Publication Information Available

Library of Congress Cataloging-in-Publication Data

The hardback version of this book was cataloged by the Library of Congress as follows:

Buel, Richard, 1933–
Historical dictionary of the early American republic / Richard Buel, Jr.
p. cm. — (Historical dictionaries of U.S. historical eras ; no. 5)
Includes bibliographical references.
1. United States—History—1783-1815—Dictionaries. 2. United States—History—1815–1861—Dictionaries. I. Title. II. Series.
E301.B79 2006
973.4'03—dc22 2005022002

ISBN 978-0-8108-6840-3 (pbk. : alk. paper)
ISBN 978-0-8108-7006-2 (ebook)

∞™ The paper used in this publication meets the minimum requirements of American National Standard for Information Sciences—Permanence of Paper for Printed Library Materials, ANSI/NISO Z39.48-1992.

Printed in the United States of America

Contents

Editor's Foreword

Looking back, the first four decades of the American Republic appear rather placid and constructive, starting with the unanimous choice of George Washington as president and ending with the so-called Era of Good Feelings. However, at the time, it was anything but, marked by often violent controversies over basic principles and institutions, bitter rivalries among persons, repeated shocks between the fledgling political parties over key issues, rejection by some states of the dictates of the nation, and the hardly glorious War of 1812. It also included an acceptance, although frequently grudging, of the institution of slavery and the crude treatment of the original inhabitants. This resort to politics as usual makes the early American Republic seem less special and admirable but does not deny the many positive achievements: the creation of a working and increasingly effective government; the establishment of a two-party system with a growing electorate; cooperation between the executive, legislative, and an emerging judicial branch; expansion well beyond the original thirteen colonies; and a more assertive foreign policy.

So it is necessary to take a closer look at this formative period to make sense of the many things that happened during a relatively brief span that left a strong mark on the rest of American history. *The A to Z of the Early American Republic* is a good place to start since it provides an overview both in the introduction and then in a year-by-year chronology before examining many specific aspects of the period in the dictionary. The entries touch not only on outstanding persons, such as the presidents, leading congressmen, and the justices of the Supreme Court, but also on significant figures in the many other aspects of the new nation's development. In addition, there are entries on crucial events; the political parties; the institutions, programs, and issues before the government; and economic, social, and cultural developments. The very extensive and carefully organized bibliography is a helpful stepping-stone to books and articles that can round out the study.

This latest volume in the Historical Dictionaries of U.S. Historical Eras series fills a crucial gap and is particularly welcome since it was written by an acknowledged authority on the early American Republic, Richard Buel Jr. He taught early American history at Wesleyan University for 40 years until his retirement in 2002. During this time, he lectured on the period to thousands of students, wrote numerous articles and other papers, and authored or coauthored five books on revolutionary America and the early Republic. He also engaged in other professional activities, serving as president of the New England Historical Association and associate editor of *History and Theory*. This reference work is the culmination of a long and fruitful career and will be of considerable assistance to specialists while written with a light enough touch to interest and intrigue the general public as well.

Jon Woronoff
Series Editor

Acknowledgments

I am indebted to Neely Bruce for assistance in writing the dictionary entry on music; to David Harlow for clarification about the New Madrid earthquakes; to the National Archives and Research Administration for portrait images of Washington, Adams, Jefferson, Madison, Monroe, and Jackson as well as for the map of the Louisiana Purchase; and to the Prints and Photographs Division of the Library of Congress for the portrait image of John Quincy Adams. John Mellish's Map of the United States in 1783 (1794) is reproduced with permission of Wesleyan University's Olin Memorial Library with the technical assistance of John Wareham. Marilyn E. Buel has reviewed the entire manuscript and has given me invaluable advice on what to include to make this volume useful to readers.

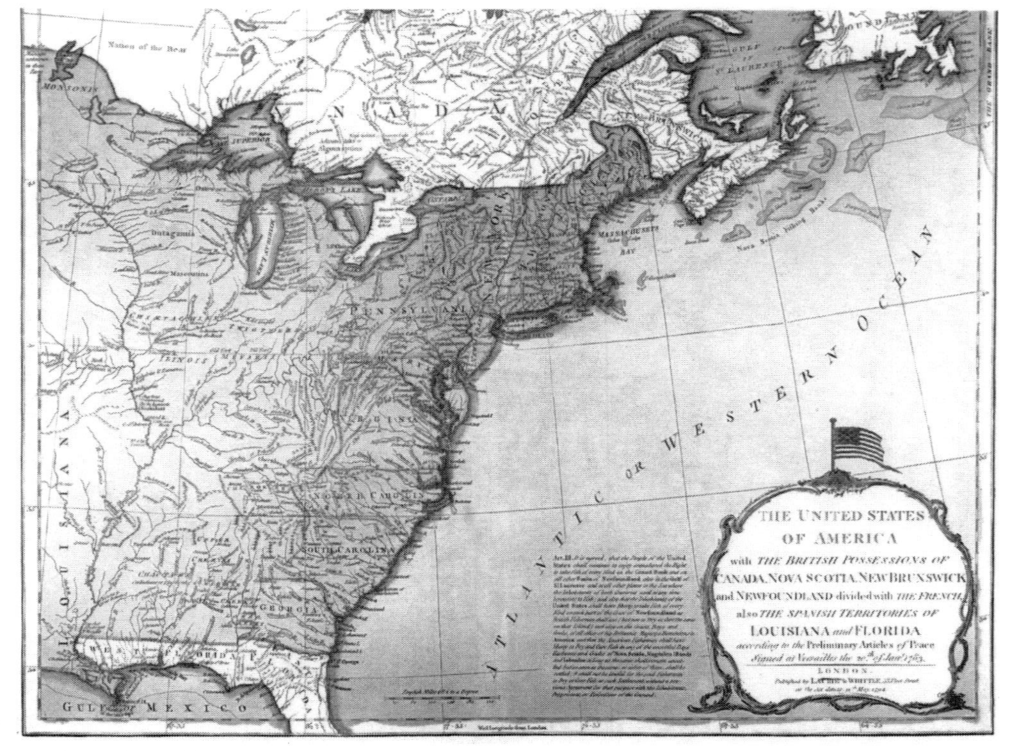

A British View of the United States as Constituted by the Peace of 1783

The Louisiana Purchase of 1803

Chronology

1789 4 February: Presidential electors in 10 states (New York had failed to designate electors because of a deadlock in its legislature) cast the first ballots to elect a president and vice president under the new federal constitution. **4 March:** first Congress begins assembling in New York City. **1 April:** House of Representatives organizes with a quorum of 30 out of 59. **6 April:** Senate has a quorum and counts the electoral ballots. George Washington unanimously elected president; John Adams vice president by a large plurality. **8 April:** House of Representatives elects its first speaker, Frederick A. Muhlenberg, of Pennsylvania. **30 April:** Washington's inauguration. **4 July:** Revenue Act of 1789 becomes law. **27 July:** Department of Foreign Affairs established.**7 August:** Department of War established. **2 September:** Treasury Department established. **11 September:** Alexander Hamilton nominated first secretary of the treasury, Henry Knox first secretary of war. **15 September:** Department of Foreign Affairs renamed Department of State. **22 September:** Office of postmaster general created. **24 September:** Judiciary Act of 1789 becomes law. **25 September:** Congress sends 12 constitutional amendments to the state legislatures for approval. **26 September:** Thomas Jefferson nominated secretary of state, Samuel Osgood postmaster general, John Jay chief justice, Edmund Randolph attorney general. **15 October–13 November:** Washington tours the New England states of Connecticut, Massachusetts, and New Hampshire. **20 November:** New Jersey becomes the first state to ratify the 10 amendments that become the Bill of Rights. **21 November:** North Carolina becomes the 12th state to ratify the Constitution.

1790 14 January: Hamilton's Report on Public Credit presented to Congress. **11 February:** Congress presented with the first petition for the abolition of slavery. **February–June:** Congressional deadlock over assuming the state debts. **29 May:** Rhode Island ratifies the Constitution, the last of the original 13 states to do so. **Late June:** Compromise between Hamilton and Jefferson and Madison in which assumption of the state debts is traded for locating the nation's capital on the Potomac. **6 July:** The House provides for the creation of the District of Columbia and designates Philadelphia as the temporary capital until 1800. **4 August:** Hamilton's plan for funding the revolutionary debt becomes law. **18–19 August:** Washington visits Rhode Island. **13 December:** Hamilton proposes the creation of a national bank. **16 December:** Patrick Henry's resolutions protesting the constitutionality of the funding law adopted by the Virginia House of Burgesses. **20 December:** Samuel Slater's water-powered spinning mill goes into production at Pawtucket, Rhode Island.

1791 February: First Bank of the United States chartered by Congress. **3 March:** A federal excise is laid on distilled liquors. **4 March:** Vermont admitted as the 14th state to the Union. **Late May–early June:** Jefferson and Madison tour New York and western New England. **31 October:** Jefferson establishes the *National Gazette* under the editorship of Philip Freneau to oppose Hamilton. **4 November:** Arthur St. Clair's military force defeated by the Ohio Indians. **26 November:** Washington consults his cabinet as a body for the first time. **5 December:** Hamilton's Report on Manufactures submitted to Congress.

1792 20 February: Post Office Act subsidizing the distribution of newspapers becomes law. **5 April:** Washington vetoes a bill for apportioning representatives in the third Congress, the first exercise of the president's veto power. **2 May:** Passage of a law enabling the president to call forth the militia to execute the laws of the Union, suppress insurrections, and repel invasions. **8 May:** Passage of a law imposing uniform standards on the state militias. **1 June:** Kentucky admitted as the 15th state to the Union. **21 August:** Four western Pennsylvania counties resolve to resist the excise on distilled liquors. **5 December:** Presidential electors reelect Washington as president unanimously; Adams reelected vice president by a majority.

1793 23 January: William Branch Giles moves that the House investigate Hamilton's management of the treasury. **12 February:** First federal statute permitting the recovery of fugitive slaves becomes law.

19 February: Supreme Court decides in *Chisholm v. Georgia* that a state can be sued without its consent. **Spring:** Eli Whitney invents the cotton gin. **11 April:** First recorded pronouncement by a republican or democratic society. **22 April:** Washington's Neutrality Proclamation. **18 May:** Edmond Genêt received as French ambassador. **31 July:** Jefferson resigns as secretary of state, effective 31 December. **2 August:** Decision made to have Genêt recalled. **14 August:** Genêt accused of appealing to the people against the Washington administration.

1794 2 January: Edmund Randolph appointed secretary of state. **5 March:** Congress proposes the Eleventh Amendment to the Constitution be adopted denying the federal judiciary jurisdiction in suits by individuals against states. **19 April:** Senate confirms John Jay as special envoy to Great Britain. **26 May:** James Monroe nominated ambassador to France. **5 June:** Passage of the Neutrality Act. **July–November:** Whiskey Insurrection in western Pennsylvania. **20 August:** Battle of Fallen Timbers. **24 September:** Washington summons 12,900 militia from four states to suppress the Whiskey Rebellion. **October–November:** The militia joined by detachments from the army suppress the Whiskey Insurrection. **19 November:** Signing of the Jay Treaty in Britain the same day Washington condemns the republican and democratic societies in an address to Congress.

1795 2 January: Timothy Pickering appointed secretary of war. **7 January:** Georgia legislature authorizes sale of 35 million acres of land in the Yazoo River basin. **29 January:** Passage of Naturalization Act requiring five years of residence to qualify for citizenship. **31 January:** Hamilton resigns as secretary of the treasury, replaced by Oliver Wolcott. **17 June:** Senate votes conditionally to ratify the Jay Treaty. **22 July:** Treaty of Greenville with the Northwest Indians signed. **12 August:** Washington decides to promulgate the Jay Treaty. **19 August:** Edmund Randolph forced to resign as secretary of state, succeeded by Timothy Pickering. **27 October:** Treaty of San Lorenzo (Pinckney's Treaty) signed.

1796 13 February: A new Georgia legislature repudiates the Yazoo land sale after much of the land is sold to northern speculators. **2 March:** Edward Livingston moves that the House of Representatives request Washington give it the diplomatic correspondence relating to the Jay Treaty. **8 March:** Supreme Court upholds the constitutionality of a carriage tax in

Hylton v. U.S. **6 May:** House votes funds to implement the Jay Treaty. **18 May:** Congress passes its first land act for the disposal of the public domain. **1 June:** Tennessee admitted as the 16th state to the Union. **Early July:** Monroe recalled as ambassador to France, replaced by Charles C. Pinckney. **17 September:** Washington's Farewell Address published. **7 December:** John Adams elected president, Jefferson vice president.

1797 **4 March:** John Adams inaugurated as second president of the United States. **31 May:** Adams responds to the Directory's rebuff of Pinckney by reappointing Pinckney along with John Marshall and Elbridge Gerry as special commissioners to France. **3 July:** Congress first learns of the Blount Conspiracy. **18 October:** Commissioners Pinckney, Marshall, and Gerry arrive in Paris.

1798 **Early April:** XYZ Dispatches from the American commissioners in Paris made public. **30 April:** Navy Department created. **28 May:** Provisional Army created. **18 June:** Naturalization Act extends the residency requirement for citizenship to 14 years. **25 June:** Alien Act and an act for the arming of merchant vessels become law. **2 July:** Washington appointed commander of the Provisional Army on condition that Hamilton exercise actual command. **7 July:** Franco-American treaties repealed by Congress. **13 July:** Commercial relations with France suspended. 14 **July:** Sedition Act and first direct tax to finance the Quasi-War with France become law. **16 November:** Kentucky Resolutions passed. **21 December:** Virginia Resolutions.

1799 **30 January:** Logan Act. **1 February:** First capture by U.S. Navy of a French armed vessel. **February:** The federal direct tax encounters resistance in northeastern Pennsylvania. **18 February:** Adams names William Vans Murray ambassador to France. **25 February into June:** Oliver Ellsworth and William R. Davie accept commissions to join Murray in negotiating with France. **7 March:** John Fries leads an armed party that frees 18 Pennsylvanians imprisoned for resisting the direct tax. **12 March:** President Adams proclaims the tax resisters led by John Fries to be traitors. **3 November:** Ellsworth and Davie sail for France. **14 December:** George Washington dies. **24 December:** Madison submits his Report of the Committee to the Virginia House of Delegates.

1800 **2 January:** Virginia House of Delegates votes to publish Madison's *Report of the Committee*. **4 April:** Federal Bankruptcy Law.

6 May: Adams asks Secretary of War James McHenry to resign. **7 May:** Indiana Territory organized. **12 May:** Adams dismisses Timothy Pickering as secretary of state, replacing him with John Marshall. **30 August:** Conspiracy of Virginia slaves known as Gabriel's Rebellion discovered. **30 September:** Treaty of Môrtefontaine (Franco-American Convention of 1800) signed. **1 October:** Treaty of San Ildefonso between France and Spain returns Louisiana to France's control. **Autumn:** Federal government moves from Philadelphia to the District of Columbia. **18 November:** News of the Convention of 1800 with France received in the United States. **3 December:** Electoral College votes.

1801 20 January: John Marshall appointed chief justice of the Supreme Court. **23 January:** Failure of the Federalist attempt to extend the life of the Sedition Act. **11 February:** Jefferson and Burr each found to have 73 votes in the Electoral College, empowering the Federalist-controlled lame-duck House to choose between them. **13 February:** Judiciary Act reorganizing the federal court system becomes law. **17 February:** Jefferson chosen president on the 36th ballot in the House. **4 March:** Jefferson inaugurated. **14 May:** Tripoli declares war against the United States. **6–12 August:** Cane Ridge camp meeting revival in Kentucky. **1 October:** Preliminaries for the Truce of Amiens between Britain and France.

1802 8 March: Judiciary Act of 1801 repealed. **16 March:** West Point established by Congress. **14 April:** Naturalization Act of 1798 repealed and the five-year residency requirement for citizenship reinstated. **24 April:** Georgia cedes western (Yazoo) lands to the United States. **30 April:** Federal government retains title to ungranted lands in the Ohio Enabling Act authorizing the drafting of a constitution preparatory to being admitted to the Union. **16 October:** Spanish intendant at New Orleans revokes U.S. right of deposit there.

1803 12 January: James Monroe appointed minister plenipotentiary to France for the purpose of buying New Orleans and West Florida. **24 February:** John Marshall declares a portion of the Judiciary Act of 1789 unconstitutional in *Marbury v. Madison*. **3 March:** Congress sets aside five million acres of the public domain to satisfy the Yazoo claimants. **11 April:** Napoleon authorizes the sale of Louisiana. **2 May:** Monroe and Robert R. Livingston sign treaty with

France for the purchase of Louisiana. **16 May:** War between Britain and France resumes. **1 June:** Ohio admitted as the 17th state to the Union. **20 October:** Senate approves a treaty with France purchasing Louisiana. **9 December:** 12th Amendment separating votes for president and vice president in the Electoral College proposed by Congress. **20 December:** United States takes possession of Louisiana. **Winter 1803–1804**: Discussions among some Federalist leaders about seceding from the Union to form a separate northern Confederacy.

1804 16 February: Destruction of the USS *Philadelphia* in Tripoli. **12 March:** Federal district judge John Pickering removed from office by impeachment. **14 May:** Meriwether Lewis and William Clark begin the ascent of the Missouri River. **11 July:** Burr–Hamilton duel. **12 July:** Death of Hamilton. **25 September:** 12th Amendment declared ratified in time for the coming presidential election. **5 December:** Jefferson reelected president by 162 out of 176 electoral votes; George Clinton elected vice president.

1805 29 January: John Randolph opposes compensating those defrauded by Georgia's repudiation of the Yazoo land sales with five million acres of the public domain. **4 June:** Signing of a peace treaty with the Barbary states. **23 July:** *Essex* decision by a British admiralty judge repudiates the doctrine of broken voyage under which the neutral colonial carrying trade had previously operated. **21 October:** Battle of Trafalgar establishing Britain's naval supremacy in the European war. **7 November:** Lewis and Clark reach the Pacific Ocean. **10 December:** Four Philadelphia insurance companies complain to Secretary of State Madison about Britain's new commercial regulations.

1806 16–21 January: New York, Boston, and Baltimore merchants memorialize Congress for redress against Britain's new commercial regulations. **25 January:** Madison's Report about the belligerents' infringements on the rights of neutrals. **7–20 February:** Merchants of Salem, Massachusetts; New Haven, Connecticut; and Norfolk and Portsmouth, Virginia, join those of the larger ports in protesting Britain's new policies. **18 April:** First Nonimportation Act against Britain, immediately suspended by Jefferson. **16 May:** Britain declares a blockade of the European coast from Brest to the Elbe. **21 November:** Napoleon's Berlin Decree declares all of Britain under blockade. **31 December:**

James Monroe and William Pinkney sign the treaty they have negotiated with Britain.

1807 7 January: British Order-in-Council bars neutral shipping from the coastal trade of France and its allies. **2 March:** Congress outlaws foreign slave trade after 1 January 1808. **March:** Jefferson decides not to forward the Monroe-Pinkney Treaty to the Senate for ratification. **22 June:** HMS *Leopard* attacks USS *Chesapeake*. **17August:** Robert Fulton's steam-powered *Clermont* successfully navigates the Hudson from New York to Albany in 32 hours. **1 September:** Burr acquitted of treason. **11 November:** A new British Order-in-Council prohibits neutral commerce with continental ports from which the British flag is excluded. **17 December:** Napoleon's Milan Decree denationalizes all neutral vessels submitting to Britain's Orders. **18 December:** Congress complies with Jefferson's request for an embargo on American shipping.

1808 9 January: First supplement to the Embargo Law. **March:** Beginning of the Spanish insurrection against French control. **9 March:** Publication of Timothy Pickering's letter to James Sullivan denouncing the embargo as a French measure that will lead to war with Great Britain. **12 March:** Second supplement to the Embargo Law. **17 April:** Napoleon's Bayonne Decree orders seizure of American vessels entering French-controlled ports. **25 April:** Third supplement to the Embargo Law. **Late May:** Federalists regain control of the Massachusetts legislature. **1 July:** Arrival of a British expeditionary force on the Iberian Peninsula. **9 August:** Boston votes to petition Jefferson to lift the embargo. **6 October:** Topsfield Convention asks the Massachusetts legislature to protect the people from the embargo if the national government refuses to repeal it. **November–January 1809:** Escalating evasions and defiance of the embargo in New England. **7 December:** Electoral College chooses James Madison president, George Clinton vice president.

1809 9 January: Final modification of the Embargo Law (the Enforcement Act) becomes law. **2 February:** Massachusetts legislature passes a bill designed to neutralize the Enforcement Act that is vetoed by Lieutenant Governor Levi Lincoln. **3 February:** Republican congressional caucus votes to lift the embargo in early March. **12 February:** Abraham Lincoln born in Kentucky. **2 March:** Embargo repealed as of March 15 and replaced with the Nonintercourse Law against

Britain and France to go into effect May 20. **3 April:** Federalist Christopher Gore defeats Republican Levi Lincoln in Massachusetts's gubernatorial election. **19 April:** Madison lifts the Nonintercourse Law against Britain in exchange for Ambassador David Erskine's pledge that Britain will repeal its Orders-in-Council. **25 May:** British government repudiates Erskine's Agreement and recalls him. **9 August:** Madison reimposes nonimportation against Britain. **29 August:** British Ambassador Francis Jackson arrives in the United States. **11 November:** Madison declares his administration will have no further dealings with Jackson and requests his recall.

1810 **16 March:** Supreme Court declares the Georgia legislature's rescinding of the Yazoo land grants unconstitutional in *Fletcher v. Peck*. **23 March:** Napoleon's Ramboullet Decree sequesters American vessels entering French ports. **1 May:** Macon's bill Number 2 becomes law, replacing the Nonintercourse Law against Britain and France with the promise to invoke it against either power should the other remove its restrictions on neutral commerce. **14 May:** Publication in France of the Ramboullet Decree made retroactive to 20 May 1809. **June:** Republicans recover control of the government of Massachusetts. **5 August:** Cadore letter conditionally revoking the Berlin and Milan decrees on November 1. **27 October:** Madison authorizes the peaceful occupation of portions of West Florida. **2 November:** Madison gives Britain three months to lift its Orders-in-Council before imposing the Nonintercourse Law.

1811 **15 January:** Congress authorizes seizure of East Florida should a foreign power (Britain) threaten to occupy it. **2 March:** Nonintercourse against Britain proclaimed. **4 March:** Charter of the Bank of the United States expires after effort to renew it fails. **1 May–Autumn:** British naval pressure on the American coast increases. **16 May:** *Lille Belt* Affair. **Mid-July:** Arrival of a new British ambassador, Augustus Foster. **5 November:** Madison recommends Congress prepare for war with Britain. **6–7 November:** Battle of Tippecanoe Creek. **16 December:** Catastrophic earthquake strikes the Mississippi Valley with an epicenter in present-day New Madrid, Missouri.

1812 **23 January:** A second major earthquake strikes the Mississippi Valley. **7 February:** Third and final major earthquake in the Mississippi Valley. **9 March:** Madison sends John Henry's Papers to Congress.

1 April: Madison asks for an embargo preparatory to war. **3 April:** Federalist Caleb Strong defeats Republican Elbridge Gerry for the governorship of Massachusetts. **25 April:** Congress creates a General Land Office under the supervision of the secretary of the treasury. **30 April:** Louisiana admitted as the 18th state to the Union. **19 June:** War declared against Great Britain. **22 June:** Britain lifts its Orders-in-Council. **2 July:** Connecticut becomes the first state officially to refuse to place its militia under federal command. **16 August:** William Hull surrenders his army at Detroit to the British without firing a shot. **19 August:** USS *Constitution* takes HMS *Guerrière*. **21 September:** Russian czar offers to mediate the Anglo-American conflict. **25 October:** USS *United States* takes HMS *Macedonian*. **23 November:** Abandonment of the American attempt to take Montreal. **28 November:** Niagara campaign abandoned. **2 December:** Electoral College reelects Madison president, Elbridge Gerry vice president. **26 December:** British proclaim a blockade of the Chesapeake and Delaware Rivers. **29 December:** USS *Constitution* takes HMS *Java*.

1813 **22 January:** Battle of Frenchtown. **8 March:** Madison receives news of czar's mediation offer. **27 April:** Burning of York, Ontario (modern Toronto). **9 May:** Siege of Fort Meigs lifted. **26 May:** British blockade extended from the race at the eastern end of Long Island Sound to the Mississippi. **27 May:** British compelled to retreat from Fort George and Fort Erie. **29 May:** Battle of Sackett's Harbor. **1 June:** Capture of the USS *Chesapea*ke by HMS *Shannon*. **6 June:** Battle of Stony Creek. **5 July:** British Foreign Minister Robert Castlereagh declines Russian mediation. **21 July:** Dispatch of American Peace Commissioners James Bayard and Albert Gallatin to join John Quincy Adams in Russia. **2 August:** British assault on Fort Stephenson. **26 and 27 August:** Napoleon's Pyrrhic victory in Battle of Dresden. **30 August:** Upper Creeks attack Fort Mims and slaughter most of those defending it. **4 September:** Boston Manufacturing Company formed. **10 September:** Oliver Perry's fleet establishes decisive control over Lake Erie. **5 October:** Battle of the Thames River. **16–19 October:** Climatic Battle at Leipzig involving more than 500,000 combatants forces Napoleon's retreat to France. **25 October:** Battle of Chateaugay. **4 November:** Britain offers direct negotiations with the United States. **12 and 13 November:** Abandonment of the attempt to take Montreal. **9 December:** Congress imposes an embargo to stop trading with the enemy. **29 December:** The British burn Buffalo.

1814 **29 March:** Battle of Horseshoe Bend. **23 May:** New England Religious Tract Society organized. **5 July:** Battle of Chippewa. **22 July:** Treaty of Greenville. **25 July:** Battle of Lundy's Lane. **2 August–16 September:** Siege of Fort Erie. **9 August:** Treaty of Fort Jackson with the Creeks. **24 August:** Battle of Bladensburg. **24–25 August:** Burning and looting of Washington. **27 August:** Monroe replaces John Armstrong as secretary of war. **3 September:** Armstrong formally resigns as secretary of war. **11 September:** Thomas Macdonough decisively checks the British invasion of New York on Lake Champlain. **12–14 September:** British attack on Baltimore repulsed. **17 September:** British retire from Fort Erie. **Mid-October:** Publication of Britain's harsh, initial terms for peace. **17 October:** Massachusetts legislature invites the other New England states to meet in convention at Hartford. **15 December:** Hartford Convention assembles. **24 December:** Peace Treaty with Britain signed at Ghent.

1815 **8 January:** Victorious conclusion to the Battle of New Orleans that had commenced 23 December. **22 January:** Madison vetoes a bill rechartering the Bank of the United States. **11 February:** Massachusetts and Connecticut commissioners arrive in Washington to arrange for New England's autonomy in defending itself the same day as the Treaty of Ghent arrives at New York. **17 February:** Senate ratifies the peace unanimously. **5 March:** Congress declares war against Algeria. **10 May:** A squadron of 10 men-of-war under Stephen Decatur sails from New York for the Mediterranean. **17 and 19 June:** Capture of two Algerian frigates. **30 June:** Dey of Algiers agrees to stop molesting American vessels. **3 July:** Commercial Convention concluded with Britain.

1816 **20 March:** Justice Joseph Story affirms that the Supreme Court has appellate jurisdiction over state court decisions in *Martin v. Hunter's Lesee*. **10 April:** Second Bank of the United States chartered. **11 May:** American Bible Society organized in New York. **27 July**: Beginning of the first Seminole War. **4 December:** James Monroe elected president, Daniel Tompkins vice president. **11 December:** Indiana admitted as the 19th state to the Union**.** **28 December:** American Colonization Society to resettle freed slaves in Africa organized.

1817 **1 January:** Second Bank of the United States opens it doors. **3 March:** Madison vetoes the Bonus Bill. **28–29 April:** Rush-Bagot Agreement. **4 July:** Construction begins on the Erie Canal. **13 and 20 September:** Publication of Congressman Daniel P. Cook's open letter to Monroe urging the abolition of slavery. **10 December:** Mississippi admitted as the 20th state to the Union. **23 December:** Most war taxes repealed.

1818 **6 January:** Andrew Jackson offers to invade Spanish Florida. **7 March:** Jackson begins operations against Florida without explicit authorization. **15 March:** Jackson tries two British subjects, Arbuthnot and Ambrister, before a military court and executes them. **25 March:** Henry Clay calls for U.S. recognition of the newly independent (from Spain) United Province of the Rio de la Plata. **20 October:** Anglo-American Convention of 1818 with Britain. **3 December:** Illinois admitted as the 21st state to the Union.

1819 **January:** Beginning of the panic of 1819. **26 January:** Taylor Amendment excluding slavery from newly formed Arkansas territory defeated. **13 February:** Tallmadge Amendment prohibiting the further introduction of slavery into Missouri and providing for gradual emancipation there. **22 February:** Adams-Onís Treaty concluded. **25 February:** Supreme Court decides that the charter of Dartmouth College protects it against state interference in *Trustees of Dartmouth College v. Woodward*. **27 February:** Senate rejects the Tallmadge Amendment. **6 March:** Supreme Court upholds the constitutionality of the Bank of the United States in *McCulloch v. Maryland*, striking down Maryland's tax on the bank's notes. **15 May:** Washington Irving's *Sketch Book* appears. **Autumn:** First treasury deficits since the end of the War of 1812. **14 December:** Alabama admitted as the 22nd state to the Union.

1820 **17 February:** Thomas Amendment to the bill for admitting Missouri to the Union excludes slavery from the remaining territories above 36°30'. **3 March:** Missouri Compromise enacted. **15 March:** Maine admitted as the 23rd state to the Union. **22 March:** Stephan Decatur dies in a duel with James Barron. **24 April:** Congress passes Land Act. **15 May:** Congress declares the foreign slave trade piracy. **19 July:** Missouri's constitution excludes all mulattoes and free blacks from the state. **6 December:** Monroe and Tompkins reelected president and vice president, almost unanimously.

1821 2 March: Missouri required to abjure laws abridging the privileges and immunities of U.S. citizens as a condition for being admitted to the Union. **4 May:** Monroe vetoes a Cumberland Road bill. **26 June:** The Missouri legislature accepts Congress's conditions for admission to the Union. **10 August:** Missouri admitted as the 24th state to the Union. **4 September:** Czar claims Pacific coast north of 51°. Calhoun announces his candidacy for the presidency. **21 December:** James Fenimore Cooper's *The Spy* published. **28 December:** Pennsylvania congressmen invite Calhoun to become a presidential candidate.

1822 27 April: Ulysses S. Grant born in Ohio. **4 May:** Congress passes act recognizing the Latin American republics. **22 May:** Monroe vetoes construction of toll gates on the Cumberland Road. **30 May:** Denmark Vesey Slave Plot is discovered. **20 July:** Tennessee legislature nominates Andrew Jackson for the presidency. **17 October:** James Fenimore Cooper publishes *The Pioneers*, the first of the Leatherstocking tales. **18 November:** Kentucky legislature nominates Henry Clay for the presidency. **31 December:** South Carolina legislature passes the Negro Seaman's Act.

1823 June: New England Religious Tract Society changes its name to American Tract Society. **17 July:** John Quincy Adams warns Russia against further colonizing the Pacific Northwest, anticipating the Monroe Doctrine. **October:** Edward Everett, editor of the *North American Review*, calls on the United States to support Greek independence. **18 October:** Charles J. Ingersoll's oration "A Discourse Concerning the Influence of America on the Mind." **2 December:** Monroe's doctrine claiming that the Americas were an exclusive sphere of influence of the United States in which the European powers should not meddle, particularly by trying to establish new colonies.

1824 14 February: Last congressional caucus nominates William H. Crawford. **15 February:** John Quincy Adams nominated for the presidency in Boston. **2 March:** Supreme Court invalidates a state monopoly because it infringes on Congress's power to regulate interstate commerce in *Gibbons v. Ogden*. **4 March:** Andrew Jackson nominated for the presidency, John C. Calhoun for vice president, by a convention in Harrisburg, Pennsylvania. **30–31 March:** Clay outlines before Congress his justification for higher tariffs on imports as part of his American system. **17 April:** Russia renounces claims to the Pacific Coast below 54°40'. **30 April:** Congress's passage of a General Survey Act lays the groundwork for the expansion of the postal service. **1 December:** Calhoun elected vice president, but none of the presidential candidates win a majority in the Electoral College.

1825 3 January: Robert Owen purchases New Harmony on the Indiana–Illinois border from George Rapp for a utopian experiment. **8 January:** Clay advises his supporters in the House of Representatives to vote for Adams as president. **9 February:** Adams elected president. **11 February:** Clay appointed secretary of state, igniting charges that Adams had concluded a corrupt bargain with him. **11 May:** New England Religious Tract Society merges with its New York counterpart to form the American Tract Society. **October:** Tennessee legislature again nominates Jackson for the presidency. **6 December:** Adams proposes an ambitious national program in his address to Congress. **26 December:** Adams nominates two delegates to attend the Panama Congress of American states.

1826 11 January: Senate Foreign Relations Committee reports unfavorably on Adams's nomination of delegates to the Panama Congress. **25 March:** Senate finally approves the Panama mission. **30 March:** John Randolph accuses Adams of a corrupt bargain to win the presidency on the floor of the Senate. **1 April:** Henry Clay challenges Randolph to a duel from which both emerge unscathed. **4 July:** Jefferson and Adams both die on the 50th anniversary of the Declaration of Independence. **26 October:** Erie Canal completed to Buffalo.

1827 2 February: Supreme Court in *Martin v. Mott* rules that the president has sole authority in determining when the state militias are to be called out to repel invasions and suppress domestic insurrections. **10 March:** Massachusetts legislature passes a law providing for public education through high school. **May:** Presbyterian synod of New York and Philadelphia calls for the abolition of slavery. **Throughout the year:** Construction of short railroad lines in Massachusetts and Pennsylvania. Samuel Slater builds an early steam-powered cotton-spinning mill in Providence, Rhode Island.

1828 Early January: Convention at Harrisburg, Pennsylvania, endorses John Quincy Adams as candidate for president. **10 May:** Congress passes a tariff known as the Tariff of Abominations. **May:** Organization of the

Workingman's Party in Philadelphia. **4 July:** Construction begun on the Baltimore and Ohio Railroad. **3 December:** Jackson elected president by an overwhelming majority of popular and electoral votes. **19 December:** South Carolina issues its "Exposition and Protest" against the tariff of 1828 and embraces a doctrine of state nullification. **30 December:** Georgia joins South Carolina in pronouncing the tariff unconstitutional.

1829 **4 February:** Virginia joins South Carolina and Georgia in condemning the tariff of 1828. **5 February:** Mississippi follows suit. **4 March:** Jackson inaugurated. **July:** Anne Royall indicted and convicted of being a common scold by a federal circuit court in Washington. **28 September:** David Walker's *Appeal to the Colored Citizens of the World* published. **8 December:** Jackson recommends distribution of surplus revenues to the states. **15 December:** First performance of John Augustus Stone's *Metamora: or the Last of the Wampanoags* in New York City.

Introduction

The drafting and ratification of the federal Constitution between 1787 and 1788 capped almost 30 years of revolutionary turmoil and warfare. The supporters of the new Constitution, known at the time as Federalists, looked to the new national government to secure the achievements of the Revolution. But they shared the same doubts that the anti-Federalists had voiced about whether the Republican form of government could be made to work on a continental scale. Nor was it a foregone conclusion that the new government would succeed in overcoming parochial interests to weld the separate states into a single nation.

During the next four decades, the institutions and precedents governing the behavior of the national government took shape, many of which are still operative today. Members of the first Congress knew that despite the greater formal powers the Constitution had granted them, they began with no more actual authority than either the Continental Congress or the Articles of Confederation had previously enjoyed. They also realized that the new government could extend its reach throughout the immense expanse of the Republic only by securing the consent of the Republic's citizenry and that the best way to do that was to solve the problems left over from the Revolution that the states had proven powerless in addressing.

CREATING AUTHORITY BY SOLVING PROBLEMS

The most intractable of these problems was the revolutionary debt. Under the Articles of Confederation, Congress had managed to reduce most of the nation's chaotic accounts to common equitable value, a process known as "liquidation." But without any revenue powers, Congress could not service that debt. The Revolutionary War had also left most of the states without the resources to do so. The few states that did have resources preferred to honor their state debts in preference to the foreign and domestic debt of the continent. Consequently, the market value of most revolutionary liquidated debts declined to a fraction of their nominal value. This undermined the authority of those responsible and attracted speculators who bought up the depreciated debt certificates, thereby arraying a minority of public creditors against a majority of public debtors. Insufficient powers also affected the new nation's relations with the European states. Dutch bankers kept the credit of the United States afloat in Europe, but the Dutch could not win U.S. merchants access to Europe's commercial empires. Without such access, full economic recovery was impossible because, despite political independence, the American economy remained essentially a colonial economy.

An imposing range of hurdles had to be overcome before the new government could address providing for the debt. Many state ratifying conventions had accepted the Constitution only on the condition that its sponsors amend it once the new government went into effect. The Federalists realized that if they reneged on this pledge, their experiment would be over before it began. That is why James Madison insisted that framing amendments to the Constitution be a priority in the initial session of the first Congress along with organizing the executive departments, creating a federal judicial system, and establishing a federal revenue. The 10 amendments that managed to meet with the approval of two-thirds of both branches of the first Congress and three-quarters of the states were appended to the original Constitution as the Bill of Rights.

After seven months of uninterrupted work, Congress wisely deferred establishing the terms on which it would honor the debt. Instead, it invited the new secretary of the treasury, Alexander Hamilton, to design a plan. When Congress reassembled in December, Hamilton was ready with his Report on Public Credit. It proposed to fund a consolidated federal debt that incorporated a large proportion of the state debts. Hamilton hoped to pay the interest due on the consolidated debt by taxing foreign imports. No one had to pay such a tax, known as an impost, unless they chose to purchase the goods so taxed. Moreover, the importing merchants would collect the impost because they expected that paying interest on the nominal sum of the debt would appreciate its value, transforming it from a liability into an asset equivalent to specie. Since the merchants held both the state and the federal debts, Hamilton was anxious to avoid arraying the two sets of creditors against each other. Combining federal and state debts into one would solve that problem but in the process create too large a consolidated debt to be serviced at 6 percent. Hamilton accordingly proposed reducing the interest to 4 percent. Though that risked alienating the creditors, Hamilton argued that funding would expand the capital resources of the nation, which in turn would drive down domestic interest rates. He may also have had his eye on the increasing turmoil of France's Revolution and have concluded that a nation that honored its debts in the New World would prove to be an attractive haven for Old World capital.

The boldness of Hamilton's scheme generated opposition among those who feared that so large a debt would perpetuate the confrontation between a majority of public debtors and a minority of public creditors that the secretary of the treasury hoped to avoid. Word of Hamilton's intentions had leaked out to interested parties before the release of his Report on Public Credit, enabling the privileged few to buy up southern state debts at bargain rates. James Madison feared that the spectacle would prejudice the public against establishing the new government's credit and proposed that the federal government instead honor its debt at 6 percent, giving the original holders roughly 50 percent of what they were due and the remainder to the final holders. Madison's discrimination also precluded assuming the state debts and was vehemently opposed by Hamilton and his followers in Congress. Though they had no difficulty defeating it, Congress deadlocked on assumption, and for a while it looked as though Hamilton's plan would come to nothing.

Jefferson, who had only recently returned from France to assume the office of secretary of state, helped orchestrate a compromise in which Madison and his followers agreed to assumption in exchange for locating the nation's capital on the Potomac. Jefferson and Madison quickly regretted the compromise when Hamilton subsequently proposed that Congress create a national bank. Hamilton proposed using the funded debt of the United States as the bank's capital on which it would issue bank notes having a common value throughout the nation. They feared that such a bank would enable the executive of the new government to manage Congress as Britain's ministers were thought to manage Parliament. But Madison was reluctant to obstruct the progress already made in establishing the new government's credit. So he opposed the bank strictly on constitutional grounds that it was neither necessary nor proper to the exercise of Congress's delegated powers, hoping that Washington would veto the bill. Washington declined to do so.

Though the federal revenue from the impost initially fell short of the funding scheme's requirements, it nonetheless proved stunningly successful. Few objected to the reduction in the interest, and by 1792 the value of the funded securities had risen close to par, in part because of the flight of capital from Europe. Hamilton exploited his success by presenting Congress with a Report on Manufactures, which advocated paying bounties for the domestic manufacture of products the nation had imported during the Revolutionary War. Hamilton also proposed an excise tax on domestically distilled liquors to help cover the revenue gap. But since it would be a while before this tax could be productive, he turned to Dutch bankers in the interim. Congressman William Branch Giles, acting for Virginians suspicious of Hamilton's success, called for an inquiry into his activities. It failed to yield the desired result because of the immediate success of Hamilton's funding system. In the longer term, war in Europe made the impost more than adequate in meeting the requirements of funding by enhancing the demand for American staples and the services of the nation's neutral flag.

RESPONDING TO THE EUROPEAN WAR

War between France and Britain followed the declaration that France was a republic and the execution of Louis XVI in January 1793. Both of the principal protagonists in this war had colonial possessions in the New World proximate to, if not bordering on, the United States. The nation also owed its independence to a strategic alliance with France that was still in force. Washington issued a proclamation requiring U.S. citizens to treat both powers impartially. Though the United States was bound to help France defend its West Indian possessions, the French republic understood that Britain's enormous sea power limited what the United States could do. Instead, the French ambassador, Edmund Genêt, wanted to use the United States as a base for privateering and conquering the New World possessions of Britain and its ally Spain. Genêt's activities led to his recall. A group of prominent Federalist gentry, who valued good relations with Britain over the French alliance, then sought to humiliate the French ambassador. Jefferson, who preferred cultivating good relations with France at the expense of an understanding with Britain, resigned as secretary of state. The British government, assuming that the United States was still allied with France, started forcing U.S. ships making for France to enter British ports and dispose of their cargoes there. Then, at the end of 1793, Britain seized more than 400 American vessels in the Caribbean. Finally, the British allowed the Barbary states to prey on American shipping while the governor-general of Canada urged the Indians on the Northwest frontier to prepare for hostilities.

Washington sent John Jay, the first chief justice of the Supreme Court, on a special mission to avert war with Britain. Both countries had failed fully to adhere to the peace of 1783: Britain by refusing to surrender the Northwest forts in American territory and to compensate masters for the value of the slaves it had carried off and the United States by neglecting to resettle loyalists and collect the private debts due to Britons. Jay came back with a treaty that settled these issues but raised another more important one. He agreed to allow Britain to force U.S. ships making for France into British ports where cargoes that were not contraband would be sold. And he failed to win the commercial concessions in the West Indies that Americans felt entitled to as compensation for Britain's retention of the Northwest forts.

The Senate conditionally approved the Jay Treaty, and Washington promulgated it in the face of widespread public disapproval. Since its terms required the establishment of a joint commission to settle the outstanding claims of both parties, a struggle took place in the House of Representatives over voting the funds needed for implementation. The prolonged battle over the treaty polarized American politics by spreading the division within the nation's political leadership over whether to court Britain or France to the public at large. The stakes were higher than at first it might appear because leaning toward one power risked provoking war with the other. France encouraged such anxieties by declaring that it intended to equalize its treaty relationship with the United States and seize American shipping as Britain did. Its ambassador also tried to interfere in the presidential election of 1796 by threatening to sever relations with the United States if Jefferson was not elected Washington's successor. The prospect of war with either power frightened Americans who remembered that victory in the Revolution had required a prolonged alliance with France. Each party thus had positive reasons for wanting to avoid war with the power it favored that were reinforced by the assumption that such a conflict would lead to dependence on the power it loathed.

France began seizing American vessels on the high seas as John Adams assumed the presidency in March 1797. Simultaneously, word arrived that France had refused to receive Charles C. Pinckney as the American ambassador. Pinckney had been appointed by Washington to replace James Monroe, who, instead of reconciling the French to the Jay Treaty, had taken France's side against his own government. Adams immediately reappointed Pinckney to an enlarged commission to which John Marshall of Virginia and Elbridge Gerry of Massachusetts were joined. But Talleyrand, the French foreign minister, refused to receive them when they arrived in Paris. Instead, he dealt indirectly with them through agents designated in the dispatches as X, Y, and Z. These agents demanded as the price of peace with France an apology for statements made by Adams about the Directory, a substantial loan that would compromise the U.S. relationship with Britain, and bribes. The commissioners broke off the negotiation and sent their report back to the United States, where their dispatches created a sensation on being made public.

The release of the XYZ dispatches shifted the even balance between Federalists and Republicans in Congress decisively in the Federalists' favor. They used the windfall to launch a limited war against France in informal alliance with Britain. American merchantmen were armed to defend themselves against French corsairs while the U.S. Navy attacked the armed vessels of France. Congress also sanctioned an expansion of the army, over which Washington assumed titular command, though Hamilton exercised actual command. While the Federalist program created many new offices to which the administration could appoint its supporters, it also cost money. To meet these costs, Congress laid its first direct tax. Many Federalists hoped France would declare war against the United States because such a development would purge the American public of their affection for France. But since they could not be sure France would oblige and did not wish to assume the responsibility for initiating a war, Congress passed several measures designed to limit French influence. First, they lengthened the residency requirement required for naturalization. Then they gave the president summary authority to deport aliens even when their nation was not officially at war with the United States. Finally, they vested jurisdiction over seditious libels against the federal government in the federal courts.

Jefferson and Madison, the leaders of the Republican opposition, had no place to turn in resisting these measures except the states. Both penned resolutions, Jefferson for the Kentucky legislature and Madison for the Virginia legislature, that challenged the constitutionality of the Alien and Sedition Laws. Jefferson's draft went further than Madison's in pronouncing federal laws "null and void" in the state of Kentucky. Madison's resolutions were worded as a legislative statement of opinion rather than a judicial declaration, or at least that was the interpretation he put on them in his 1800 Report to the Virginia legislature countering the hostile response of eight states to its Resolutions. Madison's Report argued that the Sedition Law threatened the capacity of the people to call their elective representatives to account. But the election of Jefferson to the presidency, often referred to as the Revolution of 1800, depended on peace with France as much as on the Sedition Law's incompatibility with Republicanism.

In the spring of 1799, Adams announced that he was appointing a new set of commissioners to seek a negotiated settlement with France. He acted in response to communications from Elbridge Gerry, who had tarried in Paris after his fellow commissioners had returned home, that Talleyrand was receptive to a negotiated settlement. Adams realized that if the Quasi-War with France ever became a full-scale war, it could lead to national dissolution. Most of his cabinet, inherited from the previous administration, opposed his decision but had to temper their opposition lest Adams resign in Jefferson's favor. Instability in the French government held up the mission for almost a year. After the commissioners had been dispatched, Adams moved against Hamilton, whom Adams feared intended to use the army for a coup, by dismissing James McHenry and Timothy Pickering. As secretaries of war and state, respectively, they were more loyal to Hamilton than to Adams. Hamilton responded by penning a pamphlet critical of Adams designed to persuade Federalist electors to vote for Charles C. Pinckney rather than Adams. Hamilton wrote for his fellow Federalists, but a Republican printer got hold of a copy and published it. The rift in Federalist ranks on the eve of the presidential election ensured that the Franco-American Convention of 1800 with France, which settled most of the outstanding problems between the two countries, benefited the Republicans more than the Federalists.

THE JEFFERSONIAN ASCENDANCY

The two Republican candidates, Jefferson and Aaron Burr, received the same number of votes in the Electoral College, throwing the decision to the lame-duck House of Representatives that the Federalists still controlled. After attempting in vain to secure pledges from both candidates that Federalist accomplishments would be respected, they finally elected Jefferson. Next to the dismantling of their fiscal system, the Federalists most feared that the Republicans would align the nation with France. But a truce between the great European powers later in the year temporarily relieved them of this anxiety. Instead, Napoleon's interest in New World adventures made Jefferson consider allying with Britain against France. But after losing an army to tropical disease in Santo Domingo, Napoleon decided to sell France's claims in continental North America to the United States. The Louisiana Purchase was arranged by Robert R. Livingston and James Monroe. In exchange for $15 million, France agreed to renounce its claims to New Orleans and all the lands it had ceded to Spain in 1762. The purchase eliminated France as a threat to the United States just as the European war resumed in 1803.

Die-hard Federalists were not reconciled to Jefferson's achievement because they feared it would confer permanent power on the Republicans. Republican strength was concentrated in the South and West, and they felt that the vast new lands in the West would simply add to the Republicans' supremacy. Nor were they relieved that France no longer confronted the United States on the continent because they construed France's evolution into a military dictatorship as confirmation of a course that all republics were likely to follow. This led them to perceive the Republican attack on the federal judiciary, which the Federalists had tried to monopolize, and passage of the Twelfth Amendment, designed to avoid the deadlock that had developed during the election of 1800, as replicas of France's contempt for the rule of law. Federalists also viewed Jefferson and Madison either as Napoleonic usurpers or as the emperor's terrified accomplices. When the Federalist presidential candidate garnered less than 10 percent of the electoral votes in 1804, they despaired. So bleak did the future look to some New England Federalists that they discussed among themselves the feasibility of seceding from the Union. Nothing immediately came of these discussions beyond the common knowledge that they were centered in Massachusetts.

The European war's effect on the United States changed in 1805 after a British admiralty court ruled that indirect voyages carrying French colonial goods to Europe were illegal. The ruling struck at one of the principal sources of America's wartime prosperity. Shortly afterward, Britain's decisive defeat of the combined French and Spanish fleets at Trafalgar conferred on it a naval supremacy that enabled it to enforce the Rule of 1756 denying neutral nations a trade in wartime that they had not enjoyed during peacetime. At the same time, Napoleon's successes in central Europe placed the entire continent at his mercy. With each of the great powers supreme in one element—land or sea—but unable to get at its adversary in the other, both tried to strike at the other indirectly through its commerce. This bore harshly on American ships that had become the principal neutral carriers of the world's seaborne commerce. Britain began by proclaiming a blockade of the European coast from Brest to the Elbe. France retaliated with the Berlin Decree declaring all of Britain under blockade and commerce between Britain and the continent at an end.

Jefferson responded to the European situation by dispatching James Monroe and William Pinkney on a special mission to address Britain's commercial restrictions. Its widening blockades also led the British navy increasingly to impress seamen off American vessels to man its fleet. Congress tried to strengthen the American hand by passing a Nonimportation Act barring British imports from America if the negotiations failed. Britain refused to budge on impressment or to change its interpretation of the Rule of 1756 except in minor respects. Monroe and Pinkney nonetheless signed an agreement with the British that Jefferson declined to submit to the Senate for ratification. France's actions seemed less threatening because of the inferiority of its naval force. In the Franco-American Convention of 1800, it had also forsworn taking commercial measures against the United States.

In January 1807, Anglo-American relations took a turn for the worse when a new British Order-in-Council banned neutral vessels from the coastal trade of Europe. Then in June, a British warship, HMS *Leopard*, attacked the USS *Chesapeake* as it cleared from Chesapeake Bay, inflicting 21 casualties (three fatal) in removing four seamen alleged to be British deserters. Coincidentally, the Treaty of Tilsit, which established an alliance between Napoleon and the czar, extended to operation of the emperor's continental boycott against Britain. Britain responded in November with a new Order-in-Council banning neutrals from entering European ports from which the British flag had been excluded unless they first entered a British port and paid duties there. Napoleon retaliated at the beginning of 1808 by denationalizing any neutral vessel that submitted to Britain's regulations in his Milan Decree.

Well before news of this last measure arrived in the United States, the American ambassador in France reported that the United States could no longer expect exemption from France's commercial restrictions under the Franco-American Convention of 1800. Congress responded to this information and unofficial notice of the Order-in-Council requiring neutrals making for Europe to first enter British ports by laying the general embargo on American shipping that Jefferson had requested. The measure was designed to conserve national resources in the face of the threatening behavior of both European powers and to buy time to explore alternatives to war. Jefferson and Madison also hoped the cessation of American commerce might affect the belligerent powers as much as their restrictions were affecting the United States and thus bring about a peaceful resolution to the crisis. Britain still looked like the more threatening power, but a new British ambassador, George Rose, had arrived just as the embargo was going into effect.

Unfortunately, that mission ended in Rose's dismissal just as the approach of spring brought the embargo into conflict with the seasonal scheduling of overseas voyages. Timothy Pickering, the junior senator from Massachusetts, chose that moment to attack the embargo in a public letter addressed to Governor James Sullivan of Massachusetts. Pickering alleged that the administration was contemplating war with Britain in alliance with France. The Republicans had recently captured political control of this strategic state, which was still the fourth largest in the Union. Pickering hoped to use the embargo to reestablish Federalist supremacy there. The spring elections led to Federalist majorities in both houses of the Massachusetts legislature. Massachusetts Federalists then passed resolutions condemning the embargo and insisted on naming Federalist electors in the next presidential election. After the legislature adjourned, Boston orchestrated a series of town meetings and county conventions that questioned the constitutionality of the embargo, threatening radical remedies if the measure were not repealed. The Federalists were aided in neutralizing the embargo by British proclamations assuring American vessels they would be welcome in

British ports without proper papers and by Britain's role in the Spanish insurrection against Napoleon's rule that created a demand for American staples to provision the British expeditionary force on the Iberian Peninsula.

ORIGINS OF THE WAR OF 1812

The Federalists failed to exert much influence over the presidential election of 1808 despite the embargo. Madison, the nominee of the Republican congressional caucus, won handily despite his identification with commercial restrictions. But the Federalists did succeed in increasing their strength in Congress and in recovering control over all the New England state governments except Vermont. They then forced repeal of the embargo despite Congress's passage of an Enforcement Act in early January that authorized the use of the military in its support. Instead of obedience, the Enforcement Act led to increased defiance. The Massachusetts legislature passed a bill making obeying aspects of the federal embargo a state crime. Though Lieutenant Governor Lincoln vetoed the bill (Sullivan having died in the interim), the legislature humiliated him so thoroughly as to preclude his reelection. The threatening declarations of the Massachusetts legislature also intimidated the Republicans in Congress into modifying the embargo so that it only affected commerce with Britain and France instead of declaring war against one or both powers. The new measure, known as the Nonintercourse Law of 1 March 1809, lifted the embargo on 15 March and gave the president authority to lift nonintercourse against either power should it repeal its commercial restrictions against the United States.

The British ambassador, David Erskine, took advantage of the Nonintercourse Act to strike a deal with the Madison administration. In exchange for lifting nonintercourse against Britain, he pledged that the British Orders-in-Council would be repealed on 20 May. After Madison issued the required proclamation on 19 April, hundreds of vessels that had cleared American ports with the removal of the embargo were free to make for British ports. However, the British government repudiated Erskine's Agreement when they learned of it on the grounds that Erskine had exceeded his instructions. Madison reimposed nonintercourse against Britain but not before France took offense. It regarded nonintercourse as directed principally against French interests and in the Ramboullet Decree of August 1810—made retroactive until 20 May 1809—seized all American vessels that happened to be in French-controlled ports. The Republicans' restrictive system was clearly in tatters.

Britain sent a new minister to the United States in the wake of its repudiation of the Erskine Agreement, but Francis Jackson was empowered only to listen to propositions from the U.S. government. Madison's dismissal of him in November 1809 led to a vitriolic controversy in which the Federalists took the side of the British government. They alleged that the president had known in advance of Erskine's instructions and had purposely drawn him into an agreement that his home government would repudiate so as to provoke war with Britain. However, Congress hardly behaved in a warlike fashion during the winter of 1809–1810. Under Nathaniel Macon's leadership, it fashioned a minimal alternative to nonintercourse that repealed all commercial restrictions for the moment, promising only to reinvoke them against one of the great powers should it fail to follow the other's example of abandoning its restrictions against neutral commerce.

Though criticized at the time for indecisiveness, Congress's offer was more to France's interest than Britain's because of Britain's naval superiority. In August 1810, the duke of Cadore notified the American ambassador that France would revoke its decrees against American commerce if the United States imposed nonintercourse against Britain should Britain fail to follow suit. On 2 November, Madison gave Britain three months in which to respond. Five days before, Madison had ordered the occupation of as much of Spanish West Florida as could be peacefully seized. Though Britain was currently Spain's ally, Madison did not want Britain taking advantage of the disintegration of Spain's New World empire to seize Florida for itself. Having embarked on a course of confrontation with Britain, he proclaimed nonintercourse against it on 2 February 1811.

Another British ambassador, Augustus Foster, arrived in America over the summer but fared no better than his two predecessors. He argued with some justification that France's repeal of its decrees against neutral commerce was bogus and that Britain's Orders were justified retaliation. Republicans acknowledged that France had not done everything desired but pointed out that Britain had done nothing. In November, Madison asked Congress to make such preparations for war with Britain as the temper of the country demanded. A majority of the state legislatures then passed resolves that showed they agreed with the Republican position while expressing rising anger at the continued impressments of American seamen. Foster misjudged the situation because he listened to the Federalists, who assured him that the Republicans were bluffing about war. So great was the respect the Federalists had for British power that they did not believe their adversaries meant to pick a fight with that nation while they remained unprepared for hostilities. The Federalists, who controlled most of the nation's banking capital after the charter of the First Bank of the United States expired in 1811, refused to support military preparations, while the Republicans did not wish to risk the political consequences of raising taxes.

British intransigence interacted with Republican fears of Federalism to propel the nation toward a war despite lack of preparations. Two developments pushed the Republican leaders onward. First, their constituents were thoroughly exasperated with Britain and the Federalists. If the Republicans in Congress allowed themselves to be humiliated again as a Federalist minority in association with Britain had humiliated them over the embargo, they feared that Republican principles would cease to command the loyalty of the rising generation. Second, the Madison administration had purchased the papers of a British spy, John Henry, which proved that the British government considered New England Federalists allies in subverting the American Republic. The administration released the Henry correspondence in March. On 1 April, after the latest dispatches from Europe indicated that Britain was no closer to yielding to American demands, Madison requested Congress lay a temporary embargo preparatory to a declaration of war. On 1 June, he asked for a formal declaration. The House responded almost immediately, but the Senate dickered for over a week before finally assenting. War was proclaimed on 19 June 1812.

THE WAR OF 1812

On 22 June, the British cabinet decided to revoke its Orders-in-Council. When news of their action arrived in the New World, there were immediate calls on both sides for a truce. Madison had no choice but to rebuff them given the political fragility of the Republican coalition sponsoring the war. It could not be turned on and off without risking total disintegration. But the groundswell of opposition the Federalists hoped would greet the war failed to materialize despite the disasters accompanying the first campaign. The Republicans saw Canada as a British hostage in North America and hoped that seizing it would compel Britain to respect American rights. They expected to conquer because the United States was 10 times more populous, and they assumed that most Canadians would prefer to be American if given the chance. But Americans lacked the military experience of Britain's troops, particularly its officers. Britain could also count on the loyalty of the Northwest Indians. They had rallied to the British cause under the leadership of Tecumseh and his brother Shawnee, the prophet, and William Henry Harrison's victory at Tippecanoe Creek in November 1811 had done little to shake their attachment to the British cause. The first American attempt to invade Upper Canada under William Hull ended in the surrender of the entire American force at Detroit. Subsequent efforts to attack Canada along the Niagara frontier and to move against Montreal came to naught. The only American victories occurred where they were least expected: against the British navy. In August, the USS *Constitution* took HMS *Guerrière*; in October, the USS *United States* captured HMS *Macedonian*; and at the end of December, the USS *Constitution* destroyed HMS *Java*.

The early months of the conflict hardly reconciled the Federalists to the war. Connecticut led Massachusetts and Rhode Island in refusing to put their state militias under federal command. At this point, however, New England was more interested in removing Madison from the presidency than opposing the war effort. In the election of 1812, the Federalists threw their support to DeWitt Clinton, a peace Republican and nephew of George Clinton, who had been vice president between 1805 and 1811. Though Clinton's running mate was Pennsylvanian Jared Ingersoll, Clinton's failure to carry Pennsylvania ensured Madison's reelection by a solidly Republican South and West. Federalist gains in Congress, however, would complicate the government's task of managing the remainder of the war.

Britain was slow in bringing its naval preponderance to bear in blockading the U.S. coast during 1812. The initial desire to defuse hostilities together with the capture of the *Guerrière* had forced Britain to concentrate its sea force, thus allowing American privateers to wreak havoc on British merchantmen. Only at the end of the year did they proclaim a blockade of the Chesapeake and Delaware Bays. Elsewhere, British licenses protected American vessels carrying grain to Britain's forces on the Iberian Peninsula, though these same licenses exposed them to capture by American privateers. In 1813, Britain began extending their formal blockade northward to Rhode Island and southward to New Orleans. Having failed to make much headway against Britain during the campaign of 1812, Madison was eager to accept the Russian czar's offer of mediation, which he learned of in March 1813. That, of course, did not relieve the nation from prosecuting the struggle in the near term. But it did lead to the appointment of peace commissioners, one of whom, Albert Gallatin, had to resign as secretary of the treasury to accept this appointment.

The United States fared only marginally better in the campaign of 1813 than it had in 1812. An early engagement in the West led to another American defeat at Frenchtown, Ohio, in January. But Harrison succeeded in defending Fort Meigs, to which American forces had fallen back, against enemy assault in May, and the British again were repulsed at Fort Stephenson on the Sandusky River in August. American forces in the West had no choice but to stand on the defensive while the British remained in naval control of Lake Erie. In September, Oliver Perry managed to defeat the British fleet on the lake, compelling the British to withdraw from Detroit and Malden. Harrison then invaded western Ontario and at Moravian Town, on the Thames River, defeated the British. The engagement cost Tecumseh his life, thus bringing to an end his attempt to forge a united Indian confederation against American expansion. But elsewhere along the Canadian frontier, American operations bogged down badly. Though an American force managed to take and burn York (modern Toronto) in April, it accomplished little of significance for the rest of the year. A two-pronged attempt to take Montreal also shipwrecked after one force advancing down the St. Lawrence was routed in an engagement at Chrystler's Farm, while the other, under Wade Hampton, suffered defeat in the Battle of Chateaugay. The Canadian campaign of 1813 ended with the British burning Buffalo. Six months before, the USS *Chesapeake* had fallen to HMS *Shannon* in a naval duel off Boston.

The inconclusiveness of the military campaign against Canada fueled Federalist opposition to the conflict. Though Connecticut cooperated with federal authorities in defending Stephen Decatur's squadron in

New London, it continued to refuse to place its militia under federal command. The Massachusetts Supreme Court affirmed the right of the state's governor, Caleb Strong, rather than the president, to decide when and where state forces should be deployed. Massachusetts and Rhode Island each made token cooperation with the national government dependent on receiving arms from it. In Congress, Daniel Webster proposed resolutions requiring Madison to disclose the evidence that France had repealed its decrees affecting U.S. commerce, thus challenging the moral basis for declaring war. And Federalists inside and outside Congress actively opposed loaning money to support the war effort. Many expected a negotiated settlement despite Britain's rejection of the Russian offer of mediation because of the changing course of the European war.

The combined effect of the battles of Dresden and Leipzig in 1813 placed Napoleon on the defensive and forced the withdrawal of French forces to their own borders. The decline of French power, culminating in Napoleon's abdication on 6 April 1814, led the British government to seek revenge against America as the British public had long been demanding. In the spring of 1814, renewed attempts by American forces to invade Canada on the Niagara River frontier issued in inconclusive battles at Chippewa and Lundy's Lane before Britain went on the offensive with reinforcements drawn from Europe. This compelled the American invaders to take refuge in Fort Erie, where they endured a siege lasting a month and a half before the British retired. Further to the east, a major British attempt to invade New York via Lake Champlain was eventually halted by Thomas Macdonough's flotilla in a decisive engagement with the British fleet near Plattsburgh. British forces experienced greater success in ravaging the Chesapeake area and burning Washington. After the American defenders failed to halt a British advance at Bladensburg, Maryland, on 24–25 August, the invaders torched the capitol on 24–25 August. Three weeks later, the British mounted a less successful assault on Baltimore. But in the beginning of September, they extended their July occupation of Eastport, Maine, to include Castine.

At this point, the first reports from the American peace commissioners at Ghent arrived with Britain's demands. They included retaining any territory Britain possessed when hostilities ceased, the cession of a vast portion of the Northwest to create an Indian protectorate under British control, a monopoly of naval force on the Great Lakes, and the right to navigate the Mississippi. In addition, the United States would lose a privilege it had enjoyed since independence of drying fish on the coast of Newfoundland. These demands dashed any hope for a speedy peace because no American government could accept such terms. Governor Strong of Massachusetts responded by summoning the Massachusetts legislature into emergency session. They in turn issued a call for delegates from the other New England states to meet at Hartford in the middle of December 1814. The convention would make provision for their own defense and propose amendments to the Constitution. In the interim, Americans expected to learn the fate of an expedition that the British were mounting against New Orleans.

During the summer of 1813, a portion of the Creek nation had risen in rebellion against American settlers encroaching on their lands, leading at the end of August to the massacre of 250 Americans at Fort Mims. Tennessee and Georgia retaliated by destroying several villages before the Indians dealt Tennessee forces a string of demoralizing defeats in January 1814. Only in March did Andrew Jackson manage to defeat the Creek at Horseshoe Bend and subsequently to force a peace on them that involved ceding their Alabama lands. These victories emboldened Jackson to move against Spanish Florida and seize Pensacola without authorization. They also positioned him to respond promptly when he learned that a large British force of veterans under Sir Edward Pakenham was threatening New Orleans. Rushing westward, Jackson managed to rally sufficient forces to check Pakenham's advance and decisively defeat the British in a series of engagements between 23 December 1814 and 8 January 1815. Definitive news of this victory, however, did not arrive in Washington until early February at the same time that the Treaty of Ghent, bringing an end to the war with Britain on the basis of the status quo antebellum, was received.

The conjunction of events coincided with the arrival of commissioners appointed by Massachusetts and Connecticut to convey the terms the Hartford Convention had decided to demand for their and Rhode Island's continued participation in the Union. In addition to autonomy in defending themselves, which left them free to conclude a separate peace with Britain, the Convention had framed a series of amendments to the Constitution designed to enhance New England's power at the expense of the South. Both demands were premised on the Republic's imminent collapse. Since instead of crumbling the Republic had survived despite everything the Federalists had done to ensure it would not, the commissioners withdrew in disgrace. Federalist claims that the war had failed to achieve any of the objectives for which it had been waged fell on deaf ears since everyone but the Federalist minority felt it was victory enough for the Republic to have survived with a disloyal opposition in its midst. They also assumed that the United States would not have to face such a challenge again and that they would fare better in the next contest with Britain as a united people.

THE ERA OF GOOD FEELINGS

The peace of Ghent immediately restored the nation's finances. During 1815, an avalanche of imports swelled the yields from the impost to a point where, at the end of the year, Madison could predict—accurately as it turned out—that the nation would be debt free by the 1830s. This allowed Congress to repeal many of the wartime taxes it had imposed, most of which had gone into effect only after the peace. The renewed availability of specie also allowed Congress to charter a Second Bank of the United States in 1816 based on hard-money assets. The bank's notes provided the nation with a circulating medium of uniform value that helped stimulate a dramatic economic expansion. The Depression of 1819 only briefly halted that expansion. In 1817, construction began on the Erie Canal, a project financed by the issuance of New York state bonds. By 1825, the entire canal to Buffalo had been completed, and the traffic it generated enabled the state to retire the cost of its construction in seven years. This proved to be the most successful of the many turnpike, steamboat, and canal projects that provided the infrastructure for the emergence of a truly national market. Though American business cycles would remain tied to the export of cotton until the Civil War, the U.S. economy at last had begun to transcend its colonial past.

The federal government failed to keep pace with the expansion of settlement and the development of the economy. National politics lost the unwelcome structure that the European wars had given the First Party System. The humiliation inflicted on the Federalists by a peace as favorable as it was unexpected led most older Federalists to retire from national politics, while the younger ones sought new political identities. They excused their abandonment of Federalism on the grounds that the

Republicans had finally learned the lessons the Federalists had been trying to teach them. But the first national political parties had been divided less over the powers of the federal government than with which of the belligerents the Republic should align itself. Relieved of the pressure to make this choice, the national parties degenerated into factional groupings dominated by the question of who would be James Monroe's successor after he succeeded Madison as president. The chief contenders by 1820 were John Quincy Adams, Andrew Jackson, Henry Clay, John C. Calhoun, and William Crawford.

All had distinguished themselves during the War of 1812, but since the peace, Adams had the advantage of serving as Monroe's secretary of state after 1817. Capitalizing on the Rush-Bagot Agreement of that year, in which Britain and the United States agreed to demilitarize the Great Lakes, the Anglo-American Convention of 1818 specified the 49th parallel as the northern boundary of the Republic from Lake of the Woods in Minnesota to the continental divide and provided for joint occupation west of the divide by both nations. In addition, American fishing rights along the coasts of Newfoundland and Labrador were restored. Adams's greatest diplomatic triumph, however, was the treaty he negotiated in 1819 in which Spain ceded to the United States East Florida and all its claims west of Louisiana and north of the 42nd parallel to the Pacific Ocean. He also was the principal formulator of the Monroe Doctrine. These achievements made Adams one of the most distinguished secretaries of state in U.S. history.

Only Jackson enjoyed a distinction that rivaled Adams's. In addition to his successes in the Creek War and his triumph at New Orleans, he had been the commanding officer in the war against the Seminole Indians in 1818, during which he had tried and then hanged two British subjects, Alexander Arbuthnot and Robert Ambrister. Though Jackson's preemptory conduct came under fire in the House and Senate, his success in establishing military control over East Florida had enabled Adams to issue an ultimatum to the Spanish Court to cede the province. Both Adams and Jackson had national political followings that set them apart from the other contenders. But the divided field left no candidate with a majority, thus throwing the election into the House of Representatives voting by states.

Jackson had the most popular votes, but Adams eventually became president after Clay threw his support to him. Adams then appointed

Clay secretary of state, a position that had been used as a stepping-stone by the last four presidents to the highest office in the land. Fearing that Adams was prejudicing his future, Jackson attacked Adams for making a corrupt bargain. This helped ensure that Adams's presidency would achieve little despite an ambitious national program outlined in his inaugural address. Congress tied his hands in the realm of foreign affairs, contributing to the failure of the United States to be represented at the hemispheric conference in Panama during 1826. Jackson's unambiguous triumph in the election of 1828 capped the humiliations of Adams's presidency.

The one national issue that threatened to interfere with the factional struggles of the 1820s was slavery. During the American Revolution, enslaved Africans had been ready enough to abandon their masters or to earn their freedom by fighting for the nation's independence, but they had not constituted a revolutionary force in their own right. The success of the Haitian Revolution in the early 1790s changed this. Many white masters fleeing to the United States brought their slaves with them. They in turn communicated to their fellow Africans that a slave uprising had succeeded. Masters took notice. Both Gabriel's Rebellion in 1801 and Denmark Vesey's Rebellion in 1822 were nipped in the bud, but their repression dramatized the new revolutionary potential of African slaves. After the first Congress dismissed a Quaker petition for abolition in 1790, slavery did not seriously intrude on national politics until the controversy over admitting Missouri to the Union in 1819–1821. The Missouri Territory, stretching to the continental divide, contained between 2,000 and 3,000 slaves when its territorial assembly applied to Congress for authority to draft a constitution preparatory to being admitted to the Union. The request raised questions about the status of slavery in the remainder of the Louisiana Purchase. On 13 February 1819, James Tallmadge of New York proposed an amendment to the Missouri enabling bill calling for gradual abolition. The amendment passed the House, dramatizing the growing power of the North, but was defeated in the Senate, where North and South enjoyed equal representation. In the subsequent Congress, Jesse B. Thomas of Illinois proposed an amendment to a bill admitting Maine and Missouri without reference to slavery that sanctioned slavery in Missouri but excluded its further introduction above the new state's northern boundary of 36°30'. This became known as the Missouri Compromise line.

Preserving parity between the number of slave and free states by pairing the admission of Maine with Missouri in 1820 served to quiet the agitation against slavery in Congress. But it surfaced elsewhere when South Carolina passed a law that required northern and foreign captains to lodge their black crew members in local jails while in port. South Carolina's action led Massachusetts to ask the federal government to protect its black seamen from such measures. Slavery also was a factor in the controversy over the Tariff of 1828. This began as a scheme concocted by Jackson's supporters to prejudice the middle states against Adams. They backed a high tariff desired by mid-Atlantic manufacturing interests in the expectation that the New Englanders would kill it. But they had failed to reckon with New England's growing manufactures, and the Tariff of Abominations passed. It then came under attack from southern slaveholding interests based in South Carolina that wanted to force Calhoun to choose between his national ambitions and loyalty to his home state. Calhoun subsequently spearheaded South Carolina's effort to nullify the Tariff of 1828, in the process developing doctrines that would later be crucial in the defense of slavery.

THE NATION AT THE END OF FOUR DECADES UNDER THE CONSTITUTION

In the four decades after the adoption and implementation of the federal Constitution, the United States grew dramatically. The 13 original states had grown to 24, the nation's territorial expanse had more than doubled, and its population had more than tripled. Despite the expansion, there were continuities. Roughly the same proportion of its people lived in communities of 2,500 or less in 1830 as had lived in them in 1789. Moreover, despite the success of steamboats in navigating the Mississippi and the canal boom set in motion by the Erie Canal, the focus of everyday life remained overwhelmingly local. The average person's loyalties were first and foremost to family and community, though after the beginning of the Second Great Awakening at the turn of the century, religious communities often took precedence over civil ones and sometimes even over family. Ethnic diversity and social stratification continued to provide the primary impetus for Protestant sectarianism, but economic expansion underwrote the proliferation of churches everywhere. Nor did the beginnings of Irish immigration after the conclusion of the Napoleonic wars and a proliferation of Catholic churches do much to check the multiplication of Protestant sects. The bounty of America ensured that there was more than enough resource to sustain every faith. This in turn contributed to the collapse of the religious majorities in New England that had sustained the region's Congregational establishments and the eventual separation of church and state there.

The only aspect of the federal government that remotely kept pace with the physical and economic expansion of the nation was the post office. But the absence of a strong central government in no way compromised the optimistic course on which the Republic seemed to be set. Instead, expectations of indefinite improvement prevailed, encouraging widespread experimentation in all fields of endeavor. In addition to the beginning of reform movements like temperance and antislavery, these years saw the first asylums for the insane, the first penitentiaries to redeem criminals, the first special schools for the handicapped, and the first attempts at providing women with some form of higher education. America also began to spawn a series of utopian social experiments. The failure of Robert Owen, a Scottish industrial reformer and the first foreigner accorded the honor of addressing the U.S. Congress, to establish a socialist community in New Harmony, Indiana, did little to dampen the perfectionist impulse. Instead, the millennial supposition behind much of the Second Great Awakening, that Christ's second coming was imminent, lent religious urgency to the notion that the conversion of heathen everywhere as well as of Americans would hasten the glorious redemption of God's creation. Some of the innovative energy of the age had less transcendent roots. Thus, artisans attempting to protect the value of their skills in an expanding market tried to form the first trade unions in the nation's growing cities. And an increasing stream of immigrants from abroad sought to improve the material circumstances available to them.

After 1815, the growth and prosperity of the Republic validated the claim that America was the land of opportunity. But the largess associated with American life was not equally shared. Before the introduction of modern sanitation and purified water supplies, the nation's growing cities proved much less healthy than the countryside, and neither wealth, gender, nor ethnicity provided full protection against periodic outbreaks of yellow fever, typhus, and cholera. During the first half of the 19th century, the life expectancy of Americans fell across the board. Dislocations associated with the westward movement contributed to the decline. The most vulnerable remained the poor, who were disproportionately either recent immigrants or Africans. Though by 1800 the northern states had all chosen a path that would lead to the gradual elimination of slavery, most Americans of African descent in the North were relegated to the status of an unassimilated underclass. At the same time, the calls for the abolition of slavery in the rest of the nation had the effect of tightening the constraints slaves were subjected to. Though Congress outlawed the importation of additional slaves from overseas after 1 January 1808, this had the effect of enhancing the value of Africans to their masters in the South. Slavery by all accounts remained an inefficient means of production, but few masters could have done better without it given the rising demand for southern staples, especially cotton and sugar. The continued demand for slaves to produce these crops empowered an aristocracy interested in slavery's perpetuation.

A second group experienced an equally systematic exclusion from the promise of America's future. The Constitution denied Indians recognition as Americans on the grounds that they were members of foreign nations, even though many continued to live in the midst of Europeans. Native Americans were left with no choices but displacement from the lands they occupied or absorption into an underclass that was indistinguishable from the free blacks. Serious efforts to halt the European plunder of Indian lands ceased with Tecumseh's death and the American victory in the War of 1812. It is hardly surprising that, under these circumstances, Indians who refused displacement began to merge with free blacks through marriage. Though the noble Indian warrior acquired a romantic, tragic identity denied the African, his material circumstances were hardly better.

Woman's lot in the new Republic depended on the fortunes of her family. Even the most fortunate, though, were required to cede almost all their civil rights to their husbands. The changes set in motion by the Revolution initially failed to address the anomaly that only recognized the civil independence of adult woman without husbands. However, female education received a boost from the new emphasis placed on Republican motherhood even as Republicanism relegated women to a separate, private sphere. There they were supposed to inculcate virtues in their children that could sustain the nation's form of government. The Second Great Awakening led some clergy to invade women's separate sphere by mobilizing them for religious ends. They invited middle-class women to organize missionary and maternal societies beyond the home and increasingly drew on their energies for the reform movements. The new emphasis on educating women enabled many to become teachers and some even to become writers speaking primarily to a gendered audience. Women of the early Republic benefited more from the beginnings of the industrial revolution than they did from the American Revolution. The expansion of the market progressively liberated the more privileged among them from the drudgery of household labors, expanded their leisure time, and provided the audience in which women authors, who generally identified with reform, could expand their sisters' sense of entitlement to the revolutionary promise of the Republic.

Even the most privileged Americans acknowledged that the nation's culture was inferior to Europe's. Britain continued to define the standards of literary and artistic expression for the American Republic. Religious and political rhetoric took precedence over letters, though some literary figures commanded an audience abroad as well as at home. The most prominent among them were William Ellery Channing, Washington Irving, and James Fenimore Cooper. The female authors who began to publish in this period, such as Mercy Otis Warren, Lydia Sigourney, and Anne Royall, addressed a predominantly domestic audience, but the novelist Catharine Sedgwick proved to be the modest exception. America's best painters, such as Benjamin West and John Singleton Copley, preferred Europe to America. But some notable American painters, such as Charles Wilson Peale, Gilbert Stuart, and John Trumbull, chose to pursue American rather than European careers. Washington Allston was the first American painter to explore the landscape of the American continent that would inspire so many artists later in the 19th century. Indigenous theater remained in its infancy, though some native playwrights, such as Royall Tyler, began to produce scripts that were produced on the stage. However, the site of most theatrical activity remained the emerging eastern cities that were dominated by European actors who preferred a European to an American repertory. Most indigenous musical compositions were religious in nature, William Billings being the most prolific innovator in this area. But an indigenous folk music also began emerging and would inspire the later work of Charles Ives and Aaron Copeland. The United States had begun the 40-year period more politically than economically independent. It now was more economically advanced than culturally developed. The next four decades of the nation's development would address this deficiency.

The Dictionary

– A –

ABOLITION/ABOLITIONISTS. Terms referring to the elimination of **slavery** and those who advocated such a course. Most advocates of abolition during the first years of the Republic envisioned a gradual process, and the **first emancipation** that eliminated slavery in the northern states largely conformed to that expectation. In 1780, Pennsylvania became the first state to provide for gradual emancipation by law. Gradualism served the dual purpose of compensating the slave owner and apprenticing young Africans for freedom. In the 1830s, though, northern abolitionists like William Lloyd Garrison began calling for immediate and unconditional emancipation as **antislavery** took on a harsher, more urgent tone. *See also* AFRICAN AMERICANS; ANTISLAVERY.

ADAMS, ABIGAIL (11 November 1744–28 October 1818). Wife of **John Adams**, she was born in Weymouth, Massachusetts. Though denied a formal education, she was an avid reader. In 1764, she married a young, ambitious lawyer who was soon to emerge as a revolutionary leader. They had five children: three boys and two girls. Their eldest son, **John Quincy Adams**, went on to become sixth president of the United States. Abigail joined her husband in Europe after the Revolutionary War and shared in his burden of being the nation's first official minister to Great Britain. She returned to the United States in 1788 and was First Lady during her husband's presidency between 1797 and 1801. However, her health began declining after 1791, and after many years of invalidism, she died of typhus in Quincy, Massachusetts, at the house they had acquired on their return from England in 1788. She is best known for her correspondence with her husband.

ADAMS, JOHN (19 October 1735–4 July 1826). Second president of the United States, he was born in Braintree, Massachusetts. After graduating from Harvard in 1755, he practiced law in Boston. During the 1760s and early 1770s, he emerged as a leader of the revolutionary movement. A delegate to the first and second Continental Congresses, he served on the committee charged with drafting the Declaration of Independence. Between 1778 and 1783, he acted as a congressional commissioner in Europe. In 1782, he negotiated loans with Dutch bankers and played an important role in the diplomatic negotiations leading to the Peace of Paris in 1783. In 1785, Adams became the first U.S. minister to Great Britain. Returning to America in 1788, he was elected the first vice president under the new Constitution. In presiding over the Senate, he displayed an excessive concern for protocol, which, along with his ***Discourses on Davila*** (1791), led many of his colleagues to question his **Republicanism**. Nonetheless, Adams won reelection in the **election of 1792** and became president in 1796 after **George Washington** decided not to seek a third term.

A crisis growing out of France's response to the **Jay Treaty** dominated Adams's presidency. On learning that the French government had rebuffed **Charles C. Pinckney** as U.S. ambassador, Adams appointed **Elbridge Gerry** and **John Marshall** to join Pinckney in another effort to come to an understanding with the **Directory**. The French foreign minister, **Talleyrand**, insisted on dealing with the American commissioners through intermediaries designated in the dispatches as X, Y, and Z. Talleyrand's agents demanded as the price of an accommodation apology from the president as well as money in the form of loans and bribes. The American public responded angrily when the **XYZ Dispatches** were released. Adams encouraged popular hostility to France in his formal replies to the patriotic addresses he received. He also cooperated with **Federalist Party** leaders in Congress in launching a limited naval war against France between 1798 and 1800 known as the **Quasi-War**. Adams was less enthusiastic about the congressional leadership's creation of a **provisional army** after Washington, appointed as its supreme commander by Adams, insisted that **Alexander Hamilton** assume actual command. While Adams did not request passage of the Alien and Sedition Acts, he signed both measures into law.

Federalist leaders close to Hamilton hoped the Quasi-War would purge Americans of their pro-French sympathies just as the Revolutionary War had purged them of pro-British sentiments. But Adams, also a Federalist, feared the potential of such a war for escalating into a full-scale conflict that could lead to national disintegration. Hamilton's army would be no match for a French expeditionary force acting in concert with the Republican opposition centered in Virginia. In response to signals that the Directory did not want a rupture with the United States, Adams appointed **William Vans Murray** as the new minister to France in February 1799. Subsequently, he designated **Oliver Ellsworth** and William R. Davie to join Murray in negotiating the **Franco-American Convention of 1800**. But it failed to secure Adams's reelection in 1800 because Hamilton's supporters in the cabinet opposed seeking an accommodation with France so vociferously that Adams dismissed Secretary of War **James McHenry** and Secretary of State **Timothy Pickering**. Hamilton construed the dismissals as directed against him and wrote a pamphlet highly critical of Adams's leadership on the eve of the election. Hamilton hoped it would persuade Federalist electors to vote for **Charles C. Pinckney** rather than Adams as the next president. But a Republican editor published the pamphlet just before word of the Franco-American Convention arrived in the United States. Both contributed to **Thomas Jefferson**'s narrow victory in the **election of 1800**.

An embittered Adams retired to Braintree, where he lived for the next quarter century. Though he supported the **Embargo of 1807–1809**, **Elbridge Gerry**'s election as governor of Massachusetts, and the **War of 1812**, Adams lost most of his credit with the public during these years by engaging in lengthy newspaper rebuttals of his critics. Following the War of 1812, however, he and Jefferson were reconciled and engaged in a warm correspondence for the remainder of their lives. Their Protestant countrymen interpreted their simultaneous deaths on 4 July 1826 as providential approval of the Republic they had both done so much to create and nurture.

ADAMS, JOHN QUINCY (11 July 1767–23 February 1848). Sixth president. The eldest son of **John Adams** and **Abigail Adams**, he was born in Braintree, Massachusetts. He accompanied his father to Europe in 1777 and attended schools in France and Holland, where he became fluent in the principal European languages. Later he served as secretary to several American diplomats, including his father, before returning to the United States in 1785 to enter Harvard. Adams graduated in 1787 and practiced law in Boston until **George Washington** appointed him minister to Holland in 1794. He returned to America again in 1800 after serving as minister to Berlin during his father's presidency. In 1803, a Federalist-dominated legislature named him one of Massachusetts's senators. But Adams asserted his political independence from the **Federalist Party**, supporting the **Louisiana Purchase** and the **Embargo of 1807–1809**. His rebuttal of **Timothy Pickering**'s claim that the embargo was a French measure designed to provoke war with Britain led the Massachusetts legislature to name a successor to his Senate seat a year before Adams's term expired, provoking his resignation. In 1809, **James Madison** appointed him minister to Russia. Adams remained in Europe until 1817, serving as one of the peace commissioners who negotiated the **Treaty of Ghent**, and then as ambassador to Great Britain, where, along with **Henry Clay** and **Albert Gallatin**, he participated in the negotiations leading to the **Convention of 1815**.

In 1817, **James Monroe** appointed Adams secretary of state, in which capacity he remained until he was elected president in the **election of 1824**. During those seven years, he successfully negotiated the **Anglo-American Convention of 1818** and the **Adams-Onís Treaty of 1819** and was the principal architect of the **Monroe Doctrine**. Some of Adams's diplomatic initiatives backfired, most notably his attempt to pressure Britain into liberalizing American trade with its West Indian possessions. But no secretary of state before or since did quite as much as Adams to enhance the stature of the nation. His diplomatic achievements made him a strong contender as Monroe's successor, but he still failed to win a majority in the **Electoral College**. Adams and **Henry Clay** had quarreled while serving as peace commissioners at Ghent and disagreed over when to recognize the newly independent Latin American republics. But in the early 1820s, both endorsed the **American system**. When Clay failed to command enough electoral votes to entitle him to consideration by the House of Representatives, he backed Adams against **Andrew Jackson** for the presidency.

Charges that Adams had entered into a "corrupt" bargain with Clay surfaced even before Adams appointed him secretary of state. **John**

Randolph's subsequent repetition of them in Congress led to a **duel** between Clay and Randolph. Though the administration had some foreign policy successes, its failure to be represented at the Panama Conference of 1826 confirmed Britain's claim that the United States was irrelevant to the rest of the hemisphere, thus compromising the Monroe Doctrine. At home, Adams promoted the **canal** craze ignited by the completion of the **Erie Canal** by supporting grants of federal lands along rights of way and direct governmental investment in state projects. But his national vision was not accompanied by comparable political skills, and as the nominee of the **National Republican Party** in the **election of 1828**, he was defeated by Andrew Jackson's **Democratic Party**.

After a brief retirement from public office, Adams accepted nomination as a candidate for the U.S. House of Representatives. He was elected in 1830 and remained in Congress until he died from a stroke suffered on its floor in 1848. In his remaining years, he supported Jackson's policy of pressuring France to settle claims arising from commercial plundering during the **Napoleonic Wars** but supported the rechartering of the **Second Bank of the United States**. He also assumed leadership of the emerging **antislavery** movement in Congress, first by opposing the gag rule under which the House refused to receive antislavery petitions, next the annexation of **Texas**, and finally the Mexican War. He also successfully pleaded the case of the Africans aboard the *Amisted* before the **Supreme Court** and cast his last vote in the House against a resolution thanking military officers for their service in the Mexican War.

ADAMS-ONÍS TREATY (1819). Sometimes referred to as the **Transcontinental Treaty**, by which Spain ceded **East Florida** to the United States, agreed to a boundary between Mexico and the **Louisiana Purchase** lands favorable to the United States, and renounced all claims north of the 42nd parallel to the Pacific Ocean. Secretary of State **John Quincy Adams** was able to extract these concessions from Spain in his negotiations with Luís de Onís in Washington for several reasons.

The **War of 1812** dramatized the strategic vulnerability of Spain in trying to hold East Florida. After the war, operations against the **Seminole** Indians, who had taken refuge in Spanish East Florida, led to military incursions by U.S. forces under the command of **Andrew Jackson**. Though Jackson exceeded his orders in executing two British subjects and seizing several Spanish forts, he narrowly escaped censure by President **James Monroe**'s cabinet because of Secretary of State Adams. Adams realized that Spain was in no position to defend East Florida. Immigrants from the United States threatened to overwhelm the European inhabitants of the province loyal to Spain just as they previously had in **West Florida**. In the wake of the upheavals of the previous decade that had dismantled much of Spain's American empire, the government of Ferdinand VII wanted to prevent the United States from recognizing any of the new republics emerging from the **Latin American revolutions**. Defending Mexico, still nominally under Spanish control, against the U.S. immigrants who had begun streaming into **Texas** seemed more practicable, and after a prolonged negotiation Onís was authorized to sell East Florida for the nominal sum of $5 million in exchange for agreement on the frontier between Louisiana and Mexico. The treaty defined the boundary as the west bank of the Sabine and Red Rivers, then north along the 100th meridian to the Arkansas River and west to the continental divide. Since Spain was also in no position to defend its territory north of the 42nd parallel between the divide and the Pacific Ocean, the Spanish government also accepted Adams's proposal that it renounce all claims to what was known as the Oregon territory. Spain did not get a penny of the $5 million purchase price for East Florida because the U.S. government was to use the money to satisfy the claims of American citizens against Spain arising from the **Napoleonic Wars**. This feature of the treaty ensured speedy ratification by the U.S. Senate. But the one-sidedness of the bargain provoked opposition in the Spanish government, delaying final ratification until 1821.

AFRICAN AMERICANS. At the time of the Revolution, approximately one-fifth of the population of Britain's rebellious colonies either had been born in Africa or were of African descent. Virtually all had been brought to North America involuntarily as slaves, a condition in which most remained. The North American climate proved more salubrious than the Caribbean's, enabling a far greater proportion to survive than was the case elsewhere. But beyond that, North

American **slavery** differed little in its oppressions from other parts of the Americas despite the regional variations of climates and crops.

Prior to the Revolution, only a few troubled voices worried about the un-Christian implications of slavery aside from the **Quakers**, who had turned against the institution before independence. The Revolution awakened many more Americans to the contradiction between seeking freedom from British oppression and continuing to hold Africans in bondage. And the war provided many routes through which Africans could seek emancipation. On several occasions, the British promised freedom to those who deserted their rebel masters, but many more Africans in the South found the British unable to deliver on their promise of freedom than actually made it behind the British lines. The revolutionaries' demand for labor, particularly for long-term recruits in the army, provided a more reliable route to freedom in the North. The prolonged character of the Revolutionary War also led many to the conclusion that the Deity was punishing them for the sin of slavery. This heightened sensitivity to the injustices of the institution multiplied the number of voices calling for **abolition**, leading to an increasing number of manumissions in both North and South.

All these developments combined to set the stage for the **First Emancipation**, which gradually freed enslaved Africans in those states north of the **Mason-Dixon Line**. The North could take the lead in the process not just because it had far fewer Africans in its midst than the South but also because a far greater proportion of those it did have were American born and therefore more acculturated to life in the United States than were the more recent arrivals from Africa. Eight years of warfare further contributed to the process of transforming Africans into African Americans by temporarily shutting down imports. While a former slave like **Venture Smith** demonstrated that being born in Africa was not a bar in adapting to American ways, others, like **Richard Allen** and **Paul Cuffee**, benefited from being born American in achieving their subsequent distinction in the early Republic. The vast majority of Africans who won their freedom in the North, however, usually joined a permanent underclass that was denied full access to the promise of American life. They often intermarried with the other underclass of the early Republic composed of American **Indians**.

The African slave trade resumed in the South with the peace but not before slavery had become generally controversial in the North. The division led to hard bargaining at the Philadelphia Convention, in which southern delegates insisted that their property rights in slaves be protected by the Constitution. Despite the disposition of the northern delegates to yield to the demands of the southerners, the overall effect of the Revolution had been sufficiently unfriendly to slavery to create the expectation that a general emancipation lay in the future.

The promise of eventual deliverance for the African was kept alive by Quaker petitions to the **first Congress**; by Congress's abolition of the international slave trade on 1 January 1808, the first moment permitted by the Constitution; by the reform sentiment springing from the millennial impulses of the **Second Great Awakening**; and finally by the **Federalist Party**'s hostility to the **three-fifths clause** of the Constitution. Unfortunately, as northern opinion hardened against slavery, the development of the **cotton gin** and the industrialization of textile production further entrenched slavery in the South's plantation economy. This development presaged a future in which a majority of Republican freemen would be aligned against a minority of slaveholding aristocrats. But the slaveholding aristocracy's firm control over the southern states, together with the checks that the Constitution bestowed on minorities, enabled them to defend their interests. They increasingly did so, however, by threatening to destroy the Union through **secession**.

With the controversy over the admission of Missouri to the Union, slavery became an issue in national politics. Here the matter in dispute—parity in the Senate—could be resolved by pairing the admission of a slave state with a free state, as in the **Missouri Compromise**. The device, which was used for the next 40 years, did not address the growing moral isolation of the South in a world that was becoming increasingly hostile to its peculiar institution. The **Haitian Revolution** dramatized the South's plight even as it added to its total number of slaves and slaveholders, while conspiracies like **Gabriel's Rebellion** and **Vesey's Rebellion** made the dangers of isolation more palpable. The defensiveness of the South manifested itself in acts like the South Carolina legislature's **Negro Seaman's Act** and later in **South Carolina's Exposition and Protest** against the **Tariff of Abominations**. The polarizing effect of racial slavery on the nation's politics threatened the survival of the Republic and cast a dark cloud over the nation's otherwise bright future. *See also* AFRICAN METHODIST EPISCOPAL CHURCH; AGRICULTURAL DEVELOPMENT; AMERICAN COLONIZATION SOCIETY.

AFRICAN METHODIST EPSICOPAL CHURCH. A church formed in 1816 as an outgrowth of **Richard Allen**'s black congregation. He had led a secession from St. George's Methodist Episcopal Church in Philadelphia in November 1792 after the black members of St. George's were denied their customary seating. Allen organized a new, all-black church that came to be known as the Bethel Church. St. George's contested title to Bethel's property. Despite the blessing of **Francis Asbury** and the support of **Benjamin Rush**, it took almost two decades before Bethel Church's claims were upheld by the Pennsylvania Supreme Court. Shortly afterward, Allen called a conference of black leaders that organized the African Methodist Episcopal Church. Though the 60 founding delegates may have represented as few as 400 communicants, when Allen died in 1831, the African Methodist Episcopal Church had established outposts in many of the emerging cities of the nation. At least one of the local congregations, Charleston's, was forced to dissolve after it became implicated in the **Vesey Rebellion**. The African Methodist Episcopal Church also experienced multiple secessions, the first in less than a decade leading to the formation of the African Methodist Episcopal Zion Church. Another took place during the 1830s as a result of opposition to the power of bishops and led to the formation of the Methodist Protestant Church. Despite these setbacks, the original African Methodist Episcopal Church continued to grow in response to the discriminatory pressures being encountered everywhere by blacks in the young Republic. The African Methodist Episcopal Church not only offered them a discipline through which to pursue salvation but also championed black uplift. In 1817, the church organized a Book Concern and during the ensuing half century started its own **newspaper** and eventually acquired a college. Today, it is the oldest and one of the largest black religious institutions in the country.

AGRICULTURAL DEVELOPMENT. British North America's principal agricultural exports on the eve of independence were tobacco, wheat, rice, cattle, horses, and barreled pork, supplemented by forest products. After the war, grain exports recovered much more quickly than did tobacco exports because of the disruptions the **French Revolution** imposed on Europe's market for tobacco. At the same time, the new staple of cotton assumed an importance unknown in the colonial period, thanks to the rising demand for cotton fiber from Europe's emerging textile industry and **Eli Whitney**'s **cotton gin**. Whitney's invention, together with the **labor** of **African Americans** held in **slavery**, enabled American producers to satisfy European demand with short staple cotton. Cotton could be grown only in the southern states, and the cotton boom created a demand for servile labor that obstructed the **abolition** of racial slavery there as the northern states embarked on the **first emancipation**.

Most grains, with the exception of rice, lent themselves to free family farming where hired labor made more sense than slave labor because of the irregular labor inputs required by the crop. Northern agriculture expanded as robustly as did southern staple agriculture because of the enhanced demand of the European market for American foodstuffs during the **Napoleonic Wars**. The **turnpike**, steamboat, and **canal** associated with the **transportation revolution** were the principal improvements that linked the proliferation of small producing units in the interior with the distant, expanding markets of the eastern cities and Europe.

The **War of 1812** did not lead to the collapse of agricultural production experienced in the Revolutionary War. And once the war ended, expansion resumed, hindered only by occasional financial disruptions like the **Panic of 1819**. The removal of the **Indians** in the Southwest freed cotton production from the constraints of available land, while stagnation in the tobacco regions ensured that there would be an ample supply of slaves to bring rich, new lands into production. Northern grain production also resumed its prewar expansion within the context of the family farm, thanks to the success of the **Erie Canal** in connecting the newly settled areas in western New York, Ohio, Indiana, Michigan, and Illinois with the larger Atlantic world. The railroad that was just beginning to emerge at the end of this period promised a continuation of the expansion. The productivity of American agriculture made it then, as it has since been, one of the cheapest places in the world to subsist.

ALCOHOLISM. *See* TEMPERANCE.

ALIEN LAW (Alien Friends Law of 1798). Initiated by the **Federalist Party** in the Senate of the Congress while the House of Representatives was working on an Alien Enemies Bill, the measure empowered the president to have any alien deported whom he deemed "dangerous to the peace and safety of the United States" or whom he suspected of "treasonable or secret machinations against the government." The law addressed the possibility that the crisis in Franco-American relations following the **XYZ Dispatches** might not lead to a formal declaration of war and gave the executive comparable power over alien friends (those who were subjects of a power not at war with the United States) that the fifth Congress was in the process of giving him over alien enemies from nations with which the United States was at war. Members of the **Republican Party** in Congress challenged the constitutionality of vesting such discretionary power in the executive, but **John Adams** signed the measure into law anyway on 25 June. While no alien was actually deported under this law, several prominent foreigners left the United States to avoid being forcibly ejected. **Thomas Jefferson** and **James Madison** subsequently condemned the Alien Friends Act along with the **Sedition Act** in their respective drafts of the **Kentucky and Virginia Resolutions** of 1798. The law expired after a two-year period without any Federalist effort to extend its operation. *See also* SEDITION ACT.

ALLEN, RICHARD (14 February 1760–26 March 1831). African American religious leader, he was born into **slavery** near Philadelphia. While a child, he was sold with his parents and several siblings to an owner in Delaware. There, in 1777, he was converted by a **Methodist** preacher. He and his brother succeeded in earning their freedom in 1780. Allen became a Methodist itinerant, supporting himself by woodcutting, as a wagoner, and by laying bricks. For a while, he traveled with **Francis Asbury**, the leader of Methodism in the United States, in a circuit that encompassed Maryland, Delaware, Pennsylvania, and New Jersey. When Asbury convened a conference in 1784 to organize the Methodist Episcopal Church, Allen was one of two black delegates in attendance. Allen proved almost as effective in preaching to whites as to blacks, and when he settled down in

Philadelphia several years later, he brought a black following with him to St. George's Church there. However, it was not long before white discrimination against the blacks persuaded Allen to lead a separatist movement that resulted in the establishment of St. Thomas's Church. Known later as Bethel Church, it was dedicated by Asbury. With the assistance of **Benjamin Rush**, Bethel Church successfully resisted attempts by St. George's Church to reclaim their property until 1816, when the state supreme court finally upheld Bethel Church's legal autonomy. Allen then called a conference, attended by 60 delegates, that on 11 April 1816 established the **African Methodist Episcopal Church** and elected him its first bishop.

In addition to establishing and presiding over the first African American religious organization to win legal recognition in the United States, Allen with his fellow parishioners provided heroic service to the entire Philadelphia community during the **yellow fever** epidemic of 1793. During his ministry, he also founded several benevolent societies, promoted the education of African Americans, petitioned Congress against the **Fugitive Slave Law** of 1793, and raised a black legion for the defense of Philadelphia in 1814. At the end of his life, he spoke out against the **American Colonization Society**'s program of sending free blacks to Africa because it would deprive their enslaved brothers and sisters of their most effective advocates.

ALLSTON, WASHINGTON (5 November 1779–9 July 1843). Painter, he was born in South Carolina during the Revolutionary War. When his father died in the conflict, his mother married a doctor on the staff of revolutionary General Nathaniel Greene from Rhode Island. After the war, his parents sent him to Newport to prepare for college. He subsequently entered Harvard, graduating in the class of 1800, and then embarked for Europe to study painting under **Benjamin West**. A trip to Paris and a visit to the Louvre inspired him to start experimenting with romantic themes, an inclination that was reinforced by four years of residence in Rome and acquaintance with Samuel T. Coleridge. But when Allston returned to America at the end of the decade, he found that those in a position to buy art were interested mainly in portraits. Between 1811 and 1817, he resided in England, where his artistic inclinations met with more encouragement. During a subsequent year in Paris, he began to experiment with heroic landscape as a genre. On his return to the United States in 1818, a group of Boston gentlemen put up a purse of $10,000 to support his work on an enormous allegorical painting, *Belshazzar's Feast*, which remained unfinished at the time of his death. Allston was the first American artist to write philosophically about art. His writings failed to earn him much money, however, and to make ends meet, he was reduced to doing smaller paintings that Americans would buy. As the nation's first romantic painter he failed to win the recognition at home that he enjoyed in Europe.

AMENDMENTS (to the Constitution). *See* BILL OF RIGHTS; ELEVENTH AMENDMENT; FIRST AMENDMENT; TWELFTH AMENDMENT.

AMERICAN BIBLE SOCIETY. On 11 May 1816, 28 delegates from local Bible societies, some of which traced their origins back to the missionary efforts of the colonial period, gathered in **New York City** to establish the American Bible Society. It replicated the establishment of the British Bible Society, which had been founded in 1804. Both societies sought to distribute the Bible as widely as possible. The American Bible Society cooperated with the various Protestant sects in supplying Bibles to the growing number of internal migrants who were severing their connection to their churches. It was seen as an arm of the mission movement presided over by the interdenominational **American Board of Commissioners for Foreign Missions**. The American Bible Society proved to be the largest of the many organizations spawned by the **Second Great Awakening** because all the Protestant sects initially agreed that Bibles were essential in converting heathens to Christianity. They in turn saw this as a necessary prelude to the second coming of Christ. The American Bible Society still provides Bibles in many languages throughout the world.

AMERICAN BOARD OF COMMISSIONERS FOR FOREIGN MISSIONS. The American foreign mission movement had colonial antecedents in the effort of American Protestants, particularly the **Congregationalists**, to convert the American **Indians** to Christianity. But foreign missions were the product of a cross-pollination between the religious fervor of the **Second Great Awakening** and the heroic traditions of the Revolution. In 1806, a group of Williams College students, seeking shelter from a thunderstorm, made a commitment among themselves to evangelize the non-European world. Many of the group, subsequently referred to as the Society of Brethren, attended Andover Theological Seminary, where their youthful enthusiasm proved contagious. In 1810, the American Board of Commissioners for Foreign Missions was established under the joint auspice of the **Congregationalists** and **Presbyterians**. Though national in name, the foreign mission movement remained the preoccupation of a religious elite from New England centered in Massachusetts. They saw the nation's Protestant Christianity, in association with a similar movement within British Protestantism, as a divinely ordained instrument for converting the heathen world that was a necessary prelude to Christ's second coming.

The Board dispatched its first missionaries to Asia in 1812; to India in 1813; to Hawaii, Palestine, and Turkey in 1819; and to China in 1830. The missionaries were active in founding schools to spread literacy so that converts would have access to the gospels that they translated into foreign, sometimes unwritten languages. The missionaries also sent extensive reports of their activities back home that were printed in religious **magazines** like the *Missionary Herald* founded by the Board in 1821 to help maintain home support. During its first 50 years, the Board sent a total of 1,250 missionaries overseas.

Despite the Board's ecumenical ambitions and confederated structure, the foreign mission movement became progressively more sectarian with time. In 1814, the **Baptists** established their Board for Foreign Missions, followed by the **Methodists** in 1819 and the **Episcopalians** in 1821. Eventually, in 1837, even the **Presbyterians** withdrew from the original Board. Nonetheless, in 1828, the American Board stood second only to the **American Bible Society** among Protestant benevolent societies in the resources it could deploy, and it remained the largest U.S. sponsor of foreign missions throughout the 19th century.

AMERICAN COLONIZATION SOCIETY. Established at the close of 1816 to settle free blacks in Africa, the Society attracted support from both philanthropists and **abolitionists** desiring to improve the condition of the **African American** as well as from slave owners anxious about the effect that **freedmen** were having on their enslaved brothers and sisters in the United States. **Henry Clay**, a Kentucky slaveholder of considerable prominence, was a charter member of the Society, which solicited subscriptions from both individuals and the government. A congressional appropriation of $100,000 in 1819 enabled the Society to dispatch its first vessel with 88 black emigrants and three whites to the West African coast. All the white and a quarter of the blacks quickly succumbed to **yellow fever**. But the emigrants kept going, numbering over 2,600 by 1830. They acquired additional strength from the cargoes of captured slave ships after the U.S. Navy joined the British navy in interdicting the African **slave trade** in 1842. Expanding numbers in turn enabled the American-sponsored settlers to quash the forceful opposition to their presence by native people. Until 1842, the colony was governed by white agents of the Society. After that, the settlement had black governors until the independent republic of Liberia was established in 1847.

AMERICAN FUR COMPANY. *See* ASTOR, JOHN JACOB.

AMERICAN SYSTEM. Henry Clay first formally outlined it in a speech delivered to the House of Representatives on 30–31 March 1824 advocating a protective **tariff** to encourage domestic industry. As part of his bid for the presidency in the **election of 1824**, Clay contrasted his American system with a foreign system of depending on other nations for manufactured goods. Clay recognized that the United States had made great strides from the colonial economy with which it had embarked on nationhood toward an economic independence that was congruent with its political condition. The nation's ability to wage the **War of 1812** without reliance on outside sources for military supplies heralded the change. Clay advocated developing the home market through an ambitious program of federally sponsored **internal improvements** the cost of which was to be borne by revenue raised from **tariffs** and the sale of the **public domain**. The decreasing reliance of the federal government on the **impost** for revenue enabled Clay to envision the tariff as a device for protecting the American market. The growth of the nation's population, which increased the demand for western lands, would supply the additional revenues while expanding the domestic market.

The southerners feared that the American system would make them dependent on the North for manufactures. Southern statesmen stressed the constitutional effect that concentrating power in the central government would have in annihilating the municipal powers of the states. They objected to Congress raising tariffs in 1824 and 1828, and South Carolina threatened to **nullify** the **Tariff of Abominations** of the latter year. This forced Clay to compromise on protecting the home market with high import duties. But after **Andrew Jackson** won reelection as president despite vetoing the recharter of the **Second Bank of the United States**, Clay promoted the American system as the only way the federal government could exercise some control over the nation's economic development. However, the nationalist ring of its title never quite neutralized the suspicion that its program was at odds with fundamental aspects of American liberty.

AMERICAN TRACT SOCIETY. Modeled on an English society established at the turn of the 19th century, the New England Religious Tract Society was established on 23 May 1814 in Boston. In 1823, the New England Society changed its name to the American Tract Society and in 1825 merged with the New York Religious Tract Society. Though the new, enlarged society was known as the American Tract Society, each branch retained some autonomy. Over the next decade, this new organization succeeded in printing and distributing over 32 million religious tracts, largely because of the introduction of new printing technologies in the 1830s that substantially reduced the costs of publication. Though some were sold at local bookstores, many were distributed free of charge by colporters. The American Tract Society, like the **American Bible Society**, was an offshoot of the **Second Great Awakening**. Its sponsors assumed that the printed word could have an enormous impact in promoting the millennium, and they were prepared to do what was necessary to ensure that the American public had access to the classic texts that all American Protestants drew inspiration from, such as John Bunyan's *Pilgrim's Progress*. The American Tract Society also distributed religious fiction and advice literature. The Society continues today to be a major producer and distributor of religious literature.

AMIENS, TRUCE OF. *See* TRUCE OF AMIENS.

ANGLO-AMERICAN CONVENTION OF 1818. Negotiated by **Albert Gallatin** and **Richard Rush** in London, this convention extended the **Convention of 1815** for a decade, restored to the United States the privilege of drying fish on the coasts of Newfoundland and Labrador, specified the 49th parallel to the "stony mountains" as the northern boundary between the United States and British Canada, and provided for the joint occupation of territories between the mountains and the Pacific for a decade.

ANTI-FEDERALIST. A term used to designate those originally opposed to ratifying the Constitution drafted by the Philadelphia Convention and implementing the new federal government. The success of the **first Congress** in addressing some of the reservations of the anti-Federalists with the **Bill of Rights** and in **funding** the Revolutionary War debt quickly defused anti-Federalist sentiment. By 1792, very few responsible leaders, even those who opposed some aspects of **Alexander Hamilton**'s funding policy, wanted to go back to where the Republic had been at the beginning of 1789. **James Madison**'s objections to the **First Bank of the United States** rested on a strict construction of the Constitution. As a leader of the emerging opposition, his position signaled acceptance of that document as the legitimate frame of government as much as it objected to an unnecessary addenda to Hamilton's funding policy. Though many anti-Federalists chose to become affiliated with the **Republican Party**, some eventually became **Federalists** as the **European War** reshaped political alignments among national leaders during the 1790s.

ANTI-MASONIC MOVEMENT/ANTI-MASONRY. Originating in upstate New York as a consequence of the 1826 disappearance of William Morgan, anti-Masonry rapidly emerged as a significant political movement in 1828. Morgan, an itinerant stonecutter, vanished just before a book he had written about the secrets of the Order of Masons was published. The opposition of local officials, who were also Masons, to investigating the Morgan case, together with the appearance of Morgan's book, fueled popular suspicions that a secret conspiracy was afoot. In 1827, towns in western New York started refusing to elect local officials who were also Masons. The publicity of a Rochester newspaper managed by Thurlow Weed ensured that the movement expanded not just throughout upstate New York but into Pennsylvania and Vermont as well. In 1828, anti-Masonic papers sprang up in Pennsylvania and Boston, and anti-Masons began winning state offices in New York and Vermont. Though Weed steered the nascent movement toward supporting **John Quincy Adams**'s **National Republican Party**, anti-Masonry continued to expand after Adams's defeat in the **election of 1828**. In 1830, New York's National Republicans adopted the slate of candidates the anti-Masons had put forward, while Pennsylvania's anti-Masons elected six Congressmen and Massachusetts's anti-Masons helped send John Quincy Adams back to the House of Representatives. In 1831, the party called the first national presidential nominating convention, but their candidates succeeded in winning only Vermont's electoral votes in the ensuing election. Though anti-Masonry remained a political force to be reckoned with throughout the 1830s in some northern states, by the end of the decade it had been largely absorbed into the **Whig Party**. As the nation's first third-party movement, it demonstrated the political strengths and weaknesses of concentrating on a limited agenda. *See also* FREEMASONRY.

ANTISLAVERY. Initially, racial servitude served the purpose of acculturating both Indians and Africans to the ways of the European in addition to appropriating their **labor**. But while Indians could often escape their bondage by melting into the native population, Africans were not so lucky. This is why racial **slavery** eventually came to be equated with African slavery.

From the beginning, some European colonists were troubled by the religious implications of slavery. Though many hoped slavery might be the means through which alien Africans would be converted to Christianity, the oppression entailed by bondage brutalized both the enslaved and the enslaver. In the late colonial period, the **Quakers** were the first to espouse **abolition** as a precondition for remaining in fellowship, and after the institution of the new federal government in 1789, they sponsored the first antislavery petitions submitted to Congress. Antislavery sentiment ripened in the North during and after the Revolution, leading all the states north of the **Mason-Dixon line** to make provision for freeing their slaves by 1804. The development is often referred to as the **First Emancipation**. Though the Revolution led to increased manumissions (individual emancipations) in the

South, no state south of the Mason-Dixon line followed the North's example. Northerners suspected that their failure to do so derived from the **three-fifths clause** in the Constitution entitling the southern states to count each slave as the equivalent of three-fifths of a free white in apportioning representatives in Congress.

Antislavery in the North initially derived more energy from the hatred of the **Federalist Party** leadership for the southern aristocratic leaders of the **Republican Party** than it did from the moral perplexity generated by the institution. But with the advent of the **Second Great Awakening** and the emergence of revivalists like **Charles Grandison Finney**, who followed the Quakers in condemning slavery as incompatible with Christianity, antislavery become more strident. In 1830, William Lloyd Garrison's calls for the immediate eradication of slavery elicited from the South equally uncompromising defenses of the institution. Most of those in the North who opposed slavery continued to favor a gradual, compensated abolition and colonization of the freed slaves elsewhere. But as southern slavery spread into areas like **Texas** that would otherwise have been free, those who objected to the expansion of slavery became aligned with the more radical antislavery advocates.

ARCHITECTURE. The Revolution created a demand for architectural innovation in both public and private domains. The destruction by the British of the major port towns of Boston, **New York City**, Philadelphia, and Charleston led to a major rebuilding during the prosperity of the 1790s and early 1800s. Initially, the Federal style reflected classical borrowings grafted onto Georgian designs from England instead of relying directly on Greek and Roman models. In private structures, wood usually replaced stone in applying these models because wood was much more available in North America than it was in Europe. The prototypes of antiquity were thought to be even more appropriate for the public architecture of a republic, and the era's leading architects, such as **Charles Bulfinch**, **Thomas Jefferson**, **Benjamin Latrobe**, and **William Thornton**, drew on such models in designing their stone buildings, including the capitols of Virginia and of the District of Columbia. **William Strickland**'s design for the **Second Bank of the United States** (1818) is widely credited with launching the Greek Revival movement. This semipublic building drew heavily on Greek temples for its design. Strickland's later structures added to the popularity of the movement, enabling it to supplant the Georgian high style of the late colonial period as well as vernacular styles like the saltbox in the construction of private dwellings.

ARMSTRONG, JOHN (25 November 1758–1 April 1843). Soldier and diplomat, he was born in Carlisle, Pennsylvania, and attended Princeton for two years before leaving for the Continental army. There he served as aide-de-camp to revolutionary General Horatio Gates. Armstrong saw action at Trenton, Princeton, and Saratoga, but he was most remembered for authoring the Newburgh Address in 1783, threatening rebellion by the army if Congress failed to pay the wages that had been promised. After the war, Armstrong was elected to represent Pennsylvania in the Annapolis Convention and the Confederation Congress, though he failed to win a seat in the Philadelphia Convention.

Armstrong's material fortunes changed dramatically for the better when he married **Robert R. Livingston**'s daughter in 1790. The marriage placed 25,000 acres of land at his service and aligned him with a powerful Republican family in the Hudson Valley. But Armstrong was unable to turn his good fortune to political account until New York elected him a senator in 1800. In 1804, **Thomas Jefferson** appointed Armstrong to succeed his father-in-law as ambassador to France. He immediately became embroiled in quarrels with other Americans over his handling of American claims under the **Louisiana Purchase** Treaty. **Napoleon**'s dismissive treatment of the United States exasperated him, and he repeatedly urged both Jefferson and **James Madison** to take stronger measures to resist French pressure. He returned to America in 1810, claiming credit for the **Cadore letter**, in which France conditionally promised to revoke its commercial decrees affecting the United States. Though Madison initially snubbed him, Armstrong supported war with Britain and opposed **De Witt Clinton**'s bid for the presidency in the **election of 1812**. Madison then rewarded him by appointing him secretary of war in 1813.

Had the **War of 1812** been immediately victorious, Armstrong would have had as good a chance at the presidency in 1816 as **James Monroe**. But Armstrong failed to produce the requisite triumphs, though he personally joined **James Wilkinson** and the northern army that had been ordered to take Montreal during 1813. Armstrong promoted talented junior officers like **Winfield Scott**, **Jacob Brown**, and **Andrew Jackson**. But his inability to prevent the **burning of**

Washington in 1814 led to his resignation and Monroe's assumption of responsibility for the conduct of the war. Armstrong never again held public office, though he continued to write vituperative pamphlets attacking old enemies like Wilkinson and Monroe.

ARTS. Before the development of photography in the mid-19th century, there were no alternatives to painters and sculptors for visual representations of experience. This put a premium on the detailed accuracy of an artist's work. Portrait painters were in high demand in the early Republic, and even the best painters of the period had little choice but to turn their hands to this task in order to support themselves. The only exception to the rule was **John James Audubon**, whose *Birds of America* copied nature with unparalleled exactitude. Portraiture, of course, need not limit a painter's artistry, as **Gilbert Stuart**'s famous portrait of **George Washington** demonstrates. But most aspiring artists of the early Republic thought their age required other forms of expression. **John Trumbull** excelled at painting historic scenes from the Revolution, some of which now adorn the rotunda of the nation's Capitol. Later, the **War of 1812** supplied a younger generation with ample materials for celebrating the exploits of the American navy in historic sea paintings. **Charles Willson Peale** improved on this genre by capturing history as it happened in his *Exhuming the Mastodon* (1806). Peale organized and financed the dig, which he then painted in process, though he was unable to resist the temptation to insert portraits of his entire family into the picture. **Samuel F. B. Morse** executed a similar work in his the *House of Representatives* (1821), which captured the mood of the chamber in addition to the likenesses of all 88 members present. American artists like **Washington Allston** also began experimenting with landscape themes that went beyond the more literal depictions by John Vanderlyn of Niagara Falls to touch on the wild, untamed qualities of nature. Allston's *The Deluge* (1804) anticipated the romantic interest in the American environment of a subsequent generation. Allston also pioneered the exploration of allegorical subjects in his never-completed *Belshazzar's Feast*, though Rembrandt Peale's *The Court of Death* (1820) was not far behind.

Sculpture was less tied to representation than painting in the early Republic because of its greater cost. What there was of it derived directly from indigenous craftsmen who were wood-carvers rather than from European-trained artists who had returned to America. Wood-carvers provided the figureheads for the prows of ships and supplied decorations for some of the finer private residences and churches. But only occasionally did a carver like William Rush attempt to capture a decent likeness, as in his bust of **Lafayette**. American sculpture might have developed greater resources during the early years of nationhood had not President **Thomas Jefferson** been reluctant to commission native craftsmen to do the stone works that would embellish the Capitol.

Samuel F. B. Morse's small stone sculpture *The Dying Hercules* had won a gold medal from the Royal Academy in England in 1813, but few in America were prepared to pay it much attention when he shipped it home after the War of 1812. Up until the end of the 1820s, native stonecutters had fashioned mainly gravestones, but John Frazee's portrait busts in the 1820s and Hezekiah Augur's sculptured figures suggested that American artists of the next generation would become as proficient in stone as they had already proven to be in wood. *See also* MUSEUMS.

ASBURY, FRANCIS (20 August 1745–31 March 1816). Apostle of **Methodism** and organizer of the Methodist Episcopal Church, he was born into an English farm family of modest means. Though he had little formal education, his pious mother exposed him to Methodist prayer meetings, and in 1766 he started preaching. The next year, he was appointed an unordained itinerant. In 1771, he responded to John Wesley's call for volunteers to go to America. His early ministry in the New World was conducted in the shadow of the Revolutionary War. Wesley's opposition to the American Revolution made Asbury suspect in the United States. But while other Methodist missionaries retired to Britain, Asbury remained in America, even though political pressures forced him to lie low for two years in Delaware. After the war, he formalized the split between the American and British Methodist movements. He spent the rest of his life traveling throughout the United States as an itinerant and is thought to have preached between 15,000 and 17,000 sermons. His annual circuit averaged between 5,000 and 6,000 miles a year, and it has been estimated that during his lifetime he traveled 275,000 miles, most of it on horseback. At his death, the Methodist Episcopal Church had grown from insignificant beginnings to embrace 140,000 parishioners and 2,500 preachers.

ASSUMPTION (of the state debts). Alexander Hamilton responded to the **first Congress**'s invitation to design a plan to establish the credit of the new federal government with his **Report on Public Credit** (1790). In it he proposed assuming responsibility for many of the state debts as well as the **liquidated** federal debt. Because this would increase the size of the total debt, Hamilton linked assumption to a reduction of the interest that would be paid on the new consolidated debt from 6 percent to 4 percent. He hoped to make the burden of this debt as light as possible by relying on a uniform **impost**. But he needed to eliminate competition between the claims of the state and federal creditors if such a tax were to be productive. Most merchants held one or the other of these debts, and the impost would yield little unless all importers supported its collection.

Hamilton assumed that the public creditors would agree to the reduction of interest because the creation of $65 million of new capital would lower the price of capital in the domestic market. He may also have anticipated that the French Revolution would make the U.S. debt attractive to those seeking to protect their property from disorders in Europe. In the short run, his forecasts proved to be correct, and by 1792 the subscribed debt of the United States had appreciated to par. But the impost initially failed to provide all the revenue required to meet current interest charges, and Hamilton had to make up the difference by borrowing in Europe. His financial operations fed suspicions about his intentions and prompted **Giles's Resolution** in 1793 for an investigation into Hamilton's management of the treasury. After 1795, the yield from the impost grew to the point where it was sufficient to meet the interest charges on the funded debt and even retire some of its principal, vindicating Hamilton's foresight.

ASTOR, JOHN JACOB (17 July 1763–? March 1848). Fur merchant and financier, he was born in Waldorf in the duchy of Baden in modern Germany, the son of a butcher. In 1779, he joined his older brother, a maker of musical instruments, in London. After the conclusion of the Revolutionary War, he sailed for America to join another brother. Settling in **New York City**, he quickly developed a profitable trade importing musical instruments from Europe and exporting furs. Realizing that Canada held the key to the continent's fur trade, he established contacts with fur-trading firms in Montreal. They used his overland network for moving peltry from Canada to New York in order to circumvent British trade restrictions that obstructed sending furs to China. In 1797, Astor entered the China trade in his own right, and in 1803 he began employing his own vessels as well. The profits he made with furs, supplemented by even greater ones from ginseng, were invested in New York City real estate. In 1808, he secured a charter of incorporation from New York for the American Fur Company. Shortly afterward, he sponsored the settlement of Astoria at the mouth of the Columbia River. He hoped it would facilitate the direct shipment of furs to China, but Astoria was taken by the British during the **War of 1812**. In 1813, Astor was the junior partner in a consortium headed by **Stephen Girard** and David Parish that **Albert Gallatin** organized to underwrite a $10 million government loan to sustain the war effort.

After the war, Astor employed a fleet of ships in a worldwide fur trade. The profits from his postwar ventures enabled the American Fur Company to buy out British fur-trading interests in the interior of the continent, which had begun to feel the pressure of his competition. Astor favored the establishment of the **Second Bank of the United States** in 1816 and in 1817 became head of its New York branch. But he soon resigned when his fiscally conservative views were ignored by others who wanted cheap credit. In 1819, following the death of a grandson, he retired to Europe for 15 years, returning to America for only brief visits until 1834, when he reestablished residence in New York City. By this time, the American Fur Company was suffering because of settlement in the West. Astor sold the company and turned to developing Astor House as New York's largest and most elegant hotel and the Astor Library, which eventually became part of the New York Public Library. At his death, he was criticized for not leaving more of his fortune to the city in which he had prospered.

AUDUBON, JOHN JAMES (26 April 1785–27 January 1851). Naturalist and artist, he was born Jean Rabin in Les Cayes in modern Haiti, the illegitimate offspring of a French sea captain and slave dealer, Jean Audubon, and a French servant girl. Though his mother died while he was an infant, his father cared for him and in 1791 sent the child to France. There the father and his childless wife adopted Jean in 1794. The parents indulged Jean's artistic inclinations and in 1803 sent the boy to the United States to avoid **Napoleon**'s military conscription. John tried his hand at helping to manage an estate his father had acquired outside Philadelphia and at running general stores in Kentucky, Missouri, and Louisiana. But he experienced little business success, and the **Panic of 1819** brought the latter ventures to a halt. Long before that, Audubon had begun publishing papers on American birds and quadrupeds that he had been observing and, in some cases, painting since his arrival in the United States. In 1820, he decided to compile an illustrated folio of American birds but was stymied in finding the necessary backing for the project. He and his American wife were barely managing to support themselves by teaching the children of wealthy southern families. However, a trip to Britain in 1826 yielded patrons, particularly in Scotland, and the first volume of his four-volume elephant folio, *Birds of America*, each priced at the equivalent of $40,000 today, appeared in 1831. In 1839, he returned to the United States to devote the remainder of his life to a comparable study of American quadrupeds. Senility overtook him in the 1840s, however, leaving the completion of the latter project to a son, John Woodhouse Audubon.

AUSTIN, MOSES (4 October 1761–10 June 1821). Entrepreneur, he was born in Durham, Connecticut. After a brief involvement in a dry-goods business in nearby Middletown, Austin moved first to Philadelphia and then to Virginia. In 1789, he secured the contract to roof the new state capitol in Richmond. Since the state was willing to pay a 5 percent premium if he used lead deposits in Virginia, Austin entered the mining, smelting, and refining business. Austin imported foreign workers to teach him the latest techniques and eventually improved on what he learned from them. He also sought elsewhere for lead and ended up establishing the first Anglo-American settlement in modern Missouri, which the **Louisiana Purchase** had opened to U.S. migrants. Austin's initial successes as a Missouri lead producer were eventually compromised by the end of the **War of 1812** and the **Panic of 1819**. When the newly established Bank of St. Louis, in which he had invested most of his money, folded, he turned to colonizing **Texas**, even though the **Adams-Onís Treaty** had recently confirmed it as Spanish territory. Austin journeyed to San Antonio, where he succeeded in winning the consent of the Spanish authorities to such a venture. But Austin became ill on his way home and on his deathbed voiced his hope that his son, **Stephen F. Austin**, would continue the enterprise he was in the process of launching.

AUSTIN, STEPHEN FULLER (3 November 1793–27 December 1836). Leader of the American colonization of **Texas**, he was born in Virginia, the son of **Moses Austin**. Stephen received his **education** in Connecticut schools and at Transylvania University in Lexington, Kentucky, before joining his father in Missouri. There he served in the territorial legislature from 1814 to 1820, when the collapse of the Bank of St. Louis, in the wake of the **Panic of 1819**, forced him to move first to Arkansas and then to **New Orleans**. Moses died shortly afterward, and Stephen decided to honor his father's memory by continuing his Texas venture. On arriving in San Antonio, he was informed that the concessions his father had secured from the Spanish government had been invalidated by the recent Mexican Revolution. But in 1823, Austin persuaded the revolutionary government in Mexico City to confirm his right to settle 300 American families between the Brazos and Colorado Rivers. Eventually, the government broadened Austin's authority, enabling him to attract closer to 1,500 such families. In this process, Austin occupied the role as sole mediator between the settlers and the Mexican authorities, acquiring in the process a great deal of power and land. Austin supported the Mexican government during the 1826 **Fredonia Rebellion**, but after 1827 he started encouraging American settlers to form local councils. Austin did not like **slavery** but felt that it was necessary if his colonizing venture were to flourish. The Mexican government outlawed the practice in 1824, but Austin succeeded in winning exemption from the ban by pretending the Africans were indentured servants. After 1830, the good relations with Mexico that Austin had been scrupulous about promoting began to collapse, largely over the issue of slavery. Austin was arrested by Mexican authorities while trying to negotiate a compromise between the two sides, and his subsequent imprisonment enabled those who opposed conciliation to displace him in power. A subsequent trip to the United States to recruit aid for resisting Mexico further damaged his stature, and Austin died shortly after Sam Houston defeated him in Texas's first popular election.

– B –

BALDWIN, LOAMMI (21 January 1745–20 October 1807). Civil engineer, he was born in Woburn, Massachusetts, and apprenticed as a carpenter before joining the family business in Boston. Baldwin developed an interest in hydraulics and, though largely self-taught, attended scientific lectures at Harvard. When the Revolutionary War began, he was commissioned a major and later promoted to lieutenant colonel during 1776. After poor health forced his retirement from the army in 1777, Baldwin was elected a member of the Massachusetts General Court between 1778 and 1779 and again in 1800–1804. His association with the **Middlesex Canal** began in 1793 as an investor and board member. In 1794, he assumed supervision of the enterprise, though he had no prior experience with canal construction. During a trip to Pennsylvania and Virginia to inspect other canal projects under way, he met the British civil engineer William Weston. Baldwin persuaded Weston to consult on the Middlesex Canal. Weston instructed Baldwin in English construction techniques and rented him the equipment to do a proper survey of the route. By 1803, Baldwin had presided over the completion of the nation's longest artificial waterway of 28 miles with 3.5 feet of water, 30 locks, and eight aqueducts. Baldwin was also active in the construction of **turnpikes**, and he supervised the construction of the India Wharf in Boston that had been designed by **Charles Bulfinch**. But he regarded the Middlesex Canal, whose measurements the designers of the **Erie Canal** copied, as his greatest achievement. Five of Baldwin's sons became notable civil engineers in the next generation.

BANKING/BANKS (commercial). The United States possessed only five commercial banks, located in the larger towns of the North and Providence, when the **First Bank of the United States** began operations at the end of 1791. The next year, branches of the Bank of the United States appeared in New York, Boston, Baltimore, and Charleston. During the remainder of the decade, 26 more banks joined their ranks. In some cases, corporations chartered to perform other functions, like the Manhattan Company, which provided water for **New York City** and subsequent canal companies, were empowered to act as commercial banks to facilitate their primary activities.

Initially, most banks were located in the North's larger towns. But by 1815, 210 chartered banks dotted the American landscape with a combined capital of $115 million. Though New England contained one-third of the chartered banks, it accounted for only one-fifth of the authorized bank capital, reflecting the banking aspirations of many small New England communities. Between them, **New York City**, Philadelphia, Boston, and Baltimore accounted for almost 30 percent of this capital. The Girard Bank of Philadelphia, created in 1811 when **Stephan Girard** took over the assets of the First Bank of the United States after its charter expired, was the nation's principal private bank of significance.

Most of the nation's larger commercial banks participated in efforts to finance the **War of 1812** until the Boston banks, empowered by exemption from the British blockade, succeeded in forcing them to suspend specie redemption of their bills in the summer of 1814. After the war, commercial banking expanded even more rapidly as state legislatures abandoned restraint in issuing charters. In 1818, the United States had 338 chartered commercial banks. But their number shrank dramatically after the **Second Bank of the United States** started to contract credit at the end of 1818, setting off the **Panic of 1819** and a financial downturn that persisted through much of the ensuing decade. Not until 1827 did the number of commercial banks exceed those that had been in operation during 1818. By that time, the bills issued by banks accounted for a major portion of the money circulating in the American economy. They acquired widespread currency because of the legal requirement that they be redeemed in specie. This, however, failed to keep the bills from passing at discounts proportional to one's distance from the point of issue or the issuing banks from being vulnerable to insolvency.

The Second Bank of the United States used its branches to present the bills of state banks for redemption, thus acting like a central bank to control the extension of credit. But that failed to address the need for monetary equivalency within regional markets. In 1824, the Boston banks developed a clearinghouse arrangement known as the **Suffolk system**, which allowed the notes of country banks to circulate at par in Boston. However, by requiring the country banks to keep substantial balances on deposit at the central clearinghouse, the Boston banks forced them to absorb most of the hidden costs associated with the plan. Dissident banks that refused to join the arrangement were punished with runs on their deposits. For this reason, the Suffolk system was not copied elsewhere in the nation, and monetary equivalency for most bank notes remained illusive.

BANKRUPTCY (FEDERAL) LAW. Passed by the sixth Congress on 4 April 1800, it was part of the **Federalist Party**'s strategy for enhancing the power of the judiciary in the federal government. The uniform Bankruptcy Law allowed anyone who had become insolvent to file for bankruptcy in a federal district court. If one had creditors in more than one state, this law facilitated the centralized administration of the one's assets in the federal courts and thus addressed some of the problems involved in the expansion of the domestic market. While not as blatantly political in motivation as the **Judiciary Act of 1801**, it was still viewed by members of the **Republican Party** as promoting dangerous centralization. The seventh Congress repealed the Bankruptcy Law on 19 December 1803, nineteen months after it repealed the Judiciary Act of 1801.

BAPTISTS. From the 17th century, Baptists and **Congregationalists** had shared certain key assumptions about a gathered church of believers under **Calvinist** principles. The disputed point between them was whether scripture authorized infant baptism. The Baptists subscribed to the belief that only consenting adults should undergo baptism and that it required full immersion.

Though Baptist growth had been slow during the colonial period, there were an estimated 60,000 Baptists in the United States by 1790. That represented less than 2 percent of the population, but the Baptists would make major gains during the **Second Great Awakening**, which began around 1800 and lasted into the 1830s. During this period, Baptists along with **Methodists** were the fastest-growing sects in the new nation, and they emerged as the largest denominations in the South. The explanation for the remarkable growth of both sects lay in their ability to evangelize those uprooted from their traditional origins and to order their unsettled lives. They appealed especially to the migrants streaming into the southern heartland, but migrants into the nation's emerging urban areas also responded. Congregationalists and **Presbyterians** proved less able to accommodate new congregants because they imposed too many requirements and their resources were concentrated in the North. Though the polity of the Calvinist sects seemed geared to accommodate local sentiment, only the Baptists accorded real autonomy to their separate conferences and rigorously subscribed to the separation of church and state.

The Baptists were also in the forefront of the missionary movement sired by the Second Great Awakening. The first missionaries sent overseas by the **American Board of Commissioners for Foreign Missions** departed from the United States as Congregationalists but arrived overseas as Baptists. In 1814, the sect formed its first overseas mission. In 1824, it established the Baptist General Tract Society to support its evangelical work. In 1832, it capped these efforts with the formation of the American Baptist Home Mission Society.

BARBARY WARS. One unwelcome consequence of American independence was that U.S. vessels lost the immunity from capture by North African pirates that they had enjoyed while members of the British Empire. Vulnerability was confined to the Mediterranean after the United States concluded a treaty with Morocco in 1786 because Britain's navy kept the warships of the other North African states bottled up there until 1793. Captures rose significantly beginning in 1794, when Britain abandoned its former policy, forcing the United States to pay tribute for immunity from capture as well as to ransom those already enslaved. This it did through a series of agreements negotiated by **David Humphreys** and **Joel Barlow** with Algiers (1795) and Tripoli (1796–1797) that paved the way for one with Tunis (1797–1799). But in 1801, the pasha of Tripoli upped the ante by declaring war on the United States. **Thomas Jefferson**, though preferring peace, economy, and minimal naval defenses, decided to resist and dispatched a sizable armada of frigates and warships left over from the **Quasi-War** to the Mediterranean. The **Tripolitan War** went badly at first with the capture of the frigate USS *Philadelphia*. But **Stephen Decatur** led a daring assault that destroyed the *Philadelphia* under the enemy's guns, thus depriving the pasha of the only armament that might have defeated the ensuing blockade mounted by the U.S. Navy. On 4 June 1805, Tripoli capitulated by signing the first treaty that exempted the United States from paying annual tribute.

The implications of the Tripolitan War were not lost on the other North African states, but worsening relations between the United States and the principal European belligerent powers after 1807 led Algiers to take increasing liberties with U.S vessels. Moreover, during the **War of 1812**, both Tripoli and Tunis allowed Britain to seize American vessels in their ports, contrary to their treaties with the United States. In May 1815, **James Madison** dispatched a squadron of 10 men-of-war under Decatur's command to the Mediterranean. Decatur's seizure of a 44-gun Algerine frigate and a 22-gun brig brought the dey of Algiers quickly to heel. He agreed to free all American captives and to renounce the principle that immunity had to be bought with tribute. Decatur then had no trouble getting Tripoli and Tunis to follow suit and to pay compensation for the U.S. vessels Britain had seized in their ports. This brought to an end the difficulties the Republic had experienced with the North African states.

BARLOW, JOEL (24 March 1754–26 December 1812). Poet, Republican ideologue, and diplomat, he was born in Redding, Connecticut, and educated at Dartmouth and Yale, graduating from the latter college in 1778. Barlow's poetic ambitions were nourished by the opportunity to deliver two verse orations at Yale commencements in 1778 and 1781. During the war, he served as chaplain to the Third Brigade of the Massachusetts Line. After the war, Barlow tried his hand at editing a **newspaper** and running a stationary shop in Hartford while he composed a long epic poem, *The Vision of Columbus* (1787), to which he secured such distinguished subscribers as **George Washington**, **Benjamin Franklin**, and Louis XVI. The poem portrayed the Revolution as the culmination of the heaven-ordained advancement of the human race initiated by Columbus's discovery of America, but it failed to make Barlow either rich or famous. He was also one of several contributors to a mock epic, *The Anarchiad* (1786), which was designed to suppress sympathy for Shays's Rebellion in Connecticut.

Barlow agreed to serve as agent for speculators wishing to sell lands in Ohio to European settlers and journeyed to western Europe in 1788. In England, he fell in with a group of radical Republicans who included **Thomas Paine**, William Blake, Richard Price, **Joseph Priestley**, and William Godwin, Mary Wollstonecraft's consort. In France, Barlow cultivated the acquaintance of **Thomas Jefferson**, **Lafayette**, and Brissot de Warville, an author who was familiar with the United States and who would become an influential Girondist. Though the land scheme collapsed, Barlow was well situated to witness the early phases of the French Revolution, moving between France and England as circumstance dictated. Barlow envisioned a peaceful republican revolution for all of Europe, a cause that he tried to promote in his *Advice to the Privileged Orders in the Several States of Europe, Resulting from the Necessity and Propriety of a General Revolution in the Several States of Europe* (1792). The conservative backlash against the French Revolution in Britain, together with the National Assembly's bestowal of French citizenship on him, led Barlow and his wife to settle in Paris. While running for a seat in the National Assembly, he penned *Hasty Pudding* (1793), the best known of his poems, which expressed affection for a vanishing rural simplicity as well as reservations about the course that France's revolution was taking. During the Terror, he managed to evade arrest and even rescued the manuscript of Paine's treatise on **deism**, *The Age of Reason*, from the French police when Paine was imprisoned. After de Warville's execution, Barlow and his wife settled in Hamburg for two years, where U.S. neutrality turned out to be enormously advantageous in sponsoring trade between the belligerent powers.

The Barlows returned to Paris at the end of 1795 far richer than when they had left it. Financial security allowed him to accept George Washington's request that he serve as consul general to Algiers. Since 1784, the North African states had been seizing American vessels and enslaving their crews. Between 1796 and 1797, Barlow arranged for the liberation of 119 Americans as well as negotiating a treaty with Tripoli that helped temporarily to check the piracy. Returning to Paris in 1798, he and his wife established an elegant residence in the French capital and befriended the American inventor **Robert Fulton**.

As a committed republican revolutionary, Barlow did not welcome **Napoleon**'s transformation of France into a military dictatorship. In 1804, the Barlows returned to the United States and settled in Washington, where they were on intimate terms with Jefferson and **James Madison**. Barlow declined to embark on a history of the United States despite their and **James Monroe**'s urgings. Instead, he chose to collaborate with Fulton in a poem promoting technological improvement and to rework his *Vision of Columbus*. The latter appeared as *The Columbiad* (1807), pruned of the providential millennialism that had been a prominent feature of the earlier epic. When **John Armstrong** retired as minister to France, Madison sent Barlow to Paris as his replacement in 1811. By this time, Madison had become convinced that there was no option to war with Britain. While he did not seek a military alliance with Napoleon, he did want agreement on commercial matters. Barlow died in Poland while trying to find Napoleon to sign a commercial treaty during the latter's retreat from Russia.

BATTLE OF BLADENSBURG. *See* BLADENSBURG, BATTLE OF.

BATTLE OF CHATEAUGAY RIVER. *See* CHATEAUGAY RIVER, BATTLE OF.

BATTLE OF CHIPPEWA PLAIN. *See* CHIPPEWA PLAIN, BATTLE OF.

BATTLE OF CHRYSTLER'S FARM. *See* CHRYSTLER'S FARM, BATTLE OF.

BATTLE OF FALLEN TIMBERS. *See* FALLEN TIMBERS, BATTLE OF.

BATTLE OF FRENCHTOWN. *See* FRENCHTOWN, BATTLE OF.

BATTLE OF HORSESHOE BEND. *See* HORSESHOE BEND, BATTLE OF.

BATTLE OF LAKE CHAMPLAIN. *See* LAKE CHAMPLAIN, BATTLE OF.

BATTLE OF LAKE ERIE. *See* LAKE ERIE, BATTLE OF.

BATTLE OF LUNDY'S LANE. *See* LUNDY'S LANE, BATTLE OF.

BATTLE OF SACKETT'S HARBOR. *See* SACKETT'S HARBOR, BATTLE OF.

BATTLE OF STONY CREEK. *See* STONY CREEK, BATTLE OF.

BATTLE OF THE THAMES RIVER. *See* THAMES RIVER, BATTLE OF THE.

BATTLE OF TIPPECANOE CREEK. *See* TIPPECANOE CREEK, BATTLE OF.

BEECHER, LYMAN (12 October 1775–10 January 1863). A prominent **Congregational** leader during the **Second Great Awakening**, Beecher was born in New Haven and attended Yale in the mid-1790s. During his sophomore year, **Timothy Dwight**, who had recently become president of the college, identified Beecher as a protégé. After undergoing a conversion experience and graduating with the class of 1797, Beecher stayed on to study theology until he was called to the Presbyterian Church of East Hampton, Long Island, New York. His success in stimulating a revival there won him widespread attention in the Northeast. In 1810, he accepted a call from the Litchfield, Connecticut, Congregational Church, where he remained for the next 16 years. At East Hampton, Beecher had modified mainstream **Calvinism** to make it more compatible with the dominant trends of postrevolutionary American culture. In particular, he stressed the importance of laymen in eradicating the moral failings of the early Republic, such as **dueling**.

Since Christians could not expect the millennium to take place while the nation was riddled with sin and the rest of the human family remained ignorant of Christ's salvation, Beecher was a strong proponent of both domestic and foreign missions. While at Litchfield, he expanded his reformist program to include **temperance** and the founding of the **American Bible Society**. He also established two religious **magazines**—the *Christian Spectacle* and *Connecticut Observer*—and in 1822 joined with **Nathaniel Taylor** in helping to found the Yale Divinity School. In 1825, his *Six Sermons on Temperance* helped launch the national temperance movement. In 1826 Beecher accepted a call from the Hanover Street Church in Boston. In 1828, he founded the **newspaper** *Spirit of the Pilgrims* for lay and clerical audiences.

Ever since his East Hampton days, Beecher had supported the unification of the Congregational and **Presbyterian** Churches as part of the millennial project. But during his sojourn in Boston, he helped open up a schism among evangelical Protestants by joining those who sought to temper the emotional excesses promoted by clergymen like **Charles Grandison Finney**. He also reacted to the Irish **immigration** by claiming **Roman Catholicism** was incompatible with **Republicanism**, thereby sowing seeds of the violence visited on nearby Charlestown's Ursuline Convent in 1834. Sensing that his Boston ministry was bogging down in controversy, he accepted the presidency of the newly founded Lane Theological Seminary of Cincinnati in 1832. His efforts to avoid confronting the divisive issue of racial **slavery** by supporting the gradualism of the **American Colonization Society** backfired when Theodore Dwight Weld, who had been converted by Finney, led a major secession from the student body that resulted in the establishment of Oberlin College. Thereafter, the Lane Seminary entered a long period of decline. In 1835, Beecher also faced heresy charges from the conservative wing of his presbytery. Though he was acquitted, the Presbyterian Church divided over slavery in 1837. In 1851, Beecher finally moved back to Boston from Cincinnati and lived there for over a decade, though with his mind progressively impaired, until the middle of the Civil War.

BENTON, THOMAS HART (14 March 1782–10 April 1858). Democratic congressman, he was born in North Carolina. At age 16, Benton was expelled from the university there for the misuse of funds entrusted to his care. In 1801, the family moved to Nashville, Tennessee, where he quickly entered the state legislature and befriended **Andrew Jackson**. During the **War of 1812**, he acted as Jackson's trusted aid and liaison in Washington. But Jackson's role in arranging a **duel** in which Benton's brother was both wounded and humiliated led to a falling out and a bloody brawl between the two in which Jackson was seriously wounded. Afterward, Benton moved to Missouri, where he killed a political rival in another duel. Stricken with remorse, he resolved to give up dueling regardless of the provocation.

Elected one of Missouri's first senators, Benton spent the remainder of his long career championing the nation's destiny and hard money. Reconciled with Jackson in 1824, he became a devoted partisan of the **Democratic Party** in Congress after 1828. He joined Jackson in opposing the recharter of the **Second Bank of the United**

States and subsequently supported the distribution of treasury surpluses to the states. Though a slaveholder and a senator from a slave state, he opposed the compromise **tariff** sponsored by **Henry Clay** and **John C. Calhoun** that defused the **nullification** crisis of 1833, the imposition of the gag rule on **antislavery** petitions in 1836, and early calls for the annexation of **Texas**. He championed partitioning the **public domain** among small farmers and refused to defend **slavery** at the expense of the Union. In 1850, Missouri denied him reelection to the Senate, but two years later he was elected a congressional representative and denounced the Kansas-Nebraska Act. In his last years, he opposed the Republican candidate for the presidency in 1856, John Frémont, who happened to be his son-in-law, and criticized the *Dred Scott* decision.

BERLIN DECREE. Issued by **Napoleon** on 21 November 1806, allegedly in response to the blockade Britain had proclaimed of a 200-hundred-mile section of the northern European coast on 16 May 1806. The Berlin Decree instituted a **paper blockade** of the entire British Isles without the slightest pretense that France had the naval power to enforce such a measure. The Decree also excluded all British ships and goods from access to that portion of the European continent under French control, commonly referred to as the **Continental System**.

BIDDLE, NICHOLAS (8 January 1786–27 February 1844). A banker, he was born to a prominent Pennsylvania family outside Philadelphia. Biddle graduated from Princeton with the class of 1801, having first completed a course of study at the College of Philadelphia at age 13. Between 1804 and 1807, he served as ambassador **John Armstrong**'s private secretary in Paris and then with **James Monroe** in London before returning to the United States to study law. Admitted to the Pennsylvania bar in 1809, he was elected a member of the state legislature in 1810. Though he briefly edited a Federalist **magazine**, the *Port Folio*, during 1812, Biddle supported the **War of 1812** and helped the Pennsylvania legislature frame a critical response to the resolutions issuing from the **Hartford Convention** in 1815. James Monroe appointed him a director of the **Second Bank of the United States** in 1819. While Biddle supported efforts to rein in the Bank's lavish extension of credit, he disapproved of radically contracting it. When Biddle assumed the presidency of the Bank at the end of 1822, he skillfully adjusted the availability of credit to counterbalance the Bank of England's lending policies. He also used the Bank's branches to restrain the volume of bills issued by western banks by presenting them for specie redemption. Though some of his actions provoked criticism, by 1830 he had demonstrated the beneficial impact a wisely managed central bank might have on American **economic development**.

Andrew Jackson's hostility to all **banks** posed a problem for the Second Bank of the United States because its charter would expire in 1836. Biddle decided to follow the lead of congressional supporters in the emerging **Whig Party** and to push for recharter in 1832 instead of 1835. This strategy assumed that Jackson would be reluctant to risk a veto on the eve of the presidential election. But Jackson vetoed the recharter bill anyway, and **Henry Clay**'s unsuccessful attempt to make the veto an issue in the election of 1832 paved the way for a war between Jackson and the Bank. Jackson ordered government deposits removed to state banks that were friendly to him, weakening the Second Bank of the United States both economically and politically. Biddle continued to preside over the Bank after its charter expired, but he could do little to cushion the impact of the depression that set in after 1837 without branch banks, and in 1839 he retired to private life.

BILL OF RIGHTS. During the struggle over ratifying the Constitution in 1787–1788 the state conventions had proposed a total of 210 separate amendments. **James Madison** carefully selected those that protected the individual against the power of the state in preference to those that qualified the powers of the new government. Even the Tenth Amendment, which stated that all powers not expressly granted the new government in the Constitution were retained by the states or the people, has been construed as turning the sovereignty of the people against the states. The House of Representatives eventually forwarded 17 amendments to the Senate, 12 of which were in turn sent to the states on 25 September 1789. Only 10 of these received the endorsement of three-fourths of the states. On 15 December 1791, they were appended to the Constitution and declared in force. They have subsequently become known as the Bill of Rights, of which the **First**

Amendment has proven to be by far the most important. Because **judicial review** was still in the process of developing during the early national period, the Bill of Rights proved more significant as a statement of fundamental ideological principles than in providing a legal basis for limiting the power of the government.

BILLINGS, WILLIAM (7 October 1746–26 September 1800). Composer and singing master, he was born in Boston and apprenticed to a tanner, a trade that he practiced periodically throughout his life. His real love was music, and he started a singing school and published *The New-England Psalm Singer* (1770) well before the start of the Revolutionary War. Billings was an ardent patriot, and his musical works were popular during the conflict. On the conclusion of the peace, he made a misstep as editor of the *Massachusetts Magazine* by producing an issue that drew condemnation for its off-color humor. This led to his replacement and diminished his popularity. Nonetheless, he continued to write religious music that appeared in the collections of others as well as his own tune books. In all, he produced six such works between 1770 and 1794. His last, *The Continental Harmony*, was sponsored by his friends trying to redeem his fortunes, which by then had declined disastrously. He died poor, and during the 19th century his tunes lost favor. He was rediscovered in the 20th century, and between 1977 and 1990 his complete musical works were collected and published in four volumes. Though virtually all his music was sacred in nature, he is now regarded as an innovative pioneer in a musical wilderness. *See also* MUSIC.

BINGHAM, HIRAM (30 October 1789–11 November 1869). Protestant overseas missionary, he was born in Vermont to a farming family. He attended Middlebury College, graduating in 1816, and then Andover Theological Seminary until 1819. In the latter year, the **American Board of Commissioners for Foreign Missions** (ABCFM) sent Bingham and his recent bride to Hawaii. They were joined by another cleric as well as 12 laymen skilled in medicine, farming, printing, and teaching. The ABCFM saw the conversion of the heathen as a cultural as well as a religious enterprise.

After settling in Honolulu, Bingham developed a 12-character alphabet for the Hawaiian language, translated portions of the Bible into Hawaiian, and by 1822 had published the first Hawaiian speller. He then taught members of the Hawaiian royal family and their chieftains how to read their written language. This persuaded the island's leadership that Christianity had much to offer the native population. After 1824, Bingham turned to educating the common people. Sponsorship by the native elite helped make the acquisition of literacy so much of a priority on the islands that merchants complained it was interfering with the procurement of cargoes and the provisioning of their ships. Bingham in turn used the new literacy to launch reforms that included **temperance** and monogamy as well as Protestant Christianity. The reports of Bingham's accomplishments he sent home to his sponsors helped sustain overseas missions for the next century.

BLADENSBURG, BATTLE OF. On 19 August 1814, a British force of approximately 4,000 under the command of Major General Robert Ross landed at the Patuxent River, in Maryland, from the fleet under the command of Vice Admiral Sir Alexander Cochrane. At the urging of Rear Admiral Sir George Cockburn, Ross's men marched on Washington and were met at Bladensburg on 24 August 1814 by a hastily assembled American force of about 3,000 consisting of a core of 900 army and navy regulars and 2,100 Maryland **militia**. Though **James Madison** and **James Monroe** were present on the field, Brigadier General William Winder assumed nominal command of most of the American units. The British experienced only momentary difficulty dispersing the bulk of Winder's badly positioned troops. But 400 better-positioned sailors and marines manning five heavy artillery pieces under the command of Joshua Barney, a veteran of the Revolution, put up stout resistance until Barney was wounded and captured and the rest of his men either killed or dispersed. The British victory at Bladensburg left the nation's capital defenseless before the enemy's advance. They entered the city the same night and burned Washington before withdrawing on the evening of 25 August.

BLOUNT CONSPIRACY. William Blount (21 March 1749–27 March 1802) was born in North Carolina and fought in the Revolutionary War. After the peace, he devised a scheme to pay the state's soldiers with title to lands claimed by North Carolina in present-day Tennessee. This was the seed from which an all-consuming passion for speculating in land sprang. After being denied election as a North Carolina senator, Blount moved west and settled in Tennessee. **George Washington**'s appointment of him as the territorial governor and Indian agent positioned Blount to protect his speculations. He aggressively expanded his land purchases, recruiting emerging figures like **Andrew Jackson** into his enterprise. After helping draft the Tennessee constitution in 1796, the state legislature sent him to the U.S. Congress as one of its first senators in 1797.

Blount feared that the outbreak of war between Spain and Britain might lead to France reacquiring Louisiana and a cancellation of the trading privileges that **Charles Cotesworth Pinckney** had recently wrung from Spain in the **Treaty of San Lorenzo**. If that happened, the value of his land speculations would collapse. He decided that the river's navigation would be more secure if the lower Mississippi River valley region formed a separate nation comprised of the southwestern territories of the United States and Spanish territory to the west of the river. He hoped to form this new political entity with British support and put his plans in a letter that became public. In July 1797, the House of Representatives began impeachment proceedings against Blount, inducing him to resign his Senate seat. The proceedings were eventually dropped in 1799 on the grounds that senators were not subject to impeachment. Blount's plan to detach the southwestern portion of the United States to form a new country anticipated a similar conspiracy of **Aaron Burr** a decade later.

BONAPARTE, NAPOLEON. *See* NAPOLEON.

BONUS BILL (1817). At the conclusion of the **War of 1812**, **John C. Calhoun** helped design and then led the movement to create the **Second Bank of the United States**. One provision of its charter was that the Bank would pay the government an annual bonus of $1,500,000. In addition, the government would receive dividends on the Bank stock it held. Calhoun proposed that the income the government derived from the Bank be permanently appropriated for the construction of a national network of roads and canals. On 3 March 1817, **James Madison** vetoed this legislative appropriation on the grounds that sponsoring a national network of **internal improvements** exceeded both the necessary and the implied powers the Constitution granted to Congress.

BOSTON MANUFACTURING COMPANY. *See* LOWELL, FRANCIS CABOT.

BOWDITCH, NATHANIEL (26 March 1773–16 March 1838). Mathematical astronomer, he was born in Salem, Massachusetts. He had little formal education before being apprenticed to a ship chandler. Subsequently, he went to the sea, making five long voyages between 1795 and 1803, the last as master and part owner of the vessel. Though entirely self-taught, in 1799 he published a corrected version of John Hamilton Moore's *The Practical Navigator*. By 1802, his corrections to this work had become so extensive that he issued *The New Practical Navigator* under his own name. Before his death, this work would run through 10 editions. In 1804, he retired from seafaring to become head of the Essex Fire and Marine Insurance Company in Salem. The company prospered under his supervision despite the **Embargo of 1807–1809** and the **War of 1812**. Harvard, West Point, and the University of Virginia offered Bowditch academic appointments, but he preferred the leisure and income he enjoyed in insurance. In 1823, he moved to Boston to serve as actuary for the Massachusetts Life Insurance Company. During his later years, he published many scientific papers. Between 1814 and 1817, he had translated Pierre Simon Laplace's *Traité de mécanique céleste*. Laplace's work was designed to cover advances in celestial mechanics since Isaac Newton's *Principia*, and Bowditch's translation, which did not begin to appear until 1829, similarly updated Laplace. Bowditch's many important scientific papers won him international recognition over the years, most notably in his election to the Edinburgh Royal Society and as foreign member of the Royal Society of London in 1818.

BRANT, JOSEPH (? 1743–24 November 1807). A Mohawk chief, he was born in the Ohio country but rose to prominence as a leader of the Mohawks and other members of the **Iroquois Confederation** largely because his sister was the common-law wife of Sir William Johnson. Johnson served as superintendent of Indian affairs on the northern frontier during the French and Indian War, and Molly Brant bore Sir William many children. Through Johnson's sponsorship, Joseph spent two years at Moor's Indian School in Lebanon,

Connecticut, under the tutelage of Eleazur Wheelock, who later founded Dartmouth College. There, Joseph became fluent in English while helping to teach would-be missionaries the Iroquois language. Subsequently, he assisted an Anglican missionary, John Stuart, in translating several religious texts into Iroquois. At the beginning of the Revolution, Brant journeyed to London, where he took the town by storm, at least socially, and had his picture painted by the American-born John Singleton Copley. Returning to America in the middle of 1776, he secured the loyalty of the Iroquois Confederation, with the exception of the Oneida, to the British cause. For the remainder of the war, Brant proved to be an effective leader of Indian forces, rendering essential military service to the British. After the war, he was able to secure compensation from the British government for losses of the Mohawk, who were expelled from their New York lands with the peace. Brant led over 2,000 Indians to settle along the Grand River in southern Ontario. He also tried to get the British to support his scheme for resisting the expansion of white settlement through a pan-Indian confederation. But the British never gave more than lip service to Brant's idea, and the U.S. victory at the **Battle of Fallen Timbers** in 1794 diminished its prospects still further. Brant nonetheless continued to be an influential intermediary between the British and the Indians of the Northwest until his death in 1807.

BROKEN VOYAGE. *See* ESSEX DECISION.

BROWN, CHARLES BROCKDEN (17 January 1771–22 February 1810). The novelist was born into a prosperous Philadelphia **Quaker** family that was marginalized during the Revolutionary War. Like several of his generation, Brown as a young man considered attempting an epic poem about the Revolution. Instead, he tried his hand at the law before deciding to be a professional writer, a calling in which no American had previously been able to support himself. Brown possessed enough wealth to permit an extended period of experimentation with the epistolary novel. The choice reflected the priority he attached to inner feelings over the display of exterior virtues. Between 1798 and 1801, while residing in **New York City**, he produced the six novels for which he is known today: *Wieland* (1798), *Ormand* (1799), *Arthur Mervyn, or*

Memoirs of the Year 1793 (1799–1800), *Edgar Huntly* (1799), *Clara Howard* (1801), and *Jane Talbot* (1801). Though this enormous outpouring drew some critical notice, it failed to make him much money, and after returning to Philadelphia and marrying, he turned to editing and writing for **magazines**. His later work consisted of fictional pieces and political commentary that supported **territorial expansion** and condemned the commercial restrictions of **Thomas Jefferson** and **James Madison**—particularly the **Embargo of 1807–1809**. Parts of an unfinished novel about the role of powerful Europeans in creating a dysfunctional, violent world were found after his death from tuberculosis in 1810. But neither his published nor his unpublished oeuvre did much to redeem his artistic reputation during the 19th century. Only in the 20th century has the complexity and fragmentation of his plots come to be understood as reflecting the inner turmoil of people living through a revolutionary age.

BROWN, JACOB JENNINGS (9 May 1775–28 February 1828). Land speculator and soldier, he was born in Pennsylvania to **Quaker** parents and graduated from the University of Pennsylvania in 1790. After a decade pursuing various callings, he became a surveyor and speculator in upstate New York lands, settling in modern Brownville. Though he opposed the **Embargo of 1807–1809** and Congress's declaration of the **War of 1812**, as brigadier general in the New York **militia** he mobilized his units defensively along Lake Ontario during the first autumn of the conflict. On 28 May 1813 Brown was the senior officer when a British force attacked the American position at Sackett's Harbor at the eastern end of Lake Ontario. He succeeded in rallying the militia, after they had initially given way, to support the regulars defending the post. This feat won him promotion to brigadier general in the regular army. During the remainder of 1813, he served under Major General **James Wilkinson** in the latter's abortive attempt to take Montreal.

Brown was promoted to major general in command of the Niagara frontier at the beginning of 1814. After **Winfield Scott** had trained Brown's officers, Brown invaded Canada, capturing **Fort Erie** on the Niagara River. He then moved north and at the **Chippewa** River forced the British regulars who opposed his advance to retire from the field. In a hard-fought subsequent engagement at **Lundy's Lane**, Brown received two wounds that compelled him to devolve command of his small army on a subordinate, Eleazer Ripley, who ordered a general retreat to Fort Erie. Brown resumed command in time to break a British siege of the Fort on 17 September, thus redeeming the campaign from the disgrace of the preceding year, when an American retreat had led to the burning of Buffalo.

Brown remained in the army after the war as commander of the northern department. In 1821, as the only major general in the service, he was made commanding general of the army and ordered to Washington. Shortly afterward, he suffered a stroke that disqualified him from having much effect on the subsequent development of the army. He continued to advise the administration, though, and dabbled in politics to the extent of conducting the negotiations that led to **John C. Calhoun** standing for the vice presidency rather than the presidency in the **election of 1824**.

BROWN, MOSES (12 September 1738–6 September 1836). Philanthropist and entrepreneur, he was born in Providence, Rhode Island, into a merchant family who were **Baptists**. He began his mercantile career in partnership with two brothers. Together they helped ensure that the college, which today bears their name, was located in Providence. After the death of his first wife, Moses became a **Quaker** and progressively went his own way. During the Revolutionary War, he made sure Quaker philanthropy addressed the needs of those being impoverished by the struggle. He also freed his **slaves** and lobbied for laws abolishing **slavery** and forbidding Rhode Islanders from fitting out **slave trading** voyages in the state. Initially, Moses opposed ratification of the Constitution because of the sanction it seemed to give to slavery. But in 1790, he changed his mind and helped persuade Rhode Island's Quakers to back ratification. Brown's entrepreneurial ambitions were directed as much to providing employment and sustenance for impoverished women and children as to turning a profit. He seized on the opportunity to partner with **Samuel Slater**, who was interested in transferring the new textile technology that had been developed in Britain to America. Though Moses eschewed public visibility, he remained an inspirational presence in the firm Almy, Brown, and Slater, which constructed mill sites throughout southern New England. Moses lived an exceptionally long life and had the distinction of being paid a personal visit by President **Andrew Jackson** before he died.

BRYANT, WILLIAM CULLEN (3 November 1794–12 June 1878). Poet and editor, he was born in the backcountry of Massachusetts, being educated by his physician father. At age 13 he published a verse satire of the **Embargo of 1807–1809**. After briefly attending Williams College, he trained for the law. Sometime during the **War of 1812**, he began composing the poem for which he became best known, *Thanatopsis*. First published in the **magazine** *North American Review* in 1817, the poem in its final 1821 form invited the reader to accept death with a confidence that owed nothing to the traditional religious doctrines of Protestant Christianity. In the mid-1820s, Bryant moved to **New York City** to edit a literary magazine. When it failed, he worked for and eventually became editor and part owner of the *New York Evening Post*, which he made into one of the most influential **newspapers** in the country. Though initially sympathetic to the **Federalist Party**, he became a Jacksonian **Democrat** in the 1830s with Free Soil leanings and eventually helped form a new **Republican Party** in the 1850s.

BULFINCH, CHARLES (8 August 1763–15 April 1844). Architect and public administrator, he was born in Boston into a prominent colonial family and educated at Harvard, graduating in the class of 1781. After touring Britain, France, and Italy during 1785–1787, he began giving amateur advice on design matters to his Boston friends. This in turn led him to propose a design for the Massachusetts statehouse that was executed during the 1790s. Though Bulfinch was conversant with many architectural styles, he drew most of his ideas from British neoclassical designs. Boston embarked on a rebuilding program during the prosperity of the 1790s that, despite the interruption of the **Embargo of 1807–1809** and the **War of 1812**, lasted until Bulfinch accepted **James Monroe**'s appointment to be architect of the United States in 1818. More than any other designer, Bulfinch influenced the way Boston expanded during those years because, as chairman of the board of Selectman, he supervised public works, including the lighting and paving of the city's streets. As administrator of the city's new fire code, he also oversaw the transition from the use of wood and brick to a greater emphasis on stone structures. Many of his architectural works, including the New North Church, the remodeled Faneuil Hall, and the core of the Massachusetts General Hospital, along with the statehouse, survive, albeit in modified form.

Bulfinch is best known for supervising the completion of the nation's Capitol after 1818. This structure had been initially conceived by **William Thornton** and carried forward by **Benjamin Latrobe** until the **burning of Washington** by the British in 1814 interrupted the work. Bulfinch oversaw the construction of the House and Senate wings and the beginnings of the Library of Congress. After the completion of the Capitol, he retired to Massachusetts, where in the last 15 years of his life he executed relatively few new works. His influence on public architecture, however, was felt for many years to come, not just in Boston and New England but throughout the nation.

BURNING OF WASHINGTON. *See* WASHINGTON, BURNING OF.

BURR, AARON (6 February 1756–14 September 1836). Third vice president and politician, he was born in Newark, New Jersey, a grandson of Jonathan Edwards. He graduated from Princeton in 1772 and studied law. After serving on Benedict Arnold's staff in the 1775 attempt to take Quebec, Burr was briefly part of **George Washington**'s staff before joining Israel Putnam's staff and rising to the rank of lieutenant colonel. He distinguished himself at the Battle of Monmouth Court House but afterward retired from the army because of ill health. Admitted to the New York bar in 1782, he won election to the state legislature in 1784 and was appointed New York state attorney general from 1789 to 1791 by Governor **George Clinton**. The legislature sent him to the U.S. Senate for one term between 1791 and 1797. From 1797 to 1799, he was a member of the New York Assembly and through aggressive organizing helped the **Republican Party** win complete control of the state legislature in 1800. Burr's role in capturing New York's electoral vote for **Thomas Jefferson** made Burr the leading Republican contender for vice presidency in the **election of 1800**. When it was learned that he and Jefferson had received the same number of electoral votes, Burr refused to say that he would accept only the vice presidency. This encouraged leaders of the **Federalist Party**, which controlled the majority of the House in the sixth Congress—to whom the choice now fell—to try extracting concessions from each of them in exchange for being elected president.

Though Burr scrupulously refused to make any bargains with the Federalists, Jefferson never forgave him. Realizing that his career in national politics was for the moment blocked, Burr set his sights on being elected governor of New York in 1804 with Federalist support. When **Alexander Hamilton** opposed him, Burr challenged Hamilton to a duel in which Hamilton fell mortally wounded on 11 July 1804. Barred from both federal and state advancement, Burr became involved in a conspiracy to form an independent republic in the West. When Jefferson learned of it, he issued a proclamation for Burr's arrest. General **James Wilkinson**, a suspected coconspirator, apprehended Burr and sent him east for trial, where government prosecutors decided to charge him with treason. Chief Justice **John Marshall** presided over the **Burr Treason Trial** in a way that ensured acquittal. After the trial, Burr lived in Europe for four years before returning to **New York City** to spend the remainder of his life practicing law there.

BURR TREASON TRIAL. On 30 March 1807, **Aaron Burr** was charged with treason and high misdemeanors before the U.S. Circuit Court of Appeals sitting at Richmond presided over by Chief Justice **John Marshall**. Marshall previously had ruled that the government had sufficient evidence to try Burr only for high misdemeanors. But a federal grand jury subsequently indicted Burr for treason. The case finally came to trial on 10 August. Burr was acquitted of treason after Marshall ruled that the government had failed to provide the sworn testimony of two separate witnesses to the same overt act of levying war against the United States. Marshall's restrictive definition of treason signaled to the nation's leaders that charges of constructive treason could not be used to settle political scores. Though this did not prevent members of the **Republican Party** from accusing their Federalist adversaries of "moral treason" before and during the **War of 1812**, no one was prosecuted for the offense.

– C –

CADORE LETTER. On 5 August 1810, **Napoleon**'s foreign minister, the duke of Cadore, notified the American ambassador, **John Armstrong**, that France would respond to the invitation implicit in **Macon's Bill #2** by conditionally revoking the French decrees that affected U.S. **neutral commerce**, effective 1 November 1810. In return, the United States was expected to impose **nonintercourse** against

Britain if Britain failed to follow France's example. On 2 November, President **James Madison** issued Britain an ultimatum that gave it three months in which to act before nonintercourse would go into operation against it. The ultimatum could not have come at a worse time for the British government since it was coping with one of George III's periodic descents into madness. After Britain missed Madison's deadline, the president issued a proclamation on 2 February imposing nonintercourse, even though official confirmation that France had in fact revoked its decrees had yet to arrive and French corsairs were continuing to seize American vessels allegedly under the decrees in question. Britain, seconded by the **Federalist Party** in America, argued that Madison had been duped by the French, who sought to embroil the United States in a war with Britain. Confirmation that the French decrees had been revoked was not obtained until April 1812 by **Joel Barlow**, Armstrong's replacement. Barlow was then shown a decree that had allegedly been issued at **St. Cloud** on 28 April 1811 stating that the **Berlin Decree** and the **Milan Decree** no longer applied to American vessels.

CALHOUN, JOHN CALDWELL (18 March 1782–31 March 1850). Vice president, secretary of war and state, and influential member of Congress for 30 years, he was born on the frontier of South Carolina. Schooled at Yale, he graduated in the class of 1804 and then attended **Tapping Reeve's Law School** in Litchfield, Connecticut, until 1806. After serving briefly in the South Carolina legislature, he was elected to Congress as a representative in the 12th through 14th Congresses (1811–1817). **Henry Clay** named him to the House Foreign Relations Committee, where as a **war hawk** he was elected chair and helped persuade Congress to declare the **War of 1812**. Calhoun and his colleagues vigorously supported war measures but failed to address successfully the problems the war had created. On its conclusion, however, he emerged as a vigorous spokesman for nationalist projects, such as **internal improvements** and a protective **tariff**. He also was one of the principal designers of the **Second Bank of the United States** and the **Bonus Bill** of 1817.

Calhoun resigned from Congress to accept appointment as secretary of war in **James Monroe**'s cabinet. In that capacity, he resisted Congress's attempt to completely demobilize the army. Instead, he preserved a small professional force that was deployed in the first **Seminole War**. When **Andrew Jackson** exceeded his authority by invading Spanish **East Florida** and hanging two British subjects, Calhoun favored censuring him. At the end of Monroe's second term, he agreed to be a candidate for the vice presidency in the **election of 1824**. During the presidency of **John Quincy Adams**, he joined with **Martin Van Buren** in opposing the administration's policies. Among other things, this involved Calhoun supporting the **Tariff of 1828 (Abominations)** on the assumption that it would be defeated. When it passed, the South Carolina legislature put pressure on Calhoun to resist it. He replied by drafting what became known as the "**South Carolina Exposition and Protest**" designed to protect the rights of the minority against the majority. It argued that the people of a state meeting in convention could nullify a federal law they felt violated the Constitution because the people acting through state conventions were the original parties to the federal compact. The other states had to amend the Constitution to get the nullified law reinstated, and this required three-quarters of them to agree. The South Carolina legislature officially endorsed Calhoun's ideas as its own at the end of 1828.

Calhoun still wished desperately to be president and hoped, after winning a second term as vice president in the **election of 1828**, to be Andrew Jackson's successor. Van Buren shared the same ambition and managed to undermine Calhoun's standing in Jackson's administration. This made it easier for Calhoun to yield to South Carolina's insistence that he choose between his national ambitions and the defense of **slavery** and to pursue a state's rights trajectory when he returned to Congress as a senator in 1833. Though he helped **Henry Clay** arrange the compromise that defused the crisis over **nullification** in 1833, he became an increasingly strident defender of slavery for the remainder of his political career. Aside from a brief stint as secretary of state under President John Tyler, during which he promoted the annexation of **Texas**, Calhoun opposed the Mexican War and the admission of free states from the territories acquired by it. His death in 1850 before the Compromise of that year passed probably helped postpone the crisis of southern secession for another decade.

CALVINISM/CALVINISTS. Derived from the theology of John Calvin (1509–1564), Calvinism stressed human insufficiency before

God's sovereignty in achieving salvation. Reconciliation with the deity depended entirely on the gift of divine grace that God arbitrarily chose to bestow on his fallen creatures. Calvinist governance required the church to be composed exclusively of those the deity had foreordained for salvation. Within Calvinism, distinctions were made between the New Lights, who focused on the redeeming power of God's grace, and the Old Lights, who remained more concerned with order based on reason and tradition. The polities of most of the larger Protestant sects in the early republican period, including the **Congregationalists**, the **Presbyterians**, the Dutch Reformed Church, the **Baptists**, and even, in a more limited way, the **Unitarians**, reflected these assumptions. The principal sects rejecting Calvinistic assumptions in their church polities were the **Episcopalians**, the **Methodists**, and the **Quakers**. But Calvin's assumptions about God's sovereignty placing the burden of salvation directly on the individual instead of on the mediating influence of a church affected all the Protestant sects in a greater or lesser degree.

CANALS. *See* ERIE CANAL; MIDDLESEX CANAL; SANTEE CANAL; TRANSPORTATION REVOLUTION.

CANE RIDGE CAMP MEETING REVIVAL. Local revivals, many of them in wilderness camp meetings, came to a head in August 1801 when 18 **Presbyterian** ministers were joined by several **Baptist** and **Methodist** preachers in haranguing a camp meeting in the Cane Ridge area of Kentucky. The event lasted for a week and drew an estimated 20,000 participants, many of whom had intense emotional responses to the religious message they heard. Critics of this revival focused on the hysterical behavior of the participants, which included screaming, weeping, barking, and fainting. Its defenders pointed to the hundreds who claimed they had experienced God's saving grace and were converted. The sponsors of the meeting were too theologically diverse to agree on what they had accomplished besides increasing the religious fervor that became the hallmark of the **Second Great Awakening**. Though some claimed the revival had restored Christianity to its original purity, there was little doctrinal agreement about what that involved. However, the revival demonstrated the radical potential of frontier Christianity to the extent that it inspired some who claimed the benefit of healing grace to free their **slaves**.

CATHOLICISM. The population of Britain's North American colonies, which achieved independence during the American Revolution, was predominantly Protestant. Maryland had been founded as a Catholic refuge in the 17th century, but by the 18th century its Catholics were a decided minority. During the 1790s, some Irish Catholics migrated to the United States as a result of the Irish disturbances of that decade and occasionally helped build some of the **internal improvements** undertaken in that period. With the end of the **Napoleonic Wars** and an increasing reliance on contractors who recruited **labor** from abroad, the trickle of Irish Catholics soon swelled into a noticeable stream. Though the Irish supplied much of the labor for the construction of the **Erie Canal**, many of the immigrants settled in the nation's emerging cities and quickly established Catholic institutions like churches and convents. This created unease among Protestant religious leaders, some of whom feared a resumption of the religious struggles associated with the Reformation and its aftermath. Protestant clergymen like **Lyman Beecher** inveighed against Catholicism during the 1820s, questioning whether the claims of papal authority were compatible with **Republicanism**. But a virulent anti-Catholicism, one that would lead to the destruction of convents and churches, did not emerge until the 1830s.

CHANNING, WILLIAM ELLERY (7 April 1780–20 October 1842). Unitarian leader, he was born in Newport, Rhode Island. After graduating from Harvard College in 1798 and spending a year and a half as a tutor in Richmond, Virginia, he read theology and then accepted settlement in Boston's Federal Street Church in 1803. Channing aligned himself with the **Federalist Party** of Massachusetts and felt strongly enough about the **War of 1812** to preach political sermons opposing it. In June 1814, he helped the Federalists in Boston orchestrate a religious celebration of **Napoleon**'s abdication. But after the **Treaty of Ghent** brought an end to the war, he shifted his attention to defending theological liberalism against orthodox **Calvinism**. In 1819, he delivered a sermon at the ordination of Jared Sparks in Baltimore. It was subsequently reprinted as *Unitarian Christianity* and received wide circulation as a concise statement of Unitarian principles. Channing helped establish Unitarianism as a separate sect within the Protestant tradition. He also championed the creation of a distinctive American **literature** and was one of the first American authors to establish a literary reputation not just in the British Isles but also on the Continent. Like many Federalists, he became an outspoken opponent of **slavery**, though his **antislavery** sentiments derived more from his postgraduate sojourn in Richmond than from a political animus directed at leaders of the **Republican Party**.

CHATEAUGAY RIVER, BATTLE OF. On 25 October 1813, a minor engagement in the **War of 1812** took place along the Chateaugay River in southwestern Quebec. It contributed to the unraveling of the American effort to take Montreal. In late September, Major General Wade Hampton had moved his force of 4,200 to the Chateaugay River to rendezvous with Major General **James Wilkinson**'s command advancing down the St. Lawrence from Sackett's Harbor. When Secretary of War **John Armstrong** ordered Hampton to descend the river to facilitate the rendezvous, Hampton found his way obstructed by a force of 800 entrenched British troops. He then detached a strong force to flank the British position while ordering the remainder of his men to undertake a frontal assault. But the flanking party failed to make contact with the enemy, leading those ordered to press forward to come to a halt and eventually to retreat after suffering 50 casualties compared to the enemy's 25. Hampton subsequently withdrew his entire force on the assumption that an assault on Montreal before the winter set in was no longer practical. But Armstrong and Wilkinson tried to blame Hampton's conduct at the Chateaugay River for the failure to take Montreal. Hampton certainly was in no position to attack the city by himself and had received conflicting orders from Armstrong about whether the campaign should continue. Wilkinson's far more serious defeat at **Chrystler's Farm** on 11 November 1813 played a larger role in dooming the planned assault on **Lower Canada**.

CHEROKEE. The Iroquois-speaking **Indians** occupying the southern Appalachian region were known as the Cherokee. They were probably the largest tribe in the Southeast despite being visited by a series of epidemics during the mid-18th century. In the late colonial period, they fought a two-year war against the backcountry colonists of Virginia and subsequently sided with the British during the Revolution. Despite the pressure they had experienced from states like Georgia to cede their lands after the Revolution, the Cherokee assisted U.S. forces during the **Creek War** (1813–1814). A Cherokee chief was credited with saving **Andrew Jackson**'s life during the **Battle of Horseshoe Bend**. After the **War of 1812**, the Cherokee tried to defend themselves against white pressure to abandon their lands by acculturating to white ways. They began to dress like Europeans and practice settled **agriculture**, and in 1820 they adopted a **republican** form of government and proclaimed themselves a nation. But these measures failed to heal the divide between the eastern Cherokee, who wanted to resist being dispossessed of their lands, and the western Cherokee, who were more disposed to accept **removal**. The achievement of a western Cherokee, **Sequoyah**, in creating a syllabary of the Cherokee language enabled them to adopt a written constitution modeled on the U.S. Constitution. In 1828, they even launched a **newspaper**, titled the *Cherokee Phoenix*, that published articles in Cherokee and English. These defensive maneuvers enabled them only to postpone removal until the late 1830s, not to avoid it entirely.

***CHESAPEAKE*, USS.** The ill-fated U.S. 38-gun frigate, launched in December 1799 during the **Quasi-War**, that figured prominently in two notorious naval incidents before and during the **War of 1812**. On 22 June 1807, the *Chesapeake* was intercepted by HMS *Leopard* as she cleared the capes of Chesapeake Bay for a Mediterranean cruise. When her commander, Captain James Barron, refused to submit to a search for alleged British deserters, the *Leopard* fired seven broadsides into the *Chesapeake*, killing three and wounding 18, before it surrendered and had four crew members forcibly removed. The incident further poisoned relations with Britain, already riled by other incidents of **impressment** off American merchant ships, some of them within American waters, as well as by **paper blockades** of the European continent. Though many voices called for war with Britain, **Thomas Jefferson** settled in the short term for banning British warships from American waters. The ban was not immediately heeded, and the *Chesapeake* incident continued to trouble Anglo-American relations until the matter was finally settled early in 1812.

On 1 June 1813, the *Chesapeake*, now under the command of Captain James Lawrence, accepted a challenge to a naval duel in Massachusetts Bay from HMS *Shannon*. The engagement lasted only

15 minutes and resulted in the capture of the *Chesapeake* after all the ship's officers were either killed or seriously wounded. Captain Lawrence's dying words were reported to be "Don't give up the ship," and he was accorded full military honors by the British when they buried him in Halifax. The *Chesapeake* subsequently was taken into the British service.

CHILD, LYDIA MARIA FRANCIS (11 February 1802–20 October 1880). Author and **abolitionist**, she was born in Medford, Massachusetts, and educated at schools for **women** that were appearing at this time to train them as teachers. In 1821, she moved into her brother's household. He had attended Harvard and had become a **Unitarian** minister. Lydia opened her own school for girls in his home and in 1824 published her first novel, *Hobonok, a Tale of the Time*. That was followed in 1825 by *The Rebels; or, Boston before the Revolution* and in 1829 by *The Frugal Housewife*. In 1826, she established a **magazine** designed for children titled *Juvenile Miscellany*, which she continued until 1833. She also wrote advice **literature** for **women** like *The Mother's Book* and *The Little Girl's Book*, both of which appeared in 1831. In 1829, she married David Child, who introduced her to some of the reformers of this era. Lydia Child was particularly taken with **antislavery**, and in 1833 she issued *An Appeal in Favor of That Class of Americans Called Africans*. It advocated immediate, uncompensated emancipation and opposed colonization. Her **abolitionism** adversely affected her reputation with the reading public she had so carefully cultivated until then, but she continued editing an antislavery **newspaper** and writing for the periodical press. Some of her later works found favor with the public, but once again she forfeited public approval when she expressed sympathy for John Brown after his failed raid on Harper's Ferry.

CHIPPEWA PLAIN, BATTLE OF. On 3 July 1814, an American force of 3,500 under the command of Major General **Jacob Brown** crossed the Niagara River and seized **Fort Erie**, taking British 170 prisoners. Major General Riall collected a force of 1,500 British regulars and 600 **militia** and stationed them behind the Chippewa River to block Brown from advancing farther. Then, on 4 July, Riall surprised the Americans by advancing beyond the Chippewa. On 5 July, Riall's men encountered **Winfield Scott**'s brigade of 1,300 men in the process of crossing a creek. Despite meeting intense fire, the American units persevered in their advance and broke the British line, losing only a third of the men lost by the British. This was the first time during the **War of 1812** that an American force of regulars managed to defeat a numerically superior British force of regulars, thereby conferring a much-needed boost in confidence and self-esteem on the U.S. Army.

CHISHOLM v. GEORGIA **(1793).** On 11 July 1792, the federal marshal for Georgia served notice to the governor and attorney general of the state to answer the complaint of two citizens of South Carolina acting as executors for a British subject, Alexander Chisholm, to recover property confiscated by Georgia during the Revolution. Georgia refused to appear, though it did instruct two counselors to submit a written protest against the Supreme Court's assumption of jurisdiction. After the jurisdictional issue was argued on 11 August, preliminary judgment was rendered on 19 February 1793. A majority of the justices held that the Court had jurisdiction under article III, section 2, of the Constitution and that final judgment would be rendered by default if Georgia did not appear to plead its cause at the beginning of the next term. In February 1794, the Court entered judgment against Georgia, but it was never executed because the Court's decision had given rise to a proposed amendment to the Constitution that denied federal jurisdiction in suits brought by individuals against states. The **Eleventh Amendment** was not declared ratified until 8 January 1798. During February 1798, a unanimous Court then ordered similar suits swept from its records when it declined to assume jurisdiction in *Hollingsworth et al. v. Virginia*.

CHRYSTLER'S FARM, BATTLE OF. After months of indecision during the summer of 1813, **James Wilkinson** decided on 17 October to lead a 6,000-man force down the St. Lawrence River toward Montreal, where he expected to rendezvous with Wade Hampton's 4,200-man force moving north from New York. But Wilkinson's men were not in position to descend the river until 5 November. And then they were followed by a British force of 800 that was able to move faster by boat because it was smaller. On 11 November 1813, Wilkinson's armada had progressed to Chrystler's farm on the Canadian side of the river when he learned that the pursuing British force was advancing against him. Because Wilkinson was too sick to leave his bed, the American command devolved on Brigadier General John Boyd. Boyd suffered defeat at the hands of a numerically inferior British force, sustaining twice the casualties the British incurred. The next day, on learning that Hampton had withdrawn his force after a minor engagement on the **Chateaugay River**, Wilkinson abandoned the campaign and withdrew into winter quarters.

CLARK, WILLIAM (1 August 1770–1 September 1838). Explorer and **Indian** agent, he was born in Caroline County, Virginia. In 1785, his family moved to Kentucky, where he became a renowned Indian fighter and diplomat. In 1796, he decided to renounce soldiering to become a merchant. But **Meriwether Lewis** soon recruited him to share command of an exploratory expedition that **Thomas Jefferson** dispatched to investigate the territory acquired through the **Louisiana Purchase** in the Northwest and to find a route to the Pacific. The expedition departed from St. Louis in May 1804, reaching the mouth of the Columbia in late December 1805 after wintering in present-day North Dakota. The return journey took only six months and was completed by 23 September 1806. Though the expedition failed to discover a water route through the continent, it did bring back much valuable scientific information, including maps prepared under Clark's direction.

At Jefferson's behest, Clark next undertook the excavation of the Pleistocene fossils at Big Bones Lick, Kentucky. In 1808, Jefferson appointed him Indian agent for the **Louisiana Territory**, and in 1813 **James Madison** named him governor of the newly organized Missouri Territory. Clark was more sympathetic to the Indians than most of the white settlers over whom he presided, which explains why he failed to be elected governor of Missouri when it entered the Union in 1821. But he continued to hold federal offices, such as superintendent of Indian affairs in St. Louis and surveyor general of Illinois, Missouri, and Arkansas, until close to the end of his life.

CLAY, HENRY (12 April 1777–29 June 1852). Congressional leader and aspirant to the presidency, he was born in Hanover County, Virginia. At the end of the century, he moved to Kentucky and married into the state's emerging "Blue Grass" gentry. Despite the lack of much formal education, Clay's elocutionary skills led to his election to the Kentucky legislature in 1803. The legislature then sent him briefly to the U.S. Senate in 1806 to complete someone else's term. Returning to Kentucky in 1807, he was elected Speaker of the House and in 1810 again selected to complete another unexpired term in the U.S. Senate. Whether out of inclination or a sense that the looming crisis with Britain made the House more important than the Senate, he chose to stand for election as a congressional representative in 1811 and was selected Speaker of the House in the 12th Congress. This enabled him to appoint those favoring war with Great Britain, known as **war hawks**, to the key committees. Together, they led Congress to declare the **War of 1812** in June despite the nation's lack of preparation for the conflict. Clay remained a **Republican** leader in Congress during the war until he accepted appointment by **James Madison** as one of the peace commissioners at Ghent. His quarrel with fellow commissioner **John Quincy Adams** over the advisability of ceding Britain rights to navigate the Mississippi in exchange for restoring the North Atlantic fisheries was resolved when Britain withdrew its demand that the **Treaty of Ghent** include access to the river. Clay then joined Adams in London, where, together with **Albert Gallatin**, they managed to negotiate the **Convention of 1815**.

On returning to the United States, Clay resumed his seat in Congress, where he espoused an expansive nationalist program that included chartering the **Second Bank of the United States**, protective **tariffs**, and **internal improvements** like national roads. Eventually, these projects became associated with the **American system**. When the issue of **slavery** threatened to divide the Republic over the admission of Missouri to the Union, Clay was the principal architect of the **Missouri Compromise** of 1820. But losses suffered in the **Panic of 1819** forced him to retire to Kentucky between 1821 and 1823 in order to restore his finances. He returned to Congress in 1823 with the nomination of the Kentucky legislature for the presidency but failed to win a place among the top three contenders during the **election of 1824**, in which no one candidate won a majority in the **Electoral College**. As the most influential member of the House of Representatives, though, he had no trouble prevailing on the House to elect Adams, for which he was rewarded with the office of secretary of state.

Clay proved less effective in managing the nation's foreign affairs than he had been in managing the House of Representatives, largely because of the hostility of **Andrew Jackson**'s supporters, who accused him of entering into a corrupt bargain with Adams. Clay responded to **John Randolph**'s charges by challenging Randolph to a **duel**, the only time a highly placed executive official resorted to such an expedient while in office. Both men escaped unscathed. But Clay found his attempts to cooperate with the newly independent republics produced by **Latin American revolutions** and to purchase **Texas** from Mexico barred by his opponents. He retired from the government after Adams's defeat in the **election of 1828** with little accomplished aside from a series of bilateral trade agreements. After three years back in Kentucky, he emerged on the national scene as leader of the new **National Republican Party** or **Whig Party** and as one of the dominant figures, along with **John C. Calhoun** and **Daniel Webster**, in the U.S. Senate. He was the Whig Party's unsuccessful presidential nominee in 1832 and 1844. Clay proved more effective in sponsoring legislative compromises, such as the tariff of 1833 that resolved the **nullification** controversy brought on by South Carolina's opposition to the **Tariff of Abominations** in 1828. His last great act of legislative statesmanship was to design the Compromise of 1850 to address the problems created by the annexation of Texas and the Mexican War. Though Clay owned **slaves** for most of his adult life, he favored gradual, compensated emancipation and was a founder of the **American Colonization Society** in 1816.

CLINTON, DEWITT (2 March 1769–11 February 1828). Mayor of **New York City** and governor of the state, DeWitt Clinton attended Columbia College, graduating in 1786. Following the lead of his uncle, Governor **George Clinton**, Dewitt opposed ratification of the Constitution. From 1790 to 1795, he served in the New York General Assembly and during 1797 and 1798 in the state senate and concurrently as a member of the Council of Appointment. In the latter capacity, he challenged Governor **John Jay**'s exclusive right to recommend appointments to the legislature and was vindicated in his stand by a constitutional convention in 1801. On being reelected to the Council, he purged most of the Federalists from state offices. Following a brief stint in the U.S. Senate, he became mayor of New York

City for all but two one-year terms from 1803 to 1815. From 1806 to 1811, he also served as state senator and from 1811 to 1813 as lieutenant governor.

Though nominally a member of the **Republican Party**, Clinton opposed the commercial restrictions pursed by the administrations of **Thomas Jefferson** and **James Madison**. The New York legislature nominated him for president in the **election of 1812**, and he was supported by the **Federalist Party** as a peace Republican. He paid dearly for challenging the national party's leadership, though, and would not have had a political future had not his rival, Governor **Daniel Tompkins**, accepted the vice presidency on the Republican ticket in the **election of 1816**. Clinton also benefited from his aggressive advocacy that the **Erie Canal** be built by the state. After being elected governor in 1817, he secured legislative approval for the issuance of $7 million in state bonds to finance the project. Though he lost the governorship in 1820 because of the opposition of a rival Bucktail faction led by **Martin Van Buren** and was purged from the Canal Commission, his political martyrdom led to his reelection in 1824. On completion of the Erie Canal in 1825, Clinton presided over the ceremonies attending the opening of "Clinton's Ditch." In several respects, especially his courting of the Irish vote and his success in removing any barriers to their participating in city politics, Clinton was considered ahead of his times. But his most influential achievement was to see the Erie Canal through to completion, thus ensuring New York's future preeminence in the Republic. Here again he diverged from the majority of Republicans who opposed state sponsorship for public works.

CLINTON, GEORGE (26 July 1739–20 April 1812). Soldier, governor of New York, and vice president of the United States, he was born in Little Britain, New York. During the Seven Years' War, he served both at sea on a privateer and on land. Afterward, he studied law and was elected to New York's colonial assembly in 1768. As a leader of the colony's revolutionary party, the legislature sent him to represent New York in the second Continental Congress. He was named brigadier general of the New York **militia** in 1776 and placed in charge of defending the Hudson River. In 1777, he was elected governor of New York. Despite directing the unsuccessful defense of

Fort Montgomery in 1777, he managed to preside over the formation of a stable political coalition supporting the Revolution in a state whose most prosperous regions remained under enemy occupation or control until 1783. Only with his opposition to the ratification of the Constitution did his political stature in the state begin to erode. After barely winning reelection in 1792, and then by dubious means, he retired from office in 1795. But **Aaron Burr** persuaded him to reenter the electoral fray as the **Republican Party**'s candidate for governor in 1800. After winning office once again, **Thomas Jefferson** chose him to be his vice president in the **election of 1804** in place of Burr. Clinton mounted an unsuccessful bid to succeed Jefferson in the **election of 1808** but had to accept the vice presidency instead. While presiding over the Senate in February 1811, Clinton caste a tie-breaking vote against rechartering the **Bank of the United States**. He was the first vice president to die in office.

COMMERCIAL EXPANSION. Prior to 1830, commercial exchanges in an expanding market were as significant as technological innovation in promoting increased productivity and rising standards of living through the division of labor. During much of the early republican period, the most dynamic sector of the economy remained geared to the overseas markets of the Atlantic basin and beyond. Mercantile restrictions on free access to the colonial empires of the European states inhibited the expansion of American overseas enterprise until the outbreak of the wars of the **French Revolution**. Thereafter, for almost two decades, the neutral flag of the United States conferred on its merchant vessels a unique advantage. The invisible earnings derived from being the world's principal neutral carrier were a prime source of the economic prosperity of the 1790s and helped lay the foundations for fortunes like those amassed by **John Jacob Astor** and **Stephen Girard**. A European truce between 1801 and 1803 briefly eliminated the advantage enjoyed by American vessels, but they regained it once the war resumed and maintained it until the **Embargo of 1807–1809**. **Nonintercourse** directed against Britain and France had little effect on the carrying trade, thanks to the indirect trade and the opening of the South American market that accompanied the **Latin American revolutions**. Even the **War of 1812** failed to check the nation's commercial enterprise, particularly that of New England, until the last year of the conflict.

The pacification of Europe, however, forced American carriers to compete with the other European traders after 1815. They did so by developing fast sailors with skills honed when the nation lacked much of a navy. The development of the American clipper allowed the United States to retain an advantage in the carrying trade because of the ample supply of materials needed in constructing wooden ships, materials that were in short supply in Europe. American merchants also increasingly turned to developing the internal market in this period. **Henry Clay**'s advocacy of an **American system** articulated the ideal of a nation of specialized regions knit together in mutual dependence. But the real force behind the development of the internal market was a **transportation revolution**, the most notable aspects of which before 1830 were the steamboat and **canals** like the **Erie Canal**.

COMMUNICATIONS. The first 40 years of the Republic failed to produce dramatic innovations in communications technology, like the telegraph, that would begin to replace the printed word in the 30 years before the Civil War. But two developments did expand information flows before 1830. The first was the growth of the U.S. **Postal Service**, which reached into an increasing number of localities as settlement of the West proceeded. The Postal Service in turn subsidized the transmission of **newspapers**, so that a community that lacked the critical mass necessary to sustain a press of its own nonetheless had access to information printed elsewhere. Improvement associated with the **transportation revolution**, such as the construction of **turnpikes** and the development of the steamboat, also enhanced the speed with which information circulated among an increasingly literate public.

CONGREGATIONALISM/CONGREGATIONALISTS. The 17th-century Puritan migration to New England developed Congregational principles where full church membership was reserved for those who could bear witness to a personal experience of salvation. Connecticut, Massachusetts, and New Hampshire also made legal provision for the state to support their Congregational clergy. These religious establishments were not abolished in Connecticut until 1818 and in Massachusetts until 1832. Long before that, New England's Congregationalism had split between liberal and conservative or orthodox wings. The liberals emphasized the role of human agency in salvation, while the orthodox adhered to the doctrine of the individual's total dependence on

God's grace. Liberals were especially prominent in the environs of cosmopolitan Boston, while orthodoxy tended to prevail in the interior. Harvard had since the 17th century been a seedbed of liberalism, while Yale, founded at the beginning of the 18th century, saw itself as countering Harvard's heresies.

In the 1790s, liberally inclined parishes in Boston started recruiting clergy of like sentiment for the better-paying pulpits in their region. In 1804, the liberal clergy had acquired enough influence to name Henry Ware, a suspected **Unitarian**, as Harvard's Hollis Professor of Divinity. The orthodox responded by founding their own seminary in nearby Andover in 1808. The division of New England's Congregational leadership at the top did not prevent the orthodox wing from reaching out to the **Presbyterians**, who shared the same theological premises, in the mid-Atlantic states. In 1801, the orthodox Congregationalists of New England entered into a plan of union with the Presbyterians, and in 1810 both collaborated in establishing the **American Board of Commissioners for Foreign Missions**. Led by **Timothy Dwight**, the president of Yale, and supported by graduates from rural Congregational colleges like Williams and Amherst, the Congregationalists joined the Presbyterians in sponsoring both a foreign and a home mission movement throughout the **Second Great Awakening**. But the collaboration began to break down in the 1830s when the Congregationalists turned to ministering more exclusively to migrants from their home region to western states like Ohio.

CONGRESSIONAL CAUCUS. A device developed by the **Republican Party** to make sure its national political majority did not dissipate in confusion or division. The caucus was composed of all Republicans in Congress. Its most important function was to nominate the party's presidential candidate, but it also met regularly to agree on measures the party would pursue in both branches of Congress. Occasionally, Federalists who sympathized with the Republicans on a particular issue were invited to attend, as **John Quincy Adams** did on the occasion of the **USS *Chesapeake*** incident in 1807. The Federalists questioned the legitimacy of the caucus, but to no effect. It lost its function of nominating presidential candidates after the **Federalist Party** dissolved following the **War of 1812**. Its last attempt to designate the Republican nominee occurred in the **election of 1824**, when a badly attended caucus endorsed **William H. Crawford** as President **James Monroe**'s successor. Its role in formulating party policies has survived into the present.

***CONSTITUTION*, USS.** One of six frigates authorized by Congress in 1794, the *Constitution* was built in Boston and launched 21 October 1797. It mounted 54 heavy guns, had solid oak siding seven inches thick, and displaced 2,200 tons, making it more like a ship of the line carrying 74 guns than a frigate. After patrolling the U.S. coast during the **Quasi-War**, it served as flagship for the Mediterranean squadron during and after the **Tripolitan War** between 1803 and 1806. Returning to Boston in 1807 for extensive refitting, it was in fighting trim when the **War of 1812** commenced. Under the command of **Isaac Hull**, it managed to capture HMS *Guerrière* on 18 August 1812. Subsequently, under William Bainbridge's command, it destroyed HMS *Java* on 29 December 1812. While the *Constitution* spent more of the war blockaded in port than at sea, the nation's superfrigates forced the Royal Navy to concentrate in American waters far more than had been the case during the Revolution. The American navy thereby substantially reduced Britain's ability to recapture prizes taken by American privateers. After the War of 1812, the *Constitution* returned to the Mediterranean for seven years between 1821 and 1828. It was found unfit for service on its return to Boston in 1828, but Oliver Wendell Holmes's poem "Old Ironsides" saved it from destruction, and it remains today the oldest commissioned ship in the US Navy.

CONTINENTAL SYSTEM. Napoleon's policy between 1807 and 1813 of waging indirect war against Britain by excluding her goods and vessels from the European countries under his control.

CONVENTION OF 1815. With Britain and negotiated by **John Quincy Adams**, **Henry Clay**, and **Albert Gallatin** after the conclusion of the **War of 1812**, this convention opened U.S. trade with the British East Indies in exchange for the United States renouncing the imposition of discriminatory duties on British products and ships. Britain's American possessions, including the West Indies, were specifically exempted from the agreement.

CONVENTION OF 1817. With Britain and also known as the Rush-Bagot Agreement because it bore the signatures of acting Secretary of State **Richard Rush** and the British minister, Charles Bagot. This convention provided for mutual reduction of naval armaments on the Great Lakes and Lake Champlain and contributed to improving relations between the two countries.

COOK, DANIEL POPE (? 1794–16 October 1827). Early Illinois congressman, he was born in Kentucky and did not move to Illinois Territory until 1815. After briefly establishing a law practice there, he moved to Washington, D.C., where **James Monroe** dispatched him to England to summon **John Quincy Adams** back to the United States as secretary of state. After performing this errand, Cook returned to Illinois and established a **newspaper** that promoted the territory's bid for statehood, free of **slavery**. After Illinois was admitted to the Union in 1818, Cook was elected its sole representative in Congress. While in Washington, he served on the Public Lands Committee and proposed during the debates over the **Missouri Compromise** that the public land west of the Mississippi be reserved to finance the compensated **abolition** of **slavery**. In the **election of 1824**, still Illinois's sole representative, he caste the state's ballot for John Quincy Adams. Always in poor health, he died at the age of 33. Cook County in Illinois was later named for him.

COOPER, JAMES FENIMORE (15 September 1789–14 September 1851). An author best remembered for his novels, was born in Burlington, New Jersey, and attended Yale for two years before being dismissed for misconduct. During 1806 and 1807, he served as an ordinary seaman on a merchant vessel preparatory to entering the navy as a midshipman. His father's death in 1809 left him with a substantial fortune that enabled him to leave the navy and marry into the prominent DeLancey family. By 1817, however, he had dissipated most of his inheritance and had to take up writing to support his family. His first novel, *Precaution*, appeared in 1820, followed in 1821 by a story set in the Revolution titled *The Spy*, which commanded a wide audience. In 1823, he published the first of the equally successful Leatherstocking tales, *The Pioneer*. It was followed in 1826 by *The Last of the Mohicans* and in 1827 by *The Prairie*. Sandwiched between the latter Leatherstocking novels were two sea stories, *The Pilot* (1824) and *The Red Rover* (1827), as well as *Lionel Lincoln* (1825), a story about revolutionary Boston.

The success of his more popular novels enabled Cooper to take his family to Europe, where they remained until 1833. During that sojourn, he became involved with Europe's **republican** revolutionaries, and his writing suffered as a consequence. When he returned to the United States in 1833, he encountered hostility in the **newspapers** that he had not previously experienced. Though he remained active as a writer up to 1850, experimenting with a variety of genres, including history, travel, and the defense of America against European criticism, his best work remained his romantic novels. A burst of creativity in the 1840s led to the publication of several later Leatherstocking tales, including *The Pathfinder* and *The Deerslayer*. Another trilogy of novels critical of the antirent riots in colonial New York proved less successful. At the time of Cooper's death, he was as widely known as any other American author. But his later books proved to be less financially successful than those published in the 1820s.

COTTON. *See* AGRICUTURAL DEVELOPMENT.

COTTON GIN. A machine invented by **Eli Whitney** for mechanically separating the seeds of short staple cotton from the fiber that allowed one worker to process 50 pounds of cotton per day. It broke a processing bottleneck with short staple cotton and allowed the southern states to expand production and to become the producers of three-quarters of the world's cotton by the 1850s. Whitney, however, failed to profit as much from his invention as he had hoped. His machine was easily copied, southern cotton growers were averse to paying the high fee Whitney attempted to charge for processing their cotton, and the courts failed to uphold his patent, issued in 1794, until it had almost expired.

CRAWFORD, WILLIAM HARRIS (24 February 1772–15 September 1834). Politician and cabinet member, he was born in rural Virginia to parents who then moved to Georgia. Crawford had some schooling before himself becoming a schoolteacher and then reading for the law. His ability to plead cases in court quickly won him election to the Georgia legislature, where he aligned himself with James Jackson's faction against John Clark and his followers. In 1802, Crawford accepted a challenge to a **duel** from a Clark follower and killed his opponent. In 1806, he fought Clark and emerged from the encounter badly wounded. But his willingness to engage in dueling enhanced his political following, and in 1807 the Georgia legislature sent him to the U.S. Senate.

While Crawford was critical of the **Embargo of 1807–1809,** he joined unsuccessfully in efforts to prevent the **Federalist Party** from getting it repealed. In 1811, he emerged as a **Republican Party** champion for the recharter of the **First Bank of the United States**, which failed in the Senate when vice president **George Clinton** cast the deciding vote against it. After Clinton sickened and subsequently died, Crawford replaced him as president of the Senate. Crawford supported President **James Madison**'s call for a declaration of war against Britain in 1812 but refused appointment as secretary of war. He accepted Madison's offer of the ambassadorship to France in 1813, though, and served in that capacity throughout the remainder of the **War of 1812**.

On returning to the United States in the middle of 1815, Madison again offered to appoint him secretary of war, which he accepted. Crawford forced **Andrew Jackson** to renegotiate the **Treaty of Fort Jackson**, which had compelled the **Creeks** to cede much of their lands, because the treaty encroached on **Cherokee** lands. In the election of 1816, Crawford almost prevailed over **James Monroe** in the **congressional caucus** that selected Madison's successor, even though Crawford had endorsed Monroe's nomination. He subsequently served as secretary of the treasury in the Monroe administration, reorganizing the Treasury Department, then the largest federal bureaucracy, so as to reduce its size to what it had been in 1801. Crawford was the leading candidate to succeed Monroe in 1824 and received the endorsement of the Republican Party's congressional caucus prior to the **election of 1824**. But a paralytic stroke in the fall of 1823 impaired both his vision and speech, and three-quarters of the eligible congressmen abstained from the caucus vote. Though Crawford got more votes in the **Electoral College** than **Henry Clay**, **John Quincy Adams** won the election in the House of Representatives on the first ballot after Clay endorsed Adams in preference to either Jackson or Crawford.

After the election, Crawford retired to a judicial position in Georgia, where he remained to the end of his life. He contributed to the falling out between Jackson and **John C. Calhoun** in 1830 by publishing a letter Calhoun had written in 1818 urging that the Monroe administration repudiate Jackson's aggressive actions in **East Florida**. *See also* WAR OF 1812 (DIPLOMACY OF).

CREEK NATION. A Muskhogean-speaking people living in what is now Georgia, Alabama, and Mississippi. The pressure of U.S. expansion produced division within the tribe. The Lower Creeks, or eastern portion, favored accommodation with the whites and were receptive to settled **agriculture**. The Upper Creeks, to the west, inspired by a visit in 1811 from **Tecumseh**, whose mother had been a Creek, looked to a reversion to ancestral ways for a remedy to white pressure. They became known as "Red Sticks." Civil war broke out between the two Creek factions during 1812 over the murder of isolated whites and mixed-bloods in the border lands, but the **Creek War** between the Red Sticks and whites did not begin in earnest until the summer of 1813 largely because the Upper Creeks suffered from a shortage of arms and ammunition. In the aftermath of this war, the Creek lost more than half their lands in the **Treaty of Fort Jackson**. Those who did not join the **Seminoles** in **East Florida** eventually were forced to accept **removal** to present-day Oklahoma in the 1830s. *See also* CREEK WAR; INDIANS.

CREEK WAR (1811–1814). During the summer of 1813, the civil war between the Lower and Upper Creeks escalated into a wider conflict after the Red Sticks received arms and ammunition from the Spanish in Pensacola, Florida. A detachment of Mississippi's territorial **militia** had ambushed a Red Stick supply train coming from Pensacola on

27 July. The Red Sticks responded on 30 August 1813 with the slaughter of approximately 300 mixed-bloods and whites who had taken refuge in **Fort Mims,** near modern Tensaw, Alabama. The massacre spread sufficient terror along the frontier to involve the Georgia and Tennessee **militias** in the conflict.

A decisive U.S. response was slowed by the distance between the two states, which had been placed in different military districts at the beginning of the **War of 1812**. A shortage of supplies and regular army troops, together with the temporary enlistments of the militia, precluded an effective response during the remainder of 1813. This allowed the Red Sticks to win a series of minor victories against the Georgia and Tennessee militias between November 1813 and January 1814. But **Andrew Jackson** managed to turn the tide in March after his Tennessee militia was reinforced by a regiment of regulars. On 27 March 1814, Jackson attacked a heavily fortified Red Stick position at **Horseshoe Bend**, killing most of the 800 warriors who were defending it. Those who got away subsequently surrendered or fled to the **Seminoles** in Florida. Jackson's victory was so complete that he was able to demand more than half the Creek lands as the price of peace in the **Treaty of Fort Jackson**. Though the Lower Creeks had allied with the whites against the Red Sticks, this failed to protect their lands as well as those of the Upper Creeks from white appropriation.

CUFFEE, PAUL (17 January 1759–7 September 1817). African American entrepreneur, he was born on the island of Cuttyhunk, Massachusetts, to a free African father and an **Indian** mother. The family moved to the mainland before the Revolution. There Cuffee managed to launch a shipping enterprise using the capital of his extended family connections. By the 1790s, he had a fleet of three small schooners that were manned by African crews. Local authorities of southern ports sometimes feared that his crew's presence might set off an insurrection. But Cuffee managed to dodge trouble and by 1806 was worth probably $20,000, making him the richest African American in the United States. He industriously reinvested his profits in several additional vessels, one a ship of over 250 tons burthen. The **Embargo of 1807–1809** put a temporary crimp on his enterprise, but during its operation he joined a **Quaker** meeting that gave him entry to the English Friends. They supported Cuffee's attempt to supply the colony that Britain had recently established for its former slaves in Sierra Leone. Cuffee's hopes of creating a triangular commercial network involving Britain, the United States, and West Africa were frustrated by the **War of 1812**. But after the **Treaty of Ghent**, he resumed his efforts and before his death endorsed the aim of the newly founded **American Colonization Society** to transport **freedmen** back to Africa.

CUMBERLAND (NATIONAL) ROAD. In April 1802, Congress created a fund from the sale of federal lands to be used for the construction of a national road joining the East with the trans-Appalachian West. It acted under the authority conferred in the Constitution to establish postal routes. On 29 March 1806, President **Thomas Jefferson** authorized the appropriation of $30,000 from this fund to be used in surveying a route through the mountains from Cumberland, Maryland, to Wheeling in present-day West Virginia. Though Secretary of State **Albert Gallatin** vigorously supported the building of the national road, construction did not begin until 1811. Shortly afterward, the **War of 1812** interrupted work until 1816. The first section of the road to Wheeling opened in 1818 along a route roughly corresponding to the modern U.S. 40. Subsequent extensions of the road through Ohio and Indiana to Vandalia, Illinois, encountered partisan bickering and the constitutional objections of President **James Monroe**. On 4 May 1822, he vetoed a bill for erecting toll gates along the road on the grounds that doing so exceeded the powers the Constitution had vested in Congress. By the time the road was finally completed in 1850, its functions had been largely assumed by other innovations of the **transportation revolution**, particularly the railroads and **canals**.

– D –

DARTMOUTH COLLEGE CASE (1819). *Board of Trustees of Dartmouth College v. Woodward* grew out of the New Hampshire legislature's attempt in 1816 to reorganize Dartmouth College into a university. The college trustees resisted the reorganization and sued William H. Woodward, in whom the legislature had vested the college property, to recover it. After losing their initial suit and an appeal in the state courts, the trustees appealed to the **Supreme Court**. **Daniel Webster**, representing them, argued that the prohibition in the Constitution against states impairing the obligation of contracts protected the college against the action of the state legislature. **John Marshall** delivered the opinion of the Court invalidating the state law and reversing the ruling of the state supreme court. In ***Fletcher v. Peck*** (1810), Marshall had upheld the validity of one state law by denying the validity of a legislative attempt to repeal it on the grounds that doing so abridged the obligation of contract. In the Dartmouth College case, he broadened the application of the contract clause to invalidate both a state legislature's law and a state judiciary's construction of it. This set the stage for an even broader assertion of judicial power over state legal systems in ***McCulloch v. Maryland*** two weeks later. *See also* SUPREME COURT.

DEARBORN, HENRY (23 February 1751–6 June 1829). Soldier, he was born in Hampton, New Hampshire, and trained as a doctor in Portsmouth with a prominent physician. During the Revolutionary War, he began as a company officer but eventually rose to the rank of lieutenant colonel and briefly served as deputy quartermaster general. After the war, he moved to Maine, then a part of Massachusetts, where he was appointed a major general of the **militia**. In 1797, he was elected to Congress, disclaiming all partisan affiliation. But he soon found himself opposing the policies of the **Federalist Party**. When **Thomas Jefferson** became president as the result of the **election of 1800**, he appointed Dearborn his secretary of war. Dearborn served throughout Jefferson's two administrations, dutifully reducing the army in accordance with the president's policy of retrenchment. Dearborn also saw to the establishment of West Point, but his attempt to assimilate the **Indians** was a failure. When Jefferson retired from the presidency, Dearborn was rewarded for faithful service with the lucrative collectorship of the Port of Boston.

Shortly before the commencement of the **War of 1812**, President **James Madison** appointed him the senior major general in the army. But Dearborn failed to launch a credible offensive against Canada during that year in part because of the refusal of New England's governments to place any of their state militias under his command. The absence of military pressure on **Lower Canada** allegedly contributed to **William Hull**'s humiliating **surrender of Detroit**. Dearborn was no more effective in 1813 because he undercut Secretary of War **John Armstrong**'s plan to take Kingston and move against Montreal. Instead, Dearborn concentrated the forces under his direction on the Niagara frontier. He was relieved of his command in July 1813 as much because of illness as because of ineffectiveness. He resigned his commission at the end of the war and retired from public life. However, President **James Monroe** called him out of retirement to serve as minister to Portugal between 1822 and 1824. *See also* WAR OF 1812 (LAND OPERATIONS).

DECATUR, STEPHEN (5 January 1779–22 March 1820). Naval hero, he was born on the eastern shore of Maryland into a family headed by the captain of the same name who served in the navy during the **Quasi-War**. Decatur seemed destined to pursue a career at sea. But he did not join the USS *United States* as a midshipman until 1798, after having first been tried and acquitted for murdering a prostitute in Philadelphia. In November 1803, he was promoted to lieutenant and ordered to the Mediterranean. On 16 February 1804, he led the party that burned the USS *Philadelphia* at Tripoli before the vessel's captors had a chance to transfer its technology to their own men-of-war or use the *Philadelphia* against American vessels. Subsequently, he led a fleet of gunboats in a close engagement with the pirate forces.

Returning to the United Sates a national hero, Decatur was promoted to captain. He sat on the court-martial of James Barron, who had commanded the **USS *Chesapeake*** when it surrendered to HMS *Leopard* on 22 June 1807. Barron subsequently held Decatur responsible for his being dismissed from the service. At the commencement of the **War of 1812**, Decatur was assigned to the USS *United States*, which succeeded in capturing HMS *Macedonian*. However, he spent most of the rest of the war with his squadron blockaded in New London, Connecticut, by a vastly superior British force. Only after he mothballed the vessels in this squadron in 1814 was he given command of the USS *President* in **New York City**. On 15 January, he had to surrender his ship to the enemy after unsuccessfully trying to run a British blockade. Three weeks later, news arrived from Europe of the peace **Treaty of Ghent**, signed on 24 December 1814.

After being freed, Decatur took command of a nine-vessel squadron in May 1815 ordered to the Mediterranean and rapidly extracted treaties from Algiers, Tunis, and Tripoli to cease molesting American shipping. Returning to the United States, he took a seat on the Board of Naval Commissioners in 1816. Having acquired almost as much reputation as **Andrew Jackson** by his actions in the war, Decatur might have met with success had he entered politics. But instead he perished in a **duel** fought with James Barron on 22 March 1820. *See also* BARBARY WARS; WAR OF 1812 (NAVAL OPERATIONS).

DEISM/DEISTS. The repudiation of divine revelation as the source of religious authority. Deists differed from atheists because they inferred the existence of a deity from rational, empirical observation. Many of the revolutionary leaders leaned toward deism, but only a few were prepared publicly to admit it because of the threat deism posed to the vast majority of American Protestants whose religious identities were rooted in revelation. **Thomas Jefferson** paid dearly for the rest of his public career for articulating deistic sentiments in his *Notes on Virginia* (1787), and most Americans regarded **Thomas Paine**'s deistic polemic, *The Age of Reason* (1795), as a dangerous book. The advance of deism fueled the response of alarmed orthodox religious leaders that ignited the **Second Great Awakening**. **Unitarianism** was often confused with deism, but as the leading deists were quick to point out, subjecting revelation to rational scrutiny was very different from repudiating it entirely.

DEMOCRATIC PARTY. Initially "democracy" was a pejorative term applied by members of the **Federalist Party** to their **Republican Party** adversaries. In the 1820s, in part because of **Andrew Jackson**'s rise from humble origins to national prominence, "democracy" began to take on more positive connotations, and by the **election of 1828** Jackson found it advantageous to claim to be the leader of the Democratic Party.

DEMOCRATIC SOCIETIES. *See* REPUBLICAN SOCIETIES.

DENMARK VESEY REBELLION. *See* VESEY REBELLION.

DEPRESSION OF 1819. *See* PANIC OF 1819.

DETROIT, SURRENDER OF IN 1812. William Hull, the governor of Michigan Territory, in command of a force of four regiments and local **militia** numbering no more than 1,500, received orders to invade western Ontario from Detroit shortly after the declaration of the **War of 1812**. He crossed the Detroit River to move against a British position at Malden in southwestern Ontario that threatened his lines of communication to Ohio, counting on a simultaneous American invasion of the Niagara region along with the expected disaffection of the Canadian militia for success. When he learned that British reinforcements were on their way to Malden because the Niagara frontier seemed secure and **Tecumseh** had attacked his supply lines, he retreated to Detroit. There he was besieged by a British force roughly comparable to his own. But when the governor of **Upper Canada**, Isaac Brock, summoned Hull to surrender on 15 August, Hull capitulated, largely because of Brock's threat to turn Britain's **Indian** allies loose on the civilian population. Hull was subsequently tried by court-martial; condemned for cowardice, neglect of duty, and conduct unbecoming an officer; and sentenced to death. **James Madison** approved of the court's findings but suspended the execution of the death penalty. Hull's name, however, was stricken from the army's roll.

DIRECTORY. The executive branch of the French government under the Constitution of the Year III (1795) that evolved into a dictatorship of five men after the coup d'état of 18 Fructidor (4 September 1797). It ruled France until it was in turn overthrown in the coup d'état of Brumaire (9 November 1799), led by **Napoleon**, and replaced by the Consulate.

***DISCOURSES ON DAVILA* (1791).** In this rambling book, **John Adams** advanced the unpopular thesis that France would be more free and stable if it remained a monarchy than if it adopted a purely republican form of government.

DISCRIMINATION. In the second session of the **first Congress**, **James Madison** countered **Alexander Hamilton**'s plan for the **assumption** of the debts the states had incurred during the Revolution by proposing that the federal government honor its **liquidated** debt as contracted at 6 percent but divide payment equally between the original holders and the speculators who had become the final holders. Madison's proposal precluded assumption, which could be funded only by reducing interest charges on the consolidated debt to 4 percent. Madison feared that the speculation in the southern states' debts shortly before the release of Hamilton's **Report on Public Credit** (1790) would prejudice the public against establishing the public credit of the new government unless the original holders shared in the benefits the speculators reaped. Discrimination also served Virginia interest in blocking assumption because the state feared it would pay a disproportionate amount of the **impost** in order to retire the debts of other states. But Congress decisively rejected Madison's proposal.

DISCRIMINATORY TONNAGE DUTIES. Congressman **James Madison** first proposed levying discriminatory duties on the tonnage of foreign vessels from countries not in treaty with the United States during the first session of the **first Congress**. He hoped to get Britain to agree to full diplomatic relations with the United States and then to induce it to relax its restrictions on American commerce with the West Indies. Congress rejected the proposal, but Madison renewed it in 1791 after Britain had agreed to an exchange of ministers. On this occasion, Madison hoped to extract a commercial treaty from Britain. In 1794, Madison again proposed the measure as a way of retaliating against Britain's forcing American ships sailing for France to enter British ports and sell their cargoes there and in seizing approximately 400 American vessels trading with the French West Indies. Not only did Congress, at the behest of the emerging **Federalist Party**, repeatedly defeat this proposal, but the **Jay Treaty** of 1795 explicitly barred the United States from pursuing such measures to extract concessions from Britain in the future. However, Madison, along with **Thomas Jefferson**, preferred commercial pressure to military action in settling disputes among nations and hoped that measures like his discriminatory tonnage duty would become an essential dimension of an emerging, republican world order.

DOW, LORENZO (16 October 1777–2 February 1834). Methodist evangelist, he was born into a Connecticut family of **Congregation-**

alists. At the age of 17, Dow was persuaded to renounce **Calvinism** by an itinerant Methodist preacher. He then became an itinerant himself but refused to apply for a license from Methodist church authorities. Nonetheless, his camp-meeting revivals proved hugely successful. Between 1794 and 1820, he traveled extensively throughout the United States in addition to visiting Europe three times. He eventually became wealthy by investing his earnings from his religious writings in real estate and patent medicines. Known as "Crazy Dow" because of his bizarre appearance, he was not above using specially contrived effects to stimulate conversions. More than any other preacher of the period, he used revolutionary ideology to question religious authority and to promote the notion that salvation was the individual's opportunity and sole responsibility.

DUELING/DUELS. Dueling began among members of the officer corps of the Continental army during the Revolutionary War. Since the code of honor governing duels applied only to gentlemen, it provided a convenient way of resolving disputes about precedence among the officers that did not jeopardize the fragile divide between officers and enlisted men. The rituals associated with the code of honor were designed to minimize but not completely eliminate violent encounters over questions of honor. After the war, the practice spread to the gentry of the new Republic. In a world where little could be taken for granted, some found contests of honor as available as any other means for achieving recognition if not distinction. While dueling infected the gentry everywhere, after **Aaron Burr** killed **Alexander Hamilton** in a duel in 1804, it was increasingly frowned on in the North. It continued to flourish in the South and West despite efforts to suppress it because of the weaker sanctions exercised by communities and the law in those areas and the presence of **slavery**. Slavery guaranteed the submission of the white nonslaveholders to local elites independently of any other qualification the gentry might possess because of the ever-present threat that a servile insurrection might ignite racial warfare. During **Thomas Jefferson**'s administration, some **Republican Party** congressmen challenged their **Federalist Party** adversaries to duels, which were occasionally accepted. But northern Congressmen could announce in advance that they would not accept challenges without hurting their standing among their constituents, as **Timothy Pickering** and **Josiah Quincy** did. That did not stop southerners and westerners from fighting each other. In April 1826, Secretary of State **Henry Clay** fought a duel with Congressman **John Randolph** over the latter's accusation that a corrupt bargain between Clay and **John Quincy Adams** had led to Adams winning the **election of 1824**. This duel ended without either serious injury or loss of life. But some were not so lucky. Several years before, James Barron had killed **Stephen Decatur**, a naval hero of the **War of 1812**, in a duel. The custom was not abandoned until after the Civil War.

DUNLAP, WILLIAM (19 February 1766–28 September 1839). Dramatist and artist, he was born in Perth Amboy, New Jersey, to parents who fled to **New York City** during the Revolutionary War. There he witnessed his first theatrical performance. After an accident deprived him of the sight in one eye at the age of 12, he took private painting lessons. He soon showed enough promise as a portrait artist for his merchant father, who had prospered during the war, to send him to England in 1784 to study under **Benjamin West**. While in London, he learned a good deal more about the theater than about painting. Though he continued to paint some portraits on his return to New York, much of his energy went into writing plays. *The Father; or, American Shandyism* (1789) was the first of his plays to be produced. In 1796, he took over management of the nation's first professional theatrical company in partnership with other two men. His partners eventually quarreled, and the company dissolved in bankruptcy in 1805, though not before it had produced two of Dunlap's most successful plays, *André* (1798) and *The Glory of Columbia: Her Yeomanry* (1803). In his later years, Dunlap wrote a biography of **Charles Brockden Brown** (1815), histories of New York state and of the arts and design in the United States, and the first *History of the American Theater* (1832). But his most enduring influence remained on the development of the American theater. He was responsible for more than 60 plays and adaptations, supported productions of American playwrights, pioneered the staging of sensational spectacles that theater audiences came to expect, and insisted that theater serve a moral, didactic purpose.

DU PONT, ELEUTHÉRE IRÉNÉE (24 June 1771–31 October 1834). Founder of the American chemical industry, he was born in

Paris and was trained in making gunpowder by the famous French chemist Antoine Lavoisier. The beginning of the **French Revolution** found him employed in a royal arsenal. Along with his father, du Pont was one of the few defenders of Louis XVI to survive the storming of the Tuileries on 10 August 1792. The family subsequently aligned the **newspaper** it published with the Jacobins, but his father escaped the guillotine only because Robespierre's fall brought a timely end to the Terror. The subsequent imprisonment of both father and son after the coup of 18 Fructidor (4 September 1797) persuaded the family to emigrate to the United States. They arrived in Newport, Rhode Island, in 1799 and settled briefly in New Jersey, near **New York City**, without a clear idea of what to do next. A hunting excursion with a French friend in Delaware drew Eleuthère du Pont's attention to the deficiencies of American-made gunpowder.

With **Thomas Jefferson**'s blessing and **Alexander Hamilton**'s legal assistance, du Pont established a powder mill on the Brandywine River in Delaware. The French government supplied him with their latest formulas, equipment, and some trained workers to wean the United States of its dependency on Britain. The enterprise turned a handsome profit during 1804, its first year of operation, and by the **War of 1812** had expanded sufficiently to supply American forces with more than 700,000 pounds of reliable powder during the conflict. Du Pont's enterprise survived an accidental explosion in 1818 that killed 40 people and destroyed his original mill. After rebuilding, he was thought sufficiently prominent to be appointed for two terms to the board of the **Second Bank of the United States**. The company he founded went on to become one of the country's biggest chemical firms in the 20th and 21st centuries. As E. I. du Pont de Nemours and Company, it is still a leader in the industry.

DWIGHT, TIMOTHY (14 May 1752–11 January 1817). Theologian and president of Yale, he was born in Northampton, Massachusetts, a grandson of the 18th-century theologian Jonathan Edwards. Dwight proved to be intellectually precocious and entered Yale at age 13. Excessive study while at college and afterward as a tutor there, together with his attempt to write an American epic poem titled *The Conquest of Canaan* (completed in 1775), permanently impaired his eyesight and led to a general collapse of his health in 1774. After convalescing for three years, he joined Samuel Holden Parsons's brigade in the

Continental army as its chaplain. After Dwight's father died in 1778, he resigned his commission to support his mother and his large family. During this period in his life, he represented the town of Northampton briefly (1781–1782) in the state legislature. In 1783, he was settled as the minister of Greenfield Hill parish in present-day Fairfield, Connecticut, a community he later immortalized in an elegiac poem titled *Greenfield Hill* (1794). During his residence there, he established a coeducational academy that acquired such notice that students dropped out of Yale to attend it.

Dwight succeeded Ezra Stiles as president of Yale after Stiles's death in 1795. Dwight devoted the rest of his life to restoring the college, which had fallen into ruin during and after the Revolutionary War. Among his many innovations was establishing the first professorship of chemistry in an American college, thus positioning Yale at the forefront of scientific research during the 19th century. He also founded Yale's medical school. But he exerted his greatest influence through the moral force of his personality. No student of his willingly disappointed him, and Dwight launched a sustained religious revival in the college that became one of the driving forces of the **Second Great Awakening**. Many Yale graduates, like **Lyman Beecher**, subsequently helped spread Dwight's New Light **Calvinism** throughout the nation. In addition to restoring Yale's prestige, Dwight also was a prime mover in the founding of the Connecticut Academy of Arts and Sciences in 1799.

– E –

EAST FLORIDA. Established by the British Proclamation of 1763 after Spain ceded all of Florida to it at the end of the Seven Years' War, East Florida's western boundary ran along the Apalachicola River to the confluence of the Flint and Chattahoochee Rivers. The northern boundary then extended east to the head of the St. Mary's River and from there to the Atlantic. When Britain ceded the Floridas back to Spain at the conclusion of the Revolutionary War, Spain did not dispute its East Florida boundary with the United States as it did the boundary of **West Florida**.

ECONOMIC DEVELOPMENT OF THE UNITED STATES (1789–1829). The Republic was fortunate in constructing a national legal order authorized by its new federal Constitution just as the country was beginning to recover from the economic dislocations of a prolonged war fought on home soil. A revival in the exchange of American staple exports for European and West Indian imports underwrote **Alexander Hamilton**'s ambitious program for **funding** the revolutionary debt. The yields from the **impost** were not sufficient to service the debt until after the outbreak of a general European war in 1793 enhanced overseas demand for American provisions. The war also made vessels sailing under the American flag the leading neutral carriers of the world. Well before that, the appreciation of the newly funded debt to par enabled it to provide much of the capital subscribed to the **First Bank of the United States**. The notes the Bank issued were stable enough in value to become a reliable medium in fostering exchanges throughout the entire nation. The example of the Bank in turn proved contagious. The three banks in existence in 1790 had become 28 a decade later. By the beginning of the **War of 1812**, there were 90 banks, and by 1830 their number had swollen to 329, though the **Panic of 1819** showed that increasing the number of banks did not necessarily increase the value of the notes they issued.

At best, money only facilitated exchange, though trade increased productivity through the division of labor. The economic expansion between 1789 and 1829 depended on two other critical factors. The most important was **westward movement**. The availability of a vast **public domain** in the American West drew increasing numbers of migrants after the native occupants had been displaced either by disease and purchase or, as in the case of the "civilized" tribes of the South, by coerced, mass **removal**s. The settlement of the West led to an expansion of **agriculture** throughout the first 40 years of the new Republic's existence. In the South, the **slave** plantation accounted for most of the surpluses, while in the North, surplus production remained rooted in the family farm. Technological innovation also proved to be significant. In the North, **Oliver Evans** combined a grain elevator with a grinding mill to permit the more efficient processing of grain surpluses for the market. In the South, **Eli Whitney**'s **cotton gin**, which enabled short staple cotton fibers to be separated from the parent plant both quickly and economically, led to cotton supplanting tobacco as the most valuable American export. Expanded American production was stimulated by the expanding demand for cotton accompanying the application of machine processes to the manufacture of textiles in Europe and the United States. The **Republican Party**'s commercial measures, such as the **Embargo of 1807–1809** and **nonintercourse**, followed by the **War of 1812**, brought the export boom in agricultural products to a temporary halt. But it quickly resumed after the **Treaty of Ghent** and continued unabated into the 1830s.

Agricultural production would not have flourished without the growing access to distant markets that the beginnings of the **transportation revolution** provided. Initially, this took the form of widespread investment in toll roads known as **turnpikes**. Since land transport was much more expensive than water transport, turnpikes were most effective for the short haul. The nation was liberally endowed with navigable rivers, but until **Robert Fulton** demonstrated the commercial feasibility of the steamboat on the Hudson in 1807, its rivers remained more suited for exporting than importing. Rivers also followed courses that could be made more serviceable when supplemented by **canals**. Several short canals had been completed by the beginning of the 19th century, the longest of which was the **Middlesex Canal** linking the Merrimack River with Boston. The **Erie Canal**, linking the Hudson River with the Great Lakes, was the nation's first long-distance canal. Financed by the issuance of state bonds and built by **immigrant** Irish **labor**, it proved so successful that it paid off the entire cost of its construction in the first seven years of operation. This inspired a subsequent canal craze. Soon after the completion of the Erie Canal, the first short railroad went into operation, and almost immediately afterward work began on a line designed to link Baltimore with the Ohio River. With improved transportation came speedier and more secure **communications** facilitated largely through the expansion of the U.S. **Postal Service**.

Though the first attempts at expanding **industrial** production in a factory context took place during the 1790s, the movement from the shop to the factory accelerated in the period 1808–1815 as Republican commercial restrictions and war protected the home market. Industrialists like Eli Whitney, **Eleuthère Irérée du Pont**, and **Paul Revere** freed the nation from having to seek military supplies from European sources during the War of 1812. The dumping of European goods on the American market in the immediate postwar period brought only a temporary halt to the expansion of manufacturing. But as long as water remained the principal source of power, most of the larger industrial establishments, such as the **Boston Manufacturing Company**'s plants at Waltham, Lawrence, and Chicopee, were located in what was then the countryside. Though the factory system depended for its success on its ability to enhance productivity, specialization furthered this end as much as labor-saving technology. In addition to the corporate organization of enterprise and the integration of the entire productive process under one roof, these years were notable for the willingness of men, **women**, and children to supply the labor still required by the new machine processes. Many of these workers came from the farm economy of New England, whose labor demands were contracting because of the opening up of new farmlands to the west. However, the first labor organizations that emerged at the end of the 1820s were not the creation of factory workers. Rather, they reflected the efforts of urban artisans to protect the value of their skills in an expanding market.

Financial chaos accompanied the War of 1812 because of strenuous attempts on the part of bankers sympathetic to the **Federalist Party** to obstruct the war effort rather than the absence of a national bank. However, once the war ended with the Federalists' disgrace, the nation's credit quickly revived despite the addition of almost $100 million to the national debt. In his last address to Congress, President **James Madison** called for the abolition of war taxes. He could do so because half the revenue received by the treasury during 1816 was unbudgeted surplus, suggesting that the nation would be debt free by 1835. The financial health of the nation allowed political leaders increasingly to turn the **impost** into a **tariff** for protecting the American market. There were political costs to doing so, as seen in the attempts by South Carolina to **nullify** the **Tariff of Abominations**. But by the 1820s, the expansion of the national economy, fueled by renewed **immigration** from Europe, appeared to be irreversible. If the early Republic was nothing else, it was a stunning economic success. *See also* BANKING; COMMERCIAL EXPANSION; INDUSTRY; LABOR; TRANSPORTATION REVOLUTION.

EDUCATION. The primary education of male children was highly valued at the time of the Revolution, but different provisions were made for it in the different regions. The northern colonies, some of which had laws requiring towns to provide common primary schools, devolved this function on local school districts that hired school teachers and maintained small schoolhouses. The southern colonies relied largely on itinerant teachers who would temporarily establish a school in someone's home. Alternatively, a wealthy planter would hire a tutor for his children and allow the less prosperous neighboring children to share in the instruction. Secondary education in the classical languages was relevant only to gaining admittance to the eight colonial colleges currently in existence. It could be obtained from the more learned clergy who routinely accepted students as boarders in their households. Most young men expected to complete their training for adult roles as apprentices. Though young girls came increasingly to share in the benefits of common schooling with boys, they apprenticed for homemaking duties either with their mothers or as servants in other people's homes. **Women** were excluded from receiving a college education.

The Revolution inspired several prominent figures, including **Thomas Jefferson** and **Benjamin Rush**, to propose a comprehensive educational system suited to an extended republic. These plans usually called for free elementary education for all and access to a secondary education and college for the most qualified males. The economic disruptions accompanying the war prevented these plans from being implemented. But Massachusetts reenacted its colonial laws requiring towns to provide primary and secondary schools. Beginning in 1795, the New York state legislature appropriated money for distribution to its local school districts. Connecticut also formed a fund from the sale of its western lands in Ohio and used the income from $1,200,000 it realized to support its common schools until the 1830s. Other states were less fortunate in establishing school funds during these years. Only Delaware managed some form of public support for its common schools before 1830.

The management of education by local school districts worked reasonably well for the vast majority of the population. During the 40 years between 1789 and 1829, enrollment in rural common schools continued the rise begun in the colonial period, producing almost universal literacy in the North and expanding it among white males in the South. But local school districts were not suited to the needs of the growing urban populations of the era. In 1789, most primary education in the emerging cities of the nation took place in "pay schools" for which parents paid. As the cities grew, the system increasingly failed to serve the needs of the children of common laborers and **immigrants**. At the same time, the urban elites feared that if these constituencies were not educated, they would breed civil disorder. The leaders responded with charity schools that enrolled both boys and girls, if not during the week then at least in Sunday schools. The charity school movement even led to the establishment of infant schools. As the pay schools got more expensive, the numbers seeking admission to charity schools increased. This induced their sponsors to form citywide associations for the efficient administration of limited resources. After 1830, they would give increased weight to calls for a publicly supported educational system.

Secondary education remained relatively undeveloped during the early republican era. Apprenticeship still remained the option most pursued, even in learned professions like the law. Those bent on acquiring a college education still boarded with clergymen versed in the classical languages and known to the president of a reputable college. With the exception of Boston's Latin School, which had been established by the town in the 17th century, what secondary schooling there was remained private before 1827, when Massachusetts passed a law to provide free schooling above the primary level. A few academies, such as Governor Dummer (1763), predated the Revolution, while Phillips Andover (1778) and Phillips Exeter (1781) had been established during the war years. But most were created after 1789. During the next 35 years, 14 new academies emerged, some of which survive today along with many others that have since disappeared. They resembled the independent pay schools of the cities except in the more advanced subjects they taught and their rural settings. But they did not begin to keep pace with the number of colleges founded during the early republican era.

After the Revolution, 19 new colleges were chartered between 1782 and 1802. Dickinson College (1783), Williams College (1793), and Bowdoin College (1802) reflected the religious motivations of their founders as had been the case with all but one of the colonial colleges. The nonsectarian College of Philadelphia (1752), which subsequently became the University of Pennsylvania, was more widely copied in the postwar years. In 1795, the New York Board of

Regents established Union College as a nonsectarian institution. North Carolina opened the first publicly funded college that became the state university in the same year. Georgia, which had issued a charter for a state college as early as 1785, did not succeed in establishing the institution that would become the University of Georgia until 1801. But **George Washington**'s desire to create a national university received little support despite Jefferson's and **Joel Barlow**'s subsequent endorsement of the idea.

The **Second Great Awakening** continued to play a role in the colleges founded during the next quarter century, as the establishment of Hamilton College (1812), Amherst College (1822), and Trinity College (1824) demonstrate. But publicly sponsored secular institutions also proliferated in South Carolina, Kentucky, Ohio, Tennessee, and Virginia. These years also saw the opening of professional graduate schools in a range of fields that included medicine, beginning with Harvard (1782); law, beginning with **Tapping Reeve's Litchfield Law School** (1784); and theology, with the establishment of Andover Theological Seminary (1808). In addition, the nation saw the founding of its first military academy, West Point (1802), and its first civilian engineering school with the establishment of the Renssaeler Polytechnic Institute (1824). Opportunities for higher learning significantly outstripped the development of secondary education. But the new collegiate institutions addressed the imbalance by offering preparatory courses that qualified students for admission to their higher-degree programs.

ELECTION (PRESIDENTIAL) OF 1789. In September 1788, after the Constitution had been ratified by 11 states, the Congress of the Articles of Confederation called on them to choose presidential electors by 7 January 1789. The electors were instructed to cast their ballots on 4 February. The schedule allowed little time for factional intrigue, which accorded with the intentions of the framers who had designed the **Electoral College**. **George Washington** was unanimously elected the first president of the United States. **John Adams** received the largest plurality of electoral votes after Washington and so became the first vice president. New York failed to cast its electoral votes because of unresolved differences between the two houses of its legislature.

ELECTION (PRESIDENTIAL) OF 1792. Despite the emergence of factional tensions within **George Washington**'s first administration, the president was reelected for a second term without dissent, though three electors abstained. **John Adams** fared better in this election than previously, receiving a solid majority of the electoral votes to remain vice president.

ELECTION (PRESIDENTIAL) OF 1796. A national division between the **Federalist Party** and the **Republican Party** first surfaced in this election despite **George Washington**'s postponing his **Farewell Address** until mid-September in order to minimize intrigues over the succession. The division stemmed from the polarizing impact of the **Jay Treaty** reinforced by the French ambassador Pierre Adet's clumsy attempt to influence the vote of the **Electoral College**. He announced that France would sever diplomatic relations with the United States should **Thomas Jefferson** not be elected Washington's successor. The threat had no noticeable effect on the outcome, but it did dramatize Jefferson's disagreement with President Washington's foreign policy. **John Adams** received three more electoral votes than Jefferson to become the second president of the United States. Jefferson, who in turn had more electoral votes than either **Thomas Pinckney** or **Aaron Burr**, became the second vice president.

ELECTION (PRESIDENTIAL) OF 1800. The first prolonged electoral contest between the **Federalist Party** and the **Republican Party** ended in a tie between the two Republican candidates, **Thomas Jefferson** and **Aaron Burr**. **John Adams** owed his election in 1796 to several southern states choosing their electors by district. Had they been chosen as part of a general ticket or been designated by their state legislatures, the Federalist minority would have been denied all voice in the South just as the Federalist state legislatures had denied the minority of Republicans a voice in the North. In 1800, the southern states made sure this did not happen again. The legislatures of Pennsylvania and Maryland were divided with Republicans controlling one house, the Federalists the other. They managed to avoid deadlock, and have each state's vote counted by working out compromises that divided their respective electoral votes. **Alexander**

Hamilton's attempt to swing Federalist electors from Adams to **Charles C. Pinckney** failed to influence the outcome of the election. But since neither Jefferson nor Burr had a clear majority, the final selection fell to the Federalist-controlled House of Representatives, voting by states. After vainly trying to get both Republican candidates to make concessions to the Federalists, Jefferson was elected third president of the United States on the 36th ballot. Jefferson, who thought the presidency rightfully his, never forgave Burr, who could have put a stop to Federalist intrigues by simply declaring that he would accept only the vice presidency.

ELECTION (PRESIDENTIAL) OF 1804. This was the first election under the recently ratified **Twelfth Amendment** requiring electors to vote separately for president and vice president. **Thomas Jefferson** and the Republican nominee for vice president, **George Clinton**, triumphed over their Federalist rivals, **Charles C. Pinckney** and **Rufus King**, capturing 92 percent of the electoral vote. Only Connecticut and Delaware electors voted for the Federalist ticket, reflecting the steep decline in the fortunes of the **Federalist Party**.

ELECTION (PRESIDENTIAL) OF 1808. Thomas Jefferson had no desire to violate **George Washington**'s precedent for serving no more than two presidential terms, especially after the controversy over the **Embargo of 1807–1808** had poisoned Jefferson's last year in office. In May 1808, the **Republican Party**'s **congressional caucus** chose Secretary of State **James Madison** to be Jefferson's successor with **George Clinton** continuing as vice president. Dissident southern Republicans, led by **John Randolph**, had no success in promoting **James Monroe** as an alternative to Madison. The **Federalist Party** again nominated **Charles C. Pinckney** and **Rufus King**, who fared slightly better than they had in the previous presidential election. Thanks to the embargo, the Federalists recovered political control of several New England states that had voted for Jefferson in 1804, most notably Massachusetts, which still included Maine.

ELECTION (PRESIDENTIAL) OF 1812. The disastrous beginning of the **War of 1812** failed to deny **James Madison** reelection with **Elbridge Gerry** as his vice president. Madison, who was again the choice of the Republican congressional **caucus**, faced serious competition from the dissident New York Republican, **DeWitt Clinton**, the nephew of the recently deceased vice president, **George Clinton**. As mayor of **New York City**, the younger Clinton opposed the war that had been declared the previous June. The **Federalist Party** endorsed Clinton and his running mate Jared Ingersoll from Pennsylvania. Ingersoll's candidacy represented an unsuccessful effort to court a state critical to the outcome of the election. Madison commanded solid backing from the South and the new western states in addition to Pennsylvania and Vermont. That Clinton had carried all the other states north of the Potomac suggested that Federalism's fortunes were reviving.

ELECTION (PRESIDENTIAL) OF 1816. The survival of the nation in the face of attempts by members of the **Federalist Party** to bankrupt the government and threats to conclude a separate peace with Britain deprived the **Republican Party**'s nominee of a serious Federalist challenger in 1816. **Rufus King** still received 15 percent of the electoral votes, but Federalism was clearly on the wane. The principal question in this election was whether **James Monroe** or **William H. Crawford** would be **James Madison**'s successor. Despite Crawford's record as an influential congressman, Monroe narrowly won the endorsement of the Republican **congressional caucus**. **Daniel D. Tompkins**, the war governor of New York, received the vice-presidential nomination.

ELECTION (PRESIDENTIAL) OF 1820. James Monroe faced no opponent and received all but four votes—one was cast for **John Quincy Adams**, and there were three abstentions—for the presidency. **Daniel D. Tompkins** was reelected vice president, though not by quite as overwhelming a margin. The near unanimity of this election made it emblematic of the "**Era of Good Feelings**."

ELECTION (PRESIDENTIAL) OF 1824. The unanimity of the previous presidential election vanished in the factional struggle over who would succeed **James Monroe**. With the disappearance of the **Federalist Party**, the **Republican Party**'s **congressional caucus** lost its former rationale of designating the single candidate around whom the diffuse Republican majority of the nation had to coalesce in order to defeat their adversaries. Though a poorly attended congressional caucus nominated **William H. Crawford** in 1824, the other contenders questioned its legitimacy, especially since Crawford had previously been seriously incapacitated by a stroke. **John C. Calhoun**'s supporters had first announced his candidacy at the end of 1821. The Tennessee legislature nominated **Andrew Jackson** in the middle of 1822. **Henry Clay** was nominated by the Kentucky legislature and tried to solidify his claim to the presidency by promoting his **American system**. Finally, **John Quincy Adams**'s diplomatic successes as secretary of state recommend him for the highest office in the land.

The competition among ambitious leaders intersected with a sea of change taking place in American politics. Throughout the 1820s, the last barriers to universal manhood **suffrage** collapsed, and the selection of presidential electors fell increasingly to an expanded male electorate. Though six state legislatures still named a slate of electors in 1824, the remaining 18 provided for their popular election. After Calhoun withdrew from the competition to seek the uncontested vice presidency, Jackson received the greatest number of popular and electoral votes, while Clay received the least. Since no candidate had a clear majority in the **Electoral College**, the task of choosing between the top three candidates passed to the House of Representatives voting by states.

Though Clay had been eliminated from consideration, as Speaker of the House he still wielded enormous influence. He had never been on cordial terms with Jackson, and he now used his influence to have Adams chosen president. Jackson, who felt his popular vote entitled him to the presidency, alleged that he had been cheated by a corrupt bargain between Adams and Clay. His change seemed to be confirmed when Adams appointed Clay secretary of state. That office had been the stepping-stone by which the last three presidents had come into the White House, and Jackson feared it would work the same magic for Clay. He and his supporters spent the next four years making sure this did not happen by founding the **Democratic Party**.

ELECTION (PRESIDENTIAL) OF 1828. Andrew Jackson relied on a nucleus of strategically placed politicians and **newspaper** editors to capture the White House in 1828. At their center was Vice

President **John C. Calhoun** of South Carolina—who felt no compunction about unseating President **John Quincy Adams**, **Martin Van Buren** of New York, and **Thomas Hart Benton** of Missouri. After the Tennessee legislature renominated Jackson for the presidency in October 1825, he retired from the Senate to concentrate on his campaign. His supporters eventually succeeded in taking control of Congress, where they sponsored measures like the **Tariff of Abominations** in an effort to divide Adams's mid-Atlantic supporters from his New England ones. Adams refused to use presidential patronage to defend himself against the machinations of the Jacksonians. He also declined trying to harness the nascent **anti-Masonic** movement in the Northeast for his reelection. Adams's influential supporters like **Henry Clay** and **Daniel Webster** tried to compensate for the president's reluctance about leading a political party, but they were no match for Jackson's **Democratic Party**. Newspapers committed to Adams fought back by dredging up incidents from Jackson's controversial past, including his **dueling** and the allegation that his wife had been married to someone else when she married him, making this the most scurrilous presidential campaign the nation had yet witnessed. Jackson eventually won 56 percent of the popular vote and 68 percent of the electoral vote, while Calhoun was virtually unopposed in his bid for reelection as vice president. Jackson and his supporters hailed his victory as a triumph for democracy, but superior organization was probably more important, particularly in critical states like New York and Pennsylvania.

ELECTORAL COLLEGE. Article II, section 1, of the original Constitution provided for the selection of the president and vice president by special electors appointed by the states. Each state was entitled to as many members of the Electoral College as it had senators and representatives in Congress. On a specific day prescribed by Congress, the electors were to meet in their respective states, where each would cast two votes, only one of which could be for a resident of the elector's state. If one person received a majority of the electors' votes, he would become president, while the individual with the next-highest total, not necessarily a majority, would become vice president. The drafters of the Constitution expected that in most elections the Electoral College would fail to produce a majority candidate. The selection of president and vice president would then devolve on the House of Representatives voting by states, choosing from among the three candidates with the largest tally of electoral votes. The arrangement was designed to allow the large states an advantage in nominating the president, while the smaller states would have an advantage in making the final selection.

Though designed to insulate the selection of the president from intrigues, both foreign and domestic, the **Federalist Party** and the **Republican Party** began improvising a system during the **election of 1796** whereby prospective members of the Electoral College were pledged in advance to vote for a candidate. In the **election of 1800**, the arrangement produced a tie between the two Republican candidates, **Thomas Jefferson** and **Aaron Burr**. That left the Federalist majority in the House of Representatives with the power to choose between them. The Federalists hoped to play one off against the other and thereby win concessions from the successful candidate. The effort failed, and the Republicans drafted the **Twelfth Amendment** at the end of 1803 to avoid a repetition of what had happened in the previous election. The amendment required electors to cast separate votes for president and vice president. The amendment received the sanction of two-thirds of both houses of Congress and was ratified by three-quarters of the states in time to be implemented in the **election of 1804** despite the vehement objections of the Federalists, who saw it as limiting their power to influence future presidential elections.

ELEVENTH AMENDMENT (TO THE CONSTITUTION). The Constitution grants jurisdiction to the federal courts in controversies between a state and a citizen of another state as well as in controversies between a state and the subject or citizen of a foreign country. A suit instituted by Alexander Chisholm against the state of Georgia (***Chisholm v. Georgia***) came before the **Supreme Court** during its August term in 1792 but was postponed until the following February to allow the state time to respond. When the state failed to appear on 18 February 1793, the Court ruled that judgment should be entered against Georgia by default if the state failed to appear by the first day of the next term. Two days after this decision was announced, Senator Theodore Sedgwick of Massachusetts proposed the Constitution be amended to deny the federal judiciary jurisdiction in suits by individuals against states. Connecticut and Virginia proposed a similar amendment, while the Georgia legislature declared that anyone attempting to execute judgment in the Chisholm case would be guilty of a felony. On 5 March, Congress forwarded to the states the Eleventh Amendment, which **John Adams** declared ratified on 8 January 1798. Though the Supreme Court had issued a writ of enquiry in February 1794 to begin executing its judgment, after the Eleventh Amendment was proposed, no further attempt was made to do so.

ELLICOTT, ANDREW (24 January 1754–20 August 1820). Mathematician and surveyor, he was born to a Pennsylvania **Quaker** family headed by a miller who was also a clock maker. While Ellicott was still young, the family moved to the Baltimore area and established a series of mills near to the growing metropolis. During the Revolutionary War, Ellicott served in the Maryland **militia**, rising to the rank of captain. After the war, he was made a member of the commission to establish the boundary between Virginia and Pennsylvania, a task that was completed during 1787. In 1791, the federal government commissioned him to ascertain whether the speculators who had purchased Massachusetts's claim to parts of western New York were entitled to what is now Erie, Pennsylvania. Subsequently, President **George Washington** hired Ellicott to mark off the boundaries of the District of Columbia. In 1796, Washington again commissioned him to survey the boundary between Spanish **East Florida** and **West Florida** and the United States that had been agreed to in **Pinckney's Treaty**. Later, Ellicott declined **Thomas Jefferson**'s offer to appoint him surveyor general of the United States. But he did accept President **James Madison**'s appointment as professor of mathematics at West Point. After the **War of 1812**, he helped establish the line between the United States and Canada prescribed in the **Treaty of Ghent**.

ELLSWORTH, OLIVER (29 April 1745–26 November 1807). Statesman and second chief justice of the United States, he was born in Windham, Connecticut. Attending first Yale, from which he was dismissed for disciplinary reasons, and then Princeton, he graduated in 1766. He then trained for the law and was elected to the Connecticut

General Assembly between 1773 and 1775. With the advent of the Revolution, he assumed greater responsibilities as a member of the state's Council of Safety and the upper house of the legislature. Between 1778 and 1783, he represented Connecticut in the Continental Congress and in 1787 was named a delegate to the Philadelphia Convention. There he distinguished himself by helping to craft the Connecticut Compromise, whereby the small states got equal representation with the large states in the Senate. After leading the Federalist effort to secure Connecticut's ratification of the Constitution, the legislature elected Ellsworth to the U.S. Senate in the **first Congress**. He was one of the principal architects of the **Judiciary Act of 1789** and helped manage the passage of the amendments to the Constitution that subsequently became known as the **Bill of Rights**. In 1796, **George Washington** appointed him second chief justice after **John Jay** refused to continue as chief justice in the wake of the controversy over the **Jay Treaty**. In that capacity, Ellsworth vigorously supported the judicial enforcement of Federalist laws like the **Sedition Act**, arguing that because the federal government already possessed common-law jurisdiction over seditious libel, the law actually expanded rather than abridged the freedom of speech. In 1799, he accepted **John Adams**'s appointment as one of the three peace commissioners who negotiated the **Franco-American Convention of 1800** with France. On returning to the United States in 1801 after **Thomas Jefferson**'s victory in the **election of 1800**, Ellsworth retired from national politics. However, he remained active in state affairs until his death.

EMANCIPATION. *See* FIRST EMANCIPATION.

EMBARGO. A legal ban on vessels or goods leaving the United States. *See also* EMBARGO OF 1807–1809; EMBARGO OF 1812; EMBARGO OF 1813–1814.

EMBARGO OF 1807–1809. In December 1807, **Thomas Jefferson** responded to the simultaneous news that the **Franco-American Convention of 1800** would no longer exempt the United States from **Napoleon**'s **Berlin Decree** and that Britain was about to impose sweeping new restrictions on **neutral commerce** by asking Congress to embargo American shipping. Congress complied on the assumption that this was the only way to protect the nation's maritime property from the depredations of the great powers. Over the winter, the administration sought a diplomatic resolution to its problems with the belligerents in vain. Instead, the text of a British **Order-in-Council** of 16 November 1807 forcing American vessels trading with those portions of Europe under French control to enter British ports and pay duties before proceeding arrived. Napoleon then responded with the **Milan Decree**, which subjected any neutral vessel obeying the new British regulations to condemnation if captured. The embargo accordingly acquired a new rationale during the spring as an alternative to war that would coerce the belligerent powers into an accommodation.

Continuing the embargo disrupted many commercial ventures normally initiated in the spring and proved very unpopular in New England. Massachusetts Congressman **Timothy Pickering** used it to launch a campaign motivated as much by the desire to defeat the Republicans, who controlled the state government, as by a concern for commerce. In an inflammatory pamphlet, he claimed that Napoleon had ordered Jefferson to institute the embargo to complement his **continental system** directed against Britain and that the measure was intended to provoke war with Britain. Pickering's efforts contributed to the Federalists' success in capturing control of both houses of the state legislature. The **Federalist Party** then used its newly acquired advantage to oppose the embargo in a way that encouraged wholesale violations of its provisions.

Larger developments in the Atlantic world proved as significant as Federalist agitation in subverting the embargo's effectiveness as an instrument of commercial coercion. Napoleon's attempt to place the Spanish crown on his brother's head ignited a **Spanish insurrection** against the French, which Britain nourished by dispatching an expeditionary force to the Iberian Peninsula. To sustain that force, Britain lifted its blockade of the Continent as it applied to Spain and Portugal, creating an attractive market for American grain exports that led many to defy the embargo. The Spanish insurrection also led to the gradual collapse of Spain's New World empire. British merchants rushed into the market created by the ensuing **Latin American revolutions** from which they had previously been excluded. This initially more than compensated for loss of access to the U.S. market. Military measures provided for in the **Enforcement Act of 1809** proved futile in tempering the Federalist assault against the embargo in the face of overseas developments. At the beginning of February 1809, Congress announced its intention to replace the general embargo with a modified embargo against Britain and France known as **nonintercourse**. On 4 March, Congress repealed the embargo as of 15 March, but nonintercourse was not to go into effect until 20 May. Though ostensibly evenhanded, nonintercourse favored Britain at the expense of France because it allowed Britain access to the American market through third parties that Britain could deny to France because of the former's naval superiority.

EMBARGO OF 1812. On 1 April 1812, President **James Madison** asked Congress for a 60-day embargo. Though not explicitly stated in his message, most regarded this request as preliminary to a declaration of war against Britain. The House immediately complied, but the Senate insisted on a 90-day embargo. The Embargo of 1812 came just before the spring elections in Massachusetts and contributed to the Federalist victory that ousted governor **Elbridge Gerry** from office and gave the **Federalist Party** control of the Massachusetts House of Representatives. Capturing the state senate took another year, thanks to the previous legislature's gerrymandering. Thereafter, Massachusetts remained under Federalist control for a full decade. Despite the loss of a large, strategically positioned state, Madison invited Congress to declare war on 1 June 1812. Congress finally obliged on 18 June, and the **War of 1812** was proclaimed on 19 June.

EMBARGO OF 1813–1814. President **James Madison** asked Congress to impose this embargo to cut off the thriving trade with the British that had continued through the early phases of the **War of 1812**. Though New England was not alone in conducting this trade, its exemption from the British blockade had encouraged commerce with the enemy. Congress obliged on 17 December 1813. In response, the Massachusetts legislature threatened to call a convention, which, since the release of the **Henry Papers**, had become a coded way of threatening either **secession** from the Union or its military equivalent, a separate peace with Britain.

The retreat of **Napoleon** to France during the ensuing winter shrank the scope of the **continental system** and led Britain to relax its restrictions on **neutral commerce** with most of the rest of Europe. The Republicans in Congress now rethought their system of commercial restrictions aimed at Britain. They decided that more was to be gained from repealing the embargo and the ban on importing British goods—which was unenforceable given the political control the Federalists exerted over New England—than persisting with them. They hoped that by abolishing all restrictions on the commerce of neutrals, they could gain much-needed revenue from an **impost** on imports in high demand. If Britain attempted to crack down on the trade of neutrals, it would simply alienate those nations, strengthening the hand of the United States internationally. Congress accordingly lifted its commercial restrictions against importing British goods together with the embargo on 14 April 1814. Those Republicans who were reluctant about doing so were reassured when Britain extended its naval blockade to all of New England shortly afterward.

ENFORCEMENT ACT OF 1809. This desperate attempt by the 10th Congress to increase the effectiveness of the **Embargo of 1807–1809** as an instrument of commercial coercion directed against Britain and France authorized federal officials to call on the state **militias** to help them enforce the law. But news of the Enforcement Act inflamed opposition to the embargo in New England. Federalist majorities in both houses of the Massachusetts legislature passed a bill that would have made it a state crime to obey certain sections of the new federal statute. Though the Republican lieutenant governor of the state vetoed the bill, the Republican majority in Congress concluded that the embargo could not be enforced in New England without igniting a civil war. This led Congress to abandon both the embargo, repealed on 4 March 1809, effective 15 March, and the Enforcement Act.

ENTREPÔT. A market in which the exchange of foreign imports for domestic exports was centered. Most commercial towns served as entrepôts for their immediate environs, but only the largest cites, like **New York City** and **New Orleans**, could vie for the distinction of being the commercial hub of a nation in the former case or of a substantial region in the latter.

ERA OF GOOD FEELINGS. A phrase used to describe the period from 1817 to 1825 embracing **James Monroe**'s presidency. It was coined by a Boston Federalist **newspaper**, the *Columbian Centinel*, in connection with Monroe's 1817 tour of the New England states, which had done everything in their power to obstruct the conduct of the **War of 1812**. As such, it aptly described the disappearance of the partisan competition between the **Federalist Party** and the **Republican Party** that had brought the nation to the brink of dissolution by the time of the **Hartford Convention**. However, though these years witnessed the dissolution of the **First Party System**, new problems quickly replaced the old ones as potential sources of division. The most prominent of these were disputes engendered by the economic recession originating in the **Panic of 1819**, the expansion of **slavery** that eventuated in the **Missouri Compromise**, and the selection of Monroe's successor.

ERIE CANAL. Visionaries had dreamed of joining Lake Erie with the Hudson River since the end of the 17th century, but the project became a reality only because of **DeWitt Clinton**'s leadership. In 1817, he persuaded the New York legislature to issue $7 million in state bonds to finance building the 363-mile **canal**. Construction began on 4 July 1817, and the first and middle section of the canal, joining Utica with Rome, New York, opened on 23 October 1822. A year later, it was possible to pass by water from the Genesee River to Albany. When completed in only seven years, the canal had 77 locks and an 802-foot aqueduct spanning the Genesee River. Contractors arranged for the **immigration** of Irish laborers who had experience working on the construction of British canals. But the American civil engineers under whose direction they worked had little formal training in undertaking a project of this magnitude.

On 26 October 1825, Clinton was a passenger on the first boat to pass between Lake Erie and **New York City**, where he poured two casks of lake water into the harbor to symbolize the "marriage of the waters." The canal immediately reduced shipping charges between the city and the Great Lakes to one-tenth of what they had previously been. This resulted in expanded traffic and retired the entire cost of construction in seven years. The success of the Erie Canal ignited a canal-building craze in the nation that resulted in many less profitable enterprises. One of the more lasting effects of the canal's completion was to consolidate New York City's position as the nation's preeminent commercial center. *See also* ENTREPÔT.

ESSEX DECISION. During the diplomatic rapprochement between Great Britain and the United States that began with the **Jay Treaty**, Britain relaxed its efforts to disrupt trade between the French West Indies and continental Europe to the extent of tolerating an indirect trade between the two in U.S. vessels. The legal fiction used in legitimating this commerce was the "broken voyage." As long as the American vessel carrying French colonial produce first entered an American port and broke bulk (a euphemism for unloading), the British admiralty courts would protect an American vessel transporting the colonial goods to France from condemnation after capture. American trade with the French West Indies flourished under the broken voyage rule until Britain's admiralty courts repudiated the doctrine in the *Essex* decision of 23 July 1805 and substituted in its place the **Rule of 1756**. The ruling acquired additional force after the British victory over the French and Spanish fleets in the Battle of Trafalgar gave the Royal Navy undisputed dominance in the European and Caribbean seas.

EUROPEAN WARS. *See* NAPOLEONIC WARS; WARS OF THE FRENCH REVOLUTION.

EVANS, OLIVER (13 September 1775–15 April 1819). Inventor, he was born in Newport, Delaware. While still serving as an apprentice to a wheelwright, he invented machines capable of mechanizing two operations required in making wool or cotton cards. From an early age, Evans was fascinated with the possibilities of steam-powered locomotion. But before developing either land or water vehicles, he built an automated flour mill that relied on gravity to feed grain to grinding stones from a conveyor belt in an elevator. Started in 1785 and perfected in subsequent years, Evans expected his automated mill to be widely copied, and he secured patents in the hope of being able to live off the licensing fees. But the design caught on slowly, and after it had, Evans spent almost as much on prosecuting patent infringements as he did in collecting royalties.

Beginning in 1800, Evans concentrated on applying high-pressured steam power to propulsion both on land and in the water. A contract with Philadelphia for a dredging vessel led him to build the amphibious, steam-powered *Oruktor Amphibolos*. But despite attracting considerable attention, no one else was prepared to buy such a device. After 1806, Evans was more successful in constructing steam engines in his Mars Works foundry. By 1815, he had produced more than 100 such engines that could be found in vessels navigating the Delaware and the Ohio Rivers. But Evans's vision of steam-powered land transportation would have to wait until a decade after his death to become a reality.

EXPLORATION. The **Louisiana Purchase** of 1803 ignited a flurry of government-sponsored expeditions to investigate the interior of the continent. The first, most ambitious, and therefore most famous of these was **Meriwether Lewis** and **William Clark**'s overland trek to the Pacific in 1803–1806. It signaled that the Republic entertained continental ambitions well before the nation had established any claim to the Pacific coast. Lewis and Clark were followed by **Zebulon M. Pike**'s explorations of the upper Mississippi River and the Southwest in 1805–1807 and Stephen H. Long's exploration of the region between the Missouri River and the Rocky Mountains in 1820. Exploration was not confined to government-sponsored expeditions. Fur traders, many of them associated with **John Jacob Astor**'s **American Fur Company**, contributed to an expanding knowledge of the West, as did naturalists like Thomas Nuttall. The initial reports from travelers in the interior, however, were not encouraging. Instead of a Garden of Eden, they conveyed the impression that the Great Plains was a desert. After 1830, that misconception gradually disappeared with the development of the telegraph and the railroad.

– F –

FALLEN TIMBERS, BATTLE OF. On 20 August 1794, a force of 2,000 army regulars and 1,500 **militia** under Anthony Wayne's command withstood an ambush by over 1,000 Indians supported by a few Canadian militiamen in a thickly wooded area known as Fallen Timbers in northwestern Ohio. Wayne's force then dispersed their adversaries in a bayonet charge and drove them toward the British-held Fort Miami. Not wishing to engage an American force of such numbers, the British commander refused to shelter the fleeing Indians. After defying British orders to refrain from advancing toward the fort, Wayne employed his troops in devastating the villages of Britain's Indian allies. They quickly sued for peace. The victory annulled the defeat a smaller American force had met with in 1791 under Arthur St. Clair. Wayne's victory at Fallen Timbers led directly to the first **Treaty of Greenville** in 1795.

FAREWELL ADDRESS. George Washington waited until 19 September 1796 to announce publicly that he would not accept another term as president of the United States. Though **James Madison** had drafted a valedictory address for the president in 1792, Washington relied principally on **Alexander Hamilton** for his farewell address to the nation. Substantively, the 5,000-word document stressed the advantages that Americans derived from their union and cautioned them against becoming entangled in foreign alliances with European powers. It also condemned the emergence of sectional political alignments that the struggle over the **Jay Treaty** had produced.

FEDERALIST PARTY. The phrase originally referred to a coalition of like-minded gentry leaders dedicated to securing the Revolution through the establishment of a stronger central government. They saw to drafting and ratifying the Constitution and then implemented the new government in the **first Congress**. After 1791, the original Federalists began to divide into what subsequently came to be known as the Federalist Party and the **Republican Party**. Henceforth, the distinguishing characteristic of a Federalist was desiring good relations with Great Britain no matter what the cost with France. Though Federalists continued to claim credit for the development of such national programs and institutions as **funding** the consolidated revolutionary debt, the **First Bank of the United States**, and the navy, these remained secondary to avoiding war with Britain as long as the **European wars** stemming from the **French Revolution** lasted.

The Federalists' desire to align the nation with Britain grew out of a calculation about which of the great powers was most likely to triumph.

Because they assumed that the American Republic was weak, they were especially anxious to aligned the nation with the European victor. But their assumption that the Republic was weak also reflected their sense of themselves within the nation. After the **election of 1800**, Federalism increasingly became a political sect centered in southern New England. Though there were Federalists in the South and the West, they, like their New England counterparts, had been placed on the political defensive by the strength of the Republican gentry surrounding them.

Both parties initially assumed that war with one of the principal European belligerents inevitably would involve the nation in an alliance with the other, just as the Revolution had led to the **Franco-American alliance**. The Federalists feared such an alliance would strengthen French influence over the United States, ensuring that the American Republic would pursue the same path from a revolutionary republic to a military dictatorship as France had. Indeed, the Federalists assumed that France represented the trajectory that all republics were likely to follow without proper restraint.

The Federalists' preference for monarchical Britain led many to question their loyalty to **Republicanism**. Though they saw themselves as Republicans, the course they pursued from the **Embargo of 1807–1809** to the end of the **War of 1812** was often at odds with the Republican premise that the majority should rule. Federalists also did their best during the war with Britain to hamstring the federal government. In the **Hartford Convention**, the party's New England leadership tried to coerce the rest of the nation into accepting a wholesale revision of the Constitution that would empower the Federalists at the expense of their Republican adversaries. After the war ended honorably with the **Treaty of Ghent** and **Andrew Jackson**'s victory at the Battle of **New Orleans**, the Federalist Party disappeared as a force in national politics, partly as a consequence of the pacification of Europe and partly because of the disgrace it had brought on itself.

FICTION. Independence bred a cultural nationalism in the American reading public that created the expectation that nationhood would produce a great American novel as well as a great American epic poem. Cultural nationalism easily overpowered the lingering suspicion with which religious and political elites viewed novels. Since the appearance of John Bunyan's *Pilgrim's Progress* in the mid-17th century, the devices of fiction had widely infiltrated religious literature. Many of the religious tracts issued by the **American Tract Society** would later take the form of morally instructive fiction.

The first authentically American novel was William Hill Brown's *The Power of Sympathy* (1789), a sentimental tale of seduction masquerading as a morality story. **Susanna Rowson**'s *Charlotte: A Tale of Truth* (1791) quickly became the most successful exemplar of this genre. Though men and **women** both devoured such tales under the guise of moral instruction, they disproportionately appealed to a female audience. The increasing leisure available to women after the Revolution, particularly with increased **urbanization**, broadened the demand for this kind of literary product and helped create a generation of female authors who wrote for women.

While sentimental tales of seduction proved to be the most popular novels, American authors explored other possibilities as well. Hugh Henry Brackenridge's *Modern Chivalry*, published in installments between 1792 and 1815, parodied the collapse of elitist distinctions before the advance of democracy. **Royall Tyler** exploited the potential of the adventure tale in *The Algerine Captive* (1797). The most versatile American novelist of the early period was **Charles Brockden Brown**, who in the short space of four years (1798–1801) published six major works that were early exemplars of the gothic novel. Brown explored more deeply than any other American author of his generation the inner fractured identity of those who had lived through revolutionary upheaval. Though none of his works sold as well as Rowson's *Charlotte Temple*, he was the first American writer to support himself from his literary output and was recognized by his contemporaries as a standard setter, even though few cared to follow his example.

The most successful fiction writers to follow Brown were **Washington Irving** and **James Fenimore Cooper**. Irving's early career was devoted to satire, and his most successful book was a spurious history of New York that lampooned **Thomas Jefferson**'s America. After the **War of 1812**, Irving went abroad for almost two decades. In 1819, he published two short tales that have become legends of the early Republic despite being partially inspired by exposure to German materials: "Rip Van Winkle" and "The Legend of Sleepy Hollow." After that, Irving turned to serious history and biography. Cooper's engagement with fiction proved to be more sustained. Between 1821 and 1829, he produced seven romantic novels, including three in the Leatherstocking series. He was the first American writer to use the nation's past, particularly the Revolution, as a realistic setting for his tales. By the end of the 1820s, he was sufficiently rich to take his family to Europe for six years. Like Irving, he also commanded an audience in the wider Anglophone world. But unlike Irving, Cooper continued to draw on American materials in his imaginative work. *See also* CHILD, LYDIA MARIA; HALE, SARAH JOSEPHA BUELL; SEDGWICK, CATHERINE MARIA; SIGOURNEY, LYDIA.

FINNEY, CHARLES GRANDISON (29 August 1792–16 August 1875). An evangelist, he was born in Warren, Connecticut. When he was two, the family moved to upstate New York, where he grew up. After teaching school and studying law along with the Bible, he experienced a religious crisis in 1821 in which the **Second Great Awakening** played a contributory role. As a result, he committed himself to God and, after studying theology with a local pastor, was licensed to preach by the local presbytery in December 1823. The next year, the Female Missionary Society of the Western District of New York commissioned him as an evangelist, and shortly afterward he was ordained. He became renowned for engendering revivals in the emerging urban areas of New York spawned by the **Erie Canal**.

Finney's style of preaching called for maintaining uninterrupted eye contact with his audience. His message stressed each individual's moral responsibility for achieving salvation and summoned his auditors, often individually by name, to commit themselves to Christ as he had himself. More conservative proponents of the Second Great Awakening, like **Lyman Beecher**, objected to some features of Finney's revivalist preaching. In July 1827, they summoned a conference of ministers to discuss the matter at New Lebanon, New York. From this encounter, Finney emerged victorious. The next year, he carried his revivalism to Wilmington, Philadelphia, and **New York City**. In the latter city, he recruited a circle of Christian businessmen who backed his ministry financially.

Finney's later career included an extended revival in Rochester during 1830–1831, presiding over two churches in New York City between 1832 and 1837, and a professorship at Oberlin College after 1837. By the mid-1830s, Finney had concluded that Christians were required to become **temperance** advocates who abstained from alcohol and who also opposed **slavery**. His **abolitionism** attracted students to Oberlin whom he felt he could not disappoint, though his teaching forced him to cut back on his evangelical activities. But with the development of the railroad, he soon was able to do both. In 1851, he accepted the presidency of Oberlin, though he did not let this new burden keep him from mounting urban revivals both in the East and in Britain until he retired in 1865.

FIRST AMENDMENT (TO THE CONSTITUTION). The first of 12 amendments forwarded by the **first Congress** to the states for their approval declared that Congress could make no laws establishing **religion** or prohibiting its free exercise or abridging the freedom of speech and the press or the right of the people to assemble and petition the government. It was the only original amendment whose wording helped restrain the federal government in exercising its power. During the **election of 1800**, the First Amendment served as a constitutional reference point for judging the **Federalist Party**'s sponsorship of the **Sedition Act**, even though **James Madison**'s **Report of the Committee** made less of it as a formal bar to what Congress had done than the Sedition Law's incompatibility with **Republicanism** in general. Since the doctrine of **judicial review** was still undergoing development, few wasted energy attempting to challenge the law's constitutionality in the courts as they would today, particularly as the judiciary in 1800 was assumed to be Federalist in sympathy. *See also* BILL OF RIGHTS.

FIRST BANK OF THE UNITED STATES. On 13 December 1790, Secretary of the Treasury **Alexander Hamilton** submitted a report to Congress recommending that it charter a national bank with a capital of $10 million, one-fifth of which would be subscribed by the federal government, the remainder by private investors. Hamilton had the revolutionary precedent of Robert Morris's Bank of North America to guide him. Morris's bank had proven indispensable to Congress in recovering a measure of control over the conduct of the Revolutionary War during 1782 because its bills possessed the credit of specie without any of specie's disadvantages, such as the cost of transportation over great distances. But for peacetime operations, the Bank of England provided a more suitable model. After the Glorious Revolution of 1688, the Bank of England had accepted subscriptions of the nation's funded debt as a major portion of its capital stock. Doing so allowed the debt to be transformed into money, which in turn stimulated the development of the domestic market and cemented the interests of public creditors to the revolutionary regime.

Hamilton's proposal encountered opposition from **Thomas Jefferson** and **James Madison**, the leaders of the emerging **Republican Party**. They feared that the centralizing implications of the Bank were incompatible with the nation's Republican form of government. A national bank in close alliance with the government might enable the executive to wield powers similar to those exercised by the British ministry in managing Parliament. Madison raised the constitutional objection that chartering such a bank lay beyond the powers the Constitution vested in Congress. He hoped that **George Washington** would veto the bill. The attorney general, **Edmund Randolph**, supported Madison's narrow construction of the Constitution. But Hamilton argued to the contrary and prevailed on Washington to sign the bill into law on 21 February. At the opening of subscriptions on 4 July 1791, $8 million were subscribed so rapidly that it set off a speculative frenzy. The Bank opened its doors for business in Philadelphia on 12 December 1791. During 1792, stockholder pressure led to the establishment of branches in Boston, New York, Baltimore, and Charleston. Four more branches were set up after 1800 in Washington, Norfolk, Savannah, and **New Orleans**.

The Bank had an immediate positive effect on the value of the funded debt of the United States as well as stimulating business activity in general through discounts and loans. It also acted as a central bank by regulating the availability of credit. In March 1792, it called in some of its loans, producing a brief speculative collapse that reinforced the enmity of its opponents. Thereafter, it managed to act with greater caution. In 1795, alarmed by the amount the federal government had borrowed, it forced the sale of the government's Bank shares to pay off this debt. But by the early 1800s, the rising yield from the **impost** strengthened the government's credit sufficiently to allow the administration to turn to the Bank of the United States, which by then dwarfed the nation's other banks, in financing the **Louisiana Purchase**.

Rechartering the Bank, whose original charter was to expire in 1811, first came before Congress in 1808. While Congressmen associated with the **Federalist Party** strongly supported recharter, their opposition to the **Embargo of 1807–1809** and subsequent willingness to take Britain's part against the United States prejudiced many members of the Republican Party against the Bank. Its opponents pointed out that a majority of the stockholders were foreigners, including some prominent members of the British aristocracy. Though by this time the secretary of the treasury, **Albert Gallatin**, and even President Madison supported recharter on the grounds of the institution's usefulness, recharter narrowly failed to pass in both the House and the Senate, where Vice President **George Clinton** cast the tie-breaking vote against it. The Bank ceased to exist as the Bank of the United States on 3 March 1811. **Stephen Girard** subsequently took over its assets and ran it as a private bank that supported the operations of the government during the **War of 1812**. *See also* BANKING; ECONOMIC DEVELOPMENT.

FIRST CONGRESS. It met between March 1789 and March 1791 in three sessions, the first two in New York, the last in Philadelphia, to implement the Constitution that the Philadelphia Convention had drafted and the states had ratified. It also addressed the principal problems left over from the Revolution, the most urgent of which was making some provision for the revolutionary debt.

The first session was the longest and most productive of the three. Congress created a federal revenue, organized the executive departments of the government, structured the federal judiciary in the **Judiciary Act of 1789**, and proposed a series of amendments to the Constitution. The 10 amendments that met with the approval of three-quarters of the states subsequently became known as the **Bill of Rights**.

The principal achievement of the second session was to enact **Alexander Hamilton**'s proposal for **funding** the debt contracted during the Revolutionary War. This involved the **assumption** of most of the state debts in an effort to make the **impost** cover as much of the burden as possible. But to overcome the opposition of **James Madison** and **Thomas Jefferson** to funding so large a debt, Congress had to agree that the **residency** of the nation's future capital would be Washington, D.C.

The third session created the **First Bank of the United States** despite the constitutional objections of Madison, Jefferson, and **Edmund Randolph**. The Bank further alienated Madison and Jefferson and helped lay the foundations for an opposition to **George Washington**'s administration that would ripen into the **Republican Party** with the commencement of the **European wars**.

FIRST EMANCIPATION. As a consequence of the Revolution, all the states north of the **Mason-Dixon line** either abolished **slavery** outright or, more commonly, provided for the gradual emancipation of slaves over a term of years. Vermont, though not one of the original 13 states, barred the introduction of slavery in its state constitution of 1777. In 1780, Pennsylvania passed the first gradual emancipation statute freeing all Negro slaves after they reached the age of 28. Massachusetts judicially abolished slavery in 1783 after its chief justice ruled that the institution was incompatible with the state constitution of 1780. The revised state code for Connecticut adopted by the legislature in 1784 freed all children of slaves born after 1 March 1784 when they reached the age of 25. Almost simultaneously, Rhode Island adopted a similar statute that freed all children of slaves after their first year of life. While the bill of rights in New Hampshire's constitution of 1783 seemed to preclude slavery, some argued that it applied only to those born after 1783, and the ambiguity was not fully resolved by statute until 1857. Nonetheless, very few New England Africans remained in bondage after 1800. New York finally embraced gradual emancipation in 1800, and New Jersey followed in 1804. In both states, slave owners insisted that financial responsibility for the children of freed adults be assumed by the public before they would consent to the measure. Despite foot dragging and evasions, by the first decade of the 19th century it was clear that the North would eventually be entirely free of slavery.

FIRST PARTY SYSTEM. A designation by historians intended to distinguish the first political parties from a successor system of parties that emerged in the 1830s and dominated national politics until the Civil War. The First Party System arrayed the **Federalist Party** against the **Republican Party** in an ideological struggle focused on how to manage the young Republic's security in a warring, revolutionary world. The rivalry between the two parties led to the **War of 1812** with Britain, which no one wanted and which almost resulted in the dissolution of the nation. The **Second Party System** emerged in the 1830s as a national alliance of state parties dedicated principally to controlling the patronage that the expansion of the federal government, particularly the **Postal Service**, had created.

FLETCHER V. PECK* (1810).** In 1803, Robert Fletcher of New Hampshire sued John Peck of Massachusetts for selling him Georgia lands Peck did not own. The suit was collusive because both plaintiff and defendant had a common interest in getting the federal courts to rule in favor of the validity of the **Yazoo land** sales. The Massachusetts circuit court upheld Peck's defense that the sale was valid at the time it was made. In 1810, Chief Justice **John Marshall**, in reviewing the circuit court's rulings, declared the action of the Georgia legislature rescinding the original sale of the Yazoo lands in 1796 to be in violation of the constitutional ban against state laws that impaired the obligation of contract. *Fletcher v. Peck* thus asserted the **Supreme Court**'s power to rule state laws unconstitutional just as in 1803 ***Marbury v. Madison had previously asserted that a portion of a federal law was unconstitutional. In construing the contract clause of the Constitution in the expansive way he did, Marshall also made it into a potent tool for defending private property. *See also* JUDICIAL REVIEW.

FORT ERIE. Located on the Canadian side of the Niagara River opposite Buffalo at the northeastern terminus of Lake Erie, it was the site of several engagements during the **War of 1812** and frequently changed hands between the British and the Americans.

FORT JACKSON, TREATY OF. *See* HORSESHOE BEND, BATTLE OF.

FORT MEIGS. A fort constructed at the Maumee River rapids in what is today northwestern **Ohio** at the beginning of 1813 after the disastrous defeat of American forces at **Frenchtown**. The British unsuccessfully besieged **General William Henry Harrison**'s forces here between 1 and 9 May 1813.

FORT MIMS. During the summer of 1813, a division of the **Creeks**, known as Red Sticks or Upper Creeks, who had been involved in a civil war against the Lower Creeks, turned to the Spanish in Pensacola, Florida, for arms and ammunition. The Americans, who had reason to believe that the Red Sticks meant to widen the conflict to involve them, ambushed a supply train laden with arms coming from Pensacola on 27 July at Burnt Corn in present-day Alabama. Though the ambush was only partially successful, the Red Sticks avenged it on 30 August by surprising a stockade on the Alabama River near modern Tensaw, 30 miles north of Mobile, called Fort Mims, and slaughtering most of the defending force. Of the 550 frontier inhabitants—whites, mixed-bloods, and African **slaves**—who had taken refuge there, only 15 persons escaped, though the lives of many Africans were spared to become slaves to the Red Sticks. The massacre at Fort Mims opened the **Creek War** and spurred both Georgia and Tennessee to mobilize their **militias** for reprisals.

FORT WAYNE, TREATY OF. In this treaty of 30 September 1809, five of the northwestern tribes transferred three million acres of land in the heart of what is today Indiana to the United States. The treaty reinforced **Tecumseh**'s determination to resist American expansion and impelled him to seek assistance from the British.

FRANCO-AMERICAN ALLIANCE OF 1778. After the American victory at Saratoga in October 1777, France signed two treaties with the United States that established a strategic alliance with the new Republic, guaranteeing, among other things, American independence. These treaties were in effect at the commencement of the **European wars** ignited by the **French Revolution** and led Great Britain to assume that the United States would be France's ally in the coming struggle. Britain's aggressive behavior stemming from this assumption came close to provoking another war with the United States in 1794 that was narrowly averted by the **Jay Treaty**. France, aggrieved by the Anglo-American rapprochement, acted with increasing hostility toward the United States. This led directly to the **Quasi-War** of 1798–1800 and to Congress formally abrogating the Franco-American alliance. In the **Franco-American Convention of 1800**, France accepted abandonment of the alliance of 1778 at the same time that it agreed to a liberal definition of neutral commercial rights.

FRANCO-AMERICAN CONVENTION OF 1800. Also known as the Treaty of Môrtefontaine. On 25 February 1799, over the vehement objections of Secretary of State **Timothy Pickering**, Secretary of War **James McHenry**, and Secretary of the Treasury **Oliver Wolcott**, President **John Adams** appointed **Oliver Ellsworth** and Patrick Henry to join **William Vans Murray**, previously named the new ambassador to France, as commissioners to negotiate an end to the **Quasi-War**. William R. Davies subsequently took Henry's place on the commission. Instability in the French government delayed the departure of the commissioners until the following November. Then Adams dispatched them to head off a possible coup that he feared **Alexander Hamilton** might attempt at the head of the unpopular but recently enlarged army. The commissioners arrived in Paris to find the French foreign minister, **Talleyrand**, resistant to France paying for the damage it had inflicted on American shipping. But after the American commissioners abandoned that objective, they succeeded in getting France to accept a new definition of the Franco-American relationship that scrapped the Franco-American alliance of 1778. The Treaty of Môrtefortaine, signed on 30 September 1800, provided for the restoration of peace and amity between the two countries.

The treaty, which contained an expansive definition of the commercial rights of neutral carriers, arrived in the United States just before the **Electoral College** voted in the presidential **election of 1800**. Though the Convention should have redounded to Adams's credit, news of its arrival helped **Thomas Jefferson** in the ensuing election. Adams's determination to negotiate with France had badly divided the Federalists. On the other hand, Jefferson's association with France made peace with that country necessary before the Federalist-controlled lame-duck House of Representatives could have consented to his elevation to the presidency. They possessed the power to deny him the presidency because they still controlled the House of Representatives of the sixth Congress, and the Constitution gave them authority in choosing between Jefferson and **Aaron Burr**, each of whom had received the same number of electoral votes.

FRANKLIN, BENJAMIN (17 January 1706–17 April 1790). Printer, civic innovator, scientist, inventor, and diplomat, he was born in Boston. Franklin was the most distinguished American of his generation, emerging from provincial obscurity to win international renown. However, his life was nearing its end as the early republican period began. He had attended the Philadelphia convention that framed the federal Constitution. But besides signing the final document, he contributed little to the debates that shaped the nation's form of government. One of his last acts was to pen a satire of those who defended African **slavery** by having a fictional North African ruler use their arguments to justify the enslavement of captured American seamen. When Franklin died in the spring of 1790, 20,000 mourners attended his funeral.

FREDONIA REBELLION (1826). On 22 November 1826, a small band of 36 armed men tried to settle a dispute over land titles that had arisen in Nacogdoches, **Texas**. When Mexican authorities prepared to intervene, the armed band proclaimed themselves the independent state of Fredonia. Their actions failed to find support among the majority of European Texans as well as the local **Indians**, and **Stephen Austin**'s followers joined the Mexican authorities in suppressing the rebellion on 31 January 1827.

FREEDMEN. In addition to setting in motion the **first emancipation** in the North, the Revolution also led to the relaxation of manumission laws in the South. Both created a growing body of former slaves who came to be known as freedmen. They were seldom in a position to prosper the way a few **African Americans** who had been born free, like **Paul Cuffee** and **Lemuel Haynes**, were. Instead, they faced widespread racial prejudice and economic deprivation. The best labor markets for the freedman were the emerging cities, but their poverty made them especially vulnerable to public health hazards in urban areas. Additionally, freedmen had to worry about being kidnapped and sold back into **slavery** in the South under the pretense that they were fugitive slaves. Many accepted low-paying positions as crews on merchant vessels and whalers. The growing restiveness of Africans who remained slaves after the **French Revolution** and the **Haitian Revolution**, exemplified by **Gabriel's Rebellion** and the **Vesey Rebellion**, reinforced the suspicions and prejudices entertained by both northern and southern whites about the freedmen. **David Walker**'s advocacy of violent resistance and the beginning of demands for the immediate, uncompensated **abolition** of slavery at the end of the 1820s further fanned the flames of white prejudice.

Some freedmen nonetheless had distinguished careers despite all the handicaps they had to surmount. This was especially the case with **Richard Allen**, the founder of the **African Methodist Episcopal Church**. Though Allen benefited from the support of white sympathizers like **Benjamin Rush**, he realized that African Americans needed to rely primarily on their own resources if they were to survive in the hostile environment of early 19th-century America. This was a lesson that other successful freedman, like **Venture Smith**, learned each in his or her own way. In seeking allies against oppression, African American freedmen were naturally drawn to **Indians**, who remained an underclass among the European population, with whom African Americans often intermarried.

FREEMASONRY. A fraternal organization that in England developed out of the stonemasons' guilds that had built the cathedrals of the Middle Ages. In the 17th century, their prestige had attracted men of wealth and social standing whose patronage and participation broadened the original guild mandates. In the early 18th century, these guilds united into the Grand Lodge of England. In addition to fraternal support, masonry came to be associated with religious tolerance. While it instituted various degrees through which its members could progress in their quest for virtue, it affirmed the fundamental equality of all beings.

American lodges, acting under the authority of the English Grand Lodge, began to appear in the early 1730s. By the time of the Revolution, there were 150 lodges that claimed many members of the revolutionary elite, including **George Washington**. After the war, the fraternal aspects of masonry continued to attract ambitious men, while the public was repeatedly reminded of the Masonic presence by the ostentatious funeral rites it bestowed on its deceased members. As egalitarianism came to permeate the expectations of an increasing number of early 19th-century Americans, masonry's elitist implications began to attract adverse criticism. In the mid-1820s, that criticism erupted into a full-blown **anti-Masonic movement**.

FRENCH REVOLUTION. An event comparable in significance to the Russian and Chinese Revolutions of the 20th century, the French Revolution began on 17 June 1789 when the Estates General summarily abolished all feudal distinctions and proclaimed itself to be a Constituent Assembly. Though the revolution's initial leaders, which included the Marquis de **Lafayette**, hoped to institute a constitutional monarchy, many aristocrats resisted the assault on their privileges. Louis XVI sympathized with the aristocrats but was eventually forced to accept the new constitution framed by the Constituent Assembly. A year later, he was deposed after a war undertaken against Prussia and Austria began to go badly. Not content with simply proclaiming itself to be a republic, the National Convention tried and executed Louis on 21 January 1793, setting off a general European war between France and a coalition of monarchies led by Great Britain that would last until **Napoleon**'s final defeat at Waterloo in 1815 and the restoration of the Bourbon monarchy.

Most Americans initially welcomed the French Revolution as confirmation of their own revolution, but the increasing extremes to which matters were carried culminating in Louis's execution alienated those who, like the leaders of the future **Federalist Party**, entertained reservations about **Republicanism**. The **European wars** engendered by the French Revolution forced the United States to choose between maintaining good relations with France at the expense of an accommodation with Britain or seeking good relations with Britain at the cost of alienating France. When **George Washington** chose the latter course, the opposition, which evolved into the **Republican Party**, unsuccessfully opposed ratification and implementation of the **Jay Treaty**, which they regarded as a betrayal of the **Franco-American alliance**. Meanwhile, France had begun to evolve from an embattled republic into a military threat to the rest of Europe as the result of its military successes after 1794. In 1795, an executive **Directory** emerged from the ruins of France's third constitution in almost as many years to pursue a policy of conquering its neighbors. It also sought to humiliate the United States for coming to an accommodation with Britain. **John Adams**'s administration responded to French rebuffs by launching a limited naval war against it, known as the **Quasi-War**, in 1798–1800. Napoleon's coup of 9 November 1798 (Brumaire) dissolved the Directory, replacing it with a Consulate, which soon became little more than a disguise for Napoleon's dictatorship.

The change in France's government did permit the United States to terminate the Quasi-War in the **Franco-American Convention of**

1800. But from the Federalists' point of view, peace had the far less desirable consequence of contributing to **Thomas Jefferson**'s victory in the **election of 1800**. The Federalists feared that the Republicans would court popular favor by antagonizing Britain. They also assumed that in the event of another Anglo-American war, the United States would be forced to ally with France as it had during the Revolution. The subsequent evolution of France into a military despotism led the Federalists to conclude that France's course was the natural trajectory the American Republic would pursue now that the Federalists were no longer in control of the federal government. These attitudes lay at the heart of Federalist opposition to Jefferson's and **James Madison**'s policy of trying to parry the pressure of both of the principal belligerents with commercial restrictions. It also led the Federalists to side with Britain against their own government, thus helping to provoke the declaration of the **War of 1812**. Federalist behavior after 1808 was premised on the delusion that the course they pursued was the only alternative to evolving the way France had during its revolution.

FRENCHTOWN, BATTLE OF (ALSO REFERRED TO AS THE BATTLE OF RAISIN RIVER). As part of a winter attempt to recover Detroit, General **William Henry Harrison** ordered his army of 6,000 forward at the beginning of January 1813. Brigadier James Winchester, in command of a 1,300-man detachment, yielded to the pleas of the residents of Frenchtown, in northwestern Ohio but within the British lines, to occupy their settlement before Harrison had a chance to rendezvous with him on the Maumee River. There, on 22 January 1813, Winchester's force was attacked by 1,200 **Indians** and British regulars under the command of James Proctor. Virtually all of Winchester's command were either killed or captured in the engagement. Instead of taking the offensive, Harrison was forced back to **Fort Meigs** on the Maumee, which the British besieged.

FRENEAU, PHILIP MORIN (2 January 1752–19 December 1832). Poet and editor, he was born in **New York City** to a Huguenot family of some means and educated at Princeton, where, if he was not **James Madison**'s roommate, he at least became his good friend. Freneau established his credentials as a promising literary talent with a graduation poem titled "The Rising Glory of America" and continued throughout the Revolutionary War to produce a steady stream of patriotic verse and prose in between serving in the New Jersey **militia** and on a privateer. During these years, he also briefly managed a sugar estate in the Danish West Indies, now the U.S. Virgin Islands.

After the war, Freneau oscillated between **newspaper** work and going to sea. The year 1791 found him editing the *New York Daily Advertiser*, which was critical of **Alexander Hamilton**'s fiscal policy. At Madison's suggestion, he moved from New York City to Philadelphia with the federal government and established the *National Gazette* there after **Thomas Jefferson** offered him a salary as translator at the State Department. The *National Gazette* became a vehicle for Madison's opposition to the emerging **Federalist Party**. But Freneau antagonized President **George Washington**, first by supporting the controversial French ambassador, **Edmund Genêt**, long after Madison and Jefferson had given up on him and then by portraying Washington as a cryptomonarchist. The *National Gazette* folded after two years of publication. Freneau subsequently failed to deliver on his previous literary promise and spent the rest of his life as an unsuccessful editor of minor publications or at sea.

FRIES'S REBELLION. John Fries was an auctioneer of German ancestry living in northeastern Pennsylvania. When the state legislature decided to raise its portion of the direct tax of 1798 to support the expansion of the army and navy during the **Quasi-War** by taxing land and houses, Fries tried to obstruct the assessors charged with implementing the levy. On 7 March 1799, he led an armed mob that liberated 18 demonstrators against the tax from arrest in Bethlehem. On 12 March, President **John Adams** responded by issuing a proclamation branding the rioters as guilty of treason. When the governor of Pennsylvania proved reluctant to call out the **militia** to enforce the law, officials to whom Adams had delegated authority turned to a detachment of troops from the newly raised **provisional army** to do the job. It captured Fries and, along with 40 other unresisting suspects, carried him to Philadelphia for trial. In May, Fries was found guilty of treason and sentenced to death. Adams pardoned him the day before his scheduled execution. By doing so, the president alienated the faction in the government led by Secretary of State **Timothy Pickering** that wanted to demonstrate the power of the federal government and opposed to any reconciliation with France. The use of the military confirmed anxieties about standing armies and turned many German Americans into supporters of the **Republican Party**.

FUGITIVE SLAVE LAW (of 1793). Signed into law on 12 February 1793, this statute authorized masters to arrest escaped slaves in other states and to bring them before a U.S. district court judge to prove that they had fled a service they were legally bound by in their home state. Those who obstructed masters in recovering their slaves could also be subjected to substantial penalties.

FULTON, ROBERT (14 November 1765–23 February 1815). Artist, inventor, and promoter, he was born near Lancaster, Pennsylvania, and apprenticed to a jeweler in Philadelphia for whose clients he painted miniature portraits. After his indenture ended, he sailed for England to perfect his painting skills under **Benjamin West**'s tutelage. Though Fulton occasionally exhibited at the Royal Academy in the early 1790s, the wealthy aristocrats he met in Britain encouraged him to turn his talents to more practical matters. With their blessing, he studied **canals** and published the *Treatise on Improvement of Canal Navigation*, which earned him notoriety because it recommended that locks be replaced by inclined rails. In 1797, he moved to Paris and lived with Ruth and **Joel Barlow**. Using Barlow's connections with French officialdom, Fulton tried to develop a weapon capable of neutralizing Britain's naval blockade. But when actually tested, Fulton's underwater device failed to destroy any British vessels.

Residence in France proved more useful to Fulton after **Robert R. Livingston** arrived in Paris as the U.S. ambassador in 1802. Livingston was one of the richest men in America and had secured a monopoly from the New York legislature to introduce steam navigation on the Hudson River. Livingston and Fulton quickly formed a partnership, but the consummation of their project was delayed until 1807 because the British government offered Fulton a contract to develop underwater weapons. Fulton may have had ulterior motives in moving to Britain since an earlier trial of a steamboat on the Seine had shown the need for a more powerful engine that only the British made. However, British foot-dragging after Trafalgar convinced Fulton that the principal purpose of the contract was to keep him from working for the French. At the end of 1806, he returned to America with the desired English engine, and during the following August the partnership successfully tested the steam-powered, side-wheeler *Clermont* on an upstream run from **New York City** to Albany. Before Fulton's death in 1815, steamboats were in regular operation on the Hudson, the Delaware, the Potomac, the James, the Ohio, and the Mississippi Rivers.

While expanding his steamboat ventures, Fulton also unsuccessfully tried to interest the U.S. government in the development of a torpedo. Much of his energy in his last years went into defending Livingston's monopoly on the Hudson River. However, the division of Livingston's share of the partnership after his death in 1813 among multiple heirs complicated the task. Eventually, in 1824 the **Supreme Court** ruled the New York monopoly unconstitutional in ***Gibbons v. Ogden***.

FUNDING. The provision of a hard-money (specie or its equivalent) revenue appropriated to pay interest charges on the nominal sum of a debt. As long as interest payments were made in hard money, the nominal sum of the funded debt would become the equivalent of a corresponding amount of hard money. *See also* FIRST BANK OF THE UNITED STATES; HAMILTON, ALEXANDER.

– G –

GABRIEL'S REBELLION. Thomas Prosser's **slave**, Gabriel, lived on a plantation close to Richmond, Virginia, and used the freedom he was often granted of going into the town to organize a rebellion scheduled to begin on 30 August 1800. Though Governor **James Monroe** received several warnings that some sort of disturbance was brewing, he did not mobilize the **militia** until the afternoon of the 30th. Even then, a violent thunderstorm had a greater effect in disbursing the conspirators than the militia. But over the next several weeks, the authorities made a number of arrests, and on 25 September, Gabriel himself was apprehended while trying to flee from Norfolk, Virginia, on a vessel. He was quickly tried and sentenced to death, but unlike many other slaves who were detained and questioned in connection with the conspiracy, Gabriel refused to give any information about his plans. That left the terrified imaginations of the slaveholders to infer the worst, and before long they had conjured up a plot that extended to the entire state and beyond. What particularly unsettled the whites was the idea that the rebels were counting on France's intervention. The notion acquired plausibility both from the **Quasi-War** and from the Libertarian slogans of the **French Revolution**. While the South had escaped the Revolutionary War without a servile insurrection, the successful slave insurrection on the island of Santo Domingo, known as the **Haitian Revolution**, created an entirely new situation apparently laden with peril. **Thomas Jefferson** urged Governor Monroe to act with restraint in repressing the conspiracy, but as many as 35 slaves were executed, most on the basis of dubious confessions and allegations.

GALLATIN, ALBERT (29 January 1761–13 August 1849). Congressman, secretary of the treasury, and diplomat, he was born in Geneva, Switzerland, to a noble family of modest means. Orphaned at nine, Gallatin's inheritance barely paid for his schooling at a local academy. In 1780, he ran away, sailing to America, and arrived in Boston with a parcel of tea he had difficulty selling. After several other commercial misadventures, he formed a partnership with a Frenchman who supplied the capital for the purchase of land warrants in the backcountry of Maryland and Pennsylvania. A chance encounter with **George Washington**, who had large landholdings in the vicinity, led him to settle just off the Monongehela River in Pennsylvania on the supposition that the Potomac and Ohio Rivers would form the major highway of the new nation.

Gallatin first came to public attention for his thoughtful opposition to the new federal Constitution. That led to his designation as delegate to Pennsylvania's constitutional convention of 1789 and his election to the new legislature in 1790. At the end of his first term in the state legislature, it chose him a U.S. senator. There he called for an investigation of **Alexander Hamilton**'s management of the treasury. A **Federalist Party** majority managed to unseat Gallatin by claiming that he had failed to fulfill the residency requirement for citizenship. Nonetheless, he was elected to the House of Representatives the following year and served brilliantly as a leader of the **Republican Party** between 1795 and 1801. During that period, he became a recognized expert on public finance, and after **Thomas Jefferson** became president as a result of the **election of 1800**, he appointed Gallatin his secretary of the treasury.

Gallatin shared Jefferson's and **James Madison**'s reservations about a public debt, and despite the burden of the **Barbary Wars** (1801–1805) and the **Louisiana Purchase**, he quickly reduced the funded debt by a third. When it had been fully retired, he planned on using the treasury surpluses for **internal improvements**. But the intensification of the **Napoleonic Wars** after 1805 led each of the belligerent powers to try controlling the nation's commerce in ways that hurt its adversary. Gallatin went along with the **Embargo of 1807–1809** and the **nonintercourse** that replaced it only because he had no alternative to offer. When commercial coercion was replaced by the **War of 1812**, Gallatin was happy to accept President Madison's invitation to serve as a peace commissioner in Europe. There he played an important role in the negotiations that culminated in the **Treaty of Ghent** in 1814, as well as the **Convention of 1815**.

Between 1816 and 1823, Gallatin served as U.S. ambassador to France. He failed to extract any compensation from the government of Louis XVIII for depredations committed against U.S. shipping during the Napoleonic Wars, but during a visit to London he helped negotiate the **Anglo-American Convention of 1818** with Britain. After returning to the United States in 1823, he agreed to be **William Harris Crawford**'s vice-presidential running mate in 1824. When Crawford became ill, Gallatin withdrew. In 1826–1827, Gallatin served as ambassador to Great Britain and negotiated a renewal of the boundary settlement contained in the Anglo-American Convention of 1818. On his return to America, he accepted **John Jacob Astor**'s invitation to head the National Bank of New York. During his last years, he acted as elder statesman on fiscal matters and opposed military confrontations with Great Britain and Mexico.

GALLAUDET, THOMAS HOPKINS (10 December 1787–10 September 1851). Pioneer in educating the deaf, he was born in Philadelphia and educated at Yale, graduating in the class of 1805. Subsequently, he studied theology, but since his health precluded accepting a pulpit, he traveled to Europe to learn about schooling for the deaf. There he found the French more receptive to sharing their techniques than the British. Returning to Hartford, Connecticut, where his family had moved, he established, with the assistance of the Frenchman Laurent Clerc, an asylum for the education and instruction of the deaf in 1817. This was a free school that emphasized the use of sign language instead of trying to teach the deaf, who usually were also dumb, to speak. Gallaudet wanted to offer individuals who would otherwise have remained in ignorance access to the Christian message of salvation. He saw his endeavor as contributing to an approaching millennium and, like many reformers during the **Second Great Awakening**, was attracted to other reforms, especially the **antislavery** movement. However, he made his greatest mark in developing many features of modern sign language and in fathering two children—by a congenitally deaf student he married—who went on to make important contributions to bettering the lot of the deaf.

GENERAL SURVEY ACT (1824). The law provided for a survey of plans and estimates for **internal improvements** like roads and **canals** deemed of national importance because of their commercial or military importance or because they were necessary for the transportation of the public mail. The president was to name two civilians to conduct the survey and to place the Army Corps of Engineers at their service. The survey laid the groundwork for the expansion of the **Postal Service** to keep pace with the **westward movement**. As the principal source of federal patronage, the Postal Service in turn provided the structure around which the **Second Party System** began to form at the end of the 1820s.

GENÊT, EDMUND (8 January 1763–15 July 1834). French diplomat, he was born at Versailles, the son of a court specialist in Anglo-American affairs. After serving briefly as chargé d'affaires in Russia, Genêt was appointed minister to the United States by the new republican government of France. Genêt arrived in Charleston, South Carolina, on 8 April 1793 and was accorded a rapturous welcome. As he made his way north to the seat of the government in Philadelphia, he started fitting out privateers and planning expeditions against Spanish possessions in North America. President **George Washington** did not feel that such behavior accorded with the **Neutrality Proclamation** he had just issued and gave Genêt a cool reception on his arrival.

Genêt inferred from the ecstatic popular reception he was receiving that Washington was out of touch with popular sentiment. When Secretary of State **Thomas Jefferson** warned him that the Neutrality Proclamation must be obeyed, Genêt threatened to appeal over Washington's head to the people. Washington then decided to have Genêt recalled. To destroy his influence, **Rufus King** and William Willcocks orchestrated his public humiliation by revealing that he had sought to challenge Washington's authority. Rather than return to France after his replacement arrived, Genêt was allowed to remain in the United States. He soon married a daughter of **George Clinton** and retired from public life.

GERRY, ELBRIDGE (17 July 1744–23 November 1814). Governor of Massachusetts and vice president of the United States, he was born in Marblehead, Massachusetts, the son of a British merchant **immigrant**. After graduating from Harvard in 1762, Gerry became active in revolutionary politics and, as a delegate to the second Continental Congress, signed the Declaration of Independence. He continued to serve in Congress until 1781 and again between 1783 and 1785. In 1787, Massachusetts chose him as one of its delegates to the Philadelphia Convention, where he supported the Connecticut compromise that gave equal representation to the small states in the Senate. But he refused to sign the final document because it lacked a **Bill of Rights**. Despite his public criticism of the Constitution, he was elected to serve as a representative in the **first** and second **Congresses**. In 1797, President **John Adams** chose him and **John Marshall** to join **Charles Cotesworth Pinckney** in a new mission to the French **Directory**. Their report, known as the **XYZ Dispatches**, detailed the efforts of **Talleyrand**'s agents to humiliate the United States and led Congress to mount a **Quasi-War** against France. Gerry stayed in Paris after his fellow commissioners had departed, providing Talleyrand with a conduit for relaying peace overtures that eventuated in the **Anglo-American Convention of 1800**. On returning from Europe, Gerry ran for the office of governor of Massachusetts against **Caleb Strong** and was soundly beaten.

Gerry retired from public life for almost a decade, reentering Massachusetts politics as the **Republican Party**'s gubernatorial candidate in 1810 after the death of **James Sullivan** and the resounding defeat of Sullivan's lieutenant governor, Levi Lincoln, in 1809. Gerry capitalized on the desire of moderates in both parties to leave behind the bitter partisanship the **Embargo of 1807–1809** had ignited. Control of Massachusetts, which at the time included Maine, seemed vital to the administration of **James Madison** in dealing with Britain. But Gerry's decision in 1811 to attack the **Federalist Party** leadership in Massachusetts led to his defeat just before the **War of 1812**. He lost despite an electoral redistricting, which ever since has been known as a "gerrymander." His defeat delivered Massachusetts to the Federalists for the next decade. Nonetheless, Madison chose Gerry to be his vice president during his second term, reflecting the pivotal importance of Massachusetts in a war with Britain. When Madison became seriously ill in 1813, it looked for a while as though Gerry, not in good health himself, might have to assume the burdens of the presidency. But Madison recovered, while Gerry eventually succumbed as he presided over the Senate in 1814.

GHENT, TREATY OF. On 24 December 1814, the United States and Great Britain agreed at Ghent in Belgium to bring the **War of 1812** to a conclusion. While the treaty resolved none of the issues that had led to war in the first place—including Britain's **Orders-in-Council**, its **impressment** of American seamen, and the seizure of American vessels that violated her **paper blockades**—the general pacification of Europe after 1815 removed these grievances. Members of the **Federalist Party** were unsuccessful in their attempt to label the peace a disgrace because of their unrelenting opposition to the conduct of the war. The majority felt it was victory enough for the Republic to have survived a conflict with a great power unaided by any other nation in the face of a disloyal opposition.

***GIBBONS V. OGDEN* (1824).** Chief Justice **John Marshall**, speaking for the **Supreme Court**, invalidated a 30-year monopoly of steam-powered water transport created by the New York legislature. **Robert Fulton** and **Robert R. Livingston** had assigned Aaron Ogden their exclusive rights, which Ogden then invoked in an attempt to prohibit Thomas Gibbons from operating a competing steam vessel under federal license. Marshall held that the New York monopoly infringed on Congress's power to regulate interstate commerce. This was the first use by the Supreme Court of an expanded interpretation of the commerce clause of the Constitution to invalidate a state law. The decision helped remove other state monopolies obstructing the **transportation revolution**.

GILES'S RESOLUTIONS OF 1793. During the first years in which Secretary of the Treasury **Alexander Hamilton** put his plan for **funding** the revolutionary debt into operation, the yields from the **impost** were not large enough to cover all the obligations he had incurred. He tried to make up the difference by borrowing from the **First Bank of the United States** and from abroad, temporarily increasing the public debt. This inflamed the Republican sensitivities of men like **James Madison** and **Thomas Jefferson**. They feared that if Hamilton freed himself from the fiscal supervision of Congress, he would be able to corrupt the legislature, as the British crown was thought to have corrupted the House of Commons. On 23 January 1793, William Branch Giles (1762–1830), an ambitious young representative from Virginia, proposed a series of five resolutions to the House of Representatives designed to bring Hamilton to account. The failure of the resolutions to pass confirmed the worst fears of the leaders of the nascent **Republican Party** that Congress was already under the corrupt control of the **Federalist Party**.

GIRARD, STEPHEN (20 May 1750–26 December 1831). Merchant banker, he was born in Bordeaux, the son of a French naval officer. He went to sea at an early age and was licensed as a captain at the age of 23. The beginning of the American Revolution found Girard trading between the French West Indian islands and the North American continent. Putting into Philadelphia during 1776, he decided to settle there. For the next three decades, he prospered by sending a growing fleet of vessels on voyages to the West Indies and Europe despite the enormous risks involved in such commerce. He was also a good citizen, undertaking the management of Philadelphia's Bush Hill Hospital during the **yellow fever** epidemic of 1793. When the charter of the **First Bank of the United States** expired, Girard took it over and successfully ran it as a private bank. During 1813, at the behest of **Albert Gallatin**, he took responsibility for underwriting more than

$3 million of a government loan that had not been subscribed, thus helping to sustain the government's credit during the **War of 1812**. After personally subscribing $3 million of the $35 million of the capital of the **Second Bank of the United States**, he was appointed a director. But disagreements over how that bank should be managed quickly led to his resignation. At his death, he left the bulk of his fortune to Philadelphia for the **education** of fatherless children.

GORE, CHRISTOPHER (21 September 1758–1 March 1827). Entrepreneur and politician, he was born in Boston and educated at Harvard, graduating with the class of 1776. Gore's father was a loyalist who fled with the British when they evacuated Boston, but Christopher stayed behind to serve as a patriot artillery officer. He also prepared for the law and was admitted to the Massachusetts bar in 1778. During the 1780s, Gore prospered. At the end of that decade, he supported adoption of the federal Constitution and was appointed by **George Washington** to be the federal district attorney for Massachusetts. Throughout the early 1790s, Gore supported **Alexander Hamilton**'s **funding** policies and Washington's diplomatic accommodation with Britain. In 1796, Washington appointed Gore one of the American commissioners under article 7 of the **Jay Treaty** to settle the mutual claims of Britain and the United States against each other. Gore spent the next eight years in Britain, where he was well received.

Returning to the United States in 1804, he resumed the practice of law, training such notables as **Daniel Webster**. He also increased his already ample fortune by investing in **internal improvements** and the nascent textile **industry**. He attended the meeting of **Federalist Party** leaders in **New York City** that nominated **Charles C. Pinckney** and **Rufus King** for president and vice president, respectively, in the **election of 1804**. Gore subsequently became active in Massachusetts politics. After running unsuccessfully as the Federalist candidate for governor in 1808, he was elected to the House of Representatives and drafted an inflammatory report against the **Embargo of 1807–1809**, widely referred to as the "Gore Report," that advocated joining Britain in its struggle against **Napoleon**. This helped him be elected governor of Massachusetts in 1809. But he failed to accomplish much during his one term in office. In 1813, the Massachusetts legislature sent him to the U.S. Senate, where he vigorously opposed **James Madison**'s measures for prosecuting the **War of 1812**. Though he approved of the **Hartford Convention**, he did not attend it as a delegate. During the remainder of his Senate term, he opposed national programs for internal improvements as well as a protective **tariff**, fearing that government initiatives might depreciate his substantial investments.

GREENVILLE, TREATIES OF (1795 and 1814). By the first treaty concluded on 3 August 1795 between Anthony Wayne and 12 **Indian** tribes of the Northwest, the United States secured recognition of its title under the Peace of 1783 to lands north of the Ohio. The treaty was a direct consequence of the Indian defeat at the **Battle of Fallen Timbers**. The second treaty, concluded 22 July 1814 between **William Henry Harrison** and the Wyandots, Delawares, and Shawnees with their allies, required the Indians to take up arms against Great Britain. It was a direct by-product of General Harrison's victory the preceding October in the **Battle of the Thames River**, which had resulted in the death of the Indian leader **Tecumseh**.

– H –

HAITIAN REVOLUTION. The **French Revolution** set off an upheaval in the deeply stratified society of the French colony on the western third of Hispaniola, or **Ste. Domingue**. After a prolonged and bloody conflict, Haiti finally established its independence as a black republic in 1804. Enslaved Africans, who outnumbered the free population (both whites and free blacks) by as much as 10 to 1, held the key in this conflict. Their leader over the next decade, Toussant L'Overture, emerged as the primary player in the struggle between former slaves and the European powers for control of the island. The administration of **John Adams** assisted Toussant's forces in resisting France during the **Quasi-War** of 1798–1800. In 1802, the administration of **Thomas Jefferson** was less determined in supporting him against a large army **Napoleon** had dispatched to restore French control over the island. The French eventually captured Toussant and sent him to France, where he died in 1803. But Napoleon's hope of using the island as a springboard for reestablishing French power in the New World came to naught because of the ravages of the **yellow fever** that crippled the French army there. Instead, Napoleon turned his attention to the military conquest of Europe and sold France's claims in North America to the United States in the **Louisiana Purchase**.

The Haitian Revolution had a profound impact on the early Republic because many wealthy French slaveholders on the island immigrated to the southern United States during its progress, bringing their **slaves** with them. The refugees in turn spread accounts among the mainland slaves about the military and diplomatic achievements of Toussant in leading a servile insurrection. During the American Revolutionary War, slaves had proved ready enough to desert their masters whenever the British offered them opportunity to do so, but they had not risen to claim their freedom from the revolutionaries. After the Haitian Revolution, it seemed very likely they would, at least to many southern masters. This led to a tightening of the slave codes in the states not partaking in the **first emancipation** and to the harsh repression of domestic conspiracies such as **Gabriel's Rebellion** and **Vesey's Rebellion**.

HALE, SARAH JOSEPHA BUELL (24 October 1788–30 April 1879). Author and editor, she was born in rural New Hampshire and received her education secondhand from a brother attending Dartmouth who guided her reading. She taught school between 1806 and 1813 when she married David Hale. He died in 1822, leaving Sarah with five children and little means of support. After an unsuccessful attempt at becoming a milliner, she took to writing. In 1823, friends sponsored the publication of *The Genius of Oblivion*, but most of her early work was for **magazines** that were proliferating in the early Republic. In 1827, she published a novel, *Norwood*, but she made her mark more in the capacity of editor than in that of author. In 1828, she became the first **woman** to edit a new journal exclusively for a female audience titled *Ladies Magazine*. Her policy of publishing only original American work together with her vigorous editorials on behalf of women's advancement made this magazine a financial success. In 1837, she took over editing *Godey's Ladies Book* after it merged with the *Ladies Magazine*. Though she urged women to go beyond the separate sphere allotted to them, she eschewed endorsing the suffragists and favored gradual **abolition** accompanied by colonization.

HAMILTON, ALEXANDER (11 January 1755?–12 July 1804). First secretary of the treasury under the new federal Constitution, he was born on Nevis in the West Indies, the illegitimate second son of a Scotsman and a French mother. Though abandoned by his father and without visible means of support after his mother's death when he was 11, Hamilton attracted the attention of local benefactors who sent him to the mainland for a college education. He became involved in New York's revolutionary movement while a student at Columbia and subsequently served as General **George Washington**'s principal aide-de-camp from 1777 to 1781. Retiring from the army after distinguishing himself at Yorktown, Hamilton trained himself for admission to the New York bar. By 1782, he had attracted sufficient notice to be sent by the state to the Confederation Congress. Later he was a delegate to the Annapolis Convention of 1786 and drafted its summons for the Philadelphia Convention of 1787. After serving as a delegate in Philadelphia, he joined **James Madison** and **John Jay** in drafting the *Federalist* in an effort to win New York's consent to the new Constitution. In 1789, Washington asked him to serve as the nation's first secretary of the treasury.

The most pressing problem confronting the new government was the revolutionary debt. Neither the states nor Congress had succeeded in making satisfactory provision for servicing the debt because Congress under the Confederation lacked the power to raise revenue, and most of the states were exhausted by the war. The inability to pay interest on the debt after its **liquidation** depressed its market value and led to its transfer to speculators, thus arraying a minority of public creditors against a majority of public debtors. Hamilton hoped to surmount this political obstacle by relying on a federal **impost** for revenue. No one would pay such a tax who did not *choose* to buy the goods on which it was laid, and the merchants could be relied on to collect it provided that they felt their interests were served by doing so. But to get the cooperation of the merchants, Hamilton needed to fuse the interests of the state creditors with those of the federal creditors. If one group of creditors thought their interests were being sacrificed to the other, they would subvert the effectiveness of the impost. The only way to fuse the two interests was to assume most of the state debts. Hamilton's **Report on Public Credit** (1790) proposed such an **assumption** but in so doing threatened to create a larger debt than either Madison or **Thomas Jefferson** thought advisable. To get their consent, he agreed to a permanent **residency** for the nation's capital on the Potomac that became Washington, D.C.

To distribute the benefit of funding the debt as widely as possible, Hamilton next proposed that Congress charter the **First Bank of the United States**. The Bank would issue notes based on its capital, three-quarters of which could be subscribed in the funded debt of the United States. Madison, Jefferson, and Attorney General **Edmund Randolph** protested the constitutionality of such a bank, but Hamilton succeeded in persuading Washington that it was a necessary and proper exercise of Congress's powers. President Washington also welcomed Hamilton's **Report on Manufactures** in 1792 because it promised to create a domestic source of supplies the nation had been forced to import during the Revolutionary War. But Congress proved less receptive to granting bounties and subsidies for domestic **industry**.

Hamilton favored cultivating good relations with Britain because he thought aligning with Britain's government would ensure stability and because his fiscal system depended disproportionately on revenue arising from British imports. When war erupted between republican France and a coalition of monarchies led by Britain, Hamilton urged Washington to suspend the **Franco-American alliance of 1778** to protect the United States against being drawn into the **European war** as France's ally. Washington did issue a **Neutrality Proclamation**, but that failed to insulate the nation from French pressures exercised through Ambassador **Edmund Genêt**. Hamilton supported Genêt's recall and humiliation, Washington's subsequent designation of John Jay as special envoy to head off war with Britain, and the forceful suppression of the **Whiskey Rebellion**. Even though Hamilton resigned as secretary of the treasury effective 31 January 1795 before the prolonged controversy over the **Jay Treaty** had begun, he did everything in his power to ensure its ratification and implementation.

Washington continued to call on Hamilton for advice and assistance after he left the government. Hamilton drafted several of Washington's public papers, including large sections of his **Farewell Address**. Washington also insisted that President **John Adams** appoint Hamilton acting commander of the **provisional army** authorized in 1798 as a precondition to Washington accepting appointment as its supreme commander. Adams distrusted Hamilton, apparently with justification, as Hamilton considered using the military force he commanded to coerce large states like Virginia and to seize parts of Spanish America. Adams's decision to defuse the **Quasi-War** with France was motivated in part by fear of Hamilton's military ambitions. Hamilton was aware of Adams's enmity and construed the president's decision to dismiss Secretary of War **James McHenry** and Secretary of State **Timothy Pickering** from his cabinet during the summer of 1800 as a personal attack. Hamilton responded by writing a pamphlet designed to persuade the Federalist electors in the **Electoral College** to vote for **Charles C. Pinckney** rather than Adams in the upcoming presidential election. Hamilton's scheme became public after a Republican editor published the pamphlet on the eve of the **election of 1800**. When Adams lost the election by a thin margin, Hamilton helped persuade the Federalists in the House of Representatives to break the electoral tie between Jefferson and **Aaron Burr** in Jefferson's favor. Hamilton incurred Burr's further enmity by opposing Burr's attempt to become governor of New York in 1804. Burr then pursued a course that led to the Burr–Hamilton **duel** on 11 July 1804 that brought Hamilton's brilliant career to a premature close.

HARRISON, WILLIAM HENRY (9 February 1773–4 April 1841). Political leader, general, and ninth president of the United States, he was born in Virginia into a prominent family. After dropping out of college and medical school, Harrison obtained a commission in the army and acted as General Anthony Wayne's aide-de-camp at the **Battle of Fallen Timbers**. Resigning from the army just as the **Quasi-War** began in 1798, he was then appointed secretary of the Northwest Territory, elected its representative in Congress, and eventually appointed governor of the newly organized territorial government of Indiana. Harrison tried unsuccessfully to persuade Congress to lift its ban against the extension of **slavery** into the Northwest. As superintendent of **Indian** affairs, he attempted to get the natives to part with their land by luring them into debt. **Tecumseh** contested one of the purchases that Harrison had arranged in 1809 at the **Treaty of Fort Wayne**, and on 7 November 1811, Tecumseh's followers tried to ambush a **militia** force Harrison had assembled to accompany him to a parley at **Tippecanoe Creek** in modern Indiana. Harrison barely survived this engagement, which subsequently was celebrated as a victory. But thanks to **Henry Clay**'s backing, Harrison was appointed major general in the Kentucky militia and, after **William Hull**'s **surrender of Detroit**, brigadier general in the U.S. Army and eventually commander of the Northwest Military District during the **War of 1812**.

President **James Madison** assigned Harrison the task of retaking Detroit, but Harrison suffered two costly defeats before he was able to do so. On 22 January 1813, the loss of 1,300 Kentucky militia in the **Battle of Frenchtown** on the Raisin River forced an American withdrawal to **Fort Meigs**. On 5 May, 800 more troops were either captured or killed in an effort to raise the siege of Fort Meigs. Only after **Oliver Perry**'s naval victory in the **Battle of Lake Erie** on 10 September 1813 was Harrison able to reoccupy Detroit on 29 September. Then on 15 October, he decisively defeated the British forces in the **Battle of the Thames River** in Ontario. Tecumseh fell in this action, which secured American control of the northwestern frontier for the rest of the war.

After the War of 1812, Harrison entered Congress as a representative of **Ohio** between 1816 and 1819. From 1819 to 1821, he served in Ohio's senate. Despite his promotion of an ambitious plan for Ohio **canals**, his efforts to introduce slavery into the Northwest alienated his constituents. He did manage to swing Ohio into Clay's camp during the **election of 1824** and to serve as a U.S. senator for the state from 1825 to 1828. In that year, **John Quincy Adams** appointed him ambassador to Columbia and Peru to remove him from the field in the **election of 1828**. But his diplomatic career ended abruptly on 19 October 1829, when he was expelled from Colombia for fomenting revolution.

Nonetheless, Harrison's bid for the U.S. presidency in 1840 proved successful. His reputation as a military leader recommended him to the northwestern states during the election of 1836, and in 1840 he won the **Whig Party**'s nomination, thanks to **Daniel Webster**'s decision to back him rather than Harrison's old friend Clay. Harrison in turn appointed Webster secretary of state. When Harrison died within a month of taking office, his running mate—John Tyler of Virginia—became president and proceeded to veto most of the Whigs's legislative agenda. *See also* NATIONAL REPUBLICAN PARTY.

HARTFORD CONVENTION. New England's **Federalist Party** leaders had wanted to force a revision of the Constitution by calling a regional convention ever since the **Embargo of 1807–1809**. However, the disclosure of the **Henry Papers**, which suggested that a convention might also be linked to a plan for **secession** from the Union, at least until New England's demands were met, acted to restrain Federalist leaders from actually pursuing the plan. Though they repeatedly hinted that they would call a convention as a last resort against further prosecution of the **War of 1812**, the Federalists did not act on the threat until early October 1814. Then disclosure of Britain's terms for peace at Ghent persuaded them that the **Republican Party**'s leadership would prefer to fight to the finish. The Massachusetts legislature issued the call for a convention to meet at Hartford in mid-December. The timing of its summons was geared to securing the cooperation of as many New England states as possible before their autumn legislative sessions dissolved.

Connecticut and Rhode Island responded to the invitation of Massachusetts, but the summons arrived too late for either the New Hampshire or the Vermont legislature to act. Instead, two counties from the former state and one from the latter sent delegates. The convention met as scheduled in mid-December and deliberated in secret until the beginning of January 1815, when its proceedings were released. The convention issued a report enumerating its grievances. It also demanded autonomy from the federal government in defending the region against the British and proposed a series of constitutional amendments, among them one that abolished the clause entitling the southern states to count **three-fifths** of their **slaves** in their entitlement to representation in Congress and another barring any state from providing more than one president in a row. The Constitution explicitly forbade such a regional convention meeting without Congress's consent, and everyone understood that New England meant to conclude a separate peace with Great Britain if the Federalists did not get their way. Massachusetts and Connecticut then appointed commissioners to repair to Washington to receive the administration's surrender. They arrived in the capital at the same time that news was received that an honorable peace had been concluded in the **Treaty of Ghent** and that **Andrew Jackson** had prevailed over the British in the Battle of **New Orleans**. Much to their chagrin, the commissioners from Massachusetts and Connecticut had no choice but to retire in disgrace.

HAYNES, LEMUEL (18 July 1753–28 September 1833). Mulatto Congregational minister, he was born in West Hartford, Connecticut, to an African father and a white mother, both of whom abandoned him. At the age of five months, he was apprenticed to a family in a nearby town until he was 21. Though Haynes attended a common school with other children, his passion for learning and **religion** carried him well beyond what he was formally taught. On the expiration of his indenture, he enlisted as a minuteman and joined the army that besieged the British in Boston after the battles of Lexington and Concord. During 1776, he served in the Continental army. Retiring from the service in 1777, he declined an invitation to enroll at Dartmouth and instead studied classical languages and theology with several Connecticut ministers. In 1780, he was licensed to preach and returned to the town he had grown up in. There a white school teacher proposed marriage to him. After five years ministering to the congregation of his youth, he was ordained by the Litchfield County Association and accepted an invitation to preach in Torrington, Connecticut. After two years there, he was eased out, probably because of racial prejudice, but was offered another pulpit in Rutland, Vermont, where he remained for 30 years. In 1801, he published a Fourth of July oration, *The Nature and Importance of True Republicanism*, in which he denounced racial **slavery**. As a New Light **Congregationalist**, he was best known for his defense of orthodox **Calvinism** against **Universalism**. In 1804, Middlebury College awarded him an honorary M.A. His ardent support of the **Federalist Party** during the administrations of **Thomas Jefferson** and **James Madison** failed to protect him from racial prejudice, and in 1818 he was forced to move to a church in

Manchester, Vermont. There he worked hard to win freedom for two men he was convinced had been wrongfully convicted of murder. In 1822, he moved once again to minister to a congregation in upstate New York, where he eventually died.

HENRY PAPERS. John Henry, an Anglo-Irishman, had settled in the United States after the Revolution and briefly held a captain's commission during the **Quasi-War**. Eventually, he moved to Vermont near the Canadian border, where his anti-Republican sentiments attracted the attention of the governor of **Lower Canada**, Sir James Craig. In 1809, Craig recruited Henry to assess the disaffection the **Embargo of 1807–1809** was causing in New England. Henry executed this mission during February–March 1809, when the agitation against the embargo was at its peak. He sent Craig reports that, though local leaders of the **Federalist Party** were contemplating **secession**, it would take a war with Britain before they would be prepared to risk it.

In 1812, Henry, through an imposter posing as a Spanish count, offered the administration of **James Madison** his correspondence with Craig for a price. The government paid $50,000 for the documents, and on 9 March 1812, Madison transmitted them to Congress. When released, they were widely republished both in the **newspapers** and in pamphlets throughout the United States. Henry had been careful to delete the names of any Massachusetts Federalists, so the documents did not implicate specific individuals in treasonous designs. But they did cause the Federalist leadership considerable embarrassment, and they conclusively demonstrated that British officials looked to the Federalists as allies in dealing with the American Republic. They also pointed to the role that the Federalist leadership expected a regional convention to play in any secession movement. Though the Henry Papers failed to head off the **Hartford Convention** at the end of 1814, they did raise the ante to calling such a meeting and forced its sponsors to adopt elaborate stratagems and justifications for it. The Henry Papers also persuaded most of the rest of the nation that the Federalists' intentions were treasonable and helped lead to the dissolution of their party at the conclusion of the **War of 1812**.

HORSESHOE BEND, BATTLE OF. The **Creek War** between a

portion of the Creek nation and American settlers intensified during the summer of 1813. On 30 August 1813, Creek warriors massacred most of the garrison of **Fort Mims** on the Alabama River north of Mobile. **Andrew Jackson**, as major general in the Tennessee **militia**, called for volunteers and with 2,000 men undertook a winter campaign against the Creek that proved inconclusive. However, once Jackson was reinforced by a regular army regiment, he used the regulars to impose strict discipline on the militia and turned his men into an effective fighting force. In the middle of March, he advanced into **Indian** country, even though the terms of most of his men were about to expire. Some 900 Creek warriors, accompanied by 500 women and children, retreated before the American force to a bend in the Tallapoosa River, which they fortified heavily. On 29 March 1814, Jackson attacked and took the Indians' camp, killing almost all the warriors and taking the women and children captive. The engagement marked the end of effective Creek resistance and paved the way for the cession of two-thirds of the Creek lands that was consummated on 9 August 1814 in the Treaty of Fort Jackson.

HULL, ISAAC (9 March 1773–13 February 1843). A naval officer, he was born in Derby, Connecticut, and early took to the sea, assuming command of his first overseas voyage at age 21. Through the influence of his uncle, **William Hull**, he received a commission as lieutenant in the U.S. Navy on 9 March 1798 and served on the **USS *Constitution*** during the **Quasi-War**. Between 1802 and 1806, he saw action in the Mediterranean during the early phase of the **Barbary Wars**. On returning to the United States, he supervised the construction of gunboats favored by President **Thomas Jefferson** as the most economical naval defense for the nation. In 1809, he was given command of the **USS *Chesapeake*** and in 1810 the USS *President* before assuming command of the USS *Constitution*. Under his direction, the vessel was recoppered just before the beginning of the **War of 1812**. On 19 August, the *Constitution*, sailing without orders, encountered and took HMS *Guerrière*, the first major victory in the war. News of the triumph arrived almost simultaneously with that of his uncle's disastrous **surrender of Detroit**. Hull spent the rest of the war in charge of various naval yards. After the **Treaty of Ghent**, he was a member of the first Board of Naval Commissioners. He did not go back to sea again until 1823, when he served as commodore of a U.S. squadron in the southeastern Pacific. His last command of the Mediterranean squadron between 1839 and 1841 was an unhappy one because of his nearly total deafness and the resentment of those he outranked.

HULL, WILLIAM (24 June 1753–29 November 1825). Soldier and territorial governor, he was born in Derby, Connecticut, and graduated from Yale in 1772. During the Revolutionary War, he distinguished himself, rising to the rank of lieutenant colonel in the Massachusetts Line and often exercising independent command. After the war, he settled in Massachusetts and participated in the military suppression of Shays's Rebellion. As a prominent Massachusetts **Republican**, he came to the attention of President **Thomas Jefferson**, who appointed him governor of the Michigan Territory in 1805. In that capacity, he also acted as **Indian** agent and in 1807 managed to negotiate a large cession of land from the local tribes to the federal government. President **James Madison** also appointed Hull a brigadier general in the U.S. Army. When the **War of 1812** was declared, the administration ordered him to invade **Upper Canada** with a force of Ohio volunteers supported by a few regulars. After the Canadians failed to rise against their British rulers, Hull realized that his communications were in danger and retreated to Detroit. That hardly relieved the pressure he faced from a determined British commander supported by numerous Indian allies, and he surrendered at **Detroit** on 16 August 1812. The news administered a shattering blow to the morale of those who supported the war. Hull was eventually court-martialed for cowardice and neglect of duty and sentenced to death. Madison commuted the sentence to dismissal from the service, and Hull retired to a farm in Newton, Massachusetts, for the remainder of his life.

HUMPHREYS, DAVID (10 July 1752–21 February 1818). Soldier, poet, and diplomat, he was born in Derby, Connecticut, and educated at Yale, graduating with the class of 1771. At college, he became associated with a group of like-minded writers that included **Joel Bar-**

low and **Timothy Dwight** that came to be known as the "Connecticut wits." Humphreys collaborated with Barlow and two other Connecticut authors on the mock epic *The Anarchiad* (1786–1787), which sought through ridicule to suppress the discontent in Connecticut that had erupted as Shays's Rebellion in Massachusetts. Before that, Humphreys had made a poetic splash with several other poems, especially his "The Glory of America"(1782).

Humphreys had joined the Continental army as an officer in 1776 and served under Israel Putnam and Nathaniel Greene before becoming aide-de-camp to General **George Washington** in 1780. He was constantly with Washington until December 1783 and joined his household again between 1787 and 1790 after a brief stint as secretary to a trade commission in Europe directed by **Benjamin Franklin**, **Thomas Jefferson**, and **John Adams**. In 1790, President Washington dispatched him on another diplomatic mission to Spain and Portugal. Humphreys became resident minister in Lisbon during 1791 and presided over the negotiations successfully concluded by Joel Barlow for the release of 119 American seamen seized by the Algerians as well as several peace treaties between the North African states and the United States. In 1796, he was made minister to Spain. President Jefferson recalled Humphreys in 1801 because of his loyalty to the **Federalist Party**. On his return to the United States, Humphreys started a domestic woolens **industry** in Connecticut with the hundred merino sheep he had received as a gift from the Spanish court.

***HYLTON V. UNITED STATES* (1796).** Daniel L. Hylton owned 125 carriages but refused to register and pay tax on them as required by an act of Congress passed in 1794. Instead, Hylton challenged the constitutionality of the carriage tax on the ground it was a direct tax that should have been apportioned among the states according to the ratio prescribed in the Constitution. Justice Samuel Chase spoke for the **Supreme Court** in denying Hylton's appeal. He argued that since the carriage tax was not a direct tax, the rule of uniformity rather than the rule of proportionality governed. This was the first occasion on which the high court passed on the constitutionality of a federal law.

– I –

IMMIGRATION/IMMIGRANTS. The immigration of dispossessed Europeans, which had played so large a role in peopling British North America before the Revolution, came largely to an end with the commencement of the **European wars** stemming from the **French Revolution**. A trickle of prominent French émigrés, like **Talleyrand**, bent on fleeing the European disorders continued, but only a few émigrés, like **Eleuthère Irénée du Pont** and **John Audubon**, committed themselves to an American future. The United States never benefited from a large French immigration, and the flow of Frenchmen was more than matched by the immigration of British artisans like **Samuel Slater**, merchant-industrialists who saw opportunity in the new nation's neutral status, civil engineers whose skills were at a premium in launching the **transportation revolution**, and intelligentsia figures like **Thomas Paine** and **Joseph Priestley**. Aside from a few Irish laborers under contract to dig the first **canals**, Africa remained the largest source of immigrant **labor** during the first two decades of the Republic. The involuntary flow of **slaves** persisted until Congress terminated the international **slave trade** on 1 January 1808.

At the conclusion of the European wars in 1815, the migration of northern Europe's dispossessed resumed with a vengeance. Poor harvests due to bad weather compounded the effects of 20 years of mayhem and sent an increasing stream of people westward across the ocean. The majority of the newcomers continued to be Protestants, easing the strains of assimilation when ethnic and linguistic differences needed to be overcome. But after 1815, Irish **Catholics** became a more prominent presence with the commencement of work on the **Erie Canal**. The Irish continued to be regarded as transient labor, more likely to return to their homeland than to bring their families over to join them, and they remained a distinct minority among the total number of immigrants. But even the temporary absorption of an ethnic group defined by a **religion** that the majority of Americans distrusted posed a problem for Protestant America. Anti-Catholic violence would break out in the 1830s as it became clear that they intended to stay, but the seeds of these disturbances were already beginning to sprout in the 1820s.

IMPOST. An indirect tax on goods imported from overseas. Merchants were often willing to collect this tax because they could recover it in the price they charged to consumers, while consumers paid the tax only if they chose to buy the dutied goods. Direct taxes on polls (individual males) or real estate had to be paid regardless of choice, and sheriffs were empowered to collect such taxes through the seizure and forced sale of one's property. A nation that owed its birth to a tax rebellion was far more likely to pay an impost than a direct tax since the former was paid by consent, while the latter could be coerced. *See also* TARIFF.

IMPRESSMENT. Britain's forcible removal of seamen from U.S. vessels to man its warships under the pretense that they were British subjects. As an island nation, Britain sanctioned the impressment of seamen off its merchant vessels in home waters as a necessary defense measure. During the **Napoleonic Wars**, many of its seamen chose service on American vessels to escape the press and secure higher wages. As Britain tried to tighten its blockade of Napoleonic Europe after its naval victory at Trafalgar, the Royal Navy's need for manpower increased and led to the search of American merchantmen in American waters and on the high seas. Though even in the USS ***Chesapeake*** incident British naval officers maintained the pretense that they were only seizing British subjects, they often made mistakes, as the complaints of the kin of Americans forced into the British service dramatized. Agreement protecting the legitimate interests of both nations could have been worked out had not the negotiation invariably become entangled with other issues. Popular anger over recent impressments helped steel the Republicans for war at the beginning of 1812, and Britain's revocation of its **Orders-in-Council** three days after the **War of 1812** had been officially declared left impressment the only issue that justified continued hostilities. Britain failed to provide the U.S. government with the guarantee against the continuation of the practice it sought in the **Treaty of Ghent**. But the pacification of Europe after 1815 led to its effective abandonment thereafter.

INDIANS (NATIVE AMERICANS). At the time of the initial European contact, three linguistic families of Indians blanketed the eastern woodlands area. Algonkin speakers predominated along the Atlantic coast from Newfoundland to the Chesapeake and around the western Great Lakes. Iroquoian speakers controlled the area surrounding the St. Lawrence River and Lakes Ontario and Erie, along with pockets in the southern Appalachians in western North Carolina, South Carolina, and Virginia. Muskogean speakers inhabited the Southeast to the Mississippi River. A small enclave of Sioux speakers inhabited central North Carolina, though most of their colinguists resided to the west of the Mississippi. Linguistic affinity usually did little to overcome kin, band, and tribal divisions within their respective domains. But it did provide one of the unifying elements behind the consolidation of the **Iroquois Confederation** before the European discovery of the Americas.

Contact between Indians and whites sometimes contributed to the consolidation of tribes from what had been loose bands. But the arrival of Europeans generally proved more disruptive than integrative because of the diseases and domestic animals they brought with them. The indigenous population had no immunity to the endemic diseases common among the newcomers, while the introduction of European livestock required crops and land usages incompatible with Indian cultures. The result of both developments was a major demographic catastrophe. At one time or another, virtually the entire indigene population suffered from a die-off, conservatively estimated at 90 percent over the first century of contact. Besides making survival problematic, this catastrophe severely disrupted their cultures and placed Indians at a permanent military disadvantage in relation to the Europeans. Indian populations seldom managed to recover demographically in subsequent centuries in part because the warrior orientation of their societies involved them in European struggles for mastery of the continent. This ensured periodic reexposure to the lethal pathogens to which they remained vulnerable.

At the time of the Revolution, most of the coastal Indians had been displaced from their ancestral lands. Some tribes moved west, while the remnants of others survived on the fringes of the older European settlements. Indians of the interior fared better before the expansion of European settlement brought them into more direct contact with whites. But the interior peoples paid heavily during the early republican period for siding with the British in the Revolutionary War. **Joseph Brant** ended up leading most members of the Iroquois Confederation to a new location on the northern shore of Lake Ontario, while attempts by the Indians of **Ohio**—especially the Shawnees, Wyandots, and Delawares—to stem the tide of the **westward movement** met military defeat at the **Battle of Fallen Timbers**. **Tecumseh**'s subsequent efforts to mobilize pan-Indian resistance against white encroachment crumbled before the expansionism of men like **William Henry Harrison**. The **War of 1812** led to the subjugation of the northern Indians after Tecumseh's death in the **Battle of the Thames River**. Even tribes like the **Oneida**, which had embraced the American cause against Britain during the Revolution, were eventually confronted with the choice between assimilation or **removal** to distant Wisconsin.

Some southern tribes adopted features of European culture in an effort to defend themselves against white encroachments. The **Cherokee** espoused settled agricultural practices and, thanks to **Sequoyah**'s development of a syllabary for the Cherokee language, acquired literacy, which permitted the drafting and ratification of a constitution. But pressure from the southern states, particularly Virginia and Georgia, on the Cherokee and **Creek**, respectively, proved irresistible. The Creek divided over the War of 1812, and those elements of the Red Stick faction that were not destroyed in battle joined the **Seminoles** in retreating into Florida. The Creeks that clung to ancestral lands in Georgia and Alabama soon confronted the stark alternatives of physical displacement or assimilation. The same fate awaited the Cherokee, though they managed to delay their removal until the late 1830s. Then the tribe suffered terribly on the forced march to modern Oklahoma, an event that became known as the "trail of tears." *See also* CREEK WAR; FORT WAYNE, TREATY OF; GREENVILLE, TREATIES OF; HORSESHOE BEND, BATTLE OF; TERRITORIAL EXPANSION; TIPPECANOE CREEK, BATTLE OF.

INDUSTRY. In 1789, the United States was still a colonial economy. Despite political independence, Americans traded agricultural surpluses and raw materials like unfinished iron for European manufactures that they were unable to produce in the household. During the Revolutionary War, much of the clothing, arms, and munitions used by the Continental army had been imported from Europe. **Alexander**

Hamilton hoped to eliminate this dependence by offering bounties for the production of strategic commodities. But his **Report on Manufactures** (1792) failed to meet with the approval of Congress.

Nevertheless, numerous entrepreneurs during the ensuing decade began filling the gap on their own. When **Eli Whitney** realized he would not be able to enforce his patent rights to the **cotton gin**, he turned to manufacturing arms and, in the process of applying the principle of interchangeable parts, started developing precision machine tools. However, it took Whitney until the late 1820s to eliminate all the technical difficulties he encountered. **Paul Revere** was more successful in establishing a copper-rolling mill in 1800 to satisfy the government's demand for large amounts of copper sheathing for its vessels of war. And in 1804, **Eleuthère Irénée du Pont** began manufacturing gunpowder using the latest French techniques in his mill on the Brandywine.

Most domestically produced goods for the individual consumer at the end of the 18th century were still made in the household or local craft shop in response to a specific demand. Only with the turn of the century did production for a larger, impersonal market begin to encroach on household and craft production. Occasionally, an artisan like Paul Revere pioneered such changes. But merchants, who needed goods to sell in distant markets, rather than the people who actually produced them, more frequently powered the transition. Merchants took the initiative in organizing the expansion of the domestic putting-out system, harnessing the **labor** of individual households. Eventually, they developed the factory to organize the entire productive process in one place as the most efficient way of manufacturing a standardized product with machinery. Of equal importance, the factory simplified distribution of the finished product through a single agency responsive to those in charge of production.

Samuel Slater established the first successful spinning mill powered by water in 1790. His example inspired numerous others to follow, particularly during the commercial disruptions resulting from the **Embargo of 1807–1809** and the **War of 1812**. But there was a major difference between producing thread and producing a finished piece of textile. The Boston Manufacturing Company was formed in 1813 to close that gap, and in 1814 the factory complex it built at Waltham succeeded in doing so. The Boston Associates, behind the venture, committed considerably more capital over a longer time to their enterprise than anyone previously had. In the 1820s, they established similar ventures in Lowell (1822) and Chicopee, Massachusetts (1823). Though the factory system would prove to be the wave of the future, most production for the wider market before 1830 continued to combine elements of shop and domestic production in the manufacture of finished goods. *See also* ECONOMIC DEVELOPMENT; LOWELL, FRANCIS CABOT.

INFIDELITY. A term in the late 18th and early 19th centuries that referred to lack of belief in the divine authority of the scriptures. Defenders of religious orthodoxy often leveled the charge of infidelity against their opponents in much the same way conservatives during the Cold War branded anyone with opinions that differed from theirs as "communists."

INGERSOLL, CHARLES JARED (3 October 1782–14 May 1862). Author and congressman, he was born in Philadelphia and attended Princeton for two years but returned to Philadelphia during his third year to study law. Before being admitted to the bar in 1802, he wrote a play that was produced in 1801. During 1803, he traveled throughout Europe. In 1804, he came back to Philadelphia to practice law. His European sojourn interested him in defending the nation's Republican experiment against the pressures to which foreign powers were subjecting it. He produced two widely read pamphlets at the end of the decade: *View of the Rights and Wrongs, Power and Policy, of the United States of America* (1808) and *Inchiquin: The Jesuit's Letters* (1810). As a Republican congressman, he supported prosecuting the **War of 1812** in Congress until he was removed from office in 1814, partially in response to the military reverses of that year. But he was appointed U.S. district attorney for Philadelphia in 1815 and served in that capacity until 1829. His "The Influence of America on the Mind" (1823), a scholarly version of his earlier writings on the nation's character, received considerable foreign notice. During the 1830s, he sided with President **Andrew Jackson** against the **Second Bank of the United States**. Returning to Congress between 1840 and 1849, he championed **Texas** annexation and opposed the northern **abolitionists**. During the 1850s, he finished a two-volume history of the War of 1812 that is still useful today.

INTERNAL IMPROVEMENTS. *See* TRANSPORTATION REVOLUTION.

IROQUOIS CONFEDERATION. During the 16th century, five Iroquois-speaking tribes in northern New York—the Cayuga, the Mohawk, the Oneida, the Onondaga, and the Seneca—formed a confederation to ensure that internal peace was maintained between them. In the early 18th century, they were joined by the Tuscarora, also Iroquois speakers but migrants from North Carolina. The Tuscarora did not enjoy access to the Council fire, but the Oneida represented them there.

During the Revolution, **Joseph Brant** led most of the Iroquois to side with the British. However, the Oneida and Tuscarora, after attempting to remain neutral, eventually aided the United States, though they continued to avoid outright hostilities with their Iroquois compatriots. Their actions failed to protect their lands after the war despite **Alexander Hamilton**'s collaboration with Samuel Kirkland in establishing an **Indian** academy during the 1790s that eventually became Hamilton College in 1812. Some Oneida and Tuscarora had joined Brant when he led the tribes that had sided with the British to settle new lands in Ontario well before the **War of 1812**. Others moved farther west to Wisconsin in 1822. Remnants remained behind in New York, but the price of doing so was assimilation into the culture of the European.

IRVING, WASHINGTON (3 April 1783–28 November 1859). Author, he was born in **New York City**, the son of an **immigrant** Scottish merchant who expected his male children to participate in the family business. Irving explored the law as an alternative, but his real inclination was to write. He published his first satirical essays in his brother's *Morning Chronicle* at age 20 and also did some pieces for a short-lived **newspaper** that supported **Aaron Burr**. Irving then went abroad for two years. He was finally admitted to the bar after returning to the United States in 1806. During 1807, he published, in collaboration with a brother and James Kirke Paulding, a satirical **magazine** entitled *Salmagundi*. Its success next led him to embark on a spurious history of New York by Diedrick Knickerbocker that was really a satire of Jeffersonian America. After editing the *Analectic*

Magazine for two years during the **War of 1812**, Irving embarked for Europe in 1815.

He found the European branch of the family business in desperate shape and devoted two futile years to trying to salvage it. Turning back to **literature** in 1819, he published *The Sketch Book of Geoffrey Crayon, Gent*. This work, containing, among other tales, "Rip Van Winkle" and "The Legend of Sleepy Hollow," was a success both in Europe and in America. However, his subsequent Crayon books proved less appealing, and in the mid-1820s Irving moved to Madrid, where in the course of two years he managed to produce a biography of Christopher Columbus that was widely read at the time and remained authoritative throughout the rest of the century. Irving lingered in Spain, producing several more works of history as well as of fantasy before returning to the United States in 1832.

For the next decade, he turned his attention to the American West, both imaginatively and historically. Between 1842 and 1846, he served as American minister to Spain. At the end of his life, he managed to produce a five-volume biography of **George Washington**. Irving was the first American writer to make a financial success of writing by addressing the world's expanding English-speaking audience. He was also among the first American writers to have their collected works issued by the American publisher G. P. Putnam.

– J –

JACKSON, ANDREW (15 March 1767–8 June 1845). Seventh president of the United States, he was born on the border of the Carolinas into a family that had recently immigrated from northern Ireland. Jackson's father died shortly before his birth. Jackson fought his first battle against the British at age 13, survived British imprisonment and **smallpox** at 14, and found himself orphaned by 15. Thanks to a brief period of schooling while a youngster, he was able to apprentice himself to a lawyer and be admitted to the North Carolina bar in 1787. Deciding that opportunity lay to the west, he moved to modern Tennessee, married, and prospered as a lawyer. In 1796, he was a delegate to Tennessee's constitutional convention and acted as the new state's sole representative in Congress before being elected senator in 1797.

Jackson did not feel comfortable in Congress, and he resigned his Senate seat in 1798. On returning to Tennessee, he was elected to the state's highest court. His judicial duties did not prevent him from aggressively speculating in land and running an extensive trading concern. In 1802, he was elected major general of the state **militia** in preference to John Sevier, a popular ex-governor. In 1805, **Aaron Burr** stayed with Jackson after killing **Alexander Hamilton** in a **duel**. Jackson was drawn to Burr's treasonous plans to invade Spanish territory, but Burr was arrested on President **Thomas Jefferson**'s orders before Jackson became inextricably involved.

Jackson was ordered to campaign against the **Creek** during the **War of 1812**. After several reverses, he became a skilled **Indian** fighter and decisively defeated the Creek at **Horseshoe Bend** on 27 March 1814. In the aftermath of this battle, Jackson forced the Creeks to part with 23 million acres of their land in the **Treaty of Fort Jackson**. Promoted to major general in the U.S. Army, he assumed command over the Southwestern Military District. On 7 November 1814, he seized Pensacola from the Spanish without authorization before moving to counter a large British force under Sir Edward Pakenham that was threatening **New Orleans**. Jackson hastily assembled a heterogeneous collection of regulars as well as militia drawn from Tennessee, Kentucky, and Georgia, and he even recruited the services of local pirates to counter the British invasion. In a series of engagements between 23 December 1814 and 8 January 1815, he decisively defeated Pakenham's veterans at minimal cost. Overnight, Jackson became a hero because he seemed to have secured the nation's future destiny.

Jackson participated in the **Seminole War** of 1818 and, in the process of pursuing raiding **Indians** into **East Florida**, executed two British subjects for aiding the enemy. President **James Monroe**'s cabinet, fearing that Jackson's actions might provoke war with Britain and Spain, were inclined to disavow him. But Secretary of State **John Quincy Adams** saw opportunity where others saw danger and used Jackson's escapade to persuade Spain to cede East Florida to the United States in the **Adams-Onís Treaty**. Monroe had Jackson receive Spain's cession of the province, now the state of Florida, in 1821 and appointed him its first territorial governor.

Jackson returned to Tennessee at the end of the year and was nominated for the presidency by the state legislature in 1822. It also sent him back to the Senate in 1823. Jackson received a plurality of votes in the **election of 1824**, but the House of Representatives elected John Quincy Adams after **Henry Clay**, Speaker of the House, endorsed Adams. Even before Adams appointed Clay secretary of state, Jackson complained he had been denied election because of a corrupt bargain. Retiring to Tennessee, he formed a national organization that would become known as the **Democratic Party** headed by **John C. Calhoun**, **Martin Van Buren**, and **Thomas Hart Benton** of Missouri to secure victory in the **election of 1828**. After the dissolution of the **Federalist Party**, national politics had reverted to a factionalism in which an expanding electorate that had come to embrace virtually all white males would select the winner. With no real issues at stake, the past reputations of the leading candidates became fair game. Jackson's partisans charged that Adams had pimped for the Russian czar, while Adams's supporters made much of Jackson's **dueling**. They also exploited an embarrassing ambiguity about the status of his wife Rachel when they had married, accusing him of bigamy. Though Jackson won the election handily, Rachel died shortly afterward, allegedly as a consequence of the scandal.

Jackson's presidency lasted for two terms. During his tenure in office, he exercised the presidential veto power more than any previous president, blocking federally sponsored **internal improvements** and the recharter of the **Second Bank of the United States**. He also vigorously opposed South Carolina's attempt to **nullify** the **Tariff of Abominations** and presided over the **removal** of the southern Indians from their ancestral lands in Alabama and Mississippi to Oklahoma. He pursued a vigorous foreign policy that led to the settlement of claims against France, Denmark, and Naples for their conduct during the **Napoleonic Wars** and also won American access to the British West Indies. After Van Buren succeeded him as eighth president, Jackson retired to Tennessee, where he continued to influence the Democratic Party he had founded. For many Americans at the time, his ascent from poverty to the highest office of the land made him emblematic of a new, democratic age.

JAY, JOHN (12 December 1745–17 May 1829). Diplomat and first chief justice of the United States, he was born in **New York City**. Though of Huguenot descent, his mother was a Van Cortlandt, and he would marry a Livingston, thus placing him securely among the colony's first families. Jay attended King's College (now Columbia), graduating in 1764, and became a lawyer. In 1774, New York elected him first to its Committee of Correspondence and then made him a delegate to the first and second Continental Congresses. While he sought to avoid full independence and a prolonged war, he committed himself completely to the Revolution once the more moderate options had disappeared. As a member of the New York Convention, Jay was instrumental in drafting the state constitution of 1777. Subsequently, he returned to Congress and was elected its president.

In 1780, Congress appointed Jay minister to Spain. After failing to achieve anything of significance there, he joined **Benjamin Franklin** and **John Adams** in Paris to negotiate the peace. Jay's insistence that the British envoys be instructed to acknowledge American independence as a precondition delayed the negotiating process during 1782 but eventually resulted in winning more generous terms from Britain than the United States might otherwise have obtained. On returning home after the war, Jay found he had been appointed secretary for foreign affairs under the new Confederation government. In that capacity, he negotiated an agreement with the Spanish ambassador whereby the United States would forgo navigating the Mississippi for 30 years in exchange for commercial privileges in the Spanish Empire and a mutual guarantee of both countries' territories. When news of these terms leaked out, Jay was condemned by the southern leadership for being willing to renounce navigating the Mississippi, something they regarded as essential to the West's development. Jay was not a member of the Philadelphia Convention, but he did support the adoption of the new frame of government and collaborate with **Alexander Hamilton** and **James Madison** in drafting a few essays for the *Federalist*.

President **George Washington** appointed Jay first chief justice of the United States. In that capacity, he joined with the rest of the court in ruling that an individual could sue a state in ***Chisholm v. Georgia***. The ruling led directly to the framing and adoption of the **Eleventh Amendment**. In 1794, Washington asked Jay to go to Britain as a fully accredited envoy to head off a war between the two countries resulting from Britain's disregard of the nation's neutral rights. Jay brought home a commercial treaty with Britain that avoided war but at the cost of compromising the nation's alliance with France as well as its neutrality. The **Jay Treaty** made its negotiator very unpopular, and Washington accepted the agreement with utmost reluctance. Despite the controversy over the treaty, Jay was elected governor of New York for two successive terms from 1795 to 1799. At the end of his second term, he refused to go along with a scheme proposed by Alexander Hamilton that would have stymied **Aaron Burr**'s efforts to have the state cast its votes in the **Electoral College** for **Thomas Jefferson** in the **election of 1800**. He also refused **John Adams**'s offer to reappoint him chief justice of the United States. Instead, Jay spent the remaining years of his life in retirement.

JAY TREATY. Negotiated with Britain by **John Jay** at the end of 1794, it sought to head off war between the two countries. By its terms, Britain agreed to surrender the northwestern posts it had been holding in violation of the Peace of 1783, to compensate the United States for the seizure of its neutral shipping since 1793, and to admit American vessels and merchants to limited privileges within its commercial empire. In exchange, the United States agreed to a joint commission that would pass on the claims the citizens of each country had against the other. This opened the United States to accepting responsibility for debts owed in Britain that had been acknowledged in the Peace of 1783 but never paid. The United States also agreed to a broad, British definition of contraband and accepted the British practice of intercepting American vessels sailing to France and sending them into British ports where their cargoes were sold.

Many Americans thought Jay had paid too high a price for peace with Great Britain and were afraid that France, with whom the nation was still formally in alliance, would take offense. President **George Washington**'s initial inclination was to reject the treaty, but he eventually agreed to ask the Senate's advice and consent. A bare two-thirds of the Senate endorsed the treaty but not before its terms were made public. The resulting uproar gave President Washington additional reason to reject it, but his hand was forced by the British seizure of French diplomatic dispatches that showed that the secretary of state, **Edmund Randolph**, had asked for French financial assistance in quelling the **Whiskey Rebellion**. When Randolph proved unable to explain his behavior, Washington decided that he had to accept the treaty to prove that the United States was not a French pawn as many in the British government suspected. Washington's actions further inflamed public sentiment against the treaty and set the stage for a struggle in the House of Representatives over whether it should be implemented.

The issue arose because the joint commission would cost money, which the House alone could appropriate. Representative **Edward Livingston** initiated the House struggle by calling on the president to submit all the papers relating to the treaty. Washington invoked executive privilege to deny the request. That inflamed the opposition still further. But in the last analysis, the members of the **Republican Party** in the House, led by **James Madison**, declined to push matters to extremes because they did not control the executive and therefore were unable to take responsibility for the consequences that might ensue. The treaty eventually became the law of the land after Britain accepted the deletion of a section that admitted U.S. vessels of 70 tons or less to its West Indian trade. Though many found the petty nature of this concession objectionable, it also was joined to a prohibition on exporting U.S. cotton that was deemed unconstitutional.

The Jay Treaty was the defining moment in the emergence of the **First Party System**, which would dominate national politics until the conclusion of the **War of 1812**. It revealed the essential cleavage between the **Federalist Party** and the **Republican Party**. The struggle over implementation helped expand popular involvement in national politics. The treaty led to deteriorating relations with France that culminated in the **Quasi-War** and informal alignment with Britain. Only with the election of **Thomas Jefferson** as president in 1801 did the nation recover a credible neutral stance. But the financial advantages the nation had reaped by seeking good relations with Britain at the expense of bad relations with France continued to fuel the Federalist view of international relations through 1815.

JEFFERSON, THOMAS (13 April 1743–4 July 1826). Principal author of the Declaration of Independence and third president of the United States, he was born in Albemarle County, Virginia, and graduated from William & Mary College in 1762. He emerged as a revolutionary leader after entering the Virginia legislature in 1769. Except for a brief stint in the second Continental Congress during 1776, Jefferson spent most of the Revolutionary War in Virginia, serving between 1779 and 1781 as the state's governor. Sent back to Congress in 1782, he was appointed ambassador to France in 1784 and remained there until the autumn of 1789.

President **George Washington** appointed Jefferson his first secretary of state on his return to the United States in 1789. Taking up his duties in March 1790 as the controversy over **Alexander Hamilton**'s **funding** system developed, Jefferson arranged the meeting between Hamilton and **James Madison** that resulted in the bargain that traded **assumption** of the state debts for the **residency** of the capital on the Potomac. Britain's failure fully to abide by the Peace of 1783 and its attempt to exclude American commerce from the British West Indies soon became his principal preoccupations. Jefferson favored France after the outbreak of the **European wars** in 1793, but he proved no match for the pro-British faction in the administration, particularly after ambassador **Edmund Genêt** compromised the nation's neutrality by inciting Americans to undertake warlike activities against Britain. After reluctantly consenting to Genêt's recall, Jefferson resigned from the government, expecting to remain in private life permanently. However, he quickly reemerged as the **Republican Party** candidate for the presidency in the **election of 1796** and, as the runner-up, acted as vice president during **John Adams**'s presidency.

Jefferson could do little to halt the **Federalist Party**'s march toward limited war with France as the presiding officer in the Senate. Instead, he had to sign measures like the **Alien** and **Sedition Acts**. Retreating to Virginia after the session of the fifth Congress that had authorized the **Quasi-War** against France and placed Hamilton at the head of an enlarged **provisional army**, Jefferson joined Madison in turning to the state legislatures to resist. Jefferson drafted the **Kentucky Resolutions** of 1798, which in his version declared the Alien and Sedition Acts unconstitutional and therefore "not law, but . . . altogether void, and of no force." Jefferson thus helped sow the seed for a doctrine of **nullification**, which Massachusetts would use a decade later against the **Embargo of 1807–1809** and **John C. Calhoun** would refine against the **Tariff of Abominations**. Nullification eventually became a bulwark for the southern defense of **slavery**.

Jefferson's authorship of the Kentucky Resolves was not widely known, and Kentucky's actions failed to attract the attention Madison's

Virginia Resolves did. Consequently, Jefferson benefited from Adams's peace initiative with France that led to the **Franco-American Convention of 1800**. Though again the leading Republican candidate for the presidency, he had the same number of electoral votes as **Aaron Burr** in the **election of 1800**, allowing the Federalists who controlled the lame-duck House of Representatives to choose between them. On the 36th ballot, the House finally decided to make Jefferson the third president of the United States. Jefferson, in turn, behaved in a conciliatory manner toward the Federalists, who found the **Truce of Amiens**, which produced a temporary cessation of hostilities between Britain and France, additionally reassuring. Though still critical of Hamiltonian finance, Jefferson left the funding system in place beyond paring down the expenses of government to a minimum and retiring as much of the debt as possible.

The honeymoon ended when the seventh Congress assembled at the end of 1801 and a Republican majority repealed the **Judiciary Act of 1801**. Many who had benefited from Adams's last-minute judicial appointments now lost their positions. Subsequently, Jefferson's congressional allies, led by Representative **John Randolph**, initiated impeachment proceedings against two federalist judges. The seventh Congress also framed the **Twelfth Amendment** to the Constitution and forwarded it to the states for ratification. It required electors in the **Electoral College** to vote separately for president and vice president, precluding another tied election. Three-quarters of the states ratified this amendment before the **election of 1804**. The Federalists also objected to the **Louisiana Purchase** from France negotiated at Jefferson's behest by **James Monroe** and **Robert R. Livingston**. They feared that Louisiana would permanently empower their Republican adversaries because Federalism had little foothold outside New England. Jefferson's landslide reelection in 1804 confirmed their anxieties.

In 1805, the **Napoleonic Wars** took a new turn after the battle of Trafalgar established Britain's naval supremacy and France demonstrated the potency of its armies on the Continent. With each belligerent supreme in its own sphere, they tried to strike at the other indirectly through **paper blockades**. Jefferson sent **William Pinkney** to join ambassador **James Monroe** in London to negotiate an understanding with the British, but they failed to win sufficient concessions, and Jefferson declined forwarding the **Monroe-Pinkney Treaty** to the Senate. By 1807, each of the belligerents had outlawed the neutral trade of the other. Britain, however, posed the greater threat because of the preponderance of its naval power. Britain also **impressed** seamen off American vessels to man its fleet and in June 1807 perpetrated an outrage against the **USS *Chesapeake***. HMS *Leopard* intercepted the *Chesapeake* as it left American waters and removed four alleged deserters by force, killing three and wounding 18 in the process. Though the incident could have provoked a war, Congress was not in session to declare one, and by the time it did assemble, Jefferson had learned that France no longer intended to exempt the United States from its commercial restrictions under the **Franco-American Convention of 1800**. Jefferson then asked Congress for a general embargo to buy time while other remedies, either diplomatic, commercial, or outright war, were explored. Jefferson, along with Secretary of State Madison and Secretary of the Treasury **Albert Gallatin**, preferred the former two to the latter. Though Burr had offered to conquer parts of Spanish America for the British, the **Burr treason trial** that took place as the crisis in the nation's foreign relations unfolded seemed like a minor distraction.

The New England Federalists opposed the **Embargo of 1807–1809** and wanted any war to be waged against France. In March 1808, Federalist Senator **Timothy Pickering** launched a blistering attack against the embargo. It marked the beginning of a sustained campaign that in March 1809 led Congress to replace the embargo with **nonintercourse** against Britain and France, just as Jefferson retired from the presidency. Jefferson blamed the humiliation on New England, which appeared to be on the brink of civil war. But the Republicans' aversion to war, which the Federalists did everything in their power to exploit, was equally important. This debacle, as much as Britain's commercial restrictions or impressments, eventually pushed the Republicans into declaring the **War of 1812**. Jefferson watched the spectacle unfold from his Virginia plantation, Monticello, giving counsel when he could but happy to be relieved of public responsibilities. His last years were spent in correspondence with many former friends and associates in America and Europe, most notably with his former political rival, John Adams. After the British **burning of Washington** on 25 August 1814, he donated his library to Congress. It proved to be the seed that has grown into the Library of Congress. He also helped found the University of Virginia in Charlottesville. He died fittingly on the jubilee of the Declaration of Independence, on the same day as Adams.

JOURNEYMEN. A term referring to someone who had completed an apprenticeship but was not yet in a position to establish himself as a master craftsman. As the apprentice system atrophied, a journeyman became synonymous with a wage laborer.

JUDICIAL REVIEW. The doctrine that the **Supreme Court** is empowered to review state and federal laws and to annul those it finds in conflict with the Constitution. Some state higher courts had examined the constitutionality of their laws before 1787, the *Federalist* had argued that the Supreme Court would review the actions of the legislature and executive to maintain the independence of the branches of government, and sections 13 and 25 of the **Judiciary Act of 1789** had empowered the Court to reverse state judicial rulings that involved federal laws, treaties, or the Constitution. But it was quite another matter for a new, untried government to implement judicial review, as became apparent from the response to the Court's decision in ***Chisholm v. Georgia*** (1793), which led directly to the **Eleventh Amendment**. That judicial review came eventually to be accepted at all was due largely to Chief Justice **John Marshall**'s gradual elaboration of the Court's powers in a series of decisions spanning more than 20 years. The first, ***Marbury v. Madison*** (1803), invalidated a portion of a congressional statute, but the Court did not rule that the actions of a state legislature were unconstitutional until ***Fletcher v. Peck*** (1810). Subsequently, Marshall and his colleagues expanded the grounds on which a state law might be annulled in the ***Dartmouth College Case*** (1819), ***McCulloch v. Maryland*** (1819), and ***Gibbons v. Ogden*** (1824). The Court also asserted its power to review state judicial decisions in ***Martin v. Hunter's Lesee*** (1816). By the time Marshall retired from the Court, the supremacy of federal laws and the Court's powers to review the constitutionality of all statutes was beyond dispute.

JUDICIARY ACT OF 1789. Article III, section 1, of the Constitution gave Congress the power to organize the federal court system. The

first Congress provided for a **Supreme Court** of six justices and 13 separate district courts. The district courts were given jurisdiction over violations of federal laws and concurrent jurisdiction over suits where the parties came from different states or from abroad. The Judiciary Act of 1789 also provided for three circuit courts. Though they had original jurisdiction in some cases, their principal function was an appellate one, and each was presided over by a district judge and two Supreme Court justices riding circuit. Though this meant that a Supreme Court justice might end up reviewing a previous ruling he had made if a case came to the high court on appeal, it made the federal appeals process more available to litigants. Short of asking the state courts to assume original jurisdiction in federal matters and leaving the federal courts to focus principally on hearing appeals, the first Congress had created a legal structure that remained as decentralized as was practical.

JUDICIARY ACT OF 1801. In the last days of President **John Adams**'s administration, the sixth Congress revised the judicial system instituted in the **Judiciary Act of 1789**, vastly expanding the federal courts and the functions they were to perform. The Judiciary Act of 1801 created six circuit courts, all but one of which was staffed by three specially appointed circuit judges, and expanded the number of district courts. Since each district had a marshal and a district attorney, the law substantially increased the judicial patronage at the president's disposal. Adams responded with a series of last-minute appointments to these newly created judicial posts. On assuming the presidency, **Thomas Jefferson** urged the repeal of this law, and **James Madison** refused to deliver a commission to one of Adams's "midnight" appointees, William Marbury. Marbury brought suit in ***Marbury v. Madison*** to force Madison to deliver his commission. Chief Justice **John Marshall** used the occasion to rule the section of the **Judiciary Act of 1789**, under which the Court was requested to act, unconstitutional. The sixth Congress had also sought to extend the reach of the federal court system through a federal **bankruptcy law** that the new circuit courts would be responsible for administering. The seventh Congress quickly repealed the Judiciary Act of 1801 and nineteen months later the bankruptcy law, restoring most of the legal system that had been created by the Judiciary Act of 1789.

– K –

KENT, JAMES (31 July 1763–12 December 1847). Jurist, he was born in rural New York. Kent attended Yale, graduating in 1781; was admitted to the New York bar in 1785; and settled in Poughkeepsie, New York. There Kent supported the new federal constitution in opposition to the **anti-Federalist** faction led by Governor **George Clinton**, though he was not a member of the ratifying convention that met nearby. In 1793, he moved with his family to **New York City**, where Columbia appointed him its first professor of law. In 1798, he joined the New York supreme court, where he immediately made his mark by insisting that the justices file written opinions that would be collected into published reports. As members of the Council of Revision charged with reviewing and possibly rejecting legislation, the state's supreme court had little need for doctrines of judicial review. But Kent made his mark in other ways, especially after becoming chief justice in 1804. Thus, his opinions in some of the early litigation involving the steamboat monopoly of **Robert Fulton** and **Robert R. Livingston** shaped **John Marshall**'s approach in ***Gibbons v. Ogden*** (1824) and kept alive the notion that the states had concurrent jurisdiction over regulating commerce. Kent also opposed the **War of 1812** and found himself defending the civil liberties of others with similar sentiments. But he felt no compunction about pronouncing Christianity to be part of the common law of the land in a famous blasphemy case. In 1814, Kent became state chancellor, which gave him sole authority in equity cases, subject only to the intervention of the legislature. As a member of the state constitutional convention of 1821, he vehemently opposed expanding the **suffrage** to include all white males. After his retirement from the bench in 1823, he returned to teaching and produced his classic *Commentaries on American Law*, which rivaled Blackstone's *Commentaries on the Laws of England* in their influence on 19th-century American jurisprudence.

KENTUCKY RESOLUTIONS. As vice president, **Thomas Jefferson** had reluctantly presided over the Senate during the session of the fifth Congress that had initiated the **Quasi-War** against France. He even signed the **Alien** and **Sedition Acts** despite his conviction that they were unconstitutional. When he returned to Virginia after Congress's recess, he, together with **James Madison**, turned to the two state legislatures still under the control of the **Republican Party**, Kentucky and Virginia, to resist the direction in which the **Federalist Party** was leading the nation. Jefferson drafted a set of resolutions that were introduced to the Kentucky legislature by John Breckenridge and adopted on 16 November 1798. The resolutions not only declared the Alien and Sedition Acts to be unconstitutional but also pronounced them "not law, but . . . altogether void, and of no force." The last resolution urged the other states to adopt measures to prevent the execution of these acts within their borders.

Though the word "nullify" did not appear in the final text of the resolutions, they nonetheless suggested that states had the constitutional authority to pass on the constitutionality of the federal laws and to annul those that were unconstitutional. Massachusetts Federalists subsequently had their state legislature pronounce the **Enforcement Act of 1809** unconstitutional and were blocked from passing a law that the Republican opposition claimed would nullify the **Embargo of 1807–1809** only by the governor's veto. In 1815, the Connecticut legislature pronounced a federal law permitting the enlistment of minors "repugnant to the spirit of the constitution" and passed a law subjecting anyone acting under the federal statute to heavy penalties. South Carolina came comparatively late to nullification. Its **Negro Seamen's Act** of 1822 contravened several treaties, but only at the end of the decade did the state government begin to develop, with **John C. Calhoun**'s assistance, a formal doctrine of nullification. This was initially deployed against the **Tariff of Abominations**, but nullification's real purpose was to defend **slavery**.

KING, RUFUS (24 March 1755–29 April 1827). Senator and diplomat, he was born in Scarborough, Maine (then Massachusetts), and graduated from Harvard in 1777. After a brief military tour in 1778, he was admitted to the Massachusetts bar in 1780, elected to the General Court in 1783–1785, and named a delegate to the Confederation Congress between 1784 and 1786. King represented Massachusetts in the Philadelphia Convention before moving to **New York City** in

1789 as the new federal government was being put into operation. The New York legislature appointed him to the U.S. Senate in time for him to support Secretary of the Treasury **Alexander Hamilton**'s **funding** policy and the creation of the **First Bank of the United States**. In 1793, he was a key player in discrediting **Edmund Genêt** for threatening to appeal to the people against **George Washington**'s **Neutrality Proclamation**. He also spearheaded the successful effort to bar **Albert Gallatin** from taking a seat in the Senate on the ground that he had not fulfilled the residency requirement specified in the Constitution. During the controversy over the **Jay Treaty**, King coauthored the influential *Camillus Papers* supporting ratification and implementation. Rewarded with appointment as minister to Great Britain, King was influential in preventing the leaders of the Irish Rebellion of 1798 from being deported to the United States. In 1802, he successfully negotiated a £600,000 deal with Britain that settled all remaining claims against the United States. Shortly afterward, he resigned his diplomatic post because President **Thomas Jefferson** showed no interest in revising and extending the Jay Treaty.

On returning to the United States, King was the unsuccessful vice-presidential candidate of the **Federalist Party** in the **election of 1804** and again in the **election of 1808**. After the **War of 1812** was declared, he returned to the Senate for two consecutive terms. He was critical of President **James Madison**'s conduct of the war and especially opposed the **Embargo of 1813–1814**. But he was careful to distance himself from the **Hartford Convention**. In the **election of 1816**, he was the last presidential candidate put forward by the then-disgraced Federalist Party. During his remaining time in the Senate, he voted against the bill chartering the **Second Bank of the United States** but supported excluding British vessels from American ports that sailed from British ports to which American vessels were denied entry. When Missouri applied for admission to the Union, he opposed its admission as a slave state in 1820. Subsequently, King opposed a bill for gradually abolishing **slavery** in the nation's capital, but one of the last resolutions he introduced in Congress called for devoting the revenue from public land sales to compensating slaveholders for emancipating their slaves. After retiring from the Senate in 1825, he served briefly again as minister to Britain. But ill health quickly forced him to return home shortly before he died.

– L –

LABOR. In the colonial period, the production of goods, whether they were resources extracted from the earth or finished products, required far greater labor inputs than would be required after industrialization. Despite this, there was no organized labor movement that transcended the boundaries of local markets of the sort that began to emerge in the 19th century. That was because most production initially was organized in family units devoted to satisfying local needs. Laborers, known as mechanics, living in close proximity to each other in the principal port towns, occasionally mobilized to achieve specific objectives, but these were as likely to be political as purely economic in nature.

Outside the principal ports, the family farm dominated the rural landscape of the North. Artisans living in the smaller, country towns, as well as those in the larger gateway ports, produced specialized consumer goods to satisfy the personal demand of rural consumers. Individual proprietors assisted by their kin—usually wives, sons, and daughters—and by apprentices, particularly in the trades, supplied most of the labor for these enterprises. **Slaves** and indentured servants also contributed to the northern workforce, but bound and free alike were considered part of the proprietors' family.

By the time of the Revolution, southern society had diverged from the northern prototype of family-centered enterprises clustered in country towns. The South had fewer towns and gateway ports. Instead, plantations, often manned by large concentrations of slaves, dotted the rural landscape. They specialized in the production of agricultural staples, such as **tobacco** and rice, for distant markets. Interspersed among the plantations, though, were many smaller family farms whose production addressed local rather than distant needs.

During the late colonial period, North America still relied on European imports, largely from Britain, for its access to **industry**'s products. The one notable exception to emerge was cheap women's shoes. In the two decades before the Revolution, many farmers in Lynn, Massachusetts, turned to producing more shoes in their homes than were needed in the local market, while local merchants sold the products in the expanding regional market. The Revolutionary War underscored the need for industry because the fledgling Republic found itself relying on mass-produced arms and military supplies imported from overseas. This inspired **Alexander Hamilton**'s proposal for achieving industrial self-sufficiency in strategically important commodities outlined in his **Report on Manufactures** (1791). But suspicions about central government sponsorship, together with the more pressing problem of servicing the revolutionary debt, doomed the proposal to defeat. Though government contracting subsequently led to industrial innovation in the manufacture of arms, the sponsoring entrepreneur retained the family model of production as far as possible. **Eli Whitney** was not alone in constructing industrial villages like Whitneyville outside New Haven. **Samuel Slater** and **Francis Cabot Lowell**'s Boston Manufacturing Company pursued the same strategy. The paternalistic approach of many early industrial entrepreneurs served to blunt the emergence of a labor identity by cushioning workers from the full effect of market forces.

The expansion of international trade and of domestic markets after the Revolution progressively eroded the autonomy of local markets and with it the rationale for the apprentice system. As the skills that masters communicated to their apprentices progressively lost their value, **journeymen** became increasingly dissatisfied with being relegated to the ranks of wage laborers. In the larger port towns and emerging cities, they organized, often along craft lines, in responding to the challenge posed by the introduction of cheap, industrially produced goods from overseas. Often they took their former masters to be the principal source of their difficulty rather than the expansion of the market. Their attempts at collective action were also met by prosecutions under the common law of criminal conspiracy. Despite these difficulties, journeymen sometimes succeeded in extracting significant wage concessions from their employers. But laborers proved more successful when they mobilized for political rather than economic objectives. In the mid-1780s, the artisans and mechanics of the principal trading towns mounted a concerted response to the introduction of British factors in American ports. In the late 1780s, they supported the gentry-sponsored framing and ratification of the new federal Constitution and, during the early 1800s, the **Republican Party**'s commercial policies, such as the **Embargo of 1807–1809**, that attempted to counter the pressures the great European powers were exerting on the young nation.

Outside the principal urban centers, working people had fewer options for ameliorating their lot. The heavy labor requirements of resource extracting industries like the iron industry were met by a mixed force of slaves, indentured servants, and free laborers. As time progressed, foreign contract labor came increasingly to replace indentured servitude, especially in building the **canals** associated with the early phase of the **transportation revolution**. Where the labor force remained mixed, the degraded condition of the African, who invariably got the least desirable jobs, prevented the development of any sense of shared interest among laborers against their employers. A similar fate victimized workers in the rural cottage industries. Competitive pressures exerted on New England farmers by the expansion of western **agriculture** led men and women in the older settled areas to take on increasing numbers of industrial tasks for merchants in their homes in order to make ends meet. As a consequence, the household manufacture of shoes expanded well beyond Lynn after the Revolution. But the geographic spread of the putting-out system inhibited the emergence of organizations representing the interests of working people. If the workers in one town resisted the increasingly onerous terms set by the capitalist entrepreneurs, they could be easily bypassed by the merchant cultivating another source of supply.

The depression set off by the **Panic of 1819** led to widespread unemployment, particularly among urban laborers. This in turn destroyed most of the craft organizations that had sprung up in the larger towns prior to and during the **War of 1812**. The ensuing decade saw an economic recovery that gradually restored employment opportunities. But despite the upturn, laborers in the cities found their wages depressed by having to compete with one another and with an increasing tide of **immigrants**. They responded as they had before by again organizing despite a new spate of conspiracy trials directed against them. As the decade advanced, workingmen in Boston, **New York City**, and Philadelphia started agitating for a 10-hour day. These efforts yielded mixed results, but in 1828 they led to the formation of a citywide labor federation in Philadelphia that turned itself into the first Workingmen's Party. A year later, New York's laborers followed Philadelphia's example by turning to politics. The workingman's movement developed a labor agenda that included the 10-hour day, abolition of imprisonment for debt, and the adoption of mechanics lien laws to protect wage earners against the bankruptcy of their employers. But these efforts quickly collapsed because the movement could not extend its influence to the state governments. As long as rural constituencies retained the balance of power in states like New York and Pennsylvania, collective bargaining with one's local employers would remain labor's principal remedy. *See also* AGRICULTURE; IMMIGRATION/IMMIGRANTS; INDUSTRIALIZATION/INDUSTRY; SLAVERY/SLAVES; TRANSPORTATION REVOLUTION.

LAFAYETTE, MARQUIS DE (6 September 1757–20 May 1834). The son of a minor nobleman, Lafayette was orphaned at an early age but found himself heir to a title and a fortune by the time he turned 13. After marrying into the influential Noailles family, he accepted a commission from Silas Deane, a commissioner of the Continental Congress, in the Continental army and sailed for America on a vessel chartered with his own funds. When Congress declined to honor the commission Deane had issued, Lafayette volunteered his services to General **George Washington** without pay. After he proved himself in battle, he was promoted to major general at the end of 1777 and for the rest of the war either commanded American units or busied himself reinforcing the newly established **Franco-American alliance**. After returning to France at the end of the war, he became a moderate leader of the **French Revolution**. Lafayette thought the closest France could come to adopting American principles was a constitutional monarchy. But both Louis XVI and the radicals disagreed with his program, forcing Lafayette to flee France. In the process, he was captured by the Austrians and imprisoned for five years, during which time Washington acted as guardian to his only son. Lafayette's opposition to **Napoleon**'s rise to power led President **Thomas Jefferson** to offer Lafayette the governorship of new acquired territories in the **Louisiana Purchase**. But Lafayette refused and remained in France. He tried to play a moderating role in the restoration of the Bourbon monarchy in 1815 and during the Revolution of 1830 but with limited success. He did accept President **James Monroe**'s invitation to return to the United States in 1824, though, and was greeted with tumultuous celebrations on his tour of the Union. A touching reunion with Jefferson shortly before Jefferson died dramatized to the nation that the revolutionary generation was about to pass from the scene.

LAKE CHAMPLAIN, BATTLE OF. In early September 1814, Sir George Prevost led an army of 11,000 well-equipped and -supplied veteran reinforcements recently arrived from Europe against Plattsburgh, New York. It was garrisoned by an American force of only 3,300 men, most of whom were **militia**. Accompanying Prevost was a fleet of 16 men-of-war, led by a ship mounting 37 guns. American Commodore **Thomas Macdonough** had fewer vessels and guns but could deliver more metal per broadside at close range than his adversary. Macdonough positioned his fleet in Plattsburgh Bay in such a way that the British could bring their firepower to bear only at close range. Prevost delayed attacking the American positions on land until 11 September, when the British fleet, commanded by Captain George Downie, entered the bay where Macdonough's vessels were anchored. Downie's fleet almost prevailed despite their commander being killed early in the action. But Macdonough's precaution of anchoring his fleet so that the vessels could be turned around in the middle of the battle subdued the enemy's larger warships. Meanwhile, the American land defenses withstood Prevost's assault long enough for it to become clear that Britain would not control Lake Champlain. Since advancing further without naval support was impossible, Prevost's invading force withdrew to Canada. *See also* WAR OF 1812 (LAND OPERATIONS) and WAR OF 1812 (NAVAL OPERATIONS).

LAKE ERIE, BATTLE OF. During the first half of 1813, Britain's naval supremacy on Lake Erie hampered American General **William Henry Harrison** from taking the offensive against western Ontario as much as it had hampered William Hull's disastrous campaign of 1812. On 17 February 1813, **Oliver Hazard Perry** took charge of U.S. naval forces at Presque Isle (now Erie, Pennsylvania). Perry managed to rush the completion of several men-of-war there before the end of the spring. The British evacuation of **Fort Erie** on the Niagara River (27 May) allowed Perry to augment his force with five additional vessels from a naval yard at the eastern end of Lake Erie. By the beginning of August, he had a squadron superior in firepower and manpower to anything the British enjoyed and on 10 September engaged the British fleet off the mouth of the Sandusky River. Despite being outnumbered and outgunned in terms of metal, the British almost won the engagement because a portion of the American fleet refused to engage the enemy at close quarters, where the Americans enjoyed the greatest advantage. Only after Perry transferred his flag to one of the laggard vessels and redeployed his remaining force did he manage to snatch victory from the jaws of defeat. Perry's victory forced the British to abandon Fort Malden across the strait from Detroit and cleared the way for Harrison's subsequent advance into Ontario. Though the battle gave the United States decisive naval control of the lake for the rest of the war, it did so at the cost of exceptionally heavy casualties. *See also* WAR OF 1812 (NAVAL OPERATIONS).

LAND ACT OF 1820. This measure was designed to remedy abuses in the sale of public lands that had developed under the Land Act of 1800. By the earlier act's terms individuals could purchase as little as 320 acres on four years of credit. The provision led to widespread speculation at the expense of the public revenue. In the wake of the **Panic of 1819**, Secretary of the Treasury **William H. Crawford** complained that the treasury was receiving only half its due. Congress responded in 1820 by abolishing the credit system. It also reduced both the minimum price of public lands to $1.25 an acre and the minimum purchase to 80 acres. Though intended to encourage settlers to purchase land, the measure had the effect of adding to the deflationary pressures exerted by the Panic of 1819.

LATIN AMERICAN REVOLUTIONS. Spain's American empire began to unravel after **Napoleon** invaded Spain in March 1808 and placed his brother, Joseph, on the Spanish throne. The British sent an expeditionary force to the Iberian Peninsula in the summer to contest Napoleon's attempt to control the country after widespread resistance among both Spaniards and Portuguese to French rule had developed. The **Spanish insurrection** in turn encouraged dissident elements in the American colonies of the Iberian monarchies to launch independence movements. The only one fully to succeed before 1816 was that embracing parts of modern Uruguay, Argentina, and Paraguay. But all of Spanish and Portuguese Latin America experienced political ferment after 1808 that was a direct outgrowth of political instability in the mother countries. After 1816, the Latin American independence movements were more successful despite the restoration of the Iberian monarchs, leading to the gradual liberation of most of Latin America from European control. The United States favored Latin American independence even when the new regimes assumed a dictatorial rather than a republican form but did little to aid them beyond issuing the **Monroe Doctrine** and trading with them.

LATROBE, BENJAMIN HENRY (1 May 1764–3 September 1820). Architect and civil engineer, he was born in Yorkshire, England, the son of a Moravian minister and an American-born mother. Latrobe was schooled in Germany by the Moravians but returned to England in the mid-1780s, acquiring experience as a designer of **canals** and as an architect. In early 1796, he sailed for America to flee bankruptcy, landing in Norfolk, Virginia. He immediately began designing houses in Norfolk and Richmond and received a public commission to plan the Virginia State Penitentiary. In 1798, he moved to Philadelphia, then the nation's capital, and came to the attention of **Thomas Jefferson**, with whom he would collaborate on a number of projects. During his Philadelphia sojourn, Latrobe designed the Bank of Pennsylvania and the city's water system, which relied on steam-driven pumps to distribute water from a distant source. When Jefferson moved to Washington as president after the **election of 1800**, Latrobe followed him, and together they redesigned the Capitol and the White House. The fruits of much of this collaboration were destroyed with the British **burning of Washington** on 24–25 August 1814. After the **War of 1812**, Latrobe redesigned many of the public buildings that had been destroyed. He also joined **Robert Fulton** in a steamboat venture between 1813 and 1815. At the end of his life, he moved to **New Orleans**, where he designed the Louisiana State Bank and the city's waterworks before succumbing to **yellow fever**. Though few of Latrobe's designs were fully executed and still fewer survive today, he, along with his student **William Strickland**, were responsible for popularizing the Greek Revival style in the nation's public **architecture**.

LELAND, JOHN (14 May 1754–14 January 1841). Baptist leader, he was born into a poor farm family in western Massachusetts and became a Baptist just before the outbreak of the American Revolutionary War. After serving as an itinerant preacher, Leland eventually settled in Virginia, where he supported the disestablishment of the Anglican Church. He also helped **James Madison** win election to the **first Congress**. Leland briefly succeeded in getting the Virginia Baptists to call for an end to **slavery**, but they quickly abandoned that position. Returning to New England in 1791, Leland spent the next 30 years urging a revision of the Massachusetts constitution of 1780 and the disestablishment of **Congregationalism**. He also became an ardent Jeffersonian in a region that was controlled mainly by the **Federalist Party** and prevailed on a group of Baptist women to present President **Thomas Jefferson** with a giant cheese six feet in diameter after his victory in the **election of 1800**. Toward the end of his life, Leland opposed organized missions and laws enforcing Sabbath observance because he felt that by intruding on the individual's freedom of conscience, they were incompatible with true **religion**.

L'ENFANT, PIERRE CHARLES (2 August 1754–14 June 1825). Engineer and architect, he was born in Paris, the son of a painter who specialized in military subjects. Little is known of his early life until he arrived at Portsmouth, New Hampshire, in April 1777 with a company of French engineers. He subsequently became attached to Baron von Steuben's staff and helped illustrate the manual for soldiers that was used to train the Continental army. Promoted to captain on 3 April 1779, he was wounded at Savannah, Georgia; captured at Charlestown, South Carolina; and discharged from the army on 1 January 1784 after being brevetted a major. L'Enfant was a founding member of the Society of the Cincinnati, and the eagle he developed for the society's insignia was the first emblematic association of that image with the Republic.

In 1788, he developed a plan for converting **New York**'s city hall into the temporary seat of the national government. On 11 September 1789, he applied to President **George Washington** for a commission to design the new federal city called for by the Constitution. In January 1791, Congress commissioned L'Enfant to proceed, and by July he had readied a monumental plan appropriate to the seat of a vast empire. L'Enfant's refusal to work with others led to his dismissal from the District of Columbia commission on 27 February 1792, and his intransigence in the face of the demands of others, not to mention American realities, frustrated his achieving the eminence to which his genius might otherwise have entitled him. But the layout of the nation's capital today is more a product of his imagination than anyone else's.

LEWIS, MERIWETHER (18 August 1774–11 October 1809). Explorer, he was born near Charlottesville, Virginia. After a brief sojourn in Georgia, he returned to a family plantation near **Thomas Jefferson**'s home. Responding to President **George Washington**'s call for volunteers to suppress the **Whiskey Rebellion** in 1794, Lewis found military life to his liking and joined the U.S. Army as an ensign on 1 May 1795. He witnessed the signing of the first **Treaty of Greenville** and did garrison duty in the West during the **Quasi-War**, being promoted to lieutenant in March 1799 and captain in December 1800. When Jefferson became president, he invited Lewis to become his personal secretary. After the **Louisiana Purchase** extended the nation's boundary to the continental divide, finding an overland route to the Pacific acquired great urgency. Jefferson placed Lewis in charge of planning an expedition to explore the area, and Lewis chose **William Clark** to join with him in leading it. They began ascending the Missouri River on 14 May 1804 but made it only to the vicinity of modern Bismarck, North Dakota, before the first winter set in. The next year, they reached the site of what would become Astoria, Oregon, just before Christmas. The return journey went much faster despite the two leaders separating to chart the course of two unexplored rivers. They were back in St. Louis by the end of September 1806. In addition to geographical knowledge, the daily journals of the expedition provided a wealth of scientific information about the interior of the continent. Jefferson rewarded Lewis for his achievement by appointing him governor of the upper Louisiana Territory. But Lewis waited a year to take up the post and then fell afoul of officialdom in administering it. He died on his way back to Washington to sort out his accounts, most probably by suicide.

LIQUIDATION. At the end of the Revolutionary War, the nation confronted a jumble of state and continental debts that had been contracted at different times in depreciating currencies of different value. The superintendent of finances under the new Confederation government, Robert Morris, initiated the complex process of having the continent's accounts with individuals and with the states reduced to common hard-money values. This was done by agents of Congress who used depreciation schedules to ascertain the specie value of obligations at the time they had been contracted. All the debts were then placed on a common equitable footing by crediting them with a fixed rate of interest from the moment they were contracted. The states followed Morris's example, and by 1789 most of the revolutionary debt, both state and continental, had been "liquidated." But they had retired relatively little of the revolutionary debt before **Alexander Hamilton**'s proposal for **funding** it was adopted in 1790.

LITERATURE. Americans quickly realized that their political independence from Great Britain would remain incomplete without some measure of cultural independence. The English language perpetuated American dependence on British literary models and inhibited the development of a distinctive national character. **Noah Webster**'s attempt to surmount the problem by disseminating a distinctively American version of English in his spellers and readers proved as inconsequential as **Joel Barlow**'s efforts to produce an epic poem in a heroic voice rather than the satirical one that was being perfected by the leading English poets like John Dryden and Alexander Pope. But before the beginning of the 19th century, cultural independence had to take a backseat to political consolidation, and the best literary exemplars of America's cultural independence remained political testaments like the Declaration of Independence and the *Federalist*.

Several developments after 1800 helped plant the seeds of a literary renaissance that would come into full bloom in the fourth and fifth decades of the new century. The expansion of the reading public, particularly female readers, gave rise to a growing body of **women** authors like **Lydia Maria Child**, **Judith Sargent Stevens Murray**, **Sarah Josepha Buell Hale**, **Susanna Haswell Rowson**, and **Catherine Sedgwick** who wrote primarily for an audience of women. Though these authors earned money with their work, with the exception of **Lydia Sigourney** they did not have to support families with their writing. Male authors were less privileged unless, like **Charles Brockden Brown**, they had some independent means. Most had little choice but to try to connect with a larger anglophone audience if they wished authorship to be their principal calling. Politics still remained a dominant interest with American writers, but **Republicanism** complicated the task of authors like **Charles J. Ingersoll** in cultivating a European audience. Most aspiring authors of the early 19th century published their work in urban **magazines** that catered to a Federalist readership. With the demise of the **Federalist Party** after the **War of 1812**, several former Federalists turned from politics to other subjects. **William Ellery Channing**'s treatment of religious issues, particularly his *Unitarian Christianity*, commanded an audience that transcended national as well as sectarian boundaries because of the urgency all Christians felt about reconciling faith with reason.

The most promising route open to those who aspired to support themselves as writers remained imaginative literature. **Washington Irving** was the first American author to succeed in infusing European tales with American content in stories like "Rip Van Winkle" and "The Legend of Sleepy Hollow" in a manner that appealed equally to Britons and Americans. In the 1820s, **James Fenimore Cooper**'s Leatherstocking tales began providing a reading public on both sides of the Atlantic with romantic novels made exclusively of American materials. By the time the principal writers of the American renaissance emerged on the literary stage—Nathaniel Hawthorne, Ralph Waldo Emerson, Henry David Thoreau, Edgar Allen Poe, and Herman Melville—an American voice was no longer a novelty among the English reading public. *See also* FICTION; POETRY; THEATER.

LIVINGSTON, EDWARD (28 May 1764–23 May 1836). Politician and diplomat, he was born at Livingston Manor, New York, the youngest son of the proprietor of Clermont. After graduating from Princeton in 1781, he was admitted to the New York bar in 1785 and practiced law in **New York City** until he was elected to Congress as a representative in 1794. There he opposed implementation of the **Jay Treaty** and on 2 March 1796 moved that the president provide the House of Representatives with the papers relating to the negotiation of the treaty. **George Washington** invoked executive privilege in refusing to comply, and the House eventually voted to implement the treaty anyway. But Livingston was reelected to Congress in 1796 and 1798. He opposed the **Quasi-War** and the **Alien** and **Sedition Laws**. In the **election of 1800**, he supported **Thomas Jefferson** against **Aaron Burr** and was rewarded by being appointed U.S. district attorney for New York; shortly afterward, he was elected mayor of New York City.

Livingston's career subsequently suffered a disastrous reverse when he proved unable to locate moneys belonging to the U.S. Treasury for which he was accountable. Though it turned out a subordinate had stolen them, Livingston resigned his two offices in 1803 and placed most of his remaining property in trust to pay back the treasury. After surviving a bout of **yellow fever**, he decided to move to Louisiana, which had recently been acquired from France, partially through the agency of his brother, **Robert R. Livingston**. He hoped to recoup his fortunes in **New Orleans**, but instead he was accused of conspiring with Burr. He also found himself at odds with President Jefferson over ownership of a property that had been assigned to him in payment of legal fees. Livingston eventually made a comeback in 1814 when he chaired the local committee charged with defending the city against British attack and acted as **Andrew Jackson**'s aide-de-camp in the Battle of **New Orleans**. After the **War of 1812**, Livingston won international recognition for drafting the Louisiana Code. He was elected as a Louisiana congressman first to the U.S. House of Representatives (1822–1829) and then to the U.S. Senate (1829–1831). On 24 May 1831, Jackson appointed him secretary of state, in which capacity he served until resigning on 29 May 1833 to accept appointment as minister to France. While in Paris, he advised Jackson to take a hard line in seeking compensation for the French seizure of American vessels during the **Napoleonic Wars**. This produced a crisis in Franco-American relations that led to his return to the United States in May 1835. Livingston died a year later at an estate on the Hudson that he had inherited from his sister.

LIVINGSTON, ROBERT R. (27 November 1746–26 February 1813). Diplomat, statesman, and sponsor of technological innovation, he was born in **New York City**, the eldest son of the proprietor of Clermont at Livingston Manor. After being admitted to the New York bar in 1768, Livingston became active in revolutionary politics despite holding several colonial offices and the large inheritance he came into during 1775. He was a member of New York's Provincial Congress, which appointed him a delegate to the second Continental Congress. Though a member of the committee charged with drafting the Declaration of Independence, he opposed the measure and was in New York when the document was signed. During 1777, he took an active role in framing New York's state constitution and was appointed chancellor and a member of the Council of Safety by the New York Convention. In 1779–1781, he represented the state in Congress concurrently with his state duties, and when the new Confederation government went into effect in 1781, Congress named him secretary of foreign affairs. He exercised little influence over the conclusion of the Peace of 1783, though, besides advocating expanded boundaries for the new Republic.

Livingston supported revision of the Articles of Confederation in 1787 and argued for ratification of the new government in the state ratifying convention. But **George Washington** declined to appoint him to high office, perhaps because of Livingston's opposition to **Alexander Hamilton**'s **funding** plan. Livingston also opposed the **Jay Treaty**, penning an influential newspaper series under the pseudonym "Cato" critical of it. In 1798, Livingston lost the gubernatorial race against his brother-in-law **John Jay**. But after **Thomas Jefferson** became president in the **election of 1800**, he appointed Livingston minister to France. In that capacity, Livingston pressured **Napoleon** into selling all the **Louisiana Territory** to the United States for $15 million. Though the **Louisiana Purchase** shaped the nation's destiny almost as much as the Revolution had, Livingston was not rewarded with further federal appointments on his return from France because he tried to claim most of the credit for the transaction, ignoring the contribution made by **James Monroe**.

During his last years, he brought to fruition an enterprise he had embarked on in 1798 to develop steam-powered water transportation. In 1802, he started collaborating with **Robert Fulton** on a steamboat. The project culminated in the *Clermont*'s successful navigation of the Hudson from New York City to Albany in 1807. Livingston hoped that the legal monopoly the legislature had conferred on him would secure the profits derived from this achievement. But neither he nor his heirs gained much advantage from the legislature's action. Eventually, **John Marshall** ruled against the monopoly's constitutionality in ***Gibbons v. Ogden***. *See also* LIVINGSTON, EDWARD.

LOGAN ACT. On 13 June 1798, George Logan, a **Quaker**, embarked on a private peace mission to Paris while the federal government was launching the **Quasi-War** against France. He returned in November, claiming that the **Directory** wished to conciliate the United States. The **Federalist Party** used its decisive majority in the third session of the fifth Congress to pass a law making it a federal crime to "usurp the executive authority" of the United States through private diplomacy. In making missions like Logan's a crime, the law's Federalist sponsors revealed the political interest they had in continuing if not escalating the Quasi-War. The Logan Act was still on the statute books during the Vietnam War, when antiwar activists who attempted to negotiate with the North Vietnamese and Vietcong were threatened with prosecution under it.

LOUISIANA PURCHASE. Napoleon's deployment of an army in **Ste. Domingue** to put down the **Haitian Revolution** during 1802 led President **Thomas Jefferson** to suspect that France had larger New World ambitions than simply recovering its former colony. By this time, the administration had learned that Spain had secretly ceded Louisiana to France in the Treaty of San Ildefonso (1 October 1800). Jefferson instructed **Robert R. Livingston**, the American minister in Paris, to secure land on the Mississippi River from France that could be used as a port or, short of that, confirmation of the right of deposit at **New Orleans** contained in **Pinckney's Treaty** with Spain in 1795. When on 16 October 1802 the Spanish official still nominally in charge of New Orleans revoked the right of deposit, Jefferson sent **James Monroe** to France with full powers to purchase **New Orleans** and **West Florida**. Congress appropriated $2 million for the purpose, but Monroe was authorized to offer as much as $10 million if necessary. Before Monroe got to Paris, Napoleon reconsidered his American ambitions. The French army in Ste. Domingue had been seriously weakened by disease, and the truce with Britain was collapsing. On 11 April 1803, the French foreign minister, **Talleyrand**, offered to sell all of France's **Louisiana Territory** to the United States. Though it was not clear exactly what Louisiana's boundaries were, Livingston and Monroe seized on the offer, and a treaty embodying the sale was signed on 2 May. By its terms, the United States paid roughly $15 million, $11,250,000 of which was paid in cash to France and the remainder to U.S. citizens, whose claims against France for depredations on American commerce before and during the **Quasi-War** the U.S. government assumed.

With this agreement, the United States extinguished France's claims to the vast territory between the Mississippi and the Rocky Mountains, doubling the geographic expanse of the Republic. The Constitution had failed to provide for such an acquisition, and leaders of the **Federalist Party** strenuously objected to the purchase, fearing it would make them into a permanent minority. But the leaders of the **Republican Party** were unwilling to forgo so advantageous a bargain that eliminated the claims of one of the major European powers to the North American continent. The treaty was overwhelmingly approved by the Senate on 20 October 1803. Two months later, the United States took formal possession of the territory. *See also* LOUISIANA TERRITORY.

LOUISIANA TERRITORY. In 1804, Congress divided the lands acquired by the United States from France as a consequence of the 1803 **Louisiana Purchase** lying to the west of the Mississippi River into two territories separated by the 33rd parallel. Lands to the south were to be part of the Orleans Territory, while lands to the north were designated as the Louisiana District. In 1811, Congress authorized the people in Orleans Territory to draft a constitution and apply for admission to the Union. On 8 April 1812, their handiwork proved acceptable, and the state of Louisiana was admitted to the Union. Congress then redesignated the territory north of the 33rd parallel as the Missouri Territory. In 1819, Congress divided this territory in two, preparatory to admitting Missouri as a state into the Union. The southern division of what had been Missouri Territory henceforth was known as the Arkansas Territory.

LOWELL, FRANCIS CABOT (7 April 1775–10 August 1817). Merchant industrialist, he was born in Newburyport, Massachusetts, and attended Harvard College. After graduating in 1793, he engaged in a variety of commercial ventures for the remainder of the decade. At the turn of the century, he inherited an interest in a fleet of eight ships. Deployed in the Canton trade and later in the grain trade to Spain, Lowell's commercial enterprises had made him wealthy by 1810. In that year, he took his ailing wife to Britain for her health, using the occasion to tour the water-powered textile mills that were springing up in the north of England. The power loom particularly caught his attention. Returning to Massachusetts as the **War of 1812** commenced, he, with his brother-in-law, Patrick Tracy Jackson, formed the Boston Manufacturing Company in 1813.

Lowell expected the war to disrupt his overseas commerce, and he responded by trying to manufacture a staple at home. He was the first to envision integrating under one roof the mechanized conversion of raw cotton into finished fabric. With the assistance of a local mechanic named Paul Moody, he succeeded in creating a power loom that was successfully tested in November 1813. In 1814, the Boston Manufacturing Company built a factory complex at Waltham, Massachusetts, capable of realizing his vision of an integrated production process. However, to protect the venture from the threat of British competition when the war ended, Lowell turned to Washington and lobbied congressional leader **John C. Calhoun** to get a protective duty incorporated into the **Tariff** of 1816. By that time, Lowell's health was declining, and his impact on his associates in the Boston Manufacturing Company rapidly diminished. Nonetheless, nine years after Lowell's death, he was honored in the naming of a new industrial town that the Boston Manufacturing Company had established on the Merrimack River, which is now Lowell, Massachusetts.

LOWER CANADA. The British Parliament responded to the American Revolution with the Constitutional Act of 1791 that separated **Upper Canada** from Lower Canada along the boundary that today demarcates the province of Quebec to the east from Ontario to the west. New Brunswick, Nova Scotia, and Newfoundland remained separate from Lower Canada.

LUNDY'S LANE, BATTLE OF. On 5 July 1814, Brigadier General **Winfield Scott** succeeded in driving a superior force of British regulars from the field at the Chippewa River in Ontario. General **Jacob Brown** then pursued General Riall's retreat toward Queenstown. But without naval support on Lake Ontario, Brown had to give up the chase, and, after Riall's army started receiving reinforcements from the east, Brown withdrew the American army to Chippewa Plain on 24 July. The next day, Riall advanced to Lundy's Lane expecting to be joined by further reinforcements that evening. Brown ordered Scott's brigade forward to engage Riall in the late afternoon, and his units attacked the British positions with such determination that one regiment on the right got behind the British line and captured Riall as the sun set. But Scott's units in the center could not make headway against the British artillery, which had been reinforced and was posted on an elevation in front of the British line, until two fresh American regiments advanced after dark. While one of the new regiments drew the enemy fire, the other crept within 20 paces before charging and capturing the British emplacement. Though Brown's men now occupied favorable ground and had deprived the enemy of their artillery, the Americans paid a heavy price for their tactical victory by having to withstand repeated British counterattacks. Brown eventually ordered a retreat after almost all his officers had been wounded and the men who had escaped harm were on the verge of physical exhaustion. Though neither side could claim victory, the battle earned the American army the respect of the British veterans who participated in it. *See also* WAR OF 1812 (LAND OPERATIONS).

– M –

MACDONOUGH, THOMAS (31 December 1783–10 November 1825). Naval hero, he was born in Newcastle, Delaware. The severe wounding in 1799 of an older brother in a naval engagement during the **Quasi-War** led Macdonough to become a midshipman in 1800. On his first tour in the West Indies, he contracted **yellow fever**. Next he saw duty in the Mediterranean during the **Barbary War**. Macdonough was fortunate while serving on the USS *Philadelphia* to be given command of a prize seized just before his ship was captured at Tripoli. On 16 February 1814, he distinguished himself as a participant in **Stephen Decatur**'s daring raid to destroy the *Philadelphia*. Returning to the United States, he spent several years in Middletown, Connecticut, supervising the construction of gunboats that President **Thomas Jefferson** thought should constitute the Republic's principal naval shield. When the **War of 1812** began, Macdonough got himself appointed the naval commander of Lake Champlain and applied the experience gained in Middletown to building a naval force there. When Sir George Prevost invaded New York in August 1814, Macdonough was ready to block British control of the lake at Plattsburgh. On 11 September 1814, he decisively defeated a British fleet under the command of George Downing. This forced Prevost to withdraw his 14,000-man force.

Overnight, Macdonough became a national hero, but he failed to secure command of a frigate until he was named captain of the USS *Guerrière* in 1818. After a cruise in the Mediterranean and Baltic, he returned to the United States and waited until 1824 before he was named commodore of the Mediterranean fleet with orders to raise his flag on the USS ***Constitution***. He died at sea while making his way to his new command.

MACON'S BILL No. 2. Served as the basis for an act passed by Congress that became law on 1 May 1810, just as the **Nonintercourse Act**

of 1809, which it replaced, expired. The Act of 1 May, as it became known, lifted all restrictions on American overseas commerce but empowered the president to reimpose nonintercourse against either Britain or France whenever one of the belligerents revoked its restrictions against U.S. commerce. Macon's Bill No. 2 conferred little credit on the 11th Congress because it seemed like a capitulation to the great powers' commercial restrictions. But by offering France a good deal more than it offered Britain, it paved the way for the **Cadore Letter** and set in motion a series of events that culminated in the declaration of the **War of 1812** against Britain. *See also* BARLOW, JOEL; MADISON, JAMES; NAPOLEON; ST. CLOUD, DECREE OF.

MADISON, DOLLEY (20 May 1768–12 July 1849). Wife of **James Madison**, the fourth president of the United States, she was born Dolley Payne to **Quaker** parents in North Carolina. The family moved to Virginia in her infancy and then, when she was 17, to Philadelphia at the end of the Revolutionary War. On 7 January 1790, Dolley married a Philadelphia lawyer, John Todd Jr. But she lost both her husband and one young son in the **yellow fever** epidemic of 1793. The tragedy failed to quench Dolley's zest for life, and within the year she had been introduced to James Madison by **Aaron Burr**. Though 17 years his junior, she married Madison on 15 September 1794. She was dismissed from her Quaker meeting because he was an Episcopalian. Freed from the restraints of the Quaker meeting, she quickly mastered the art of entertaining large numbers of people and used this skill to promote her husband's political career. During **Thomas Jefferson**'s administration, Dolley served as his official hostess at the White House, and when Madison succeeded him in the presidency, Dolley instituted regular Wednesday evening receptions that became the focus of Washington's social life. Her counsel on political matters proved invaluable to Madison. When the British were threatening Washington in August 1814, she personally supervised the removal of important state documents and treasures such as **Gilbert Stuart**'s portrait of **George Washington**.

The Madisons retired to Montpelier in Virginia in 1817 at the end of Madison's second term and lived there quietly until Madison died in 1836. Then the profligacy of her one surviving son by John Todd forced her to sell most of the property Madison had left her. Dolley moved back to Washington in reduced circumstances and lived there until she died in her 81st year.

MADISON, JAMES (5 March 1751–28 June, 1836). An architect of the federal Constitution and fourth president of the United States, he was born in Virginia and graduated from Princeton in 1771. During the Revolution, he served in Virginia's legislature and council of state prior to sitting in Congress between 1780 and 1783. Returning to the Virginia legislature between 1784 and 1786, he participated in the Annapolis and Philadelphia Conventions of 1786 and 1787. Together with **John Jay** and **Alexander Hamilton**, he coauthored the *Federalist* and was instrumental in securing Virginia's ratification of the new government.

In 1789, Madison was elected to the House of Representatives of the **first Congress**. There he took the initiative in levying an **impost** (after unsuccessfully proposing **discriminatory tonnage duties** on British ships), organizing the executive departments, and drafting the amendments known as the **Bill of Rights**. Subsequently, he opposed Hamilton's plan to assume the state debts with a proposal to discriminate between the original and eventual holders of the federal debt. When Congress rejected **discrimination** and deadlocked over **assumption**, Madison was party to the compromise that rescued Hamilton's **funding** plan from defeat in exchange for the permanent **residency** of the nation's capital on the Potomac. Madison opposed chartering the **First Bank of the United States** on constitutional grounds. After **George Washington** declined to veto the bill that created the bank, **Thomas Jefferson** and Madison established the *National Gazette* to check Hamilton's growing influence in the government.

In 1793, the war between Britain and France changed the nature of their quarrel because Hamilton wanted to align the United States with Britain. Madison and Jefferson thought Britain was on the verge of bankruptcy that would be followed by revolution and wanted to cultivate good relations with France. Madison's fears that the **Neutrality Proclamation** might lead to abandonment of the **Franco-American alliance** increased when President Washington selected John Jay to seek an accommodation with Britain. Madison unsuccessfully opposed implementing the **Jay Treaty**, in which the United States forswore imposing the discriminatory duties he had long advocated, and retired from Congress in March 1797.

Madison disapproved of the **Quasi-War** with France and was appalled by the **Alien** and **Sedition Laws**. In the autumn of 1798, he drafted resolutions adopted by the Virginia legislature asserting that the laws were unconstitutional. Though Madison's **Virginia Resolutions** were more temperate than Jefferson's **Kentucky Resolutions**, they attracted the critical response of eight states. Madison reentered the Virginia legislature in 1799 and drafted the ***Report of the Committee*** (1800), which answered these criticisms. The partisan way in which Secretary of State **Timothy Pickering** administered the Sedition Law bore out Madison's claim that it was incompatible with Republicanism and helped galvanize the **Republican Party** in the **election of 1800**, which secured Jefferson's selection as president.

Appointed secretary of state in 1801, Madison backed the **Louisiana Purchase** of 1803. After the **Napoleonic Wars** took an ominous turn in 1805, Madison protested Britain's attempt to subject American commerce to the **Rule of 1756**. France's retaliatory measures posed less of a problem because the **Franco-American Convention of 1800** legally exempted the United States from them, while France's lack of naval power practically exempted them, at least until 1808. Madison approved of the **Embargo of 1807–1809** and found the **Federalist Party**'s efforts to subvert it deeply disturbing. But neither President Jefferson nor Madison after he had been elected president supplied the leadership needed to sustain the embargo in the face of mounting opposition during the early months of 1809. Jefferson was anxious to retire to private life after the **election of 1808**, while before his inauguration in March 1809, Madison lacked the power to lead.

By then, Congress had replaced the embargo with **nonintercourse**, which amounted to a capitulation to Britain. Nonetheless, the British minister, David Erskine, promised that Britain would lift its **Orders-in-Council** against the United States if President Madison exempted Britain from nonintercourse while maintaining it against France. Madison accepted Erskine's offer, only to learn that the British government had repudiated the Erskine Agreement on receiving it. Federalist attempts to justify Britain's repudiation led Madison to conclude that the Republic's future was equally threatened by internal and external enemies. He especially feared Britain exploiting the collapse of Spain's American empire to seize **East Florida** and **West Florida**. When nonintercourse proved to be as unenforceable as the embargo had been, the only measure Congress could agree to replace it with was the one outlined in **Macon's Bill No. 2**.

When **Napoleon** accepted the disguised invitation in Macon's Bill No. 2 that favored France by conditionally revoking its decrees in the **Cadore letter**, Madison issued Britain an ultimatum to follow suit. At the same time, Madison ordered the peaceful occupation of West Florida. When Britain declined to comply with Madison's ultimatum, denying that Napoleon had repealed his decrees, Madison reimposed nonintercourse against Britain in 1811. He also asked **James Monroe** to replace **Robert Smith** as his secretary of state. After Monroe failed to extract concessions from the British ambassador, Augustus Foster, Madison asked the newly elected 12th Congress to prepare for war. Republican leaders like **John C. Calhoun** and **Henry Clay** felt they could command a majority for a war only by postponing war taxes until after the conflict began. Secretary of the Treasury **Albert Gallatin** expected to borrow money, while the Republican leadership hoped the ranks of the army would swell with volunteers. Despite disappointment on both scores, the Republicans felt they had to fight Britain to defend **Republicanism** against the aspersions of the Federalist Party. Congress followed a temporary **Embargo of 1812** in April with an official declaration of the **War of 1812** on 18 June 1812.

The conflict began with a failed attempt to conquer **Upper Canada** culminating in the humiliating surrender by **William Hull** at **Detroit**. After learning in early August 1812 that the British government had revoked its Orders-in-Council three days after the war had begun, the Federalists portrayed Madison as the only obstacle to peace. Nonetheless, he won the **election of 1812** despite Federalist support for the candidacy of **DeWitt Clinton**, a peace Republican from New York. Military and financial reverses led Madison to accept Russia's offer to mediate the conflict. He selected Albert Gallatin and James Bayard, a Delaware Federalist, to join **John Quincy Adams** in Europe for the Russian mediation, only to learn that Britain had rejected the offer. But the British foreign minister, Lord Castlereigh, offered direct negotiations after **Oliver Perry**'s decisive naval victory in the **Battle of Lake Erie**. Madison then added Henry Clay and Jonathan Russell to the nation's negotiating team in Europe. The British began the negotiations at Ghent by presenting the American commissioners with a set of unacceptable demands. Napoleon's abdication in April 1814 had left Britain free to redeploy much of its military power against the United States, and its government expected that the coming campaign would leave Madison no choice but to submit.

Though the British **burned Washington** and seized a third of the Maine coast, an attempt to invade New York by Lake Champlain was checked by Commodore **Thomas Macdonough**'s naval flotilla at Plattsburgh, New York, and the British attack on Baltimore failed. Still, the nation's prospects looked dark because the Federalists, taking advantage of asymmetries in the British blockade, had managed to force most of the nation's **banks** to abandon redeeming their notes in **specie**. Massachusetts Federalists also summoned the New England states to meet in convention at Hartford at the end of the year. Many saw the **Hartford Convention** as preliminary to New England concluding a separate peace with Britain. But shortly after the convention issued its report, news that the British had granted honorable terms in the **Treaty of Ghent** and that **Andrew Jackson** had triumphed in the Battle of **New Orleans** made all associated with the proceedings at Hartford, not to mention the Federalists in general, look like traitors.

Though Madison continued to be blamed for the military disasters of the war, he was vindicated by the peace. In his last annual message to Congress, he predicted correctly that the nation would be debt free by the mid-1830s. Simultaneously, the Federalist Party had begun dissolving. Its members claimed that Madison's acceptance of Federalist measures like the **Second Bank of the United States** meant there was no reason for them to continue, but that conveniently ignored that they had lost their wager over whether the Republic could survive a war with Britain. Madison retired to private life in 1817 knowing that the nation was secure from both its internal and its external enemies. However, his last 19 years of retirement would be troubled by the realization that **slavery** posed a new threat to the survival of the Republic he had done so much to create.

MAGAZINES. Seventeen magazines were established between 1741 and 1776 in that part of British North America that would become the United States. They differed from **newspapers** because they depended almost exclusively on subscriptions, carrying few advertisements. As a consequence, they lasted only as long as the subscribers' interest could be maintained. Very few endured for more than a year, and some expired after the first issue. However, by scheduling less frequent appearances, they freed publishers from the pressure to remain as current, something that affected the newspapers, and this is why new magazines kept appearing. They also permitted one to target an audience and to specialize in ways that a newspaper could not. While most of the early magazines tried to maximize their appeal by offering an eclectic mix of literature—usually essays and **poetry**—with political commentary, the period prior to 1789 saw the brief emergence of two **religious** magazines and one that specialized, however briefly, in publishing musical scores.

Magazine publishing exploded after 1789 with the establishment of more than 260 separate ventures in the next 40 years. Most of the activity was concentrated in New England and the growing cities of the mid-Atlantic, where printers congregated. But Charleston, South Carolina, made its debut into the magazine world of the early Republic in 1797, followed by Richmond, Virginia, in 1799, and Savannah, Georgia, in 1802. A few of the magazines successfully utilized illustrative material as specialization became more widespread. The first children's and the first farmers' magazine were established in 1789, the first magazine addressed exclusively to a female audience in 1792, the first explicitly sectarian along with the first medical magazine in 1797, the first theatrical magazine in 1798, the first law journal in 1808, and the first scientific magazine that went beyond medicine in 1810. Though the shelf life of almost all these ventures remained brief, new magazines replaced failed ones more rapidly than before because of the expanding reading public. Most magazines continued to cater to a local audience despite an amendment to the **Postal Act of 1792**, which, beginning in 1794, empowered local postmasters at their discretion to grant magazines the same preferential rates as newspapers.

Despite the difficulties they faced, several magazines emerged that would have a major impact on national development. The first of these was the *Port Folio*, established at Philadelphia in 1801 with a subscription base of almost 2,000. Under the editorship of Joseph Dennie, it served as the ideological mouthpiece of the declining **Federalist Party** through 1808. After that, Dennie increasingly moved away from politics, and, with his death in 1812, the *Port Folio* began a long decline. In contrast, Hezekiah Niles's *Weekly Register*, established at Baltimore in 1811 as a fierce defender of the **Republican Party**, prospered despite the **War of 1812**. With the advent of the **Era of Good Feelings**, Niles dedicated his magazine to keeping a political, economic, and social record of the era. He was one of the first to publish accurate statistical data, which makes his magazine a valuable historical resource even today. Finally, the *North American Review*, founded in 1815 by a group of demoralized Federalists, managed through skillful editing to overcome the prejudices that attached to its backers because of the War of 1812 to become the leading national magazine of contemporary opinion and **literature** by the end of the period. *See also* HALE, SARAH JOSEPHA BUELL; MURRAY, JUDITH SARGENT STEVENS.

***MARBURY V. MADISON* (1803). John Adams** made a series of judicial appointments to fill vacancies created by the **Judiciary Act of 1801** in the last hours of his presidency. As the new secretary of state, it fell to **James Madison** to deliver these commissions. Since the **Republican Party** regarded the Judiciary Act of 1801 as a desperate attempt by the **Federalist Party** to maintain its hold on power despite losing the **election of 1800**, Madison refused to do so. William Marbury, whom Adams had appointed justice of the peace in the District of Columbia in the last hours of his administration, applied to the **Supreme Court** for an order that would compel Madison to deliver his commission to him. Chief Justice **John Marshall** declined to grant Marbury's request on the grounds that the Constitution did not authorize Congress to vest the Court with the power of issuing orders in such cases. While Marshall's opinion avoided a direct challenge to Congress, which had recently repealed the Judiciary Act of 1801, it did assert the Court's power to review the constitutionality of congressional laws and to strike down those the Court decided were unconstitutional. Establishing the power to review state laws and judicial decisions came later as the Marshall court took its time in fleshing out the doctrine of **judicial review**.

MARSHALL, JOHN (24 September 1755–6 July 1835). Third chief justice of the United States, he was born in Virginia, the son of a moderately prosperous planter. Though he had little formal schooling, he joined the Continental army as an officer in the Virginia Line early in the Revolutionary War. Retiring from the field in 1780, he studied law, was elected to the Virginia legislature in 1782, and was admitted to the Virginia bar in 1784. As a member of the state ratifying convention in 1788, he outlined a notion of **judicial review** and vigorously supported adoption of the new federal Constitution. But he refused public office until 1797 despite a growing identification with the **Federalist Party** over issues like the **Jay Treaty**. President **John Adams** then asked him to join **Elbridge Gerry** and **Charles C. Pinckney** in negotiating with the **Directory**. Marshall wrote the **XYZ Dispatches**, which—on their release to the public in 1798—delivered the fifth Congress into the control of the Federalists and led to the **Quasi-War**. Marshall was elected representative to the sixth Congress and in May 1800 was appointed secretary of state in the wake of **Timothy Pickering**'s forced resignation. At the end of Adams's presidency, Marshall was appointed chief justice of the **Supreme Court** after **John Jay** refused the office because he thought the federal courts lacked sufficient power to have significant influence.

Marshall proceeded to show how mistaken Jay had been. Though Marshall had to buck Republican hostility to the courts fueled by the **Judiciary Act of 1801**, he managed to do so by cleverly choosing his battlegrounds and avoiding serious dissent on the Court. Thus, he persuaded the Court to acquiesce in the repeal of the Judiciary Act of 1801 and then used ***Marbury v. Madison*** (1803) to rule a section of the **Judiciary Act of 1789** unconstitutional as justification for denying Marbury the judicial commission Adams had issued him. In the **Burr treason trial**, Marshall established the principle of strictly construing the Constitution to preserve individual rights against the federal government. But Marshall also used an expanded interpretation of the contract clause along with the notion that the Constitution was the supreme embodiment of the people's sovereignty to keep the states from encroaching on the federal government. Additionally, he asserted the right of the Supreme Court to reverse state judicial rulings that were incompatible with the supremacy of federal laws. Only once in Marshall's long career as chief justice did he find himself dissenting from the majority. This is why under his leadership the Court managed to establish a reputation for being an impartial umpire overseeing the evolution of the federal system. He was also notable among his contemporaries for writing a five-volume life of **George Washington**, who had promoted his career on several occasions.

***MARTIN V. HUNTER'S LESEE* (1816).** The case originated in 1791 over title to a parcel of land on the Northern Neck in Virginia held by a British subject. After moving through the Virginia courts, it came to the **Supreme Court** on appeal in 1813. When the high court reversed the decision of the Virginia court of appeals, the state appeals court refused to honor the decision on the grounds that the Constitution did not extend the Supreme Court's appellate jurisdiction to such cases. When the plaintiff again appealed, Justice **Joseph Story**, speaking for the Court, with Justice Johnson concurring, affirmed the Court's jurisdiction and power to reverse the decisions of the highest state courts on appeal.

***MARTIN V. MOTT* (1827).** During 1814, Jacob E. Mott of the New York **militia** twice refused to obey the summons of the governor of New York to report to the commanding officers of the third military district of the United States. After the war, Mott was tried by court-martial, found guilty of dereliction of his duty, and fined $96 for his delinquency. Mott then brought an action against a local deputy, Martin, who had seized his property to pay the fine. Mott won a favorable judgment restoring his property from a New York court, which the state supreme court sustained. Martin appealed to the **Supreme Court**, where Justice **Joseph Story** found the New York courts in error for failing to uphold the constitutionality of Mott's court-martial on the grounds that the president had sole authority under an act of Congress passed in 1795 to judge whether the United States was threatened by invasion. In rendering his opinion, Story also ruled against the grounds on which Massachusetts, Connecticut, and Rhode Island had refused to place their militias under federal command during the **War of 1812**.

MASON-DIXON LINE. The boundary line separating Pennsylvania and Maryland. After the **first emancipation**, it also came to mark the boundary between states in the North that were committed to eventually freeing their **slaves** and the states in the South that would retain the institution of slavery until the Civil War.

MASONRY. *See* FREEMASONRY.

***MCCULLOCH V. MARYLAND* (1819).** In 1818, the Maryland legislature passed a law requiring branches of **banks** not chartered by the state legislature but operating within the state's boundaries to pay a tax on the notes they issued. The treasurer of the Baltimore branch of the **Second Bank of the United States** appealed his conviction in the Maryland courts for violating this law to the **Supreme Court**. Justice **John Marshall**, speaking for a unanimous Court, ruled that Congress had authority to charter the Second Bank of the United States because the institution was both necessary and proper to exercising the limited powers vested in the legislature by the Constitution. He then ruled the tax laid by the Maryland legislature on the Bank's notes unconstitutional because the power to tax could be used to destroy the Bank. Though the Supreme Court had shortly before in the **Dartmouth College Case** invalidated a state law on constitutional grounds, Marshall's opinion in *McCulloch v. Maryland* is considered his most carefully argued justification for the **judicial review** of state laws.

MCHENRY, JAMES (16 November 1753–3 May 1816). Physician and administrator, he was born in northern Ireland and immigrated to Philadelphia in 1771. After studying medicine with **Benjamin Rush**, he volunteered for the Continental army in 1776, was captured at Fort Washington, and paroled until exchanged in 1778. On rejoining the army, he became **George Washington**'s secretary and in 1780 the marquis of **Lafayette**'s aide-de-camp. On leaving the army in 1781, McHenry was elected to the senate of Maryland, where his kin had settled and grown prosperous, and then to Congress in 1783 and 1784. He was part of the Maryland delegation to the Philadelphia Convention but attended infrequently. Subsequently, he urged the Constitution be adopted in the Maryland ratifying convention. Though holding only state office as the new government went into effect, Washington consulted him about whom to appoint to federal offices from Maryland and finally offered McHenry the post of secretary of war in January 1796.

In that capacity, McHenry oversaw a congressionally sponsored reorganization of the U.S. Army. President **John Adams** retained him as secretary of war. At the beginning of the **Quasi-War**, McHenry was instrumental in forcing Adams to name **Alexander Hamilton** as second in command of the expanded **provisional army**. McHenry carefully selected only Federalists as officers for this force. He then deployed a detachment from it to suppress **Fries's Rebellion**. He joined **Timothy Pickering** in resisting Adams's peace initiative during 1799, and in May 1800, Adams demanded his resignation. McHenry never held another public office after he returned to private life.

MEMORIAL. A public statement of grievances, often drafted by a corporate body like a state legislature, addressed to a political superior, like Congress.

METHODISM/METHODISTS. An 18th-century offshoot from the Church of England that addressed the needs of the poor more effectively than the official church did by emphasizing habits that encouraged spiritual development rather than the sacraments. Methodism first came to the American colonies in the 1760s through the ministry of men like **Francis Asbury**. It took hold during the Revolutionary War because it offered its followers techniques for affirming their religious identities in the midst of revolutionary turmoil. The Methodist message was spread through circuit riders rather than settled ministers, sparing the faithful the expense of supporting a full-time religious leader. Methodism emphasized the role of human agency in attaining salvation and derived its name from disciplined routines designed to inculcate virtuous behavior. Its emphasis on personal religious experience and its implicit promise that all could achieve salvation led to the sect's dramatic expansion between 1790 and 1830. In the course of 50 years, especially during the **Second Great Awakening**, it became the most dynamic religious sect in the early Republic.

Methodism differed from the other Protestant sects in two additional respects. First, because it valued spiritual fervor over learning among its clergy, it did not found a permanent college until 1831 and only then with an eye to keeping the sons of the faithful from converting to other denominations. Second, despite its Episcopal form of governance, the Methodist Church proved prone to division. In the 1790s, **Richard Allen** led a secession movement from a white Methodist church in Philadelphia that had subjected its black members to degrading treatment. Early in the 19th century, Allen's followers joined with similar secession movements in New York and Baltimore to form the **African Methodist Episcopal Church** (AME). But centralization proved to be no more effective in governing the religious fervor the AME had been so successful in generating than it had been in preventing the original separation between white and black members of the Philadelphia Church. The AME subsequently underwent multiple divisions, one within 10 years of its establishment.

MIDDLESEX CANAL. The nation's longest, completed artificial waterway before the construction of the **Erie Canal**, the Middlesex linked Boston with the Merrimack River 27 miles away. It utilized 20 locks and eight aqueducts and between 1793 and 1803 cost its backers, organized by **James Sullivan**, half a million dollars to complete. **Loammi Baldwin** recruited local **labor** from New England's farm communities that were making the transition to stock raising to build the **canal**. For 50 years, the canal carried freight and passengers until the railroad replaced it. During its operation, it had a profound effect on the development of the Massachusetts communities that bordered it as well as on the Merrimack Valley as far north as Concord, New Hampshire.

MILAN DECREE. Napoleon's response to the British **Order-in-Council** of 11 November 1807, which required all neutral vessels making for ports closed to British vessels by the Berlin Decree to enter and pay duties before proceeding to their continental destinations. Issued on 17 December 1807, the Milan Decree proclaimed that any neutral vessel complying with the British Order-in-Council would lose its nationality, be deemed a British vessel, and be condemned when captured.

MILITIA. Every state in the early Republic passed laws requiring all adult white males who were not otherwise exempt to join military companies in their localities and to train a certain number of days each year. The militia thus became a military extension of society. Noncommissioned and junior commissioned officers were usually elected from the ranks, while field officers were appointed by the state governments. Though there was some divergence between the military and the political hierarchies, there was also considerable overlap. The militia was regarded as the first line of defense in case of a local emergency, such as an invasion. It also could be summoned by the executive to maintain civil order and help execute laws. But if the law were intensely unpopular, as was the case with the **Embargo of 1807–1809**, a measure like the **Enforcement Act** of 1809 could backfire. The South looked to the militia to help suppress **slave** insurrections like **Gabriel's Rebellion** and **Vesey's Rebellion**. Militia forces were not as a rule effective in conducting extended operations because they were less disciplined than regular army troops and were often deficient in arms. However, the militia was valued as a resource from which regulars could be recruited for long-term service.

MISSOURI COMPROMISE (1820). Early in 1819, Congress moved to separate Arkansas Territory from Missouri Territory in preparation for admitting Missouri to the Union. On 26 January 1819, John W. Taylor of New York proposed that the further introduction of **slavery** into Arkansas be prohibited. Known as the **Taylor Amendment**, it was roundly defeated in the U.S. House of Representatives on 19 February. When Missouri, which contained 2,000 to 3,000 slaves, shortly afterward requested admission to the Union, James Tallmadge of New York introduced an amendment to the enabling legislation. The **Tallmadge Amendment** barred the further introduction of slavery and provided for the gradual emancipation of the slaves already in Missouri. It carried in the House despite fierce opposition from spokesmen for the South but was decisively defeated in the Senate. The success of Tallmadge's amendment in the House showed that the free states were growing more rapidly than the slaves states and put the South on the defensive despite Alabama's admission to the Union on 14 December 1819, which restored parity between the slave states and the free states.

Though the Senate experienced no difficulty in agreeing to pair the admission of Maine and Missouri when both petitioned for admission to the Union at the end of 1819, Senator Jesse B. Thomas proposed that Congress prohibit the introduction of slavery north of 36°30' in what remained of the **Louisiana Purchase** territories to make the proposal more acceptable to northern representatives. The Senate accepted the **Thomas Amendment**, but the House initially rejected it in favor of a total exclusion of slavery from the entire territory as a precondition for Missouri's admission to the Union. The willingness of northern representatives to accept Thomas's amendment as the price required to win Maine's statehood paved the way to a compromise. Under its terms, both Maine and Missouri were admitted to the Union, and slavery was excluded from the remainder of the Louisiana Purchase above 36°30'. The arrangement reserved most of the unorganized western territory for freedom.

Missouri's full statehood was delayed, though, because of an objectionable feature in its state constitution that offended northern opponents of slavery. Only after the state legislature assured Congress that the constitution would not be used to deny U.S. citizens any privileges or immunities they were entitled to under the U.S. Constitution did President **James Monroe** proclaim Missouri to be part of the Union on 10 August 1821.

MONROE, JAMES (28 April 1758–4 July 1831). Fifth president of the United States, he was born in Westmoreland County, Virginia. After attending William & Mary College for two years, he joined the Continental army as a lieutenant and distinguished himself during the campaign of 1776, particularly at Trenton. Though he was promoted to major while still in his teens, thereafter Monroe's military career stalled, and in 1778 he retired from the army to study law under **Thomas Jefferson**'s supervision in Virginia. He was elected to the Virginia House of Delegates in 1782 and represented the state in Congress between 1783 and 1786. Though Monroe favored strengthening the national government, he opposed adoption of the federal Constitution in Virginia's 1788 ratifying convention.

In 1790, Virginia elected him to the U.S. Senate, and in 1794 to balance the appointment of **John Jay** as special envoy to Britain, President **George Washington** sent Monroe to France to preserve the

Franco-American relationship. When good relations with Britain turned out to be incompatible with good relations with France, Monroe's sympathy for France led Washington to recall him in 1796. Monroe was elected governor of Virginia from 1799 to 1802, and his decisive action was credited with suppressing **Gabriel's Rebellion**. In 1803, President Jefferson sent him back to France to join **Robert R. Livingston** in negotiating the purchase of **New Orleans**. On finding **Napoleon** ready to sell all of the **Louisiana territory**, Livingston and Monroe ignored their instructions and agreed to a treaty with France consummating the **Louisiana Purchase**. Between 1803 and 1807, Monroe served as minister to Britain. In 1806, Monroe, assisted by **William Pinkney**, negotiated a treaty with her they hoped would resolve some of the differences between the two nations. But Jefferson subsequently declined to forward the **Monroe-Pinkney Treaty** to the Senate for ratification. Dissident Republicans tried unsuccessfully to promote Monroe instead of **James Madison** as Jefferson's successor in the **election of 1808** after Monroe returned to the United States in 1807. In 1810, he was again elected governor of Virginia, and in 1811 Madison enlisted Monroe to be his secretary of state. Though Monroe was known to favor an accommodation with Britain, when his efforts at negotiating the removal of the **Orders-in-Council** led nowhere, he embraced the **War of 1812** as the nation's only remedy.

During the second war with Britain, Monroe's military ambitions were blocked by Secretary of War **John Armstrong** until the **burning of Washington** in 1814 forced Armstrong's resignation. Monroe then served concurrently as secretary of war and state for the remainder of 1814 and most of 1815 before surrendering the War Department to **William S. Crawford** for the rest of Madison's second term. As secretary of state, Monroe guided American negotiators in concluding the **Convention of 1815** and the **Rush-Bagot Agreement** of 1817 with Britain. After narrowly securing the endorsement of the Republican **congressional caucus** as Madison's successor in 1816, Monroe had no difficulty (with **Daniel Tompkins** as his running mate) in defeating the Federalist challenger, **Rufus King**.

During the summer of 1817, Monroe's tour of New England offered a region that had behaved in a disaffected manner throughout the War of 1812 a chance to reconcile itself to the rest of the nation.

But on domestic matters, President Monroe remained a minimalist, and the federal government did little to cushion the effects of the **Panic of 1819**. Monroe responded to the **Tallmadge Amendment** by letting it be known he would veto any bill for Missouri's statehood that made **abolition** a precondition. Nonetheless, he supported the **Missouri Compromise**, and his near unanimous victory in the **election of 1820** suggested that he had successfully contained the divisiveness of the **slavery** issue.

The principal achievements of Monroe's presidency were in the realm of foreign relations. He and his secretary of state, **John Quincy Adams**, experienced no difficulty in collaborating because they shared the common goal of establishing the United States as the preeminent power in the Western Hemisphere. After diffusing the remaining boundary difficulties with Britain in the **Anglo-American Convention of 1818**, Monroe and Adams turned to securing the Floridas from Spain. Their efforts, to which General **Andrew Jackson** contributed with his unauthorized campaign against hostile **Indians** in the **Seminole War** during 1818, culminated in the **Adams-Onís Treaty** of 1819. In it, Spain renounced title not only to the Floridas but also to all of the Louisiana Territory north to British Canada and west to the Pacific Ocean. During his second administration, Monroe and Adams capped their previous achievements by formulating the **Monroe Doctrine**, which Monroe announced in his last address to Congress, before retiring to private life in 1825.

Monroe's last years were troubled by personal debts he had accumulated during years of government service. Congress was slow in settling his accounts for the diplomatic service because of then-President Jackson's opposition. Jackson learned that Monroe had been critical of his incursion into Spanish territory in 1818, which had proved instrumental in persuading Spain to cede so much of its continental claims to the United States. Monroe eventually received $30,000 for his past expenses, but the sum failed to cover other debts amassed through lavish entertaining while he occupied the White House. Monroe died in **New York City**, to which he had moved from Virginia after his wife's death, in 1830.

MONROE DOCTRINE. After **Napoleon**'s overthrow of the Spanish monarchy in 1808, Spain's overseas empire had begun to disintegrate in a series of anticolonial rebellions. The restoration of the European monarchies accompanying the end of the **Napoleonic Wars** in 1815 led Spain and the other continental powers supporting it to consider recovering its former colonies that had undergone republican revolutions. But 20 years of devastating warfare slowed Europe's enthusiasm for military adventures. France did not seek authority from the Holy Alliance (France, Austria, Prussia, and Russia) to intervene in the New World on Spain's behalf until 1822, just as the administration of **James Monroe** began to recognize the independence of the new Latin American republics.

As the principal commercial beneficiary of the Latin American independence movements, Britain strongly opposed the French plan and sought the cooperation of the United States in opposing it. Secretary of State **John Quincy Adams** persuaded Monroe that the United States would be better served by standing alone against all the European powers than by cooperating with Britain. Monroe outlined the doctrine that bears his name in an address to Congress on 2 December 1823, when he declared that the Western Hemisphere's political system differed from Europe's and cautioned the European powers against further colonizing the Americas. At the same time, the United States forswore interfering with existing colonies or participating in future European wars. In effect, he was declaring the Americas to be the exclusive sphere of influence of the United States in which European meddling would not be welcome. The Monroe Doctrine attracted little attention at the time and acquired practical influence only later in the 19th century. *See also* LATIN AMERICAN REVOLUTIONS.

MONROE-PINKNEY TREATY. Negotiated with the British government at the end of 1806 by **James Monroe** and **William Pinkney** at President **Thomas Jefferson**'s behest, the treaty attempted to diffuse the tension that had arisen between the two countries over Britain's **Orders-in-Council** regulating the commerce of neutrals with Europe and the **impressment** of seamen off American commercial vessels. The British government refused to renounce impressment, though it was willing to confine the practice to the immediate vicinity of the British Isles, the "narrow seas." While it appeared to be more flexible about its commercial restrictions, the final draft of the treaty was accompanied by a note making any concession contingent on the

United States defending its neutral rights against France's commercial restrictions. The note was prompted by **Napoleon**'s recent **Berlin Decree**, which proclaimed a **paper blockade** of the British Isles. Jefferson refused to send the treaty to the Senate for its advice and consent. His action contributed to a rift between Monroe and Secretary of State **James Madison** that was not fully healed until Madison as president persuaded Monroe to become his secretary of state in 1811.

MORSE, SAMUEL FINLEY BREESE (27 April 1791–2 April 1872). Painter and later inventor, he was born in Charlestown, Massachusetts, and educated at Yale, graduating in 1810. After studying painting and sculpture in England during the **War of 1812**, Morse returned to the United States in 1815 and made a name for himself, primarily as a portrait artist. In 1826, he helped found and then served as the first president of the National Academy of Design until 1842. This did not prevent him from returning to Europe in 1829 for three years or from dabbling in politics on his return to America. Though among the best-trained and most talented artists of his generation, around 1837 Morse abandoned the **arts** to devote himself to the development of what became the electromagnetic telegraph. He is remembered today chiefly for the Morse code.

MURRAY, JUDITH SARGENT STEVENS (1 May 1751–6 July 1820). Author, she was born in Gloucester, Massachusetts; received her **education** at home; and married a local sea captain. No children were born to the couple before her first husband died. Judith then married John Murray, a **Universalist** minister who took the theological position that everyone had been saved by Christ's atonement. In 1793, the couple moved into Boston to establish a Universalist congregation there. Judith had always entertained an ambition to be a writer, and she had started contributing **poetry** to **magazines** in 1782. In the 1790s, she wrote two series under the pseudonyms "The Gleaner" and "The Repository" for the *Massachusetts Magazine*. In them, she advocated educating women to an audience sympathetic to Federalism. But her "On the Equality of the Sexes," written in 1779 when the Revolution seemed to have gone awry but not published until 1790, has commanded modern attention because its sassy deflation of masculine pretensions makes Murray appear to be a protofeminist. In 1809, John Murray was incapacitated by a stroke. After he died, Judith devoted most of her writing to promoting Universalism.

MURRAY, WILLIAM VANS (9 February 1760–11 December 1803). Diplomat and politician, he was born in rural Maryland. Poor health during his youth kept Murray from taking an active role in the Revolution but did not prevent him from studying law in the English Inns of Court between 1784 and 1787. While in London, Murray became friendly with **John Adams** and **John Quincy Adams**. Returning to the United States, Murray was elected to Congress in 1791 as a representative from Maryland. He served three terms in the House, during which time he acted as a moderate member of the **Federalist Party**. He opposed William Branch **Giles's Resolutions** with their implied censure of **Alexander Hamilton**'s **funding** policy and **James Madison**'s proposal to levy **discriminatory tonnage duties** on British imports, but he supported implementing the **Jay Treaty**. President John Adams appointed Murray American minister to the Batavian Republic, a puppet state that France had established in what is today the Netherlands. Murray was roundly chastised by Secretary of State **Timothy Pickering** for prematurely recognizing the perpetrators of a coup against the French-sponsored regime. But Murray did succeed in having French **privateers** banned from the Batavian Republic's coast. **Talleyrand** chose Murray as the official conduit for the peace overture he sent the Adams administration in hopes of bringing the **Quasi-War** to a conclusion. President Adams then named Murray minister to France. His cabinet insisted that Murray was not up to negotiating a settlement with France by himself, so **Oliver Ellsworth** and William R. Davies joined him in negotiating the **Franco-American Convention of 1800**. It released the United States from all the obligations of the **Franco-American alliance**, but at the price of the United States having to satisfy the claims of those who had been injured by the depredations the French had committed against American commercial vessels. The convention also helped secure **Thomas Jefferson**'s election as president. Jefferson then replaced Murray as ambassador to France with **Robert R. Livingston**. Murray retired from public life to an estate in Maryland, dying shortly thereafter.

MUSEUMS. Urbanization created resources for cultural enterprises that could not be sustained in the countryside because of the wealth the larger towns generated and the leisure of their denizens seeking entertainment. One such diversion, pioneered by Robert Barker in London, was a rotunda displaying a 360-degree painted image that gave the viewer the illusion of being someplace else, in a manner similar to Imax theaters today. In 1795, William Winstanley opened such a facility in **New York City** with a view of London. In 1810, he replaced London with Rome, and in 1813 a new facility displayed a representation of the battle between the **USS *Constitution*** and HMS *Guerrière*.

Charles Willson Peale had started the nation's first **art** museum in Philadelphia during 1784 when he displayed his portraits of revolutionary leaders in his home. Over the years, Peale tried to broaden the public appeal of his displays by branching out into historical curiosities. By 1818, natural history items had taken primacy over paintings, which were relegated to the upper wall. Two of Peale's sons, Rembrandt and Ruben, established a similar museum in Baltimore between 1814 and 1830, though Rembrandt also used their museum to display one of his more unusual paintings, *The Court of Death*. Both the father and the sons were disappointed that their ventures did not generate more interest, and they had only limited success in getting public subsidies for them.

Charles Willson Peale developed a better way to display the work of artists when in 1805 he helped found the Philadelphia Academy of Fine Arts. He saw the mission of this institution to be encouraging the development of native artists by providing them with models of artistic elegance and encouraging them with modest commissions. New York City quickly followed Peale's example, first with its own academy presided over by **John Trumbull** and then by **Samuel F. B. Morse**'s drawing association, which soon became the National Academy of the Arts of Design. Boston was not far behind with the establishment of the Athenaeum in 1807, and by the early 1830s Cincinnati and Charleston had similar institutions. The sponsors of all these institutions saw themselves as contributing to the nation's cultural autonomy as well as the uplift of its citizenry.

MUSIC. Several European musical traditions brought by immigrants into Britain's North American colonies influenced the development of the new nation's musical culture. One was a sacred tradition of hymns and psalm tunes, which dominated in New England. Another was a folk tradition of ballad music. Finally, Celtic music crossed the ocean with the Scottish-Irish **immigration** to the middle and southern colonies. During the 18th century, Charleston, South Carolina, became a major portal through which European musical influences entered the colonies. Only the Ephrata Cloister and the Moravians of Pennsylvania developed indigenous musical cultures in the colonial period about which much is known, though their influence failed to extend much beyond the boundaries of their sects.

American composers began to emerge in late colonial New England, but they followed British models until the Revolution. Thereafter, as typified by **William Billings**, they began experimenting in the composition of psalm and fugue tunes as well as anthems and canons, sometimes mixing elements from folk melodies with unconventional rhythms and harmonies. By the early 19th century, however, native-born composers were being displaced, at least in New England, by the work of European composers who found more favor with the local arbiters of taste. The founding of the Handel and Haydn Society in 1815 by a group of Boston merchants signaled the shift.

The other emerging cities of the nation accommodated European musical influences with local influences more gracefully. In **New York City**, **William Dunlap** collaborated with the Englishman Benjamin Carr, who wrote the music for an adaptation of the story of William Tell in *The Archers* (1796), the first American opera performed in the United States. Carr also contributed to the development of American culture by establishing a music shop in Philadelphia after arriving there in 1793. While it sold the music of distinguished European composers like Hayden, Mozart, and Hummel, Carr also encouraged amateur musicians with the **magazine** *Musical Journal*, which he edited between 1800 and 1804. Finally, Carr wrote numerous compositions, including the "Federal Anthem" and the "Dead March and Monody," the latter of which was used in the ceremony organized by Philadelphia on the occasion of **George Washington**'s death.

The New England tradition of sacred music fared best in the rural South after the turn of the 19th century. Under the influence of the revivalism of the **Second Great Awakening**, northern and southern traditions merged to create a new amalgam. In Kentucky, the **Cane Ridge Revival** started a process that ultimately led to the publication of distinctive compilations like the *Kentucky Harmony* and eventually *The Sacred Harp* (1844), the most influential and long lived of these collections.

The camp meeting also became the site where a non-European musical tradition merged with and enriched European-inspired music. The introduction of **slavery** into North America brought with it African musical influences. During the first century of their enslavement, a vigorous musical culture emerged among the Africans in their quarters. As long as slavery lasted, this music's principal venues remained work, ceremonies like weddings and funerals, and the newly established black churches that were organized in the larger cities. In 1801, **Richard Allen** had issued a special hymnal, some of whose songs came from the slave quarters. **African Americans** were more open to European influences than the whites were to African influences. But the camp meeting bridged some of the separation between the races and gave the Negro spiritual a currency among whites that it might not otherwise have obtained. The emergence of minstrel songs during the second and third decades of the 19th century that denigrated Africans can be seen as a defensive response by whites to the versatility of black music.

Independence also inspired the composition of secular, patriotic music. Several poets of the early Republic, including **Timothy Dwight**, **David Humphreys**, and **Joel Barlow**, wrote songs for the Continental army during the Revolutionary War. Few of these have survived, but later the **Quasi-War** inspired the composition of Joseph Hopkinson's "Hail! Columbia," first performed in New York on 25 April 1798. Both Hopkinson's tune as well as the words were American compositions. This was not the case with Francis Scott Key's "Star-Spangled Banner," written at the end of the **War of 1812**. Though the words were composed during the defense of Baltimore against British attack on 15 September 1814 and published the next day as "The Defense of Baltimore," the tune was borrowed from the Anacreon Society of London and had been written around 1775.

– N –

NAPOLEON (15 August 1769–5 May 1821). A Corsican by birth who won a scholarship to a French military academy, he rose from obscurity to become emperor of the French in the era of the **French Revolution**. Trained as an artillery officer just as technical improvements in the casting of cannon made artillery more mobile, Napoleon's military prowess depended on concentrating overwhelming force against his adversaries on the battlefield. His military successes in turn enabled him to exploit the instability of France's republican institutions to establish his unchallenged political power by 1800. After unsuccessfully attempting to reassert French power in the Americas, in 1803 he turned France toward conquering all of Europe. Napoleon proved to be an enlightened innovator in civil affairs, giving many of the nations he conquered their first written constitutions and single-handedly drafting the Napoleonic code, which today provides the basis for French law. But his military exploits left the British no choice but to oppose him, feeding hostilities that between 1803 and 1815 consumed most of Europe.

After the battle of Trafalgar established Britain's uncontested naval superiority at the end of 1805, its principal weapon against France became the sea blockade. Napoleon retaliated with less effective but no less sweeping measures of his own, making it impossible for the United States to enjoy good relations with one of the belligerents without incurring difficulties with the other. Napoleon viewed the new Republic as a weak, peripheral state that he valued only as a possible adversary of Britain. While he played a role in precipitating the **War of 1812**, Napoleon's simultaneous invasion of Russia deprived him of an opportunity to profit from American hostilities. Leaders of the **Federalist Party** regarded Napoleon as a threat to the nation's security not just because he was trying to subdue Britain, which they saw as the only bulwark standing between the United States and his military tyranny, but also because he had presided over the transformation of France from a republic to a despotism. Leaders of the **Republican Party** viewed Napoleon with suspicion but after the **Louisiana Purchase** saw Britain as a greater potential threat to the nation's future destiny.

NAPOLEONIC WARS. The portion of the **wars of the French Revolution** in which **Napoleon** took the leading role, beginning with his assuming command of the Army of Northern Italy in 1796 to Waterloo in June 1815.

NATIONAL REPUBLICAN PARTY. A designation adopted by the supporters of **John Quincy Adams** during the **election of 1824** and the **election of 1828** after the **First Party System** had collapsed and before the **Second Party System** took shape. The National Republican Party subsequently evolved into the **Whig Party**.

NATIVE AMERICANS. *See* INDIANS.

NATURALIZATION ACT OF 1798. The first of the laws passed by the fifth Congress in the wake of the **XYZ Affair** tried to limit the power of the **Republican Party**. **Immigration** from Ireland in response to British efforts to suppress the United Irishmen's movement for independence was viewed by leaders of the **Federalist Party** as a threat because the immigrants' hostility to Britain would make them natural supporters of the then vice president, **Thomas Jefferson**. Proposed initially by the House Committee on the Defense of the Country and for the Protection of Commerce, the act extended the residency requirement for full citizenship from five to 14 years. It also compelled aliens desiring naturalization to declare their intention five years in advance of their application to become citizens and required all white immigrants to register with the federal government. Aliens who had arrived in the United States before 1795 were grandfathered under the previous naturalization system and had to declare their intention to be naturalized only one year in advance. The legislation passed both houses of Congress and was signed into law by President **John Adams** on 18 June. The seventh Congress, elected in the aftermath of the **Election of 1800**, repealed the law on 14 April 1802 and reinstated the five-year residency requirement for citizenship.

NEGRO SEAMEN'S ACT (1822). Passed by the South Carolina legislature in the wake of the discovery of the **Vesey Conspiracy**, the act required that all black seamen be lodged in local jails while their vessels remained in port. Execution of the act led to protests from British and northern shipowners. South Carolina continued to enforce the statute despite a **Supreme Court** finding that it was in conflict with a federal treaty that was the supreme law of the land. South Carolinians acknowledged the conflict but argued that the treaty rather than their law was unconstitutional, claiming the states reserved a right to nullify such laws.

NEUTRAL COMMERCE. Under international law, vessels registered under the flag of a neutral nation had certain rights during wartime that were denied to vessels sailing under the flag of a belligerent nation. These rights included immunity from seizure and detention on the high seas. *See also* NEUTRALITY PROCLAMATION; PAPER BLOCKADES; RULE OF 1756.

NEUTRALITY ACT (1794). In the wake of **Edmund Genêt**'s violations of American neutrality, Congress passed a law making it a federal crime for a U.S. citizen to accept the commission of a foreign prince or government that would be exercised within the jurisdiction of the United States. The law also forbade a range of activities relating to the vessels of war of a foreign prince or state, including enlisting on them, fitting them out, and procuring U.S. commissions for them. If necessary, the president was authorized to call out the **militia** to enforce this law.

NEUTRALITY PROCLAMATION. The outbreak of war between Britain and France early in 1793 had serious implications for the United States. Both of the belligerents had Western Hemisphere colonial possessions, which meant their naval forces were bound to come in contact with American vessels. Moreover, the United States still had a formal treaty of alliance with France dating from the Revolution. President **George Washington** was sensitive to the peril the young nation faced, and on 22 April 1793 he issued a proclamation advising Americans of the new international situation. The proclamation exhorted them to behave impartially toward both belligerents. The majority of Washington's countrymen sympathized with France and were not about to disguise their feelings. But the intention behind the Proclamation, which did not use the word "neutrality," was more to persuade the British government of the American government's neutrality than to purge Americans of their anti-British feelings. When Britain refused to take notice, Washington appointed **John Jay** as a fully empowered minister to head off another war with Britain for which the nation was ill prepared, having hardly recovered from the previous one.

NEW HARMONY. The name the British visionary Robert Owen gave to the settlement on the Wabash River in present-day Indiana that he purchased in 1825 from a separatist group from the German Lutheran Church led by Johann Rapp. The Rappists had immigrated from Germany to Pennsylvania in 1804. In 1814, they moved to a larger site on what would become the border between modern Indiana and Illinois. Within the course of a decade, they had established a prosperous community that went beyond economic self-sufficiency to turn a handsome profit selling agricultural and manufactured surpluses as far away as the eastern seaboard. In 1824, they were looking for a site closer to the growing **urbanized** markets when they came to the attention of Owen, a radical reformer and industrialist. He was looking for a site to put his educational theories based on environmentalism into operation. At the time, "Harmonie" had over 100 dwellings ready for occupancy in a location that was free from political pressures. In 1825, Owen purchased the Rappists' community and, with the support of internationally known figures like the Scottish geologist and philanthropist William Maclure, tried to establish a **utopian** community that abolished all distinctions relating to class and property and provided everyone with a free **education**.

Owen left the management of New Harmony to his eldest son, David Dale Owen, while he returned to Europe. The community failed to live up to Owen's expectations and was unable to sustain the Rappists' economic success because of the community's reformist objectives. Owen's opposition to giving his experiment a religious focus also hindered the integration of its heterogeneous participants. New Harmony did, however, become a center for training geologists and over the next 30 years was the headquarters of the U.S. Geological Survey.

NEW MADRID EARTHQUAKES (1811–1812). The first of a series of four giant earthquakes originating in the New Madrid area of modern Missouri struck around 2:00 A.M. on 16 December 1811. It was followed six hours later by a second massive tremor that is regarded by seismologists as being another event rather than an aftershock. The third quake took place on 23 January 1812 and the fourth and largest on 7 February. In between the four principal shocks and for some time after the last major tremor, the Mississippi, Missouri, and Ohio River valleys experienced repeated aftershocks. The effects of these earthquakes were felt as far away as Boston, Charleston, and Washington. Closer to the epicenter, they were responsible for tsunami-type waves on the Mississippi that temporarily reversed the flow of the river, collapsed embankments, eradicated and created islands and lakes in a matter of minutes, changed the river's channel, and damaged most of the man-made structures in the vicinity. This set of earthquakes was not directly related to another major seismic event that took place in modern Venezuela on 26 March 1812. However, the damage to man-made structures and to human life in North America was far less than in South America because the area affected was thinly populated.

NEW ORLEANS. Situated near the mouth of the Mississippi River, New Orleans held the strategic key to a vast drainage system bordered by the Appalachian Mountains on the east and by the Rocky Mountains on the west. As such, the city was vital to the future of the United States. France and Spain held it at one time or another between 1789 and 1803. In 1795, **Charles Cotesworth Pinckney**, as minister to Spain, secured the right of the United States to deposit and transship goods in and from New Orleans in the **Treaty of San Lorenzo**. But his success was threatened when Spain conveyed Louisiana back to France in 1800. Though the **Louisiana Purchase** of 1803 secured the nation's title to the city, during the **War of 1812** it looked as though Britain would be able to conquer it, thus compromising the future development of the West. When **Andrew Jackson** succeeded in defeating the British in the Battle of **New Orleans**, his victory was hailed as confirmation of the nation's destiny.

George Washington

John Adams

Thomas Jefferson

James Madison

James Monroe

Alexander Hamilton

John Quincy Adams

Andrew Jackson

NEW YORK CITY. During most of the colonial period, the province of New York and the city that shared its name existed in the shadow of larger and more powerful neighbors: Massachusetts and Boston to the east and Pennsylvania and Philadelphia to the south. But in the late colonial period, New York benefited from **immigration** from New England as well as from overseas, and the city began overtaking Boston and rivaling Philadelphia. During the Revolutionary War, the British occupation continued the trend—despite the physical damage inflicted on the city by the presence of a foreign army—because its strategic position lent itself to becoming a command and supply center. So advantageous did the British find New York City that they abandoned it only reluctantly on 26 November 1783, more than seven months after the Treaty of Paris officially ended hostilities.

In the immediate postwar period, New York City served as the **entrepôt** for southern New England and New Jersey as well as the expanding settlements in the western part of New York State. Because of the strategic importance of the Hudson River, New York had been defended during the war by the Continental army. This meant that the state entered the peace with a relatively modest debt that it could **fund** with the yields derived from a state **impost** collected principally in the city. This advantage made New York the envy of the other states in the Confederation and fed the anti-Federalist opposition of Governor **George Clinton**'s to the new federal Constitution. The city responded by threatening **secession**, but fortunately it never came to that. Though the state accepted the Constitution reluctantly, it benefited enormously from Secretary of the Treasury **Alexander Hamilton**'s **funding** policy, which led to the abolition of most state taxation. This stimulated a general expansion that underwrote the vigorous growth of the city during the years before the **War of 1812**.

The emergence of New York City as the nation's principal entrepôt was sealed in the early part of the new century by its entrepreneurs' success in broadening their market reach through two key developments. The first was the *Clermont*'s demonstration in 1807 that steam-powered navigation of the Hudson River was technically and economically feasible. The second was the **Erie Canal**, which linked the city with the waterways of the Great Lakes, stimulating settlement and an economic development in the old Northwest that far exceeded anything taking place in the South. New York City's preeminence as a distribution point for European imports even enabled it to assume control over the marketing of the South's cotton crop in Europe by the 1830s. By then, the city had surpassed Philadelphia as the central entrepôt of the nation. Its new wealth in turn helped make it the cultural capital of the new Republic, a distinction it still retains.

NEWSPAPERS. In 1790, the nation had 96 newspapers, most of them located in the larger towns along the eastern seaboard, but very few had circulations of more than 2,000. By 1828, the nation had 859 newspapers, with a far greater percentage of them distributed outside the older population centers. Since newspapers were supported as much by advertisements as by subscriptions, their emergence reflected the development of local markets in the interior. A printing technology that still relied on the hand-powered press led to the proliferation of separate newspapers even in the larger population centers associated with **urbanization**. But the **Postal Act of 1792** facilitated the flow of information between publishers in different locations and made the newspaper the chief influence through which the leaders of the **First Party System** tried to shape public opinion. Political theater had many sites beyond the state and national legislatures, but only the newspapers had the capacity in an expanded Republic to distill the cacophony of voices into something approximating a coherent whole. For the same reason, a free press was thought to be essential to the preservation of responsible government. When the **Alien** and **Sedition Acts** seemed to violate that principle during the **Quasi-War**, members of the **Republican Party** protested not only that the **First Amendment** had been violated but also, more importantly, that **Republicanism** itself was being assaulted.

Regardless of their disclaimers, most newspapers during the life of the First Party System acquired partisan identities. The most important party newspapers during the 1790s were published in Philadelphia, the seat of the national government. They included John Fenno's Federalist *Gazette of the United States*, **Philip Freneau**'s Republican *National Gazette*, and Benjamin Franklin Bache's *Aurora*. After the national government moved to Washington in 1800, the *National Intelligencer*, established by Samuel H. Smith, became the unofficial organ of the Republican administrations of **Thomas Jefferson** and **James Madison**. In 1810, Smith took Joseph Gales Jr. into partnership. After Smith retired two years later, the paper was carried on by Gales in partnership with William W. Seaton. It remained the most influential Republican paper through the administrations of **James Monroe** and **John Quincy Adams** and began to lose stature only after it unsuccessfully opposed **Andrew Jackson** in the **election of 1828**. The nearest thing to a rival Federalist paper in the nation's capital was Samuel Snowden's *Alexandria Advertiser*, later the *Alexandria Gazette*. But the most influential Federalist publications after 1800 were Boston's *New England Palladium* and New York's *Evening Post*. *See also* MAGAZINES.

NONINTERCOURSE. Initially proposed as a modification of the **Embargo of 1807–1809** and adopted by Congress in March 1809, it applied only to commerce with Britain and France. As a coercive measure, it affected France more than Britain because Britain could get American exports from neutral ports, which, through its naval power, it was able to deny France. **Napoleon** responded to the Nonintercourse Law with the Ramboullet Decree, which sequestered American vessels entering ports controlled by France on the continent of Europe. The Nonintercourse Law was allowed to expire in 1810 because it proved as unenforceable and ineffectual against the great powers as the embargo. Congress replaced it with a measure based on **Macon's Bill No. 2**, which lifted all commercial restrictions against the belligerents, but promised to reinstate nonintercourse against either power that failed to lift its **Orders-in-Council** or decrees against U.S. commerce once the other had done so. Since France lacked the naval power to enforce its decrees, it partially responded to this one-sided invitation, and on 2 November 1810, President **James Madison** gave Britain three months to follow suit. When the British failed to act, claiming that France had not actually revoked its decrees, Madison imposed nonintercourse against Britain on 2 February 1811. The new measure operated more as a nonimportation than as nonintercourse since American merchants selling cargoes in other European countries often accepted remittances on Britain in payment.

Nonetheless, it caused more economic distress in Britain than either the embargo or the previous nonintercourse had because British industry had saturated the Latin American market between 1809 and 1810 and was undergoing a painful contraction during 1811 and 1812 that made the closing of the U.S. market to British goods especially hurtful.

NULLIFICATION. The **South Carolina Exposition and Protest** (1828) against the **Tariff of Abominations** contained a theoretical rationale for a state nullifying a federal law. It was the work of **John C. Calhoun**, who argued that since the people acting through their states had established the federal government, they could also nullify an act of Congress that violated that compact in a state convention. Calhoun sought to go beyond the idea that federal authority was supreme because the Constitution was an expression of the people's sovereignty rather than a compact among sovereign states, to which Chief Justice **John Marshall**'s **Supreme Court** had committed itself. Calhoun sought to protect minorities against hostile majorities without entirely scraping the idea that the Constitution embodied a higher law.

South Carolina had several precedents previously used by minorities that it could draw on in seeking to nullify a federal law. **Thomas Jefferson**'s drafts and the final text of the **Kentucky Resolutions** had declared the **Alien Law** and the **Sedition Law** unconstitutional and therefore void and of no effect. In the struggle over the **Embargo of 1807–1809**, the leaders of the **Federalist Party** in Massachusetts repeatedly declared the embargo to be unconstitutional. They also had the legislature pronounce it unconstitutional in a bill that would have made it a state crime to execute parts of the **Enforcement Act of 1809**, had the Republican lieutenant governor of Massachusetts not vetoed it before he was voted out of office. At the end of the **War of 1812**, the Connecticut legislature empowered the state's municipalities to pass bylaws regulating the activities of federal recruiters within their jurisdictions. After the **Hartford Convention**, Hartford adopted a set of bylaws criminalizing standard recruiting practices in response to an act of Congress authorizing the enlistment of minors, which the state's

Federalist Party leadership regarded as unconstitutional. Shortly afterward, the state legislature passed a law imposing heavy penalties on anyone attempting to enlist a minor on the grounds that the federal law violated "the spirit of the Constitution." Connecticut authorities then prosecuted Captain Elijah Boardman for violations defined by Hartford's regulations after the war had ended, though Boardman—a Republican Party member of long standing—was convicted under the common law of public nuisances rather than the municipality's bylaws. Between them, Hartford and the state legislature had gone further than any other public body would in nullifying a federal law until South Carolina became interested in nullification following the **Vesey Rebellion**. The state legislature's **Negro Seamen's Act** of 1822 conflicted with federal treaties, and the state subsequently tried to nullify the federal **tariffs** of 1828 and 1832 in an effort to develop a weapon for defending **slavery**.

– O –

OHIO. The land north of the Ohio River and east of the Mississippi, was originally known as the Northwest Territory. On 30 April 1802, Congress authorized the people in the first surveyed and settled eastern division to form a constitution and apply for admission to the Union as a separate state bounded on the west by a line running due north from the junction of the Ohio and Grand Miami Rivers. The area had commonly been referred to as the Ohio Territory, and the state took that name. The lands to the west were designated as being part of the newly constituted Indiana Territory.

ORDERS-IN-COUNCIL. After the American Revolution, Parliament vested in the king and his Privy Council the authority to regulate British trade with the rest of the world—and particularly its trade with her former American colonies—through executive orders known as Orders-in-Council. The practice continued throughout the 40-year period from 1789 to 1829 and proved particularly contentious during the **Napoleonic Wars**.

OTIS, HARRISON GRAY (8 October 1765–28 October 1848). Politician, he was born in Boston and educated at Harvard, graduating in 1783. He then trained for the law and was admitted to the bar in 1786. Otis served briefly with the Massachusetts forces that suppressed Shays's Rebellion. He also invested heavily and profitably in Boston real estate as well as innovative textile ventures and helped found a commercial **bank** in Boston. In 1796, he was elected to the Massachusetts General Court and in 1797–1801 represented Massachusetts in the U.S. Congress. While in the House, he supported passage of the **Alien** and **Sedition Acts** and restrictions on **immigration**.

When Otis retired from Congress in 1801, President **John Adams** appointed him district attorney for Massachusetts. But after **Thomas Jefferson** became president, he removed Otis from the federal office. Between 1802 and 1817, Otis served as leader of the **Federalist Party** in Massachusetts, acting either as speaker of the house or president of the senate, depending on which branch he chose to be elected to. Otis orchestrated the state legislature's resistance to the **Embargo of 1807–1809** and its invitation to the other New England states in 1814 to send delegates to Hartford. He attended the **Hartford Convention** and was probably the principal author of its lengthy report. When the **Treaty of Ghent** brought the **War of 1812** to an honorable conclusion, Otis's reputation suffered. In 1817, the Massachusetts legislature elected him to the U.S. Senate, where he refused to accept Congress's condition for reimbursing the state for its war expenses because it involved an explicit disavowal of the grounds on which Massachusetts had withheld its **militia** from the federal government.

Otis's attempt to defend the Hartford Convention in Washington generated such hostility that he retired to Massachusetts before the end of his Senate term. His subsequent attempt in 1824 to run for governor of Massachusetts became a referendum on the Hartford Convention and the state's refusal to place its militia under federal command. Otis lost this election. He succeeded **Josiah Quincy** as mayor of Boston in 1829 but did little of note besides resist southern pressure to curtail the publication of **David Walker**'s *Appeal* and to muzzle William Lloyd Garrison's calls for the immediate **abolition** of **slavery**. In his last years, he became a **Whig** and a supporter of **Henry Clay**.

– P –

PAINE, THOMAS (29 January 1737–8 June 1809). Revolutionary republican and **deist**, he was born in Norfolk, England, to **Quaker** parents. After several unsuccessful careers in England, he followed Benjamin Franklin's advice and immigrated to Pennsylvania in 1774. There he quickly emerged as a leading advocate for the revolutionary cause and in 1776 penned *Common Sense*, which argued persuasively that the colonies should declare their independence from Great Britain. After brief service with the Continental army, he was employed by the Continental Congress, the Pennsylvania Assembly, and Robert Morris in various capacities until the end of the war.

In 1787, he returned to Britain and in 1791 published *The Rights of Man* in response to Edmund Burke's critical *Reflections on the French Revolution* (1790). In 1792, a second *The Rights of Man*, referred to as part 2, called for revolution in Britain and led to Paine being declared a traitor. Moving across the English Channel, he became a French citizen and was elected to the National Convention after France declared itself to be a republic. However, Paine's Girondist associations, based largely on his ignorance of the French language, created difficulties after the Jacobins came to power. He was stripped of his French citizenship, imprisoned, and narrowly averted the guillotine during the Terror. Ambassador **James Monroe** managed to secure Paine's freedom after Thermidor (27 July 1794). While under French arrest, Paine gave his *The Age of Reason* to **Joel Barlow** for publication. This **deistic** tract attacked revealed **religion** and came to be regarded by most professing Christians as a threatening and therefore a forbidden book. Paine returned to the United States in 1802 and spent his last years in the United States living in obscurity in New Jersey and New York. Ten years after his death, the English radical William Cobbett had Paine's remains exhumed for reburial in England but never succeeded in finding a proper resting place for them. Paine's final resting place is unknown today.

PANIC OF 1819. Scholars disagree over whether the dramatic price declines of 1819 were attributable to the first national business cycle recession experienced by the American economy or were simply another example of the postwar depressions that had repeatedly plagued the colonial economy during the 18th century. D. C. North argues that the recession that resulted from the Panic of 1819 was the first of three pre–Civil War cyclical downturns tied to a periodic inelasticity in the cotton supply. According to this argument, cotton was the key commodity in regulating the price structure of the American economy. As long as the supply of cotton remained elastic, prices were relatively stable. But once the available land for cultivation ran low, land prices and cotton prices rose in tandem to a point where new lands followed by new cotton production saturated the market.

No one disputes that the Panic of 1819 was preceded by speculative land purchases and that after the bubble broke, land prices collapsed. But an alternative interpretation stresses the agency of the nation's **banking** system in precipitating the price collapse. Led by the newly chartered **Second Bank of the United States**, most of the nation's commercial banks had responded to improving conditions after the **War of 1812** by recklessly extending credit. Rising prices for domestic commodities eventually came into equilibrium with falling prices for imports but not before the banks had overextended themselves. Faced with having to repay foreign debts in hard money, the larger urban banks led by the Bank of the United States radically contracted credit and precipitated the general price collapse of the following year. The federal government then made matters worse with the **Land Act of 1820**, which eliminated all credit in the purchase of public lands. This protected the treasury much better than it did the public.

Both interpretations have validity. North is right in identifying a structural basis for the recession, while the monetarists have ample reasons for holding the banks responsible. In fact, the two interpretations can be seen as complementing each other. The demand for cotton soon caught up with existing capacity during the 1820s, and under the leadership of **Nicholas Biddle**, the Second Bank of the United States, sobered by the distress it was accused of causing, pursued a more restrained policy for the rest of the decade.

PAPER BLOCKADES. International law recognized blockades only of specific ports or limited sections of a coast where the blockading power had assembled the necessary naval force to bar entry by third parties. All vessels captured running such blockades were recognized as legal prizes. Paper blockades referred to proclamations by a belligerent power that an extended portion of an adversary's coast was under blockade. Both Britain and France proclaimed paper blockades during the **Napoleonic Wars**, but Britain had the naval power to give their blockades more effect than France did, often by seizing vessels as they sailed in other seas for destinations under paper blockade. *See also* NEUTRAL COMMERCE.

PAYNE, JOHN HOWARD (9 June 1791–9 April 1852). Actor and playwright, he was born in **New York City** and at an early age demonstrated extraordinary precocity by becoming the assistant editor and drama critic of a well-received **magazine**. At the age of 14, though an apprentice in a counting house, he started another magazine while writing and producing a play, though the play was not a success. Patrons recognized his genius and sent him to Union College for two years, but he broke with them to make a triumphant debut on the New York stage before completing his studies, rising instantly to stardom. When the **War of 1812** dampened New York's theatrical life, Payne moved to England in 1813, performing in provincial theaters. Then he traveled to Paris, where he began adapting continental plays to the English language. In addition, he wrote many original scripts, including the first major tragedy, *Brutus* (1818), to be conceived by an American playwright. Throughout much of the 1820s, Payne stayed in Europe managing the Saddler's Wells Theater in London and collaborating with fellow expatriate **Washington Irving** in producing popular comedies. A profligate with money, he often found himself in debt and on several occasions was imprisoned by his creditors. This, however, proved a spur rather than a deterrent to his creativity. One of his more lasting creations were the lyrics to the song "Home, Sweet Home," which was part of a musical play titled *Clari* (1823). In 1832, he returned to the United States and took up the cause of the **Cherokee**, defending them against President **Andrew Jackson**'s **removal** policies. Friends later secured him two appointments as consul in Tunis, first in 1843–1845 and again in 1851–1852, where he died.

PEALE, CHARLES WILLSON (15 April 1741–22 February 1827). Painter and cultural entrepreneur, he was born in Queen Anne's County, Maryland, to a recent **immigrant** family from England. Peale married advantageously in America and through his wife's family acquired patrons. They recognized his talent as an artist and sent him to study painting with **Benjamin West** in London between 1767 and 1769. Returning to America, Peale quickly established a reputation as a portrait painter. In 1776, he moved his family from Maryland to Philadelphia and subsequently, while serving as an officer with the army, did numerous portraits, mostly miniatures, of the leaders of the Revolution. They remain today one of the best sources of information about the appearance of this extraordinary group of men.

Returning to Philadelphia in 1779, Peale dabbled in Pennsylvania politics until it became clear that his activities were competing with his portrait commissions. During the mid-1780s, he began converting his home into a **museum** of natural history and the **arts**. He wanted to provide the public at large with an opportunity for learning about the rational order of nature, assuming that this lesson would in turn lead a republican people toward social and moral improvement. Peale had difficulty securing public support for his museum. Most of the expenses of the project were met from charging the public admission. The American Philosophical Society gave his museum a new home in 1794, and he received some support from the Pennsylvania legislature between 1802 and 1816. But this no more covered the costs of expensive projects, such as the exhuming of the mastodon he undertook at the beginning of the 19th century, than his painting of the excavation did. Though he experimented with historical and allegorical subjects and helped found the Pennsylvania Academy of Fine Arts (1805), Peale would be remembered for his portraits. By the end of his long career, he had executed over 1,000 of them, including seven of **George Washington** between 1772 and 1795. His other major contribution to the emerging culture of the early Republic was to train three sons—Raphaelle (1774–1825), Rembrandt (1778–1860), and Titian Ramsey (1799–?)—who became leading artists in their own right.

PERFECTIBILITY. A notion that began to pervade both secular and religious thought during and after the American Revolution. "Perfectibility" did not refer to the possibility that anyone or anything, through their own agency, might become perfect. Instead, it referred to the expectation that there were no limits to the improvement of the human condition. This notion infected all aspects of human endeavor in a revolutionary age. It was the inspiration behind the early **reform** efforts of individuals like **Thomas Gallaudet**, Robert Owen, and **Frances Wright**. It inspired equally the **poetry** of **Joel Barlow**, the technical innovations of **Robert Fulton**, and the scientific claims of **Benjamin Rush**. In the hands of great revivalists like **Charles Grandison Finney**, it harnessed **religion** to secular reforms like **temperance** and **antislavery**, communicating to them energy they would not otherwise have enjoyed. Though perfectibility was often dismissed as utopianism, it was a dynamic concept in tension with the objective of **utopian** societies to insulate their achievements from change. *See also* NEW HARMONY; REFORM.

PERRY, OLIVER HAZARD (23 August 1785–23 August 1819). Naval officer, he was born in South Kingston, Rhode Island. On 7 April 1799, he entered as midshipman aboard the USS *General Greene* and saw action in the Caribbean during the **Quasi-War**. During the Tripolitan phase of the **Barbary Wars**, he was promoted to lieutenant on board the USS *Adams* and in 1805 was placed in command of a schooner, the USS *Nautilus*. Returning to the United States, he served on a gunboat enforcing the **Embargo of 1807–1809** before being placed in command of the schooner USS *Revenge*. On 8 January 1811, Perry lost his vessel in a wreck off Watch Hill, Rhode Island, but was exonerated of any dereliction of duty in a subsequent court-martial. When the **War of 1812** commenced, Perry was given responsibility for defending Newport, Rhode Island. He chafed at this assignment and in the spring of 1813 finally got himself made commander of U.S. naval forces on Lake Erie. Once he took charge, he pressed forward with the construction of five war vessels. By the beginning of July, the fortunate capture of four British ships gave him a naval force capable of challenging Robert Barclay's British squadron. He then moved his fleet of warships westward to place Barclay's force in the Detroit River under surveillance.

On 10 September 1813, the British squadron appeared off Perry's anchorage at Put-in-Bay (modern Sandusky Bay). Perry, who enjoyed the advantage in short-range firepower, signaled his fleet to engage the enemy at close quarters. But his flagship, the brig *Lawrence*, was left by a companion vessel, the *Niagara*, to do this on its own. After absorbing most of the enemy's fire for almost two hours, Perry transferred his flag from the disabled *Lawrence* to the *Niagara* and sailed into the midst of the British fleet. Shortly afterward, Barclay surrendered the six vessels under his command, conferring unchallenged naval superiority in Lake Erie on the Americans. This permitted General **William Henry Harrison** to reoccupy Detroit and to invade western Ontario, where he won a victory the following month in the **Battle of the Thames River**.

Perry's victory made him a national hero and won him promotion to full captain as well as command of the USS *Java*. But on that vessel's first postwar cruise to the Mediterranean, Perry quarreled with the captain of the ship's marines in a way that led both to be tried by court-martial. The quarrel also provoked a **duel**, though both survived unhurt. Perry was next given the task of securing from the government of Venezuela satisfaction for piracies committed on American vessels from its ports. He died from **yellow fever** while returning from successful negotiations with the Venezuelan authorities. *See also* LAKE ERIE, BATTLE OF.

PICKERING, TIMOTHY (17 July 1745–29 January 1829). Political and military leader, he was born in Salem, Massachusetts, and graduated from Harvard in the class of 1763. Pickering's public career began when he accepted a **militia** commission from the royal governor, Sir Francis Bernard. But he quickly distanced himself from royal officialdom and by 1774 was a member of Salem's Committee of Correspondence and the elected colonel of the local militia regiment. During the Lexington and Concord alarm of the following year, he slowed his unit's arrival on the battlefield and the next day opposed the creation of a provincial army to lay siege to Boston in a council of war. This earned him the reputation of being a lukewarm revolutionary, and for the next two years he remained largely inactive at Salem. In 1777, he finally accepted General **George Washington**'s invitation to serve first as adjutant general of the Continental army and later as its quartermaster general. After the peace, Pickering tried unsuccessfully to restore his economic fortunes in Philadelphia before moving his family to western Pennsylvania. There he was elected to local offices and was a delegate in the state convention that ratified the new federal Constitution.

Once the new government had been organized, Washington invited Pickering to serve as agent to the Seneca **Indians**. In 1791, he was appointed postmaster general, and in 1795, he succeeded Henry Knox as secretary of war. Pickering strongly supported ratification and implementation of the **Jay Treaty** and was appointed secretary of state after **Edmund Randolph**'s forced resignation from the office. In that role, he championed good relations with Britain to the point of an informal alliance with her at the cost of bad relations with France to the point of going to war with her. During the **Quasi-War**, he took charge of prosecuting Republican **newspaper** editors under the **Sedition Act** of 1798. He also tried to sabotage President **John Adams**'s effort to avoid a full-scale war with France by opposing the dispatch of the American commissioners who negotiated the **Franco-American Convention of 1800**. Adams demanded his resignation in May 1800.

After another brief sojourn on the Pennsylvania frontier, Pickering's friends bought out his homestead at an inflated price and settled him on a small farm in Essex County, Massachusetts. Then, in 1802, they had him selected to fill the unexpired term of a U.S senator from Massachusetts. He became prominent among the extreme members of the **Federalist Party** in 1804 who were willing to consider **secession** from the Union in response to the **Louisiana Purchase**. In 1808, he successfully intervened in Massachusetts state politics to restore Federalist control over the state government. His *Letter to **James Sullivan***, which accused President **Thomas Jefferson** of instituting the **Embargo of 1807–1809** in response to **Napoleon**'s orders, argued that **Republican Party** leaders were bent on provoking a war with Britain. After the embargo's repeal, Pickering's continued opposition to Republican measures led the Massachusetts legislature, now back under the control of the Republicans, to deny him reelection to the Senate. But he was elected to the House of Representatives, where he vehemently obstructed the conduct of the **War of 1812**, even to the point of advocating that the debt contracted during the conflict be repudiated. When contrary to his desire and expectations the British failed to take **New Orleans**, which might have provided the occasion for dismantling the Union in 1815, he suddenly began to sound like a Republican Party nationalist. But it was too late, and in 1816 his constituents declined to reelect him. He spent the remainder of his days farming and pursuing old grudges against his former rivals in public life.

PIKE, ZEBULON MONTGOMERY (5 January 1779–27 April 1813). Soldier and explorer, he was born in New Jersey and entered the army at an early age, serving during the late 1790s in various western posts. In 1805, **James Wilkinson**, governor of the newly acquired territories in the **Louisiana Purchase**, selected him to lead an exploratory expedition to discover the source of the Mississippi River. Though Pike's party of 20 men mistakenly identified a Minnesota lake as the river's source, Wilkinson dispatched him the next year to explore the Arkansas and Red River valleys with an eye to ascertaining the extent of Spanish settlement in the Southwest. Pike's Peak in Colorado bears his name, though his attempt to climb it failed. Turning south, Pike's band stumbled on the Rio Grande, which he mistook for the Arkansas River. The fort he built there attracted the attention of Spanish authorities, who then arrested him and his followers. Though the Americans were released in June 1807, Pike was suspected of being concerned in a scheme for dismantling Spain's American empire similar to **Aaron Burr**'s by virtue of his association with Wilkinson. He managed to clear himself, though, and by 1813 had been promoted to brigadier. In that capacity, he commanded the assault on York, Ontario, and died as a consequence of wounds received in the engagement.

PINCKNEY, CHARLES COTESWORTH (14 February 1745–16 August 1825). Military and political leader, he was born in Charleston, South Carolina, and educated at Winchester, Oxford, and the Middle Temple in England. Returning to America in 1769, he quickly emerged at the forefront of South Carolina's revolutionary movement. He served as a brigadier during the Revolutionary War, participating in the Florida expedition of 1778 and the unsuccessful assault on Savannah in 1779. His capture in 1780, when Charleston,

South Carolina, surrendered, ended his military career but not his political one. In the postwar period, he helped initiate many civic projects, including the **Santee Canal** and the attempt to establish a college in the state. As one of South Carolina's representatives in the Philadelphia Convention, he opposed the popular election of federal representatives and protested the provision under which a slave would count for only **three-fifths** of a Caucasian in apportioning federal representation and direct taxes.

After the establishment of the new government, he refused President **George Washington**'s invitation to sit on the **Supreme Court** but supported Secretary of the Treasury **Alexander Hamilton**'s **funding** proposal and the policy of coming to an accommodation with Britain. In 1796, Washington replaced **James Monroe** with Pinckney as ambassador to France, but the **Directory**, angered over the **Jay Treaty**, refused to receive him. Reappointed by President **John Adams** to join **John Marshall** and **Elbridge Gerry** in another effort to resolve the crisis in Franco-American relations, Pinckney was adamant about refusing the humiliating terms offered by **Talleyrand**'s agents, as reported in the **XYZ Dispatches**. After Pinckney returned to the United States, he accepted appointment as third in command of the **provisional army**, under Washington and Hamilton. Pinckney was the **Federalist Party**'s candidate for vice president in the **election of 1800** but would have nothing to do with Hamilton's intrigue to have him supplant Adams as its presidential candidate. Pinckney did emerge as the Federalists' presidential candidate in the **election of 1804** and the **election of 1808**, but in neither did he stand a chance of winning, and his own state supported first **Thomas Jefferson** and then **James Madison**. In his later years, Pinckney helped found the University of South Carolina and was active in establishing the **American Bible Society** and local Bible societies that emerged during the **Second Great Awakening**.

PINCKNEY, THOMAS (23 October 1750–2 November 1828). Soldier and diplomat, he was born in South Carolina. Like his older brother, **Charles C. Pinckney**, he was educated largely in England, though he also studied briefly in France. Returning to

America in 1774, he participated in the Florida campaign of 1778 and served as Comte D'Estaing's liaison in the unsuccessful siege of Savannah in 1779. He was fortunate in escaping capture when Charleston fell in 1780 but shortly afterward was taken at Camden, South Carolina. After being exchanged, he was present at Yorktown in October 1781.

In the postwar period, Pinckney was elected governor of South Carolina in 1787 and 1788, presided over the state convention that ratified the new federal Constitution, and played a leading role in drafting a new constitution for the state in 1790. In 1791, President **George Washington** appointed him minister to Great Britain, a diplomatic rank below ambassador, because of the British court's refusal to reciprocate full diplomatic relations with the United States. This did not help Pinckney in resolving the many problems that remained between the two countries in the wake of the Revolutionary War. Only after the wars ignited by the **French Revolution** erupted in 1793, creating a crisis with Britain, did Washington send **John Jay** as minister plenipotentiary to the court of St. James. Pinckney watched the negotiations that led to the **Jay Treaty** from the sidelines.

Realizing that Pinckney had reason to feel slighted, Washington sent him to Madrid to deal directly with the Spanish court over the disputed boundary between the United States and **West Florida** and the navigation of the Mississippi River. Because Spain was in the process of abandoning its alliance with Britain and joining France, the Spanish court thought it expedient to head off a possible Anglo-American alliance against Spain by settling the border issue in favor of the United States and opening the navigation of the river. The treaty signed at San Lorenzo on 27 October 1795, known as **Pinckney's Treaty**, was much more popular than the Jay Treaty in the United States and earned Pinckney the informal designation as **John Adams**'s running mate in the **election of 1796**. When **Thomas Jefferson** instead became vice president, Pinckney served as a representative of South Carolina in the fifth and sixth Congresses before retiring to private life. President **James Madison** appointed him major general in command of the southern military district during the **War of 1812**, but his theater did not prove to be a particularly active one.

PINCKNEY'S TREATY (ALSO KNOWN AS THE TREATY OF SAN LORENZO). In the peace of 1783, Britain restored **East Florida** and **West Florida**, which it had acquired at the conclusion of the Seven Years' War, to Spain. Britain also recognized the southern boundary of the United States as running from the head of the Saint Mary's River west along the 31st parallel to the Mississippi. Spain treated the new Republic less generously. It maintained that West Florida extended northward to the Tennessee River and from there to the Mississippi. It also closed off commercial access to its American empire and threatened to close U.S. navigation of the lower Mississippi and with it the economic future of the trans-Appalachian West. In 1785–1786, **John Jay** tried to get Spain to accept Britain's definition of West Florida's boundaries, offering at one point to trade the right to navigate the Mississippi for 25 years in exchange for commercial access to the rest of Spain's American empire. Such a bargain was unacceptable to the southern and western states. The Spanish ambassador also opposed it, fearing that commercial access would accelerate the growth of a revolutionary Republic whose influence Spain had good reason to fear.

The Spanish government's attitude toward the United States changed in 1795, when Spain abandoned its alliance with Britain to join France. Fearing the **Jay Treaty** was the beginning of an Anglo-American rapprochement that would work to their disadvantage in North America, the Spanish court sought to appease the United States by yielding on both the boundary issue and the navigation of the Mississippi. Under the terms of the Treaty of San Lorenzo negotiated by **Thomas Pinckney**, Spain agreed to Britain's definition of West Florida's boundaries, granted Americans free navigation of the Mississippi, and gave them the right to deposit their goods at the mouth of the river, for three years in **New Orleans** and after that at another point to be designated.

PINKNEY, WILLIAM (17 March 1764–25 February 1822). Diplomat and jurist, he was born in Annapolis, Maryland, to Loyalist parents. Pinkney nevertheless enjoyed the patronage of Samuel Chase, later appointed to the **Supreme Court**, who trained him for the bar. After opposing the ratification of the new Constitution in Maryland's ratifying convention, he was active in state politics until President

George Washington appointed him to be one of the commissioners under article 7 of the **Jay Treaty** assigned the task of adjudicating the claims of individual Britons and Americans against each other's governments. From 1795 to 1804, Pinkney resided in Britain. On his return, he caught the nation's attention in January 1806 by writing the *Memorial of the Merchants of Baltimore on the Violation of Their Neutral Rights*, protesting recent changes in Britain's policy regarding **neutral commerce**. Later that year, President **Thomas Jefferson** sent him to join **James Monroe**, the U.S. minister to Britain, in negotiating a new commercial treaty with Britain. Though Jefferson refused to submit the **Monroe-Pinkney Treaty** to the Senate for its advice and consent, Pinkney remained in London as the nation's diplomatic representative there between 1807 and 1811.

After returning to the United States, he became President **James Madison**'s attorney general from 1811 to 1814 and during the **War of 1812** helped establish the doctrine that trading with a British license was the equivalent of trading with the enemy. In 1814, as an officer in the Maryland **militia**, Pinkney participated in the **Battle of Bladensburg**, where he was seriously wounded. Between 1816 and 1819, he served as minister to Russia. On his return to the United States, he was elected to the U.S. Senate. There he delivered an impassioned protest against the **Tallmadge Amendment**. Its rejection contributed to pairing the admission of Maine and Missouri in the **Missouri Compromise**. Several of his arguments in cases before the Supreme Court proved to be influential. Thus, **John Marshall** followed the outline of Pinkney's plea in behalf of the **Bank of the United States** in the landmark decision of ***McCulloch v. Maryland***.

POETRY. The Revolution inspired several attempts to provide the new nation with an epic poem. The aspiring poets hoped to define the Republic's revolutionary achievements as Homer's great epic poems had defined the emergence of Greece as a distinct civilization in antiquity. Americans of the revolutionary generation also drew inspiration from the success of Alexander Pope's *Essay on Man* in articulating the aspirations of the rational Enlightenment and James Thomson's *Liberty* and *Britannia* in giving midcentury voice to a triumphant British nationalism. **Timothy Dwight** and **Joel Barlow**, both members of the literary circle known as the Connecticut Wits, led in this enterprise, the former with *The Conquest of Canaan* (1785) and the latter with *The Vision of Columbus* (1787). But neither poem succeeded commercially, despite the endorsement Barlow's poem received from prestigious subscribers like Louis XVI of France and **George Washington**. Barlow's attempt to issue a substantially reworked version of his earlier epic as *The Columbiad* (1807) fared little better than the original had. **James Fenimore Cooper**'s fictional Leatherstocking tales came closer to supplying the new nation with an epic than any of the poetic works of the period.

When it came to poetry, Americans preferred shorter works, as the early success of **David Humphreys**'s "The Glory of America" (1782) suggested. Both Barlow's and Humphreys's serial contributions to the mock epic *The Anarchiad* (1786–1787), which helped face down those elements in Connecticut inclined to follow the lead of the Shays rebels in Massachusetts, were well received. Barlow's elegiac *Hasty Pudding* (1793), penned in France while he campaigned for a seat in the National Convention, commanded a wide readership. Dwight then followed Barlow's lead with a celebration of the virtues of rural Republicanism in *Greenfield Hill* (1794). The greatest poetic success of the early Republic, though, was shorter than either Barlow's or Dwight's best work and eschewed politics entirely. It was **William Cullen Bryant**'s *Thanatopsis* (1817, 1821), a meditation on death that helped Americans come to terms with the revolutionary changes in which they were participating. *See also* FICTION; SIGOURNEY, LYDIA; WARREN, MERCY OTIS.

POINSETT, JOEL ROBERTS (2 March 1779–12 December 1851). Diplomat and naturalist, he was born in Charlestown, South Carolina, but educated at **Timothy Dwight**'s Greenfield Hill Academy in Connecticut and the university at Edinburgh. Poinsett had a gift for acquiring languages. As a young man, he traveled widely in Europe and the Middle East, meeting many of the age's leading figures, including the financier Jacques Necker, cultural leaders like Madame de Staël, and statesmen like Metternich and **Napoleon**. Returning to the United States in 1804, he sought a military career but ended up serving as a commercial agent for American interests in South America. While on this assignment, he incurred the wrath of local authorities by meddling in the region's internal politics. He missed the **War of**

1812 but afterward served briefly in Congress before President **James Monroe** dispatched him on a secret mission of observation to report on conditions in Mexico and Cuba. After Mexico achieved its independence, President **John Quincy Adams** appointed him ambassador to Mexico. He remained there until he requested his own recall in 1830 after failing to secure a portion of **Texas** for the United States. He briefly joined forces with **Andrew Jackson** to oppose South Carolina's attempt at nullifying the **Tariff of Abominations**. Eventually, President **Martin Van Buren** appointed him secretary of war during his administration. In this capacity, Poinsett not only reorganized the armed services and managed the second Seminole War but also sponsored aggressive **exploration** of the West and the polar regions. His interest in the natural world led him to help establish the Smithsonian Institute and resulted in his name being attached to a Mexican plant known as poinsettia. Retiring from office with Van Buren, Poinsett spent the rest of his life opposing the growing movement in the South for **secession**.

POSTAL ACT OF 1792. On 22 February 1792, a bill organizing the Postal Service became law. It permitted any **newspaper** publisher in the country to send individual copies of his paper to any other publisher free of charges. This facilitated the circulation of information among newspaper publishers at a time when the technology of printing made it difficult for any paper to print more than 2,000 copies of an issue. Congress's intention here was to promote the Republic's newspapers as the principal conduits through which the citizenry would become informed. The act also cut the cost of sending newspaper subscriptions through the mails to between one-sixth and one-twenty-fifth of the rates charged for an ordinary letter. In 1794, Congress extended parallel privileges to **magazine** publishers, subject to the local post master's discretion as to whether doing so would jeopardize the circulation of newspapers. The Postal Service would expand in the early 19th century to become the first nationwide extension of the federal government reaching into virtually every locality.

PRESBYTERIANISM/PRESBYTERIANS. Though theologically indistinguishable from **Congregationalism,** Presbyterianism embraced a different form of church government. Instead of the male members of each congregation of visible saints selecting their ministers and passing directly on all important church matters, the Presbyterians developed a more hierarchical system of governance. The congregation, not necessarily composed exclusively of those who could bear witness to the spiritual gift of God's grace, chose lay elders as well as a pastor. Together these men governed the parish church. Each congregation was also a member of an association of churches that was governed by all its pastors together with representatives elected by the elders. Known as the presbytery, this body ordained the pastors of the separate congregations. At the pinnacle of Presbyterian governance was the synod, composed of elected clergy and lay elders.

Presbyterianism came to British North America with English and Scottish **immigrants**. It took root in the mid-Atlantic section of the country because the greater ethnic heterogeneity of the population there made it more difficult to collect and maintain the congregations of visible saints required by Congregationalism. In 1801, the Presbyterians and Congregationalists concluded a formal union, and in 1810, they joined forces in establishing the **American Board of Commissioners for Foreign Missions**. Both sects collaborated closely throughout the **Second Great Awakening** in supporting foreign and domestic missions. But in the 1830s, the Congregationalists began withdrawing from the collaboration on domestic missions so that they could pay more attention to the emigrants from New England settling in the West.

PRIESTLEY, JOSEPH (13 March 1733–6 February 1804). Theologian, scientist, and educator, he was born in Yorkshire, England, and trained to be a dissenting clergyman. But Priestley's affinity for heretical positions, like questioning the Trinity, made him more successful as an educator. He favored a curriculum that replaced the classics with modern languages and science. His teaching led to scientific inquiries that resulted in the discovery of oxygen and the oscillatory characteristics of electric currents. In 1772, he attracted the patronage of Lord Shelburne in whose household he resided until 1780 and from whom he received an annual pension until his death. In 1782, he published his controversial *The Institutes of Natural and Revealed Religion*, followed in 1785 by *The Importance and Extent of Free Enquiry in Matters of Religion*, which **Thomas Jefferson** acknowledged had been important in shaping his religious beliefs.

Priestley had supported the American cause during the Revolution and made no secret of his approval of the **French Revolution**. But his house and the school he taught in were destroyed in July 1791 by a Birmingham mob responding to his attempt to celebrate the anniversary of the fall of the Bastille. Remaining in Britain was further jeopardized when the National Convention in 1792 made him an honorary citizen of France. After war broke out between Britain and France in 1793, Priestley began making plans to **immigrate** to Northumberland, Pennsylvania. In July 1794, he joined some of his children who had preceded him there, hoping to transform a frontier town into a wilderness retreat for like-minded European intellectuals. In this, he was to be disappointed. But at the end of the decade, he contributed two pamphlets critical of the **Federalist Party**'s sponsorship of the **Quasi-War**, *Maxims of Political Arithmetic* (1798) and *Letters to the Inhabitants of Northumberland* (1799), despite the risk he ran of being deported under the **Alien Act**. He continued writing largely on theological subjects, which he considered more important than scientific ones, during his last years, even though most of the Protestant clergy shunned him as a heretic.

PRIVATEER. A private vessel of war licensed by a legitimate government to seize the merchant vessels of an enemy nation as an act of war. The prizes taken by a privateering vessel were legally vested in the syndicate that owned and outfitted it once they had been formally condemned in an admiralty court. *See also* WAR OF 1812 (NAVAL OPERATIONS).

PROVISIONAL ARMY (1798). On 28 May 1798, Congress authorized the president to raise a provisional army of 10,000 men and to accept volunteer companies into the regular army that at the time consisted of only four regiments. In July, Congress formally added 12 new regiments to the regular army. Though legally distinct from the provisional army, the new army of 16 regiments was often referred to as being "provisional" because of the widespread suspicion of standing armies. President **John Adams** got **George Washington** to accept command of the enlarged army only by agreeing to have **Alexander Hamilton** serve as its inspector general, which made Hamilton its de facto commander. In March 1799, Congress provisionally authorized an additional dozen regiments. While the president was allowed to appoint the officers for these units, the men were not to be enlisted until war was actually declared or invasion threatened. But the only additions made to the army were the dozen new regiments authorized in July 1798, though their ranks never entirely filled. Hamilton's efforts to mobilize them were undermined by Adams, who suspected that Hamilton entertained Napoleonic ambitions. The president used his power of appointment contained in the law of March 1799 to overwhelm a weak and poorly led War Department with extraneous paperwork.

The army had to contend with other problems besides Adams's hostility toward its commander. Whatever initial popularity the new army had enjoyed evaporated as the states began to implement the direct tax Congress had laid to pay for it. Then Washington's death in December 1799 removed any protection that his prestige as titular commander had previously lent it. And the reception of the peace commissioners, whom Adams had dispatched to France, suggested that the **Quasi-War** was winding down. When in May 1800 Congress bowed to these developments by authorizing the president to demobilize the new regiments, Adams immediately complied to diminish Hamilton's power.

PUBLIC DOMAIN (OF THE UNITED STATES). The Revolution established the nation's title to a vast domain bounded on the south by the 31st parallel, on the west by the Mississippi River, and on the north by the Great Lakes and Saint Lawrence River. Various states claimed virtually all of it, which, under the Articles of Confederation, they could not be dispossessed of without their consent. Since many of these claims overlapped and some states, like Maryland and Rhode Island, had no claims, Congress recommended that the landed states renounce their claims to create a public domain that could be used to pay for the Revolution. Virginia obliged by ceding most of its claims north of the Ohio River, helping to make the old Northwest part of the newly constituted public domain. But it retained title to Kentucky, where there were no conflicting state claims, as North Carolina did to Tennessee and Georgia did to Alabama and Mississippi. North Carolina confronted a secession movement in its western reaches during the 1780s that it found expedient to resolve by ceding its claims to what became Tennessee. And Georgia eventually ceded much of its western lands to the federal government to settle the **Yazoo Land** claims. However, **Ohio** was the first "public land" state to be admitted to the Union in 1802. The **Louisiana Purchase** of 1803, to which no state had a previous claim, extended the public domain to the continental divide.

The Ordinance of 1785 had called for the public domain to be surveyed into six-square-mile townships and 640-acre sections before it could be sold. But very little land was disposed of under these terms before the inauguration of the new government in 1789 because of the presence of hostile **Indians** in the Ohio Territory. This changed after the **Battle of Fallen Timbers** and Congress responded on 18 May 1796 with a Land Act that extended the regular surveys of the Ordinance of 1785, established two land offices, and fixed the minimum price at $2 per acre for the purchase of a 640-acre section. On 10 May 1800, another law allowed four years of credit on the purchase of a 320-acre half section. It also doubled the number of land offices. Under the Ohio Enabling Act of 1802, the federal government retained title to most of the ungranted land within the state's boundaries, setting a precedent for future states created out of the public domain. In 1804, the government reduced the minimum price of public lands to $1.64 per acre and the minimum purchase to 160 acres.

The approach of the **War of 1812** forced Congress to turn to land sales for revenue. On 25 April 1812, it created a General Land Office under the authority of the secretary of the treasury. But sales remained sluggish during the war and did not begin to blossom until after the **Treaty of Ghent**. Speculators taking advantage of the four-year credit provision in the Act of 1800 then set off an explosive expansion of sales that contributed to the **Panic of 1819**. The panic also dramatized to the government that it had received payment for only a fraction of the land it had conveyed, leading to a new policy instituted in the **Land Act of 1820**. This legislation abolished all credit and reduced the minimum price to $1.25 per acre and the minimum purchase to 80 acres. Though ostensibly favoring settlers over speculators, the credit contraction following the Panic of 1819 left few able to take immediate advantage of its provisions. The Land Act of 1820 remained government policy in disposing of the public domain for the next decade.

– Q –

QUAKERS (ALSO KNOWN AS THE SOCIETY OF FRIENDS). Quakerism was an offshoot from 17th-century English Puritanism. A lay preacher, George Fox (1624–1691), rejected the fundamental premise of **Calvinism** that a creature's alienation from its creator could be bridged only by the deity's arbitrary dispensation of grace. Instead, Fox held that all humans had been endowed with a divine spark that they had the power to develop once they recognized its existence. Cultivating this inner light led Fox and his followers to question such practices as **slavery**, the violence of war, and the authority of the Church of England. The result was a persecution that led many English Quakers to migrate to America during the late 17th and early 18th centuries. Though the **immigrants** were persecuted in Puritan colonies like Massachusetts and Connecticut, they were welcomed in Rhode Island, Pennsylvania, and West Jersey, where the church and state were separated and all Protestant faiths tolerated. In the latter colonies, the Quakers organized themselves into meetings that supervised the spiritual development of their members. While Quakers rejected all religious authority imposed from without, influential men and **women** could exert almost as much weight in a Quaker meeting as an ordained minister did in the other Protestant sects.

The Quakers generally opposed the American Revolution and the war that was waged to secure independence from Britain. This made them unpopular in the early republican period. Their support for the **abolition** of slavery did little initially to alleviate that unpopularity. However, their ideas about the proper relationship of church and state helped shape the way the **First Amendment**'s prohibition against Congress "passing any law respecting an establishment of **religion**, or prohibiting the free exercise thereof" was construed into a doctrine of strict separation between the two. They also were early advocates of several 19th-century reforms besides **antislavery**, including **temperance**, prison reform, and poor relief. In the late 18th century, Elias Hicks (1748–1830) began to carry the notion of the inner light in a direction that raised questions about many biblical beliefs, such as Christ's virgin birth, the crucifixion, and the resurrection. In 1827, a formal separation took place between the Hicksites and the more orthodox Quakers.

QUINCY, JOSIAH (4 February 1772–1 July 1864). Congressman, mayor of Boston, and president of Harvard, was born in Boston. He received his education at Phillips Andover Academy and Harvard, graduating in the class of 1790. Quincy trained for the law but had little inclination for its practice. Instead, he turned to politics and, what at the time was closely associated with it, oratory. After several unsuccessful bids for office, he was finally elected to represent Massachusetts in the ninth Congress in 1805. By this time, Quincy had become convinced that the only way in which the **Federalist Party** could make a national comeback was to exploit divisions in the **Republican Party**. Quincy deployed his considerable elocutionary talents in pursuing this objective. The controversy over the **Embargo of 1807–1809** alerted him to a division among the Republicans over whether the nation could survive a war with Great Britain. He accordingly taunted them with their irresolution and, when they responded by claiming they meant business, egged them on. He assumed that they were bluffing and would be humiliated when their bluff was eventually called.

When this strategy led to a declaration of the **War of 1812**, Quincy retired to Massachusetts and took a seat in the state senate. His new position failed to provide Quincy with the commanding platform for his inflammatory rhetoric that the House of Representatives had, and he gradually drifted apart from the local Federalist leadership. That proved a blessing in disguise since it freed him from direct involvement in the **Hartford Convention**, the activities of which would be regarded as treasonous during the postwar period.

In 1821, Boston replaced its town meeting government with a common council over which a mayor presided. Quincy became the second mayor of the city in 1823. He then proceeded to make Boston one of the most progressive cities in the nation. Quincy's style of politics was nothing if not contentious, and in 1828 he had stirred up enough controversy to make retirement seem preferable to seeking reelection. But a year later, Harvard, which had been plagued by student riots, appointed him its 15th president. Here again, Quincy displayed a contentious streak, suspending the entire sophomore class for disciplinary reasons. He survived a threatened boycott of commencement by the senior class, brought student disorders under control, and strengthened and reformed the curriculum before retiring in

1845. The last years of his long and active life were spent supporting the **antislavery** movement.

– R –

RANDOLPH, JOHN, "OF ROANOKE" (2 January 1773–24 May 1833). Congressman, he was the scion of a prominent Virginia family. Though he attended both Princeton and Columbia, he was too mercurial to bother with getting a degree. He stood for Congress in 1799 only because the deaths of his father and brothers had made him the head of the family and he thought it the duty of a Randolph to serve. On being elected to the House of Representatives, he mounted a virulent attack on the military policies of the **Federalist Party** in the **Quasi-War**. When **Thomas Jefferson** emerged from the **election of 1800** as president, Randolph became one of his congressional lieutenants prepared to support the **Louisiana Purchase** despite the constitutional problems it raised. But he broke with Jefferson at the beginning of the president's second term over a proposal to compensate northern investors who had been victimized in the **Yazoo lands** scandal and over Jefferson's request for a secret fund the president wanted to use to acquire **West Florida**. Thereafter, Randolph headed a small faction of "old Republicans" who called themselves the **Tertium Quids**. They joined the Federalist Party in opposing the expansion of the nation into new territories, the use of commercial restrictions against the great powers, and war with Britain. Randolph's constituents removed him from office during the **War of 1812**, but he returned to the House in 1817 and remained there until 1825 before briefly serving in the Senate. Between 1827 and 1829, he returned for one more term to the House and then served for a short time as minister to Russia. His public career ended with him opposing President **Andrew Jackson** over **nullification** in the early 1830s.

A youthful illness had left Randolph without many of the visible signs of manhood, such as a deepened voice and a beard. He made up for these differences with a biting rhetorical style and a readiness to fight anyone who slighted him. Yet when **Henry Clay** challenged him to a **duel** in 1826 over Randolph's accusation that Clay's appointment as secretary of state was part of a corrupt bargain that had made **John Quincy Adams** president, Randolph threw away his shot after Clay had fired and missed. In the latter part of Randolph's congressional career, he was as quick to identify threats to **slavery** as he was determined to defend the institution. However, he freed his slaves in his will. Throughout his career, no one knew what he would do next. This trait commanded considerable attention but failed to make him effective.

REFORM. The "age of reform" is a term that is applied to the period beginning around 1830. But most reform causes that emerged then had originated during the preceding 15 years. These reforms included **education** for **women** and individuals with special needs like the deaf and dumb, penitentiaries and asylums for criminals and the insane, **temperance**, and **abolition**. Much of this reform agenda sprang from a **perfectionist** expectation that could be traced back to the American Revolution. But it found reinforcement in the millennial beliefs of the **Second Great Awakening**. According to many Protestant revivalists, because Christ's second coming was imminent, it was incumbent on citizens of the Republic to prepare for his arrival, presumably in America, by converting the heathen and perfecting society. The reform movements also derived inspiration from a realization, enhanced by the passing of the revolutionary generation, that the past was no longer a reliable guide to the future. Finally, some new technologies helped validate the rising expectations of the reformers. Thus, the widespread use of vaccination after 1800 constituted a major medical advance in controlling **smallpox**. Technology could work in less direct ways. The development of woodstoves capable of bringing indoor temperatures up to modern levels at an acceptable cost reduced the metabolic demands on the average person and made the use of alcohol to escape the cold seem more gratuitous. This in turn justified the increased intolerance of the **temperance** movement directed at all drinking.

RELIGION. The vast majority of European immigrants to the portion of British North America that became the United States were Protestants. The only exception was Maryland, which had been established initially as a refuge for **Roman Catholics**. However, this colony soon came to be dominated by Protestants. In most places where Protestants of a particular denomination constituted the majority of the settlers, they made provision for the public support of the clergy through local taxes. However, Rhode Island and Pennsylvania rejected such a relationship between church and state, known as an establishment, on the grounds that it was inconsistent with religious liberty and purity. At the same time, colonies like New York and New Jersey, which lacked sectarian majorities, settled for allowing the dominant sect in each community to claim public support but avoided burdening all with supporting one sect.

The first Great Awakening, between 1740 and 1760, enhanced both the religious fervor of Americans of European descent and their sectarian differences. This development gradually subverted the political base of the existing establishments. In several southern colonies, most notably Virginia and the Carolinas, the Anglican establishment gradually withered before the enthusiasm of **Baptist** and then **Methodist** dissent. The religious complexity of late colonial America was further enhanced by the arrival of a few Jewish merchants in the principal ports. Finally, some of the slaves imported to the Americas from Africa were Muslims, though the vast majority were initially unfamiliar with any of the religious traditions to which Europeans had previously been exposed.

The Revolution accelerated the growth of sectarian dissent at the expense of the established sects like the Anglicans (known after the war as Episcopalians), the **Congregationalists**, and their **Presbyterian** theological cousins. In Virginia, it led to the disestablishment of the Anglican Church, which—thanks to **Thomas Jefferson**'s drafting of the state's statute on religious freedom and the religious ideas contained in his *Notes on Virginia*—gave currency to the idea that a separation between church and state was desirable. **James Madison** contributed almost as much to advancing religious freedom first by skillfully arranging for the Virginia legislature to pass Jefferson's statute six years after it had been drafted and then by writing the principle of separation of church and state into the **First Amendment** of the **Bill of Rights**.

The secular ramifications of the Revolution triggered the **Second Great Awakening**, from 1798 through 1830. As with the first Great Awakening, the increased fervor among all Protestants multiplied the number of separate sects. Among them, the **African Methodist**

Episcopal Church became the first Christian church composed exclusively of **African Americans**. The fervor associated with the Awakening released an enormous amount of energy. During the first Great Awakening, much of that energy had gone into political struggles for control of existing pulpits and the founding of sectarian colleges. The same was true of the Second Great Awakening, though there was also a major difference. Preparing for the second coming of Christ was much more at the forefront of the agenda of early 19th-century religious fervor than previously, and this led to a more widespread mobilization of **women** as missionaries, writers, teachers, and moral reformers. Religious fervor initially blurred sectarian differences, as was evident in the **Cane Ridge Camp Meeting Revival** and such institutional offshoots of the Awakening as the **American Board of Commissioners for Foreign Missions**, the **American Tract Society**, and the **American Bible Society**. As fervor cooled, however, denominational claims tended to reassert themselves. But they did not do so before the Second Great Awakening had communicated its energy to many secular reform movements like **temperance** and **antislavery**, as exemplified in **Charles Grandison Finney**'s preaching. Indeed, the anticipated millennium can be seen as a religious version of the secular idea of **perfectibility**, which became current during and after the Revolution. Having witnessed two great revolutions in America and France, Americans of the early Republic recognized that the past should no longer be looked to in defining the parameters of a religious or a secular future. *See also* ASBURY, FRANCIS; DOW, LORENZO; DWIGHT, TIMOTHY; LELAND, JOHN; TAYLOR, NATHANIEL WILLIAM; UNITARIANISM; UNIVERSALISM.

REMOVAL (OF INDIANS). The Europeans in Britain's North American colonies thought the **Indians** made wasteful use of the land. After the conclusion of the Revolutionary War, the **westward movement** of white settlers began to pressure the native occupants to move farther west. Since the majority of Indians had sided with the British during the war, many tribes, particularly in the North, moved away from their ancestral lands and resettled under British protection. **Joseph Brant** exemplified the process when he led most of the **Iroquois Confederation** to settle in modern Ontario. Some tribes had allied with the Americans, but this failed to protect their lands as the Oneida later found out when they were confronted with the stark alternatives of moving to modern Wisconsin or being absorbed into white culture.

Some southern Indians tried to defend themselves against European encroachment by adopting settled agriculture and entering into treaties with the states or the nation in which they ceded some lands to secure the remainder. The **Cherokee** went to the extreme in adopting white ways by developing a written language and framing a constitution modeled on the U.S. Constitution. But none of these strategies availed because the military potential of the Indians failed to match that of white Americans. First the states and eventually the federal government broke previous guarantees with impunity, and whatever solidarity this might have generated among the Indians dissolved before the overwhelming preponderance of the European. Removal was a fate that could only be postponed, not avoided, as the Cherokee tragically found out at the end of the 1830s when the eastern portion of their nation, who had not voluntarily moved west, were forcibly dispossessed of their lands.

REPORT OF THE COMMITTEE (1800). Eight state legislatures framed replies critical of the **Virginia Resolutions** drafted by **James Madison** protesting the constitutionality of the **Alien Law** and the **Sedition Law**. On being elected to the Virginia House of Delegates that assembled at the end of 1799, Madison was assigned the task of writing a reply vindicating the position taken by the legislature when it adopted his resolutions in 1798. Madison submitted his lengthy report on 24 December. It defended the Virginia Resolutions line by line, reiterating the argument that the acts were unconstitutional because they exceeded the limited powers the Constitution entrusted to the federal government. The report also defended the right of the states to judge when flagrant violations of the Constitution had dissolved the federal compact and argued that the Alien and Sedition Acts were incompatible with the fundamental principles of **Republicanism**. On 2 January 1800, the Virginia legislature accepted Madison's Report of the Committee and voted to publish it. Though it strikes a modern reader as stilted, the report had considerable influence on the outcome of the **election of 1800**.

REPORT ON PUBLIC CREDIT (1790). *See* ASSUMPTION; FUNDING; HAMILTON, ALEXANDER; IMPOST.

REPUBLICAN PARTY. A coalition of like-minded gentry leaders that initially began forming in 1791 because of the suspicions they entertained about **Alexander Hamilton**'s **funding** system. After 1793, the Republican gentry were distinguished from their counterparts, who formed the **Federalist Party**, by their desire to maintain good relations with France no matter what the cost with Britain. The national leaders of the Republican Party, **Thomas Jefferson** and **James Madison**, saw enhanced value in the Franco-American relationship after Europe's monarchies led by Great Britain declared war on the French republic. They thought the nation's destiny would not be well served by aligning itself with a monarchy that they regarded as teetering on the verge of bankruptcy and revolution. France's subsequent transformation into a military dictatorship alienated them from France but failed to push them closer to Britain because by then they felt the United States was strong enough to stand on its own. Their confidence derived from the security they enjoyed in the states and regions where they were dominant. Though some of their confidence stemmed from their involvement with racial **slavery**, it also derived from the assumption after the **election of 1800** that the majority of the political nation, as well as the expanding West, agreed with them.

The Republican's confidence in turn allowed them to view the relationship between the United States and the rest of the world more realistically than the Federalists did. After the **Louisiana Purchase** eliminated France from continental North America, the Republicans understood that Britain posed more of a threat to the nation's future destiny than France. They also were the first to realize that a war with one European nation need not entail military dependence on the other, as had been the case during the Revolution. The core of Republican identity remained ideological, and the Republicans responded to Federalist assaults on it by declaring the **War of 1812**. Still the Republicans adhered to republican values throughout the contest with Britain, even when doing so meant tolerating disloyal behavior from the Federalists. When the nation survived the war despite Federalist obstructionism, the Republicans emerged triumphant on the domestic scene, leaving the Federalists little choice but to dissolve during the **Era of Good Feelings**.

REPUBLICAN SOCIETIES. The first republican societies formed in 1793 in response to news that France, on becoming a republic, was being assaulted by a coalition of monarchies led by Britain. Some critics traced their emergence to the arrival of citizen **Edmund Genêt** as minister of France in April 1793. But the earliest societies sprang up independently of any influence he could have exerted. Some patriotic societies like Tammany Hall, founded in 1786, subsequently behaved in ways that made them indistinguishable from the democratic or republican societies of the 1790s. Though all were responding to overseas developments and resembled the Jacobin clubs that had assumed power in France, they drew more on the precedent established by the Sons of Liberty and committees of correspondence during the Revolution than on foreign models. Their principal function was to alert the citizenry to threats to their liberty. They were especially worried that the administration of **George Washington** might seek an accommodation with Britain at the expense of the **Franco-American alliance** of 1778, and they uniformly opposed the **Jay Treaty**. In all, more than 30 such societies, from Maine to South Carolina and as far west as Kentucky, issued declarations and resolves. Their presence complicated Washington's policy of avoiding war with both powers, as did the **Whiskey Rebellion** in western Pennsylvania that erupted during 1794. Washington held the societies responsible for the insurrection in Pennsylvania, though no society had endorsed it, and many explicitly condemned it. Washington's message to Congress in September 1794 condemning the societies as "self-created" set off a debate about their legitimacy. While the agitation over the Jay Treaty kept some societies active into 1796, most started dissolving once the public had been thoroughly aroused. A few societies were reconstituted in 1799 and 1800 to resist Federalist policies during the **Quasi-War**, and Tammany Hall played a significant role in swinging New York into the **Republican Party**'s camp in the **election of 1800**. But by then, the other democratic societies had disappeared.

REPUBLICANISM. A republic is a form of government in which an elected executive shares formal power with elected representatives of the people. Republicanism was an ideology that affirmed the superiority of this form of government. It differed from democracy—the rule of the many—in that the people acted through their elected representatives instead of directly in their own behalf. Such an arrangement allowed people to benefit from the guidance of the best men while at the same time protecting them from being oppressed by the elite. The common interest that elected representatives shared with the people would compel their faithful attendance to the public trust. If they sacrificed the common interest to personal advancement, the people retained the right periodically to reduce their representatives to the status of common citizen and place someone else in office.

RESIDENCY (OF THE CAPITAL). The permanent location of the federal city called for in the Constitution was hotly contested in the **first Congress**. In the absence of modern **communications**, proximity to the seat of power was much more important than it currently is. The issue was settled by the bargain **Alexander Hamilton** struck with Virginians **James Madison** and **Thomas Jefferson** in 1790 in which Madison and Jefferson accepted **assumption** in exchange for locating the capital permanently on the Potomac.

REVENUE ACT OF 1789. One of the first acts of the **first Congress** was to lay a uniform **impost** that the Congress of the Confederation had been seeking in vain since 1781. The Revenue Act of 1789 imposing a tax on imports from foreign countries passed on 4 July 1789, though it would take some time before money would actually flow into the government's coffers. A year later, on 4 August 1790, Congress permanently appropriated the revenue that was not required to support the operations of the government to servicing the revolutionary debt. Since President **George Washington** could be relied on to veto any measure from Congress that reversed this appropriation, it would take a two-thirds majority of both houses of Congress to do so, providing protection for the public's credit against hostility to taxation, such as that which the state of Massachusetts had experienced in Shays's Rebellion.

REVERE, PAUL (1 January 1735–10 May 1818). Silversmith and industrialist, the son of a French **immigrant**, he was born in Boston and apprenticed as a goldsmith with his father, inheriting the business in 1754. Though most remembered by history as a courier and especially for his ride on 18–19 April 1775, contemporaries knew him best as a silversmith. Nor was he content with one craft, however proficient he became at it. In the 1760s, he had branched out into copperplate engraving, and after the Revolutionary War he diversified into hardware before establishing his own foundry in 1788. Soon his previous experience as an artillery officer during the Seven Years' War and the Revolution led him to cast brass cannon as well as church bells. Then, at age 65, with the assistance of his sons, he established the first copper-rolling mill in Canton, Massachusetts. Between the foundry and the mill, Revere produced many of the metal fittings, armaments, and eventually much of the copper sheathing for the **USS *Constitution***. Revere also built the steam boilers used in some of **Robert Fulton**'s early steamboats. Thanks to the ingenuity of Americans like Revere, the United States was able to fight the **War of 1812** without depending on foreign sources for its supply of metal products.

ROMAN CATHOLICISM. *See* CATHOLICISM.

ROWSON, SUSANNA HASWELL (? February 1762–2 March 1824). Author and educator of **women**, she was born in England, the daughter of a naval officer. When her mother died, her father remarried a Massachusetts woman and brought Susanna to America shortly before the outbreak of the Revolutionary War. After being imprisoned when hostilities commenced, the family was finally exchanged and returned to Britain in 1778. Adrift in what for her was a foreign land, Susanna started writing songs and novels. Eventually, she married William Rowson, an erstwhile actor who failed to provide her with regular support. Fortunately for both of them, in 1791 she published a short novel that would be her principal claim to fame and fortune, *Charlotte: A Tale of Truth*. In 1794, the first of over 150 editions of this book appeared in the United States just after Susanna and her husband arrived in Philadelphia with a theatrical company that folded almost immediately. They then moved to Boston with no better luck. After 1797, Susanna was employed mainly in running a female academy she established in Massachusetts. Though she continued to write until the end of her life, *Charlotte* remained her principal literary success.

ROYALL, ANNE NEWPORT (11 June 1769–1 October 1854). Author and journalist, she was born in Baltimore and spent her early years on the Pennsylvania frontier. After her father died, she and her mother entered the domestic service of William Royall in western Virginia, who first educated Anne and then married her. When he died in 1812, he left her his property in a contested will that the family succeeded in overturning in 1819. They filed many charges against Royall, though the only one she would admit to was cohabiting with her husband before marriage. Royall had spent some of the interval between her husband's death and being dispossessed of his estate traveling through the southern states. She now made Washington her base and proceeded to collect materials for *Sketches of the History, Life, and Manners of the United States* (1826). This was followed by three volumes of *The Black Books* (1828–1829) and the two-volume *Mrs. Royall's Pennsylvania* (1829). Royall acquired notoriety for the acerbic sketches of prominent personalities and for her outspoken criticism of political corruption as well as of **anti-Masonry** and the evangelicals of the **Second Great Awakening**. Her sharp tongue, which many openly feared, resulted in her being prosecuted as a common scold and public nuisance in a District of Columbia federal court during 1829. Though convicted by a male jury, sympathetic fellow journalists paid her fine and posted bond for her. During the remainder of her career, she published two small **newspapers** devoted to uncovering corruption, promoting **Freemasonry**, and exposing what she considered to be the hypocrisy of the revivalists. While she defended Roman **Catholics** against Protestant prejudices, she opposed the abolition of **slavery**.

RULE OF 1756. In 1756, the British Privy Council decided that a commerce forbidden to neutral nations during peacetime should not be open to them during wartime. Known as the Rule of 1756, it became a focus of the dispute between the United States and Great Britain over the nation's neutral rights between 1805 and 1812.

RUSH-BAGOT AGREEMENT. *See* CONVENTION OF 1817.

RUSH, BENJAMIN (4 January 1746–19 April 1813). Doctor and reformer, he was born in Pennsylvania near Philadelphia and educated at Princeton, graduating in 1760 at the age of 14. Subsequently, Rush studied medicine in Edinburgh, Scotland, before touring Britain and France to observe the leading practitioners of the age. Returning to America in 1769, he opened his own practice in Philadelphia and before long had attracted enough attention to be appointed professor at the College of Philadelphia. As a supporter of American independence, he helped write Pennsylvania's first constitution and represented the state in the second Continental Congress. During 1777–1778, he acted as surgeon general in the Continental army until he incurred the enmity of General **George Washington**. Retiring from the army, he resumed his medical practice and academic career. He developed a unitary theory of disease that has since been discredited. At the end of the 1780s, he supported the new federal Constitution in Pennsylvania's ratifying convention. During the **yellow fever** epidemic of 1793, he utilized heroic remedies in accordance with his medical theory. Though he claimed impressive results, his techniques were controversial. He served as treasurer of the U.S. Mint between 1797 and 1813. Rush published the first American work on psychiatry, opposed **slavery** and capital punishment, and was a leading advocate of free public **education** for **women** as well as men. He was also one of the first to caution against the consequences of excessive drinking. He died of a fever that he insisted on treating in the manner he had developed during the yellow fever epidemic of 1793. *See also* ALLEN, RICHARD; TEMPERANCE MOVEMENT.

RUSH, RICHARD (29 August 1780–30 July 1859). Diplomat, he was born in Philadelphia, the son of **Benjamin Rush**. After attending Princeton and graduating in 1797, he studied law and was admitted to the bar. Rush first attracted public attention in a speech he made condemning the British attack on the **USS *Chesapeake***. In November 1811, he started working for **Albert Gallatin** in the Treasury Department. A Fourth of July Oration defending the **War of 1812** confirmed his loyalty to the **Republican Party**. In 1814, President **James Madison** offered Rush his choice between appointment as attorney general or secretary of the treasury. He preferred the less challenging former post but was present with Madison on the field of the **Battle of Bladensburg**. In 1817, President **James Monroe** appointed Rush acting secretary of state until **John Quincy Adams** could return from

Europe. In that capacity, he signed the **Rush-Bagot Agreement** of 1817. After Adams became secretary of state, Rush was dispatched to Britain as the American minister.

With Gallatin's assistance, he negotiated the **Anglo-American Convention of 1818** with Great Britain, which extended the **Convention of 1815** for 10 more years, specified the boundary between the United States and Canada west of the Great Lakes as running along the 49th parallel to the continental divide, and provided for the joint occupation of the Oregon Territory west of the mountains. In 1823, the British foreign secretary approached Rush about issuing a joint declaration against France, which had just restored a deposed Spanish monarch to his throne, to refrain from reconquering any of the independent republics that had emerged from the **Latin American revolutions**. Rush demanded that Britain first recognize at least one of the new republics, which it proved politically impossible for the British government to do. This set the stage for the **Monroe Doctrine** later that year.

In 1825, Rush returned to the United States to serve as secretary of the treasury in the administration of John Quincy Adams. He was Adams's unsuccessful running mate in the **election of 1828** but declined the offer to be the presidential nominee of the **anti-Masonic** Party in 1832. Though he favored **Henry Clay** in the early 1830s, he eventually came to support **Andrew Jackson**'s **Democratic Party**. In 1847, he was appointed ambassador to France just before the Revolution of 1848. Rush recognized France's republican revolutionary regime without authorization, though that did not suffice to save it from a coup by Louis Napoleon. In his last years, Rush opposed the **antislavery** agitation because he felt it threatened the Union.

– S –

SACKETT'S HARBOR, BATTLE OF. Sackett's Harbor at the eastern end of Lake Ontario held the key to establishing American control of the lake. In the spring of 1813, Secretary of War **John Armstrong** had wanted to press the offensive against nearby Kingston in Ontario, preparatory to moving against Montreal. But Major General **Henry Dearborn** and Captain Isaac Chauncey chose instead to invade the Niagara region. This left Sackett's Harbor vulnerable to British attack. On 27 May 1813, a British fleet arrived off the port and disembarked 800 men for an assault. Brigadier General **Jacob Brown** had 500 **militia** posted at the disembarkation point who were quickly routed. But he stopped the British as they entered the town with 400 regular army troops and some 250 volunteers, even though the naval lieutenant in charge of the shipyard mistakenly ordered that it be set on fire. The British eventually withdrew after one in three of their attacking force became casualties. The defense of Sackett's Harbor helped earn Jacob Brown, heretofore a militia officer, a brigadier's commission in the regular army. *See also* WAR OF 1812 (LAND OPERATIONS).

ST. CLOUD, DECREE OF. In early May 1812, Ambassador **Joel Barlow** was handed a copy of a decree allegedly issued by **Napoleon** at St. Cloud on 28 April 1811. It declared that the **Berlin Decree** and the **Milan Decree** no longer applied to American vessels and was a belated response to Barlow's repeated requests for proof that France's decrees affecting American commerce had been repealed, as promised in the **Cadore Letter**. The Decree of St. Cloud raised more questions than it answered since it had failed to halt France's continued seizure of American ships. The suspicious circumstances surrounding the revocation of the French decrees fueled the opposition of the **Federalist Party** to the **War of 1812** and provided **Daniel Webster** with the opening he exploited in the summer of 1813 when he proposed a resolution in the U.S. House of Representatives calling on President **James Madison** to submit to Congress all the evidence in his possession pertaining to the alleged revocation.

STE. DOMINGUE. *See* HAITIAN REVOLUTION.

SANTEE CANAL. The nation's first major canal to go into operation was constructed in South Carolina between 1793 and 1800 by 700 laborers, mostly slaves, under the direction of the Swedish-born engineer Christian Senf. The Santee canal was 22 miles long, had 10 locks, and joined the Santee and Cooper Rivers. Though it cost $650,000 to build, it vastly simplified the movement of bulk freight from the interior to Charleston and facilitated the movement of goods into the interior. During 1817 and again in 1819, droughts forced a temporary suspension of traffic. But for most of the remaining years until the railroad between Charleston and Columbia took its traffic away in the 1840s, it contributed to the **economic development** of this region.

SCOTT, WINFIELD (13 June 1786–29 May 1866). Soldier, he was born in Virginia. He studied briefly at William & Mary College before apprenticing to a lawyer and being admitted to the bar. The **USS *Chesapeake*** incident in 1807 led him to join a volunteer cavalry unit in 1808 and to the personal discovery that he had a military calling. Commissioned by President **Thomas Jefferson** a captain in the U.S. Army, he was assigned to **New Orleans**. There he quarreled with General **James Wilkinson** and was disciplined with a yearlong suspension from the service. Despite that reverse, Scott had been promoted to lieutenant colonel by the beginning of the **War of 1812**. Though Scott was taken captive at Queenstown, Ontario, after only eight days in the Lake Erie theater, a preempt exchange allowed him to lead the American advance on Fort George on 27 May 1813. Promoted to brigadier under General **Jacob Brown**'s command, he undertook to train the officers in the northern army to professional standards. His efforts paid off the next year at the **Battle of Chippewa Plain** and the **Battle of Lundy's Lane**, where American regulars showed they could stand up to British regulars and even defeat them.

Scott stayed in the army after the War of 1812 despite what looked like diminished career opportunities and his penchant for quarreling with his superiors. Service in the Black Hawk War and in defusing tensions along the Canadian border between the U.S. and British forces in Canada during the 1830s led to his being considered by the **Whig Party** as a possible presidential nominee in 1840, though they chose **William Henry Harrison** instead. Scott's subsequent fame derived from his role in the Mexican War. As the senior officer in the U.S. Army, he planned and executed the assault on Vera Cruz and, when this failed to produce the desired peace, boldly struck at Mexico City. In 1852, he was the unsuccessful Whig candidate for the presidency. Though a Virginian by birth, he remained loyal to the Union in the secession crisis of 1860–1861 but yielded to the younger generation when hostilities commenced.

SECESSION. A term referring to states withdrawing from the United States to establish an independent country. Though no state or states seceded from the Union until Abraham Lincoln was elected president in 1860, secession was repeatedly threatened by political leaders in the national government who confronted hostile political majorities. The threat proved effective because it put the majority on notice that the minority was prepared to destroy the Republican experiment if it did not get its way. Though secession became the trump card of the beleaguered slaveholding aristocracy of the South, in the first years of the Republic northerners were much more likely to threaten secession than southerners. During the 1790s, these threats were made in private to congressional colleagues, but by the beginning of the 19th century it was an open secret, publicized by the **Henry Papers**, that the **Federalist Party** leadership of New England was contemplating secession. **Timothy Pickering** had tried to promote a secessionist movement in 1803–1804 on the assumption that the remaining states in the Union would be so anxious to recover the seceding states that they would accept the secessionists' terms. Many suspected that the **Hartford Convention** at the end of 1814, which implicitly threatened a separate peace with Britain, was the first step in the direction of secession. South Carolina started talking about secession only in the late 1820s, ostensibly over the **tariff** but actually in response to growing **antislavery** pressure from the North. Secession was more powerful as a threat than as a political option because any state that seceded risked penalizing itself as much if not more than the states it left behind. This explains why it took another 30 years before anyone actually acted on the threat.

SECOND BANK OF THE UNITED STATES. It was chartered in 1816 after the financial difficulties experienced during the **War of 1812** convinced Congress of the utility of a national bank. Under the initial leadership of William Jones, it helped fuel a postwar economic boom by lavishly extending credit. When it became clear that retrenchment was necessary, the Bank acted in a way that helped precipitate the **Panic of 1819**. Langdon Cheves reversed the course Jones had pursued by harshly contracting credit, in the process adding to the Bank's enemies. This paved the way for **Nicholas Biddle** to assume leadership of the Bank in 1822. Biddle managed the Bank's operations wisely, laying the foundations for sustained growth through the rest of the decade by responding countercyclically with expansions and contractions in the availability of credit. However, local interests continued to view the Bank's activities with hostility, particularly the power it exercised through its branches of presenting the bills of state banks for specie redemption. This, together with **Andrew Jackson**'s known hostility to all banks, made recharter in 1836 seem politically problematic.

Biddle allowed a group of congressmen led by **Henry Clay**, who supported the Bank, to pass a recharter measure in 1832. They assumed Jackson would accept their initiative rather than risk the consequences of a veto, but Jackson vetoed the recharter measure. The Whigs then circulated Jackson's veto message, hoping that it would gain them popular support. But Jackson was reelected anyway and revenged himself on the Bank by removing government deposits and placing them in the state banks that were friendly to him. That set in motion an expansion of credit that ultimately ended in the Panic of 1837 and was followed by depression that lasted for four years. Though the debacle seemed to demonstrate the need for a central bank, the diffuseness of the American economy and political system precluded any such measure until the early 20th century. *See also* BANKING.

SECOND GREAT AWAKENING. A widespread eruption of Christian piety that began around the turn of the 19th century and persisted into the 1830s. It affected all the Protestant sects in one way or another, dramatically expanding the number of Americans actively affiliated with a religious community. But the newer sects like the **Baptists**, **Methodists**, and **Universalists** fared better than the older, established ones like the **Congregationalists**, the Episcopalians, and the **Presbyterians** despite the heroic efforts of religious leaders like **Timothy Dwight** and **Lyman Beecher** to harness the Awakening's energies in the service of orthodoxy. Though the Second Great Awakening failed to generate as many new sects as had the first Great Awakening (1735–1750), the roots of one uniquely American religious movement, Mormonism, can be traced directly to it.

The Second Great Awakening also left a wider imprint on the culture of the early Republic than the first Great Awakening had on late colonial culture. The Second Great Awakening's evangelism merged with the revolutionary quest for **perfectibility** to mobilize religious energies for larger, social purposes. The resulting synergy led to manifestations of piety in the participatory context of the camp meeting, exemplified by the **Cane Ridge Revival** in Kentucky, and of a wide array of new, religious organizations. These included missionary societies (both foreign, under the **American Board of Commissioners for Foreign Missions**, and domestic), Bible societies like the **American Bible Society**, and maternal societies in which **women** were urged to participate. The deployment of all this energy was sustained by many new religious **magazines**. Before long, efforts to mobilize religious commitment spilled over into the secular realm. Thus, concern for observance of the Sabbath led to a struggle over whether the mails should be delivered on Sundays. Figures like **Charles G. Finney** focused religious attention on social ills like **alcoholism** and **slavery**. Eventually, the Awakening contributed to efforts to **reform** a wide range of social evils, from treatment of the mentally ill and the redemption of criminals to the eradication of illiteracy. Like the first Great Awakening, it spawned many new sectarian colleges, most of which had to reach beyond the narrow confines of the founding sect to survive. Finally, it created a congenial environment for the initiation, if not perpetuation, of experimental communities like Robert Owen's at **New Harmony**.

SEDGWICK, CATHERINE MARIA (28 December 1789–31 July 1867). Novelist, she was born in Stockbridge, Massachusetts, the daughter of Theodore Sedgwick, a prominent Federalist politician. Though Catherine Sedgwick had little formal schooling, she was an avid reader and in 1822 produced her first novel, *A New England Tale*, which criticized the rigidities of orthodox **Congregationalism**. Two other novels quickly followed, *Redwood* (1824) and *Hope Leslie* (1827). The latter's success in sketching the character of a heroine established her literary reputation in the wider English-speaking world. She remained active as a writer for the remainder of her life in addition to supporting causes like **antislavery**, the rights of **women**, and reform in **education** and the prisons. Though she never married, her novels usually ended with the heroine's marriage. She enjoyed the friendship of some of the leading authors of the day, including **William Cullen**

Bryant and **Washington Irving**. As an imaginative author, she did as much as **James Fenimore Cooper** to create American characters who were defined by their distinctively American settings.

SEDITION LAW (1798). The statute made it a federal crime to "unlawfully combine or conspire . . . to oppose any measure . . . of the government of the United States . . . or to impede the operation of any law of the United States" through "insurrection, riot, unlawful assembly, or combination" as well as "to print, utter or publish . . . any false, scandalous and malicious writing . . . against the government of the United States." The measure was sponsored by the **Federalist Party** in the fifth Congress after the disclosure of the **XYZ Dispatches** had given it control of the national legislature. Among other things, the law was designed to provide insurance against the possibility that the **Quasi-War** would not ripen into full-scale war with France. The Federalist leadership looked to such a war to purge the American public of its affection for France. But if that failed, the administration would still be able to control the opposition press through the federal courts. Members of the **Republican Party** objected that the law violated the **First Amendment**. Federalists replied that a provision allowing the accused to plead the truth of a statement and entrusting to a jury the authority to pass on that claim expanded rather than abridged the freedom of the press. Under the common law of seditious libel, the jury could decide only the fact of publication, and truth was not admitted as a defense.

The partisan administration of the Sedition Law by Secretary of State **Timothy Pickering** led to the prosecution of most of the leading Republican **newspapers** prior to the **election of 1800**. The pattern of prosecutions convinced many that empowering juries to pass on the truth of a political opinion provided little security for the freedom of the press. **James Madison**, in his **Report of the Committee**, also argued that vesting such a power in the federal government was incompatible with **Republicanism**. Federalist efforts to extend the life of the Sedition Act beyond March 1801 failed in the sixth Congress. But the Republican critique of the "truth" test led many Federalists to conclude that the Republican press had lied the Federalists out of power. This in turn authorized the licentiousness of the Federalist press during the remainder of the **First Party System**.

SEMINOLE WAR (FIRST) (1817–1818). Refugees from the Upper **Creeks**, who joined their Seminole cousins in **East Florida** at the end of the **Creek War** (1811–1814), inflamed **Indian** resentment over the failure of the United States to return their lands taken in the course of the **War of 1812**, in accordance with the terms of the **Treaty of Ghent**. Hostilities were initiated when U.S. authorities arrested the Seminole chief Neamathla for sheltering runaway African **slaves** at the end of 1817. **Andrew Jackson** then raised a force of 4,000—half of whom were Creek warriors who had allied with the whites during the Creek War—to attack the Seminoles. During the winter and spring of 1818, Jackson's operations in northern Florida scattered the Seminoles, ushering in a prolonged period of deprivation and demoralization. After crushing Indian resistance, Jackson proceeded without authorization from Washington to occupy the Spanish settlements of St. Marks and Pensacola. He also seized and executed two British subjects whom he accused of collaborating with the Seminoles. Jackson's excesses played into the hands of Secretary of State **John Quincy Adams**, who was trying to get Spain to cede Florida to the United States without disrupting the gradual rapprochement taking place in Anglo-American relations. Jackson's behavior led to a debate in President **James Monroe**'s cabinet about whether Jackson should be censured for his unauthorized actions. When the public later learned of the debate, it affected the factions jockeying for the presidential succession during the 1820s. Jackson's military victory over the Seminoles quieted the Indians until 1835, when white encroachments on their Florida lands led to a second Seminole War.

SEMINOLES. Seminole derives from the Spanish word *cimarron*, which means "runaway." During the 18th century, the Seminole **Indians** had run away from several southeastern tribes, but particularly from the **Creek**. They had also welcomed runaway African slaves from southern frontier plantations. Southern planters regarded them as a threat because they provided Africans with an alternative to **slavery**. The Seminoles responded to white pressure by retreating farther into Florida.

SEQUOYAH (1770?–August 1843). Inventor of the **Cherokee** syllabary, he was born in eastern Tennessee. Though his mother was **Indian**, his father may have been either a European or a half-breed. In any case, he was known among whites as George Guess or Gist. Because of an early lameness, he became a silversmith rather than a warrior, though there are indications that he played some role as an ally of the Americans in the **Creek War** (1813–1814). Sequoyah had no formal schooling and seems not to have known English. But his perception of the advantages the European reaped from being able to communicate in writing inspired him to develop a system of 86 symbols that embraced all the distinct syllables of the Cherokee language. The syllabary was the work of many years, probably begun in 1809 and not completed until 1821. In the interval, Sequoyah had joined the western Cherokee, who, in response to controversial land cessions, had moved to modern Arkansas. Once the syllabary was completed, Sequoyah moved back to the Southeast, where his invention contributed to Cherokee efforts to resist white pressure. It did so by enabling any Cherokee who so wished to become literate in a matter of days. In 1824, the Cherokee national council awarded Sequoyah a silver medal for his invention. In 1828, the first issue of the *Cherokee Phoenix*, a **newspaper** that published in English and the syllabary, appeared. Though Sequoyah's invention helped the Cherokee adopt a written constitution resembling the U.S. Constitution, Sequoyah distanced himself from attempts by the eastern Cherokee to resist **removal** from their tribal lands by agreeing to exchange Arkansas lands for Oklahoma lands. When the eastern Cherokee finally were forced to join the western Cherokee in the late 1830s, Sequoyah helped mediate the antagonism between the two groups and avert a civil war within the nation. It is thought that Sequoyah died looking for lost Cherokee in what is now Mexico.

SIGOURNEY, LYDIA (1 September 1791–10 June 1865). Author, she was born Lydia Huntley in Norwich, Connecticut. With minimal formal schooling, she and another woman established Norwich's first female academy in 1811. When her partner's early death forced the dissolution of this school in 1816, Huntley moved to Hartford and established another female academy in the home of her friend and patron, Daniel Wadsworth. Huntley also experimented with writing, publishing *Moral Pieces in Prose and Verse* (1816). In 1819, she married Charles Sigourney, who disapproved of her literary ambitions. This did not stop her from publishing *Traits of the Aborigines* (1822) anonymously and *Sketch of Connecticut Forty Years Since* (1824). After her husband's business collapsed, her writing became the principal economic resource of the family. In 1827, her *Selected Poems* became one of the first books of female verse to be published in the early republican period. She continued to produce a steady stream of miscellaneous literature for the next 30 years. Simultaneously, she supported a variety of **reforms**, including **Thomas Gallaudet**'s school for the deaf, **temperance**, and women's **education**. But she never seriously questioned the notion that men and **women** should stay within their separate spheres, though many of the causes she endorsed ultimately would take women beyond their homes.

SILLIMAN, BENJAMIN (8 August 1779–24 November 1864). Scientist and educator, he was born in Fairfield, Connecticut, and graduated from Yale College in 1796 at the age of 17. **Timothy Dwight** persuaded him to study chemistry in order to instruct Yale students in this developing science. After attending lectures at the University of Pennsylvania, Silliman toured Britain and France to buy laboratory equipment for instructional purposes. On returning to the United States in 1806, he offered courses in both geology and chemistry. Though he conducted some original experiments, Silliman's great talent was as a communicator rather than a developer of knowledge. His public lectures on chemistry were widely attended, and in 1818 he established the *American Journal of Science (and Arts)*, which he edited unaided for 20 years. He also wrote texts on chemistry and geology that were widely used and trained many of the nation's next generation of academic scientists.

SLATER, SAMUEL (9 June 1768–20 April 1835). Industrial innovator, he was born the son of a farmer and timber merchant in Derbyshire, England, at a time when the world's first water-powered textile mills were being constructed nearby. After an apprenticeship with the former partner of the British inventor Richard Arkwright, Slater immigrated to **New York City** in 1789. In April 1790, Slater contracted with the firm Almy and Brown, in which **Moses Brown** acted as a silent partner, to construct a water-powered spinning mill at Pawtucket, Rhode Island. The mill went into production on 20 December 1790 and was sufficiently successful to inspire the construction of an additional mill in 1793. By this time, Slater had married. With his in-laws as partners, he formed Samuel Slater & Co. and built a third mill in Rehoboth in 1798 and fourth in 1801 on the Blackstone River, both in Massachusetts. Though important primarily for transferring technology from Britain to America, Slater also pioneered new management techniques by employing parents as well as their children in his mills. His example was widely followed throughout southern New England, which, during the period between the **Embargo of 1807–1808** and the end of the **War of 1812**, saw the construction of many similar enterprises. Toward the end of his life, Slater also constructed one of the first steam-powered cotton mills in Providence, Rhode Island. At his death, he owned a total of 13 textile mills. *See also* INDUSTRY.

SLAVE TRADE. The Constitution barred Congress from prohibiting the importation of slaves until 1808, and the states ratifying the document bound themselves not to amend this provision before then. But the seventh Congress passed a law that was to go into effect on 1 January 1808 making subsequent importations illegal. Southern slaveholders supported the legislation because domestic fertility, combined with a depression in tobacco culture, meant there was no shortage of slaves. Over the longer term, the prohibition would serve to inflate the domestic prices of slaves. Southern interests eventually accepted U.S. cooperation with Great Britain in policing the African coast to suppress slave traders. However, these measures never led to a complete abandonment by Americans of involvement in the foreign slave trade. *See also* SLAVERY.

SLAVERY/SLAVES. According to the first census in 1790, Africans accounted for roughly 20 percent of the nation's population. Despite widespread public and private manumissions during the Revolution and shortly thereafter, the vast majority remained enslaved. Pennsylvania began gradually abolishing slavery in 1780, taking the lead in what has become known as the **First Emancipation,** partially to win the **Quakers** over to the Revolution. Quakers were also behind the first **antislavery** petition submitted to Congress in 1790. After New Jersey adopted a policy of gradual emancipation in 1804, the nation north of the **Mason-Dixon Line**, including the northern tier of western territories covered by the Northwest Ordinance of 1787, could look forward one day to being completely free. The South, which contained nine-tenths of the African population, retained slavery despite the periodic threat that insurrections like **Gabriel's Rebellion** (1800) and **Vesey's Rebellion** (1822) posed to the white population after the **Haitian Revolution**. Some states south of the Mason-Dixon Line considered gradual emancipation, and some politicians from slaveholding states like **Henry Clay** supported the **American Colonization Society**, hoping that African colonization would provide an eventual solution to the problem. But no southern state had succeeded in adopting a program of gradual emancipation before the Civil War. Congress's prohibition on the importation of slaves from abroad ironically strengthened the South's commitment to slavery by creating a domestic market for surplus slaves no longer needed in the less productive, northern areas of the region. Proposals in the 1820s to devote the proceeds reaped from selling the **public domain** to a compensated emancipation of all slaves and their transportation either to Africa or the American West were resisted by the slaveholding oligarchy.

The emerging geographic division between a free North without slaves and a slave South reinforced the sectional division between the **Federalist Party** and the **Republican Party** that emerged in the **First Party System**. Initially, it had seemed unlikely that the free states would ever match the political power of the slave states because of the territorial advantage the latter possessed in their access to the West and because of the political advantage the **three-fifths clause** of the Constitution conferred on them. But when Missouri applied for admission to the Union, the sanction the House gave to the **Tallmadge Amendment** calling for gradual emancipation in Missouri signaled that the free states were developing more dynamically than the slave South. The **Missouri Compromise of 1820** avoided a clash between proslavery and antislavery forces by pairing the admission of Missouri as a slave state with Maine as a free state, thus preserving formal parity between them in the Senate. But by prohibiting the introduction of slavery in what remained of the **Louisiana Territory** north of 36° 30', it also favored the free states in the longer term. This had the effect, along with the growth of worldwide sentiment against slavery, of putting the South politically on the defensive. South Carolina took the lead in defending slavery with such measures as its **Negro Seamen's Act**. The state's subsequent attempts to nullify the **Tariff of Abominations** (1828) and the **tariff** of 1832 also had the defense of slavery as their object as much as the equalization of tax burdens. Efforts to defend the institution of slavery by expanding its geographical and political base eventually led to the Civil War after continuing efforts in the **Second Party System** to suppress the issue finally collapsed in the 1850s. *See also* ABOLITION/ABOLITIONISTS; CALHOUN, JOHN; SLAVE TRADE; SOUTH CAROLINA EXPOSITION AND PROTEST.

SMALLPOX. The disease was common enough in Europe to have brought host and parasite into endemic equilibrium. But by the time of the Revolution in North America, a century and a half of relative isolation had made much of the population of the British colonies more vulnerable to the disease than Europeans were. The Creole population still was not as vulnerable as were the American **Indians**, who had evolved over the centuries without acquiring any genetic immunities to smallpox. In the 1720s, the practice of inoculation began to be introduced after medical authorities recognized that taking the disease in a controlled manner diminished mortality. But inoculation remained controversial because, during the four weeks over which the infection ran its course, those being inoculated could transmit the infection to anyone coming in contact with them. Smallpox particularly affected armies, and during the Revolutionary War, General **George Washington** had to have the Continental army inoculated. But any civilian in a city that had been occupied by the British was at far greater risk than those living in the country.

In 1798, an Englishman, Edward Jenner, discovered that cowpox, which scarcely affects humans, could be used to immunize people against smallpox without the risks and complications associated with inoculation. Because the process was as simple as it was safe, vaccination spread rapidly through the English-speaking world after 1800, dramatically reducing the mortality from smallpox. Benjamin Waterhouse is credited with introducing American physicians to the technique. City physicians were more likely to use vaccination than country doctors because the disease affected mainly urban populations. Nonetheless, Jenner's innovation led to a dramatic improvement in public health.

SMITH, VENTURE (1729?–19 September 1805). Black entrepreneur, he was born to a royal family in Guinea and captured at an early age by a band of African **slave** raiders armed by the Europeans. Despite being assimilated into this band, Venture was sold to the mate of a Rhode Island slaver who gave him his name. This slave ship carried Venture first to Barbados, where most of its cargo was sold, and then to Rhode Island, where he arrived sometime around 1737 at age eight. He remained a slave, serving various masters, until he managed to buy his freedom in 1765 at age 36. As an industrious freedman of unusual physical strength, he then purchased the wife he had married at age 22 and their four children. Eventually, he moved to East Haddam, Connecticut, where he purchased 100 acres of land, on which he built three houses. Smith never learned to read or write and complained that his ignorance of arithmetic resulted in his being repeatedly cheated by both black and white creditors. But toward the end of his life, he told his story to an unidentified white who wrote it up as the autobiographical account of a self-made man. It was first published as Venture's *Narrative* in 1798 and has been republished several times since.

SOUTH CAROLINA EXPOSITION AND PROTEST (1828). Hastily drafted by **John C. Calhoun** in 1828, after he had been elected to another four-year term as vice president, to make accommodations to the opposition of South Carolina to the **Tariff of Abominations**, the Exposition provided a theoretical rationale for the **nullification** of federal laws. Calhoun located ultimate sovereignty in the people who had acted through their respective states to create a federal government inferior to them. If the people of an individual state felt the compact between the states had been violated by a congressional law, they had the right to meet in convention to nullify it. This did not compromise the people's sovereignty in the other states because they could still sponsor a constitutional amendment that, once it had been accepted by three-fourths of the states, would be binding on the nullifying state. Calhoun's complex formulation was designed to preserve his nationalist credentials and at the same time defend the institution of **slavery** against growing **abolitionist** sentiment in the North.

SPANISH INSURRECTION. Napoleon's invasion of the Iberian Peninsula in late 1807 forced the abdication of Ferdinand, the Spanish monarch early in 1808. He was replaced by Joseph Bonaparte, igniting widespread resistance to the French aggression. Britain quickly took advantage of the turmoil by sending an expeditionary force to the Iberian Peninsula. For the next six years, Spain and Portugal were torn by a civil war in which Britain played a major role. As long as its forces needed to be provisioned, Britain encouraged American merchants to supply the Iberian market by exempting their vessels from the general blockade it was mounting against much of the rest of Europe. Britain's policy contributed to the subversion of the **Embargo of 1807–1809** instituted by the administration of **Thomas Jefferson** and ensured that a thriving trade between New England and southwestern Europe would continue under British licenses throughout most of the **War of 1812**.

STEVENS, JOHN (1749–6 March 1838). Visionary inventor, he was born in **New York City** and educated at Columbia (then Kings College), graduating in the class of 1768. His family then moved to New Jersey, where he served as treasurer for most of the Revolutionary War following a brief stint in the Continental army as a captain. After the war, Stevens became fascinated by John Fitch's 1787 experiments with steam propulsion on the Delaware River. Thereafter, Stevens devoted his energies to perfecting steam-powered engines. In 1790, he helped push the first patent law through the U.S. Congress. During the 1790s, Stevens entered into a partnership with Nicholas Roosevelt and **Robert R. Livingston** to introduce steam navigation on the Hudson River. When Livingston left for France in 1801, Stevens turned briefly to designing a public water system for New York City to be powered by steam pumps. He was the first to conceive of the propeller and was in the process of developing a steamboat that used a propeller to navigate the Hudson when the *Clermont*, a side-wheeler promoted by Livingston now in association with **Robert Fulton**, beat him to it in August 1807. Stevens felt betrayed by Livingston, but the vessel he and Roosevelt built, the *Phoenix*, was soon navigating the Delaware River.

Stevens next turned to experimenting with what would become the railroad, conceptualizing all its essential components during the 1810s. Building such a road was another matter, and though New Jersey issued him a charter that was supplemented by one from Pennsylvania in 1825, investors were reluctant to venture the capital required after the opening of the **Erie Canal**. Stevens had to settle for building a small prototype on his Hoboken property. Before he died, he also conceptualized armor for naval vessels, bridges and tunnels crossing the Hudson, and an elevated railroad for the city.

STONY CREEK, BATTLE OF (1813). Two American brigades under the command of Brigadiers John Chandler and William H. Winder pursued a small British force that was retreating along the shore of Lake Ontario in the Niagara region. On 5 June 1813, the American force reached Stony Creek and divided into separate encampments. An alert British officer reconnoitering the American camps saw an opportunity in the disposition of the Americans. The British managed to surprise the American brigades early on the morning of 6 June and to take both brigadiers prisoner. However, the numerical superiority of the Americans eventually enabled them to drive off the attackers. Though the British suffered greater losses than the Americans, the leaderless American brigades soon retreated. Stony Creek was the farthest penetration of American forces in the Niagara region of Canada during the **War of 1812**.

STORY, JOSEPH (18 September 1779–10 September 1845). Prominent jurist, he was born in Marblehead, Massachusetts, and educated at Harvard, graduating in 1798. He was admitted to the Massachusetts bar in 1801. With the patronage of the prominent Crowninshield family, Story was elected first to the Massachusetts legislature and then to the 10th Congress in 1808 to complete the term of Jacob Crowninshield, who had recently died. While there, he incurred the wrath of President **Thomas Jefferson**, allegedly for urging repeal of the **Embargo of 1807–1809**, though Story's more significant indiscretion was to inadvertently reveal how divided the **Republican Party** was over the prospect of a war with Britain. In 1810, his pleas on behalf of New England investors, who had been defrauded in the **Yazoo lands** scandal, laid the basis for **John Marshall**'s decision in ***Fletcher v. Peck*** upholding their rights.

President **James Madison** appointed Story to the **Supreme Court** in 1811. Taking his seat early in 1812, Story quickly gravitated toward Marshall's expansive definition of federal powers, even to the point of trying to get the Court to subscribe to the notion that there was a federal common law of crimes. Though the Court rejected Story's recommendation that the federal courts invoke admiralty common law in *United States v. Coolidge* (1813), Story was allowed to speak for the Court in affirming its jurisdiction over the state courts in ***Martin v. Hunter's Lesee*** (1816). His opinion arguing the supremacy of the Constitution on the grounds that it was an act of the people rather than of the states paved the way for some of Marshall's subsequent nationalist decisions, particularly ***McCulloch v. Maryland*** (1819).

In addition to his expansive ideas about the federal judiciary, Story exercised a profound influence over the development of American law by drafting much of the federal criminal code adopted in 1825, through his legal writings, and, after 1828, as Dane Professor of Law at Harvard. Under Story's tutelage, the Harvard Law School became the best in the country. Its graduates, who had been deeply influenced by Story, would shape American law and institutions in the Civil War era.

STRICKLAND, WILLIAM (1788–6 April 1854). Architect and engineer, he was born in Philadelphia, the son of a humble carpenter, but apprenticed to **Benjamin Latrobe**. This connection later helped him get his first commission to build a Masonic hall in Philadelphia. Though the structure commanded attention, Strickland had to support himself as an engraver, a painter, and an engineer constructing fortifications until he was commissioned to design the headquarters of the **Second Bank of the United States** in 1818. This structure was not completed until 1824, but it is often credited with being the single most important influence in launching the Greek Revival movement in American **architecture**. Strickland continued a parallel career as a civil engineer, surveying a route for the Chesapeake–Delaware Canal between 1821 and 1823. In 1826, he published *Report on Canals, Railways, Roads, and Other Subjects* after an extensive tour of Europe, which proved influential in winning public support for the innovative technologies that drove the **transportation revolution**. His last major project involved an ambitious Greek Revival design for the Tennessee state capitol in Nashville.

STRONG, CALEB (9 January 1746–7 November 1819). Politician, he was born in Northampton, Massachusetts. After graduating from

Harvard in 1764, he studied law with Joseph Hawley, the leading revolutionary of western Massachusetts. Like his mentor, Strong became active in the revolutionary politics of the state. He was a member of the committee that wrote the final draft of the Massachusetts constitution of 1780. In 1787, he was a member of the Massachusetts delegation to the Philadelphia Convention and played an important role in the Massachusetts Ratifying Convention by explaining to the delegates the reason behind some features of the new federal Constitution. Between 1789 and 1796, the Massachusetts legislature sent him to the U.S Senate, where he supported Secretary of the Treasury **Alexander Hamilton**'s **funding** program and President **George Washington**'s foreign policy. Returning to Massachusetts in 1797, he was elected governor of the state between 1800 and 1807 until he lost to **James Sullivan**. Strong was elected governor of Massachusetts again between 1812 and 1815. During the **War of 1812**, he was instrumental in denying the United States the services of most of the Massachusetts **militia**. Though he was not publicly implicated in organizing the **Hartford Convention**, before the convention met he dispatched an agent to sound out the governor of Nova Scotia about whether Britain would lend military support to **secession** by the New England states.

STUART, GILBERT (3 December 1755–9 July 1828). Portrait painter, he was born in Rhode Island and attracted the attention of a visiting Scottish painter who took him on as an assistant. Stuart had acquired enough skill at portraiture before his teacher's death to support himself. In 1776, the Revolution led him to move to London, where he failed to prosper. Desperate, he appealed to the American painter **Benjamin West**, who first hired him as an assistant and then took him on as a pupil. While Stuart was an attentive apprentice, he declined to follow West in branching out from portraiture. Instead, he established his reputation in London with his first commission, *The Skater* (1782), which attracted a great deal of attention because of its unconventional pose. Thereafter, commissions came tumbling in, and it looked as though he was poised to follow in the footsteps of Sir Joshua Reynolds and Thomas Gainsborough, the great portrait artists of the previous generation. However, he drank heavily, spent lavishly—he may have been bipolar—and in 1787 was forced to flee to

Ireland to escape his creditors. There he painted the Anglo-Irish aristocracy until 1793, when his debts again forced him to flee, this time back to America.

New York City's leading denizens flocked to have him paint their portraits, and Stuart was happy to oblige. At the end of 1794, he moved to Philadelphia, then the seat of the national government, to paint President **George Washington**'s portrait. Stuart did five different portraits of Washington, apparently not fully satisfied with any of them. Stuart's specialty was capturing the inner essence of his subject's personality, and he never entirely penetrated Washington's reserve. Nonetheless, his half view of Washington done in 1796 is the image of the first president Americans are most familiar with. After the national government moved to the District of Columbia, Stuart followed in 1803 and painted President **Thomas Jefferson** and **James Madison** before moving to Boston in 1805. There he remained for the remainder of his life, painting the Boston aristocracy and training younger artists who would subsequently become prominent, including Thomas Scully and John Neagle. *See also* ARTS.

SUFFOLK SYSTEM. *See* BANKING.

SUFFRAGE. Comparatively little attention was focused on the franchise—the right to vote—during the initial phase of the Revolution. Most agreed that the vote should be restricted to the male stakeholders, usually defined by residency and the possession of a minimal amount of property. Some state constitutions required increased property qualifications for public offices, with higher amounts of property being necessary to qualify for the more important offices. New Jersey's first constitution opened up the possibility for **women** to vote by vesting the franchise in "inhabitants" otherwise qualified to vote rather than explicitly restricting the franchise to adult males. But in the first phase of the framing of constitutions, other issues, particularly the division of powers between the legislature, executive, and judiciary, took precedence. Though the assertion that the franchise was a natural right to which all males were entitled was sometimes heard, few advocated universal suffrage because in many minds that was the equivalent of rule by the worst or a **democracy**. Revolutionary circumstances instead demanded guidance by the moral and intellectual elite of the Republic.

The Philadelphia Convention of 1787 that drafted the federal Constitution finessed the question of the franchise by leaving the matter to the states. Most of the states, in turn, gradually expanded the suffrage to embrace all adult white men by the 1830s. Again, the dynamic behind this expansion received relatively little attention. Ferocious rivalry between the **Federalist Party** and the **Republican Party** promoted it in some instances as each sought to outflank the other by drawing more people into the electoral process. But this worked only where the two parties contended for control of a given state or area. In much of the South and West, the Federalist Party was not a serious contender, and voter turnout remained feeble.

Broadening the franchise depended as much on the expansion of settlement and the market as it did on party rivalries. The development of the market and the expansion of credit made property, whether real or personal property, a less reliable measure of one's stake in society. The settlement of new areas also put pressure on the region's developing institutions to seek legitimacy by opening the vote to all comers.

The ascendancy of the Republican Party after the **War of 1812** precluded the Federalists from opposing the broadening suffrage. Federalists, who had repeatedly maligned the Republicans as "democrats," found to their surprise that the word had lost its invidious associations. That democracy now came to be celebrated as a virtue measured by the disgrace the Federalists had brought upon themselves by their behavior during the War of 1812. While rival wings of the Republican Party continued occasionally to bicker with each other over expanding suffrage, the Federalists had few options but to side with one or the other faction among their former adversaries. By 1830, universal manhood suffrage was celebrated as the hallmark of the new age. Though a few states like Rhode Island continued to adhere to its former ways and **African Americans**, **Indians**, and **women** were denied the franchise, democracy was on the ascendant.

SULLIVAN, JAMES (22 April 1744–10 December 1808). Lawyer and politician, he was born in Maine, then part of Massachusetts. He trained at the law with his older brother, John, who became a major general in the Continental army. A youthful accident with an ax precluded a military career, but Sullivan played a prominent role in Massachusetts revolutionary politics, serving as one of the original judges on the state's supreme court of judicature and in the convention that framed the Constitution of 1780. Though he pursued a state-oriented career throughout his life, he urged Massachusetts to ratify the new federal Constitution in an influential series of *Cassius* (1787) letters. In 1790, he became attorney general of the state, an office that he held until he was elected governor in 1807. Though Sullivan identified with the emerging **Republican Party** during the 1790s, he played a moderating role during the agitation over the **Jay Treaty**. He also acquired a reputation as a constitutional thinker. His *Observations upon the Government of the United States* (1791) helped pave the way for acceptance of the **Eleventh Amendment**. His *The Paths to Riches: An Inquiry into the Origins and Use of Money; and into the Principles of Stocks and Banks* (1792) urged that the state create a single **bank** instead of chartering many banks that would be only nominally under public control. Sullivan also was a leader in promoting **economic development**, acting as president of the **Middlesex Canal Company** from its inception in 1793 until his death. Additionally, he was a major investor in the New England Mississippi Land Company, which had acquired title to some of Georgia's **Yazoo lands**.

Sullivan's civic activities commanded the respect of many prominent members of the **Federalist Party** in Massachusetts even after **Thomas Jefferson**'s victory in the **election of 1800** placed the Federalists increasingly on the defensive. Federalist forbearance began to change after Sullivan became the Republican Party nominee for governor in 1805. His initial term as governor coincided with the imposition of the **Embargo of 1807–1809**, which bore especially hard on the state's commercial interests. Though Sullivan survived the blistering attack that Senator **Timothy Pickering** launched against him in March 1808, he confronted a solidly Federalist legislature the following May, which his opponents used to attack the embargo and Jefferson's administration, just as Sullivan's health began to decline. His efforts to defuse the bitter political controversy by issuing liberal exemptions from the embargo's restrictions helped undermine the measure without having the desired effect. At the time of his death, the Republican Party in Massachusetts had weakened to the point where the Federalists were poised to capture complete control of this pivotal state's government.

SUPREME COURT. Article III, section 1, of the Constitution vested the judicial power of the United States in a Supreme Court and such inferior courts as Congress chose to establish. Under the **Judiciary Act of 1789**, Congress created a system of 13 inferior district courts in an effort to make the justice of the United States accessible to everyone. Above the district courts, Congress instituted three circuit courts. Each was to be presided over by two Supreme Court judges joined by a district court judge. This arrangement of the lower courts determined the number of judges sitting on the high court. Initially, Congress provided for a Supreme Court consisting of five associate justices and one chief justice. The early justices of the high court, which the Constitution specified were to be appointed by the executive subject to the approval of the Senate, found riding circuit onerous, and two chief justices, **John Jay** and **Oliver Ellsworth**, had resigned their seats by 1800. In the **Judiciary Act of 1801**, Congress relieved them of the burden of doing so and reduced their number from six to five. The act also doubled the number of circuit courts and provided for the appointment of 16 circuit court judges.

With the repeal of the Judiciary Act of 1801 in March 1802, the federal court system reverted to its previous structure. Men like Chief Justice **John Marshall** who were members of the **Federalist Party** were not deterred by the burden of riding circuit after the **election of 1800** placed the **Republican Party** in control of the other two branches of the national government. Marshall and his colleagues, in a series of decisions beginning with ***Marbury v. Madison*** (1803) affecting federal laws and ***Fletcher v. Peck*** (1810) affecting state laws, gradually asserted the power of the Supreme Court to strike down legislation it found contrary to the Constitution. This positioned the Court to become the final arbiter of the American federal system. In the course of his long tenure, Marshall—aided by associate justices like **Joseph Story**—succeeded in shaping the nation's legal system in a way that affirmed the supremacy of the federal government over the state governments and promoted the expansion of the market and **economic development**. *See also* DARTMOUTH COLLEGE CASE; *GIBBONS V. OGDEN*; *HYLTON V. UNITED STATES*; *MARTIN V. HUNTER'S LESEE*; *MCCULLOGH V. MARYLAND*; *MARTIN V. MOTT*.

SURRENDER OF DETROIT. *See* DETROIT, SURRENDER OF IN 1812.

– T –

TALLEYRAND-PERIGORD, CHARLES-MAURICE, DUC DE (2 February 1754–17 May 1838). French diplomat, he was born into a noble family in France. A clubfoot destined him for the church rather than the army, and just before the beginning of the **French Revolution**, he became a bishop. Elected to the Estates General to represent the clergy, he advocated the fusion of the three estates into one constituent assembly, the abandonment of the tithe, and the appropriation of church property to pay the national debt. When the pope excommunicated him in 1790, he left the church and in 1791 was sent on a diplomatic mission to London. When his situation there became untenable after the overthrow of the French monarchy and the outbreak of war between France and Britain, he departed for the United States. While in America, Talleyrand explored numerous speculative ventures and personally took the measure of the new Republic's leaders. Allowed to return to France in 1796, he was appointed foreign minister by the **Directory** in 1797. In that capacity, he enriched himself by demanding bribes in exchange for diplomatic concessions and promoted **Napoleon**'s rise to power. His diplomatic dealings backfired when attempts to extract large sums from the commissioners appointed by President **John Adams** led to the release of the **XYZ Dispatches** and the **Quasi-War**. Napoleon's ascent minimized the damage this did him after the coup of 18th Brumaire, and Talleyrand was foreign minister during the negotiation that led to the **Franco-American Convention of 1800**. He remained in charge of French foreign relations until growing differences with Napoleon forced him into retirement in 1807. Talleyrand again surfaced as a member of the provisional government that took Napoleon's place after the emperor's abdication in April 1814, and he represented the restored Bourbon monarchy at the Congress of Vienna in 1815.

TALLMADGE AMENDMENT. On 13 February 1819, congressional representative James Tallmadge of New York proposed an amendment to the legislation authorizing Missouri statehood that barred the further introduction of **slavery** there and required the state to provide for the gradual **abolition** of slavery as a condition for admission to the Union. Though both propositions commanded decisive majorities in the House, they were defeated in the Senate. The northern majority of representatives who voted for the amendment drew the South's attention to the growing power of the northern free states. **Thomas Jefferson** referred to this development as a "firebell in the night." Tallmadge's amendment turned Missouri's admission to the Union into a fierce struggle over the future status of slavery in the territories that was only temporarily resolved by the **Missouri Compromise**.

TAPPING REEVE'S LITCHFIELD LAW SCHOOL. Tapping Reeve (October 1744–13 December 1823) graduated from Princeton in 1763 and settled in Litchfield, Connecticut, in 1773 after marrying **Aaron Burr**'s sister, Sally. Almost immediately, he started accepting students who lived with his family in order to study law. In 1783, the students had become so numerous that he began formalizing instruction in a series of comprehensive lectures. He also moved his school into a separate building. During the next 30 years, he trained over 1,000 young lawyers who were to have a major influence on the development of the new nation. Among his graduates were two vice presidents, 101 congressmen, 26 senators, and three justices of the U.S. **Supreme Court**. The renown of Reeve's school was sufficient to draw students from great distances. One of his famous pupils was **John C. Calhoun** from South Carolina. Though the College of William & Mary had established a law school in 1779, Reeve's Litchfield Law School predated the founding of Harvard's Law School (1817) and the Yale Law School (1823). It continued in existence for a decade after Reeve's death. *See also* EDUCATION.

TARIFF. As long as the national government relied on taxing imports for most of its revenue, the levy was referred to as an **impost**. After the **War of 1812**, when the financial strength of the nation seemed beyond dispute, import duties also came to be used to protect domestic **industry** from foreign competition. Protective duties were much higher than duties levied for raising revenue and came to be referred to as "tariffs."

TARIFF OF ABOMINATIONS (1828). As the nation recovered from the **Panic of 1819** and land sales increased in the West because of **immigration** and the **westward movement**, the nation ceased to rely on taxing imports for its revenue. Instead, what came to be referred to as the **tariff** was used for political and economic objectives. In the **election of 1828**, the supporters of **Andrew Jackson** attempted to court two apparently irreconcilable constituencies with the tariff they proposed that year. The South felt that tariffs taxed them unfairly because of their dependence on imports; the mid-Atlantic states welcomed the protection high tariffs gave to their nascent **industries**. Jackson's supporters drafted a high tariff that they assumed the Northeast, where most of **John Quincy Adams**'s support was concentrated, would defeat. The region had described itself as being primarily commercial, and it seemed probable that its congressmen would construe a high tariff as inimical to commerce. In this manner, Jackson's supporters hoped to court both the mid-Atlantic and the southern states. When northern congressmen instead supported the tariff of 1828 to protect their region's industries, the strategy went awry. Though Jackson won the election by portraying the tariff as an "abomination," South Carolina embarked on a course that led to the **nullification** crisis in 1832.

TAYLOR AMENDMENT. Proposed to the House of Representatives on 29 January 1819 by John W. Taylor of New York as an amendment to the bill creating the Arkansas Territory out of what had been the **Louisiana Territory** and after 1812 became the Missouri Territory, it would have prohibited the further introduction of **slavery** into Arkansas. Though a precursor of the **Tallmadge Amendment**, the House defeated it on 18 February after passing both parts of the Tallmadge Amendment. By doing so, a majority of representatives sent the message that they were prepared to accept the expansion of slavery in some of the territories, paving the way for the **Missouri Compromise** of 1820.

TAYLOR, NATHANIEL WILLIAM (23 June 1786–10 March 1858). Theologian, he was born in Connecticut and graduated from Yale in 1807. While at Yale, he was exposed to **Timothy Dwight**'s effort to defend **Calvinism** both from the rigidities of Jonathan Edwards's New Light determinism and from **infidelity** masking under the guise of **Unitarianism**. With Dwight's blessing, Taylor continued his theological studies and in 1812 was ordained by the First Congregational Church of New Haven. Taylor used this influential pulpit to defend **Congregationalism**, which was the established church in Connecticut, against attack until the constitutional revision of 1818 led to its disestablishment. Thereafter, he focused on defending Calvinism by emphasizing the moral agency of man in his redemption and the utility of means in promoting that agency. Taylor welcomed the religious fervor of the **Second Great Awakening** and mounted a series of revivals in his own parish. In 1822, after Dwight's death, he became the first Dwight Professor of Theology at Yale. He then joined forces with **Lyman Beecher** as coeditor of the **magazine** *Christian Quarterly Spectator* to defend their moderate Calvinism against theological challenges. Taylor is credited with turning Connecticut Congregationalism away from strict adherence to Edwards's theology toward a brand of Calvinism that came to be known as the "New Haven school."

TECHNOLOGICAL INNOVATION. The dependence of Americans on European technology during the colonial and revolutionary periods persisted in the early republican period. Technological transfers, particularly in British techniques of **canal** construction and British textile machinery, were facilitated by the migration of skilled artisans like **Samuel Slater**, who sought greater opportunities in the United States, as well as by Americans like **Francis Cabot Lowell**, who toured Europe specifically with a view to imitating its superior technology. But one of the most important transfers from England occurred in the medical field, where Edward Jenner's discovery of vaccination made it possible to eliminate the mortality previously associated with **smallpox**.

In addition to technological transfers, many Americans pioneered on their own substantial technological innovations specifically suited to the continent's needs. The most significant of these innovations related to resource extraction and the **transportation** of these resources to the market. **Eli Whitney**'s invention of the **cotton gin** in 1793 had the greatest impact on the subsequent development of both the United States and Europe. **Oliver Evans's** construction of an automated flour mill was the first in a long line of innovations increasing the productivity of **agriculture**. These included improved plows, mechanical seeders, and eventually the first mechanical reapers in the early 1830s.

In transportation, Britain's naval supremacy led to an emphasis on nautical designs that maximized speed and, on land, to the construction of improved roads known as **turnpikes**. Bridges over rivers, by eliminating ferries, facilitated inland alternatives to the coastal trade in case it were again interrupted by a naval blockade. American inventors also turned to steam power in an effort to unlock the transportation potential in the continent's riverine systems. Several, including Evans, James Fitch, **Robert Fulton**, James Rumsey, and **John Stevens**, made significant contributions that led to the first successful steamboats. The success of vessels like the *Clermont* in turn inspired attempts to harness steam power for overland transport. At the end of the 1820s, construction began on the first railroads that would go into operation during the 1830s, laying the groundwork for a national transportation grid capable of keeping pace with the **westward movement**.

American inventors devoted relatively little of their energy to military technologies. Only Robert Fulton experimented with the development of submarines and torpedoes, though John Stevens eventually built an ironclad vessel in 1813. But neither of these efforts would have much effect on the **War of 1812**. Of greater significance were the efforts of **Eleuthère du Pont** and **Paul Revere** to perfect the domestic manufacture of gunpowder and copper plating. Finally, Eli Whitney's contracts with the federal government to manufacture arms led him to introduce standardized parts and to develop tools for manufacturing them. Whitney's innovations would have a major impact on the nation's subsequent **economic** and technological **development**.

In 1790, the United States tried to encourage continued innovation by creating a Patent Board. Every patent it issued conferred on the inventor an exclusive right that the courts were supposed to honor. This, of course, was no guarantee that a patent would not be violated, as Eli Whitney quickly found out. But it did help encourage innovation in the early Republic, which in turn helped underwrite the nation's growth into an economic and industrial power.

TECUMSEH (1768?–5 October 1813). Indian warrior and visionary, he was the son of a Shawnee chief killed by the Virginians in the Battle of Point Pleasant in 1774. After the Revolutionary War, Tecumseh joined in the Shawnee effort to prevent white settlement of **Ohio** and, when the **Indians** suffered defeat in the **Battle of Fallen Timbers**, emerged as their most farsighted leader. Though not a signer of the **Treaty of Greenville**, Tecumseh initially was prepared to abide by its terms while he attempted with his brother, Tenskwatawa (the Prophet), to sponsor an Indian religious revival in an effort to resist social disintegration among native Americans. The brothers stressed traditional tribal values and condemned the use of **alcohol**, reliance on witchcraft, and contact with whites. Their efforts were resisted by other Indians who had a vested interest in opposing these reforms and who tried to set the American authorities against Tecumseh with reports that he was in league with the British. In 1808, he moved his band to what is now Indiana.

In 1809, after **William Henry Harrison** negotiated the transfer of three million acres of Indian land in the **Treaty of Fort Wayne**, Tecumseh vowed to resist the white occupation of the territory. He argued that no one could alienate the common possession of Indian lands without the consent of all who would be affected. Eventually, he saw a pan-Indian confederation as the only way to resist white encroachment. He courted British support with extravagant claims about the progress of his confederation that aroused American fears. Harrison took advantage of one of Tecumseh's recruiting absences among the southern tribes to attack a Shawnee base at Tippecanoe Creek on 7 November 1811. Though less than a decisive victory, it destroyed Tenskwatawa's influence and left the Shawnee destitute. With no place to turn but the British, Tecumseh with his Indian followers played a crucial role in frustrating Governor **William Hull**'s attempt to invade **Upper Canada** and in persuading him to surrender at **Detroit**. Tecumseh also rendered valuable service to the British during their unsuccessful siege of **Fort Meigs**. But he was dismayed by the British decision to pull back to the eastern end of Lake Erie after the American commodore **Oliver Perry** established naval supremacy over it. When Harrison's forces caught up with the retreating British at the Thames River in western Ontario, Tecumseh and his dwindling band of followers fought with more determination than his European allies did. Tecumseh perished in the engagement, reputedly at the hands of Colonel Richard Johnson, who owed his vice presidency under **Martin Van Buren** partially to this claim. With Tecumseh's death, effective Indian resistance to white encroachments in the Northwest collapsed.

TEMPERANCE MOVEMENT. Before safe water supplies became widely available, distilled beverages often proved healthier than nonalcoholic ones, particularly in the larger towns and cities. Alcohol also appeared to protect people from the effects of severe heat and cold. Soldiers on fatigue duty as well as sailors in general routinely expected to be served liquor as compensation for the hardships they endured. Distilled beverages were widely available in the late colonial period, and much of the sugar imported from the West Indies was distilled into rum. All ages and ranks drank some alcohol with the inevitable occasional excess.

In the early 19th century, medical reformers like **Benjamin Rush** began to speak against the dangers of excessive drinking as part of a revolutionary agenda for improving public health. Simultaneously as an outgrowth of the early phases of the **Second Great Awakening**, some religious groups became more sensitive to the issue of alcohol abuse. In 1811, the General Association of the Congregational Church created a committee on intemperance, and in 1813, the Massachusetts Society for the Suppression of Intemperance held its first meeting. These early efforts stressed moderation rather than abstinence and failed to generate much appeal beyond the narrow confines of their members until **Lyman Beecher**'s *Six Sermons on Temperance* (1825). Beecher proposed forming voluntary societies to restrain the excesses he denounced. In 1826, a national organization, taking the name of the American Temperance Society, formed in Boston with the aim of creating local societies of the kind Beecher advocated. When the American Temperance Society reorganized in 1836, it adopted total abstinence, or prohibition, as its goal. Prohibition became the objective of the Washington Temperance Societies that sprang up after 1840. Over the years, the movement succeeded in writing prohibition into a number of state constitutions and eventually in the early 20th century incorporated it into the federal Constitution as the Eighteenth Amendment.

TERRITORIAL EXPANSION. *See* LAND ACT OF 1820; LOUISIANA PURCHASE; LOUISIANA TERRITORY; PUBLIC DOMAIN; WESTWARD MOVEMENT.

TERTIUM QUIDS. A phrase connoting a third political alternative to the division between the **Federalist Party** and the **Republican Party**

in the **First Party System**, the "Quids" declared their independence from the dominant Republican Party in Congress during **Thomas Jefferson**'s second administration. Alternatively known as the "old Republicans," they formed around representative **John Randolph**'s opposition to compensating northern investors for their losses in the **Yazoo lands** and to giving the president a secret fund to facilitate the acquisition of **East Florida** and **West Florida** from Spain. During the diplomatic crisis with Britain and France leading up to the **War of 1812**, the Quids often sided with the Federalists. However, they never held the balance of power between the principal parties, and once war was declared, they suffered eclipse after Randolph failed to win election to the 13th Congress.

TEXAS. Spanish efforts to promote European settlement in Texas met with limited success before 1800, when France acquired an ill-defined claim to the region through the Treaty of San Ildefonso. The United States subsequently took over that claim in the **Louisiana Purchase** and maintained it until it was surrendered by **John Quincy Adams** as part of the **Transcontinental Treaty** with Spain of 1819.

Despite the government's actions, individual Americans like **Moses Austin** were attracted to Texas by the prospect of cheap land. They also saw opportunity in the political ferment within the Spanish Empire that **Napoleon**'s attempt to place his brother on the Spanish throne had set in motion. In 1821, Austin secured the approval of Spanish authorities to settle 300 families in Texas, and his son **Stephen Austin** continued what his father had begun after a revolution led to the establishment of an independent Mexican state in 1824.

The Mexican constitution of that year had abolished **slavery**, but the American migrants who started flooding into the area disregarded the prohibition. In 1826, a small band of North Americans in alliance with some displaced **Cherokee** seized the Spanish settlement of Nacogdoches and proclaimed the independent state of Fredonia. The **Fredonia Rebellion** failed to find support among the majority of European Texans as well as the local **Indians**, and Stephen Austin's followers even joined the Mexican authorities in suppressing it. But as the number of settlers migrating from the United States with their African slaves grew over the next decade, Texas independence began to seem more attractive. In 1835, hostilities between the Texans and Mexican authorities erupted, resulting initially in the defeat of the rebels at San Antonio and the massacre at the Alamo. But a subsequent engagement at San Jacinto led to victory for the Texans, who proclaimed their independence from Mexico in 1836.

The growing number of Americans in Texas had led to unsuccessful efforts by the United States to buy it from Mexico. Texas independence created the opportunity for annexation, but such a course was opposed by a growing **antislavery** movement. The United States eventually annexed Texas at the end of 1845, precipitating the Mexican-American War. Though the conflict led to the acquisition of vast new territories, including modern California, Arizona, and New Mexico, it also ignited a struggle over the status of slavery in the West that would lead to the Civil War.

THAMES RIVER, BATTLE OF THE (1813). Immediately after Commodore **Oliver Perry** had established U.S. naval supremacy in the **Battle of Lake Erie** in September 1813, Major General **William Henry Harrison** invaded western Ontario with a force of 5,500, 1,000 of them mounted **militia** under Colonel Richard Johnson's command. The British commander, Major General Henry Proctor, abandoned Detroit and the British base at Malden despite **Tecumseh**'s protests and retreated eastward. On 5 October, Harrison's army, which had been pressing the British for several days, forced the British to fight with the Thames River at their rear. Half of Johnson's mounted militia charged the British regulars opposing them, shattering their line. Casualties on both sides were light, but almost 500 British soldiers were captured in the brief engagement. The other half of Johnson's militia encountered stiffer resistance from Proctor's **Indian** allies. But they melted away once the Americans turned their flank. Among the 30-odd bodies the Indians left on the field was Tecumseh's. The Battle of the Thames River crushed Britain's power in the Northwest for the remainder of the **War of 1812** and destroyed the Indian confederation that Tecumseh had worked so hard to construct.

THEATER. The predominantly rural character of the population, together with religious suspicions about the moral licentiousness of the theater, inhibited its development in colonial America. Nonetheless, theatrical companies from England started visiting North American population centers during the 18th century. By the end of the colonial period, New York, Philadelphia, Williamsburg, and Charleston had enjoyed repeated, short seasons. Though New England proved more resistant to such intrusions, Newport, Rhode Island, had sampled theatrical performances under the guise of moral instruction, while **Mercy Otis Warren** turned satirical verse plays lampooning royal officialdom into vehicles for promoting the revolutionary cause. While none of her plays were performed, they were printed and widely read.

The Revolutionary War led to the occupation of most of the sites where theater had flourished as well as to the exodus of the professional players. But their place was taken by officers of the British army who were familiar with the British theatrical tradition and during the long winters staged performances to ward off the boredom of inactivity. **New York City**, an early leader in the development of the American theater, benefited the most because it was occupied the longest. **William Dunlap**'s theatrical ambitions were fired by witnessing one of these performances as a youngster, just as **Royall Tyler**'s subsequent introduction to New York theaters early in 1787 inspired him to write *The Contrast*, which quickly became an American classic.

With the end of the war, theaters sprang up in all the principal cities, including Boston, after Massachusetts finally repealed its 1750 prohibition in 1793. New theaters and theatrical companies prospered as the urban centers grew until the **War of 1812** briefly interrupted their development. Though the growth of the theater went hand in hand with the growth of American cities, urban locations also posed problems. Cities were notoriously less healthy than the countryside, and theatrical seasons were repeatedly affected by the outbreak of local epidemics, like the **yellow fever** epidemic in Philadelphia during 1793. In addition, fire was a hazard because of the need to illuminate large spaces required to accommodate the audiences. Few fires were as disastrous as the one that destroyed a theater in Richmond, Virginia, on the evening of 26 December 1811, in which 71 perished. But theaters were victimized by more than their fair share of conflagrations. In addition, urban sites were open to foreign influences, which inhibited the development of a native theatrical culture. Most of the best actors were members of the English touring groups that favored performing a British repertory centered on Shakespeare over nourishing native talent. This did not prevent the emergence of truly gifted American actors and writers, like **John Howard Payne**, who became a star both in Britain and in America. But Payne experienced difficulty in creating an American tragedy despite his success as a performer of tragic roles. He eventually produced a highly successful *Brutus* (1818), which enjoyed a long stage life in America and Europe. But it failed to make use of American materials. The first American playwright to produce an authentically American tragedy was John Augustus Stone. His *Metamora: or the Last of the Wampanoags*, premiered at the end of 1829, set off a rage for similar **Indian** dramas that endured for more than a decade.

THOMAS AMENDMENT. It linked the admission of Missouri as a state that legalized **slavery** with the exclusion of slavery from the remainder of the **Louisiana Territory** north of 36° 30'. The first issue confronting the 16th Congress was to find a solution to the problem raised by the preceding Congress's rejection of the **Tallmadge Amendment** and the **Taylor Amendment**. In the interim, Maine had won independence from Massachusetts and was petitioning Congress for admission as a free state. After Congress had admitted Alabama as a slave state on 14 December 1819, a majority of northern representatives still opposed admitting Missouri as a slave state despite the Senate's attempt to link the admission of Maine to that of Missouri. Senator Jesse B. Thomas of Illinois then came up with the idea of pairing the admission of Missouri with the future exclusion of slavery from what remained of the Louisiana Territory north of the southern boundary separating Missouri from Arkansas at 36° 30'. The majority in the House initially opposed accepting this compromise, but enough northern representatives eventually relented to pass it.

THORNTON, WILLIAM (20 May 1759–28 March 1828). Architect and civil servant, he was born on the West Indian island of Tortola, educated in England, and graduated from the University of Aberdeen, Scotland, with a degree in medicine. Soon after returning to Tortola, he immigrated to the United States, becoming a naturalized citizen in 1788. Settling initially in Philadelphia, he was quickly elected a member of the recently established American Philosophical Society.

He also dabbled in architecture and designed a building for the Library Company of Philadelphia (1789). Thornton had no training as an engineer and was far better at conceiving a structure than actually building it. But his design for the U.S. Capitol in the District of Columbia met with President **George Washington**'s and Secretary of State **Thomas Jefferson**'s approval in 1793. Though Thornton served as a member of the commission that supervised the construction of the nation's Capitol between 1794 and 1802, it would fall to **Benjamin Latrobe** and **Charles Bulfinch** to bring his plans for the Capitol to completion. In 1802, Secretary of State **James Madison** asked Thornton to preside over the Patent Office, which until then had been part of the State Department. Despite the absence of congressional support, Thornton experienced modest success in protecting patent rights against subsequent infringement. He had acquired a personal interest in such matters through his partnership with John Fitch in developing one of the nation's first steamboats. This venture did not prove financially successful despite Thornton's attempts to protect it from the competition of **Robert Fulton**'s more profitable *Clermont*. Though Thornton's financial independence rested on the ownership of **slaves**, he favored **abolition** through a general compensated emancipation. While he never freed any of his slaves, he became a founding member of the **American Colonization Society**. He also supported Greek independence and the new republics emerging from the **Latin America revolutions** and hoped for the eventual emergence of a hemispheric confederation of republics. Finally, he advocated for the establishment of a national system of **education** and was awarded a prize for an essay on educating deaf-mutes.

THREE-FIFTHS CLAUSE (OF THE CONSTITUTION). Article I, section 2, of the Constitution apportioned representation in the lower house of the federal Congress according to the total number of free persons plus three-fifths of "all other persons" excluding **Indians**. The "other persons" were Africans held in **slavery**. Though the South gained additional weight in the House of Representatives because of the three-fifths clause, all the states were equally represented in the Senate, which conferred an advantage there on the smaller states. Since there were more small states north of the **Mason-Dixon Line** than south of it, the advantage the North enjoyed in the Senate came to balance the advantage the South had in the House. This gave additional symmetry to the bargain struck in the Philadelphia Convention whereby representation in the House had been paired with the apportionment of any direct taxes that were laid by the national government. However, once experience demonstrated that direct taxation was an inexpedient way for the government to raise a revenue, given the productiveness of the **impost** and the sale of the **public domain**, the three-fifths clause came to look less fair to some than it had when originally agreed to.

TIPPECANOE CREEK, BATTLE OF (1811). Tecumseh used the settlement at Tippecanoe Creek as a model community in his drive to rejuvenate **Indian** culture through the renunciation of alcohol and as the headquarters of his attempt to unite the western **Indians** against white expansion into their territory. At the beginning of November 1811, **William Henry Harrison**, who was both a governor and a general, responded to pleas from expansionists on the western frontier and advanced toward Tippecanoe with a force of approximately 1,000 regulars and militia after Tecumseh had departed to rally the southern tribes to his pan-Indian confederacy. Harrison sought to extract the consent of the Prophet (Tenskwatawa) and the remaining chiefs in the settlement to further land concessions. On 6 November, the American force advanced to within a mile or two of the Tippecanoe settlement and camped, professing, as did the Indians, the desire to negotiate rather than to fight. Early the next morning, the Indians attacked but were repulsed after a two-hour battle that left a quarter of Harrison's force casualties. Harrison held his position for the next 24 hours. He had little choice despite the potential superiority of his enemy in the area until he was reinforced by a column of dragoons and mounted riflemen on 8 November. Then he retreated in haste. Though the Battle of Tippecanoe helped establish Harrison's repu-tation as a western hero and temporarily diminished Tecumseh's influence, it failed to destroy Britain's sway among the western Indians. Instead, everyone concluded that a British war would be accompanied by an Indian war.

TOBACCO. *See* AGRICULTURAL DEVELOPMENT.

TOMPKINS, DANIEL (21 June 1774–11 June 1825). Vice president and governor of New York, he was born in modern Scarsdale and educated at Columbia, graduating in 1795. Influenced by **James Kent**'s Columbia law lectures, Tompkins trained as a lawyer. After briefly practicing, he was appointed to New York's supreme court in 1804. When no other member of the faction headed by **George Clinton** and **Dewitt Clinton** was available in 1807, they nominated him for governor, a position to which he was reelected until 1816. Throughout that period, he vigorously supported the national **Republican Party**'s policies, including the **Embargo of 1807–1809** and the **War of 1812**, despite the Clintonians' disapproval of both and the absence of a sympathetic Republican majority in the state legislature until 1814. At the end of that year, President **James Madison** invited him to be secretary of state, but Tompkins refused on the grounds that he was essential to New York's war effort. While governor, he supported numerous reforms and resisted the legislature's indiscriminate issuance of corporate charters. During a crucial 60-day period in 1812, he prorogued the New York legislature to prevent it from nominating DeWitt Clinton for the presidency before the **congressional caucus** nominated Madison. Tompkins was reluctant to support the construction of the **Erie Canal** because he feared it would enhance Clinton's reputation. After the War of 1812, Tompkins was rewarded for his wartime service by being elected **James Monroe**'s vice president but was absent from Washington for more than three years of his two terms in that office. In 1821, he presided over New York's constitutional convention. His last years were clouded by alcoholism and financial anxieties arising from his personal endorsement of notes to finance the war effort in New York. A faction of New York Democrats led by **Martin Van Buren**, known as the Bucktails, together with Republican admirers in Congress, saved him from bankruptcy through a series of special legislative acts.

TRANSCONTINENTAL TREATY. *See* ADAMS-ONÍS TREATY (1819).

TRANSPORTATION REVOLUTION. The geographic dimensions of the United States were without precedent. Indeed, some thought the nation was too large to survive. Notions such as these rationalized, though they did not necessarily fuel, northern **secession** thinking during the first decades under the new Constitution. Innovations in transportation would eventually allay most structural anxieties about the nation's size. The earliest improvements were comparatively modest both in cost and in reach, involving the construction of toll roads called **turnpikes**. They facilitated the transport of freight by wagon over relatively short distances by providing graded surfaces that were free of obstructions like boulders and washouts. Even so, the ton-mile cost of wagon transportation remained almost 10 times that of waterborne transport. The discrepancy between the two inspired innovations that were designed to expand the use of the nation's waterways.

The first and most cost effective of these innovations was the application of steam power to propel vessels, thus making upstream traffic on the rivers as economical as downstream traffic. Steam engines had been undergoing development in Britain for almost a century before they were successfully utilized in steamboats. Though **Robert Fulton** was not the first American to attempt such an application, he was the first to demonstrate a steamboat's commercial potential in 1807, when his *Clermont* succeeded in completing a voyage upstream from New York City to Albany in roughly 30 hours. In the next decade, steamboats flooded the rivers and protected waterways of the nation. It took longer for steam power to be applied to oceangoing vessels. But by 1820, even that innovation seemed to be only a matter of time.

The second important development in water transportation was the **canal**. The nation's earliest successful canals were constructed by publicly chartered corporations of private investors. The **Santee Canal** Company was chartered in 1785 to join the Santee River with the Cooper River near Charleston. It was begun in 1793 and completed in 1800 at the cost of $650,000. When finished, the Santee Canal extended for 22 miles and had 10 locks. Construction of the **Middlesex Canal**, linking Boston to the Merrimack River 28 miles away, began in the same year as the Santee. It took 10 years to build at the cost of $500,000. Though it is not clear that either lived up to its promoters' expectations, both aided economic development around their focal cities. They also helped inspire the far more ambitious **Erie Canal** to link **New York City** with the Great Lakes. Though this project involved a much greater distance of 363 miles and cost far more than either the Middlesex Canal or the Santee Canal, the Erie was completed in seven years partially because it was financed by the state issuing bonds instead of a private corporation that raised its capital by taxing its members. The Erie's success in paying off its entire construction cost in the first seven years of operation inspired many other states in the Union to undertake similar projects.

The era of the canal was brief because of the competition it received from the railroads in the 1830s. Though the first lines to be constructed carried passengers rather than freight, it was only a matter of time before the use of steel rails, together with heavier engines and rolling stock, would supplant the canals. They would do so because railroads were capable of operating around the year at much higher speeds and were able to negotiate terrain that canals could deal with only at prohibitive cost. Canals like the Erie continued to haul bulk freight for the rest of the 19th century, but no other canal project proved as successful.

TREATY OF FORT JACKSON. *See* HORSESHOE BEND, BATTLE OF.

TREATY OF FORT WAYNE. *See* FORT WAYNE, TREATY OF.

TREATY OF GHENT. *See* GHENT, TREATY OF.

TREATIES OF GREENVILLE. *See* GREENVILLE, TREATIES OF.

TREATY OF MORTEFONTAINE. *See* FRANCO-AMERICAN CONVENTION OF 1800.

TREATY OF SAN LORENZO. *See* PINCKNEY'S TREATY.

TRIPOLITAN WAR (1801–1805). *See* BARBARY WARS.

TRUCE OF AMIENS. On 1 October 1801, Great Britain and France signed a preliminary treaty for a European truce, bringing the war that had been waged between them since the beginning of 1793 to a brief halt. On 27 March 1802, the truce was expanded to include Spain and the Batavian Republic, or the Netherlands. It gave Europe peace until 16 May 1803, the only peace it would know until **Napoleon**'s abdication in April 1814. The truce briefly deprived American merchant vessels of the advantage they had derived from the nation's **neutral commerce**. This had made the American merchant marine the world's leading seaborne carriers and the indirect earnings of the carrying trade one of the mainstays of the prosperity of the 1790s.

TRUMBULL, JOHN (6 June 1756–10 November 1843). Painter, he was born in Connecticut, the son of the state's governor at the time of the Revolution. After graduating from Harvard in 1773, he served briefly on General **George Washington**'s and Horatio Gates's staffs in 1776–1777. In 1779, he went to France, probably on a secret mission the objective of which has never been revealed. When that failed, he moved to England to study painting with **Benjamin West**. As the son of an American war governor, he was eventually arrested and imprisoned as a spy and, when released, expelled from the kingdom. With the end of the war, Trumbull set out for England again and studied there from 1784 to 1789. Under West's influence, he conceived his first historical paintings, *The Death of General Warren at the Battle of Bunker's Hill* and *The Death of General Montgomery in the Attack on Quebec*, in 1785. While Trumbull was looking for a suitable engraver in Paris who could reproduce these epic images, Ambassador **Thomas Jefferson** suggested that *The Signing of the Declaration of Independence* might also make a suitable subject.

Returning to the United States in 1789, Trumbull started painting the portraits of the revolutionary leadership. Included in his oeuvre are three depictions of George Washington. Despair over the death of his fiancée led Trumbull to abandon painting in 1793 and to serve instead as **John Jay**'s secretary in the negotiations leading to the **Jay Treaty** in London. He remained in Europe during the crisis in Franco-American relations that led to the **Quasi-War** and played a pivotal role in transmitting the **XYZ Dispatches** to America. After marrying, he returned to the United States in 1804 and painted the portraits of prominent Americans until his commissions dried up in the wake of the **Embargo of 1807–1809**. He again returned to England, where the **War of 1812** kept him until the **Treaty of Ghent**. In 1817, he suggested the Capitol's rotunda, which was being rebuilt after the **burning of Washington**, be adorned with four of his historical paintings, including *The Signing of the Declaration of Independence* and *The Surrender of Lord Cornwallis at Yorktown*. In 1826, Congress finally accepted his proposal. Between 1817 and 1836, Trumbull acted as president of the American Academy of Fine Arts. He left his unsold paintings to Yale on the understanding that they would be housed in a building he designed and in doing so created the first collegiate art **museum** in the country.

TURNPIKES. After the Revolutionary War demonstrated the difficulty of integrating the American economy during a conflict with an adversary enjoying naval superiority, Americans started constructing turnpike roads. Typically, local investors pooled capital in corporations chartered by their state legislatures to clear and grade preexisting roads. They hoped to recover their investment by levying tolls on those using the improved roads. Between 1790 and 1810, more capital was invested in building turnpikes and bridges than any other improvement contributing to the **transportation revolution**. Though turnpikes failed dramatically to reduce ton-mile costs or to provide their investors with much of a return, they did contribute significantly to connecting local communities with existing systems of water transport and thus helped broaden the reach of the market.

TWELFTH AMENDMENT. The Constitution empowered the House of Representatives voting by states to choose the president should the ballots of the **Electoral College** fail to select one candidate by a majority. In the **election of 1800**, both candidates of the **Republican Party**, **Thomas Jefferson** and **Aaron Burr**, received the same majority of electoral votes. The Federalists in the lame-duck sixth Congress then tried to use their majority in the House to extract concessions from them. Though no deals were cut, the Republican leadership responded with an amendment to the Constitution designed to preclude future tie votes between candidates of the same party by requiring members of the Electoral College to cast separate votes for president and vice president. Congress did not get around to sending a draft of the amendment to the states until 12 December 1803. But three-quarters of the 17 states then in the Union managed to ratify it by 25 September 1804, in time for it to be implemented in the **election of 1804**. Disgruntled members of the **Federalist Party** complained that the amendment violated the principles of constitutionalism in the same way the French had been doing since the beginning of their revolution. But what the Federalists really lamented was loss by the minority of the chance to influence the decisions of the majority.

TYLER, ROYALL (18 July 1757–26 August 1826). Author and jurist, he was born into a prominent merchant family in Boston and educated at Harvard, graduating with the class of 1776. Though he participated briefly as a major in the unsuccessful attempt to recover Newport, Rhode Island, from the British in 1778, he spent most of the war qualifying for the bar. During the 1780s, he unsuccessfully courted the daughter of **John Adams**, whose parents disapproved of him. He participated in the suppression of Shays's Rebellion during 1786–1787 and was sent by the Massachusetts government to New York to apprehend any rebels seeking refuge there. While in **New York City**, he became enthralled by the **theater** and in very short order wrote *The Contrast*, which was first produced in 1787 and then published in 1790 with President **George Washington** as one of the subscribers.

Despite the attractions of the metropolis, Tyler settled in Guilford, Vermont, in the early 1790s after marrying a Bostonian. He rose to prominence as a lawyer there and between 1807 and beginning in 1813 served as chief justice of the Vermont supreme court. But he is remembered today mostly for his literary productions. These included satirical verses published in the **newspapers**, several other plays that followed *The Contrast*, and, most important, a novel, *The Algerian Captive* (1797), which became the first American work of **fiction** to be republished in Britain. He also issued two volumes of reports of cases decided by the Vermont supreme court and a series of epistolary essays under the title *The Yankee in London* (1809), which developed in prose the themes he had treated poetically in his first play.

– U –

UNITARIANISM/UNITARIANS. A religious belief almost as old as Christianity that denied the Trinity on both scriptural and rational grounds. Such ideas had occasionally surfaced among the New England clergy and laity during the 18th century, but the first American church formally to embrace Unitarianism was a former Anglican congregation at King's Chapel in Boston in 1796. That inspired others similarly inclined to declare their Unitarian belief. In 1804, the liberal faction governing Harvard College succeeded in appointing Henry Ware, a known Unitarian, to the Hollis Professorship. By 1815, 120 New

England churches had become Unitarian, rejecting the divinity of Christ, original sin, and notions of everlasting punishment. The term "Unitarian," though, did not achieve wide currency until **William Ellery Channing** published his sermon delivered at Jared Spark's Baltimore ordination in 1819 titled *Unitarian Christianity*. In it, Channing defended these doctrines with unparalleled eloquence. Unitarians were often accused by Trinitarians of being **deists**. But they vigorously rebutted the notion by arguing that subjecting revelation to rational interpretation was very different from rejecting its authority entirely.

UNIVERSALISM/UNIVERSALISTS. A religious belief that rejected the doctrine of original sin on the grounds that a benign God would never have created a species, only to doom the vast majority to damnation. Notions of universal salvation as a reaction to the **Calvinist** doctrine of predestination had a long history in European Protestantism. Universalism was brought to America in 1770 by John Murray, a **Methodist** who had been expelled from its fellowship for this heresy. He preached to largely hostile audiences until 1779, when a portion of the first **Congregational** Church of Gloucester, Massachusetts, seceded to organize a Universalist congregation. The Universalists became so accustomed to resisting pressures from orthodox bodies that they had trouble organizing their own movement. The Universalist Church in America did not take formal shape until 1833, after it had begun to benefit from the reaction to which the evangelicalism of the **Second Great Awakening** had given rise.

UPPER CANADA. In 1791, the British Parliament passed a constitutional act dividing Quebec along the boundary now used between the province of Quebec and Ontario, in effect making the Ottawa River the principal line of division between the two jurisdictions of Upper and **Lower Canada**. Upper Canada lay to the west of Lower Canada as well as of New Brunswick, Newfoundland, and Nova Scotia.

URBANIZATION. During the first 40 years of the new Republic, the portion of the nation's population living in communities of more than 2,500 remained constant at roughly 7 percent. Nonetheless, the nation's principal gateway ports along the Atlantic seacoast, including

Boston, **New York City**, Philadelphia, and Charleston, continued to grow, though at different rates, and Baltimore, which before the Revolutionary War had been less than half the size of Newport, Rhode Island, joined the ranks of the fastest-growing cities. By the end of the 1820s, New York was by far the nation's largest city, reflecting its emergence as the principal gateway port or **entrepôt**—thanks largely to the completion of the **Erie Canal**—with a total of 242,228, followed by Baltimore and Philadelphia with roughly 80,500 each and Boston with 61,392. The rapid development of these cities outran the capacity of local authorities to provide adequate supplies of water or waste disposal. This, together with crowding and the importation of diseases like **yellow fever**, made them considerably less healthy than the neighboring countryside, initiating the retreat to suburbs—like Brooklyn, New York—in the larger ones.

While the port cities would not become manufacturing centers until the 1840s after the development of coal-fired steam engines, the commerce that flowed through them provided enough resource to sustain the development of a rich cultural life in the form of **theaters**, **museums**, and learned societies that had been unknown in the colonial era. The growing enrichment of life that became characteristic of the eastern metropolises in turn inspired emulation by new cities that were emerging in the West by 1830, including Cincinnati, the largest settlement in the Northwest, with 24,831 and **New Orleans**, the largest city of the Southwest, with 46,082.

USS *CHESAPEAKE*. *See CHESAPEAKE*, USS.

USS *CONSTITUTION*. *See CONSTITUTION*, USS.

UTOPIAS. *See* PERFECTIBILITY.

– V –

VAN BUREN, MARTIN (5 December 1782–24 July 1862). Eighth president of the United States, he was born outside Albany, New York, and with minimal formal schooling apprenticed himself to a lawyer affiliated with the **Federalist Party**. Despite this influence, Van Buren chose to support **Thomas Jefferson** in the **election of 1800**. After a brief sojourn working in a **New York City** law firm and fraternizing with **Aaron Burr**'s wing of the **Republican Party**, he returned to the Albany area and joined the Clinton–Livingston wing of the state party. Elected to the state senate in 1812, he was instrumental in securing New York's electoral vote for **Dewitt Clinton** in the **election of 1812**. But shortly afterward, he parted company with Clinton over the **War of 1812**, which Van Buren supported. In 1815, he was made attorney general of the state, but his subsequent opposition to building the **Erie Canal** led to his dismissal in 1819. Van Buren then organized an opposition movement within the Republican Party known as the Bucktails. After they won control of the state government, they sent Van Buren to the U.S. Senate. There his support for **William H. Crawford**'s unsuccessful candidacy in the **election of 1824** gained him little advantage. Eventually, he helped build a nationwide coalition, resembling the statewide one he had constructed in New York, of southern planters and northern republicans that helped **Andrew Jackson** win the **election of 1828**.

Van Buren's chief rival for the presidential succession was **John C. Calhoun**. When President Jackson appointed Van Buren secretary of state, Van Buren had no trouble outmaneuvering Calhoun and becoming Jackson's running mate in 1832. Though Van Buren suffered during Jackson's second term for his opposition to Jackson's strong nationalist position on **nullification** as well as the way Jackson conducted the war against the **Second Bank of the United States**, Van Buren won the Democratic nomination in 1836 by representing himself as loyal to Jackson's policies of **Indian removal** and the defense of **slavery**. The depression of 1837 made any identification with Jackson a liability, and Van Buren lost the election of 1840 to **William Henry Harrison**. After a brief retirement from politics, he was again a contender for the Democratic nomination in 1848. But his opposition to the annexation of **Texas** led the Democrats to pass over him, and he ran unsuccessfully as the Free Soil candidate. In the 1850s, he again aligned himself with the Democratic Party on the erroneous assumption that it was most likely to preserve the Union, and he died during the Civil War without the consolation of knowing that the Union would be preserved.

VESEY'S REBELLION (1822). An aborted slave uprising planned and organized by a **freedman** named Denmark Vesey (1767?–2 July 1822), who was born in either Africa or the West Indies. Somehow he came to the attention of the captain of a Bermuda slaver carrying a large cargo of African **slaves** to Santo Domingo, where Vesey was sold as a field hand. But he proved unsatisfactory in the field, and the captain, Joseph Vesey, took him back and subsequently settled in Charlestown, South Carolina. There he became known as Denmark Vesey. He proved to be a versatile though unschooled linguist, quickly became a skilled carpenter, and in 1799 was lucky enough to win a local lottery. This enabled him to purchase his freedom and to prosper as a skilled craftsman, acquiring a sizable property over the years despite being paid considerably less than white craftsmen. He also became influential in an all-black **Methodist** congregation in Charleston associated with the recently formed **African Methodist Episcopal Church**. He used his position as class leader in the church to plan an insurrection at the end of the 1810s. The plot called for the black majority of the town, supported by slaves from outlying plantations, to rise against their enslavers, seize the powder magazine, torch the town, and kill most of the whites. Vesey hoped to use the shipping in the harbor, navigated by the few white captains he intended to spare from a general racial slaughter, to make for Haiti or Africa.

The insurrection was initially scheduled for 14 July 1822 (Bastille Day), but as the date approached, word of the conspiracy began to seep out from slaves who feared the consequences of such an insurrection. At first, the white authorities discounted the information they received. But when they learned from a credible slave informant on 8 June that Vesey had moved the date for the uprising to 16 June, they started rounding up the conspirators. Vesey himself went into hiding and was not found until 22 June. In all, 131 blacks were eventually charged in connection with the insurrection, 77 of whom were convicted and sentenced, 35 of them to either death or banishment. Most of what was learned about the planned uprising was extracted from terrorized captives under pressure to cooperate with the white authorities. This probably led to an exaggerated estimate of the conspiracy's extent, but the fact that it had come to the attention of the whites at all is an indication that many people were privy to Vesey's plans. Vesey himself stood mute throughout his trial and was hanged on 2 July. The abortive rebellion subsequently led to South Carolina's **Negro Seamen's Act** and to a hardening of the state's defense of slavery.

VIRGINIA RESOLUTIONS (1798). In the autumn of 1798, **James Madison** drafted a series of resolves challenging the constitutionality of the **Alien Law** and the **Sedition Law** recently passed by Congress. The Virginia legislature then adopted them. Unlike **Thomas Jefferson**'s draft for the **Kentucky Resolutions**, which were planned in conjuncture with the Virginia Resolves, Madison had declined to pronounce the laws null and void within the state of Virginia. This enabled him subsequently to defend the course pursued by the Virginia legislature against the objections of eight other state legislatures in his **Report of the Committee** (1800). He argued that Virginia's Resolves were a legitimate attempt to rally public opinion rather than an usurpation of the role of the judiciary by one state trying to **nullify** laws enacted by a legislature representing all the states.

– W –

WALKER, DAVID (? 1796–6 August 1830). African American activist, he was born free in Wilmington, North Carolina, to a free black woman. But his father was probably a slave, as were most of the African community of Wilmington. Sometime between 1815 and 1820, Walker moved to Charleston, South Carolina, in pursuit of greater economic opportunity and became involved with the recently formed branch of the **African Methodist Episcopal Church** there. He was present in Charlestown during the **Vesey Rebellion** but does not seem to have been implicated in it. Nonetheless, soon afterward, he moved to Boston, where he established a used clothing business. He also became involved with the black community there, joining the Prince Hall Masonic Lodge and collaborating with the local African Methodist Episcopal preacher, Samuel Snowden. Both promoted *Freedom's Journal*, the first black **newspaper** published in the United States. In 1829, Walker helped found the Massachusetts General Colored Association, the first black political organization in the country, and on 29 September of that year, his *Appeal to the Colored Citizens of the World* appeared. The *Appeal* defended the humanity of the enslaved Africans and urged them to resist white oppression by force if necessary. Walker's efforts to circulate the *Appeal* in the South led to laws against black literacy there. He died of tuberculosis contracted in Boston shortly after publication of the *Appeal*. *See also* SLAVERY.

WAR HAWKS. A term applied to those members of the 12th Congress who supported declaring war against Britain in 1812. *See also* WAR OF 1812 (CAUSES OF).

WAR OF 1812 (CAUSES OF). The ostensible grievances of the United States when it declared war on Britain on 19 June 1812 were Britain's claim to regulate the nation's **neutral commerce** through its **Orders-in-Council** enforced by its naval power and its **impressing** seamen it claimed were British subjects off of American vessels. In addition, the administration of **James Madison** complained of Britain's **paper blockades**. Beneath the ostensible grievances lay another more pressing concern. The **Federalist Party** had succeeded in subverting the commercial restrictions sponsored by the **Republican Party** to obtain redress from both belligerents without going to war. The Federalists had then defended any policy the British government chose to pursue toward the United States. The Republicans feared that the humiliation entailed in the abandonment of the **Embargo of 1807–1809** and the failure of **nonintercourse** to wring concessions from Britain would prejudice the rising generation of young Americans against **Republicanism**. The Republicans concluded they could defend the Revolution only by demonstrating that the nation could stand up to the bullying of a monarchy in league with the powerful domestic faction. Britain thus served as proxy for the Federalist enemy in their midst. But their Republicanism prevented the Republicans from striking directly at this other adversary.

WAR OF 1812 (DIPLOMACY OF). Four days after Congress declared war, Great Britain lifted its objectionable **Orders-in-Council,** leaving **impressment** as the principal issue in dispute between the two nations. However, President **James Madison** had experienced so much difficulty in putting together a war coalition that he was loathe to accept an immediate truce that did not address all American grievances. Federalist attempts to portray him as the only obstacle to peace prior to the **election of 1812** proved unsuccessful despite the military reverses of the campaign of 1812. But Madison did accept the 21 September offer of mediation by the Russian czar in March 1813. Madison then appointed Secretary of the Treasury **Albert Gallatin** and Senator James Bayard to join Ambassador **John Quincy Adams**

in St. Petersburg, only to learn that the British had declined the czar's offer. After the British defeat in the **Battle of Lake Erie** in November, however, Britain's foreign minister, Lord Castlereagh, offered direct negotiations. Madison accepted and added **Henry Clay** and Jonathan Russell to the American negotiating team that was to meet with British negotiators at Ghent in present-day Belgium.

At the first meeting in late July 1814, the British commissioners presented the Americans with a set of demands that anticipated the triumph of British arms during the current campaign. These included substantial territorial concessions, the establishment of a neutral **Indian** buffer state in the Northwest under British protection, a monopoly of naval force on the Great Lakes, a right to freely navigate the Mississippi, and the revocation of the American right to dry fish on Canadian shores. As news of the repulse of the British at the **Battle of Plattsburg** and the failure of their attack on **Baltimore** arrived in Europe, the British began to recede from these initial demands. Eventually, they agreed to an American proposal that both parties accept the status quo prior to the war. Adverse political developments on the continent of Europe that eventually led to **Napoleon**'s brief return to power in 1815 proved persuasive. The peace **Treaty of Ghent** was signed on Christmas Eve 1814, effectively bringing the war to a conclusion.

WAR OF 1812 (LAND OPERATIONS). American strategy called for attacking Britain where it was thought to be weakest in Canada. Throughout the conflict, American forces encountered difficulty in raising the men needed to execute this strategy. The campaign of 1812 began with Brigadier General **William Hull** surrendering an army at **Detroit** after a failed attempt to conquer **Upper Canada** (now western Ontario). This disaster was followed by the collapse of an attempt by American General Stephen Van Rensselaer to seize Queenstown in the Niagara region. Finally, a large force under General **Henry Dearborn** that was supposed to attack Montreal failed to move beyond the New York border.

Forces under General **William Henry Harrison** tried to take the offensive in the West early in 1813. However, the Americans' advance was checked at the **Battle of Frenchtown**, and they were forced to fall back to **Fort Meigs** at the rapids on the Maumee River in Ohio, where the British besieged them until May. At the beginning of August, a British attack on Fort Stephenson on the Sandusky River was also repulsed. However, all American positions near Lake Erie remained in jeopardy until Commodore **Oliver Perry** succeeded in destroying Britain's naval power in the **Battle of Lake Erie** on 10 September. Harrison then renewed his invasion of Upper Canada. The British retreated northward until Harrison caught up with them and defeated them in the **Battle of the Thames River** on 5 October. The **Indian** leader, **Tecumseh**, died in this engagement, which secured the Northwest frontier. But American operations around Lake Ontario remained hampered by the absence of the decisive naval superiority enjoyed on Lake Erie. An American force seized and burned **York** (present-day Toronto) in April, but it had to retreat to Niagara in May. Colonel **Winfield Scott** took the offensive again at the end of that month, forcing the British to abandon Fort George and **Fort Erie**. But a subsequent British success at **Stony Creek** in the Niagara region compelled the abandonment of Fort Erie. Farther to the east, General **Jacob Brown**'s forces repulsed a British attack on Sackett's Harbor. But ineffective coordination between troops under the command of Generals **James Wilkinson** and Wade Hampton doomed a second attempt to take Montreal. The British stopped Wilkinson's eastward movement at the **Battle of Chrysler's Farm** in what is now southeastern Ontario, while Hampton's forces retreated after a severe engagement at the **Battle of Chateaugay River**. These setbacks enabled the British to retake Fort George as well as Fort Niagara and to burn Buffalo at the end of the year. General **Andrew Jackson**'s campaign in the Southwest against the **Creeks** met with some initial successes at Talishatchee and Talladega; however, these were quickly reversed at Emuckfaw, Enotachopco, and Calibee Creek.

After **Napoleon**'s abdication on 6 April 1814, the British reinforced their armies in Canada. On 4–5 July, they attacked Jacob Brown's troops on the **Battle of Chippewa Plain** but suffered defeat. However, Brown was unable to capitalize on the victory because of the failure of Commodore Isaac Chauncey to cooperate with him. Brown's force was again attacked at **Lundy's Lane**, after which the Americans retreated to Fort Erie. They successfully defended this position for a month and a half until the British abandoned their siege on 21 September. Meanwhile, a large force of recently arrived British veterans invaded northeastern New York, moving against Plattsburg on Lake Champlain. They were supported by a flotilla under George Downie's command. Commodore **Thomas Macdonough**'s success in destroying most of Downie's vessels in the **Battle of Lake Champlain** forced the British to withdraw to Canada. A British expeditionary force of veterans under General Robert Ross was more successful in the Chesapeake. After defeating the Americans in the **Battle of Bladensburg** on 24 August, the British occupied and carried out their **burning of Washington** on the 25th. But Ross died in a subsequent unsuccessful attack on Baltimore, and the British withdrew from the Chesapeake. The only American territory they held as commissioners began negotiating the **Treaty of Ghent** was the coast of Maine from New Brunswick south to Castine. The British seized that territory between July and September.

As 1814 ended, an additional force of British veterans threatened **New Orleans**. Jackson's campaign against the Creeks had taken a turn for the better on 27 March 1814 with a decisive victory in the **Battle of Horseshoe Bend**. Though Jackson was preoccupied with seizing Pensacola and Mobile during November, he succeeded in organizing a last-minute defense of New Orleans that decisively defeated the British in a series of engagements between 23 December and 8 January 1815. Jackson's victory brought the land operations of the war to a triumphant conclusion.

WAR OF 1812 (NAVAL OPERATIONS). The war at sea began in a more promising way than that on land with **Isaac Hull** in command of the **USS *Constitution*** taking HMS *Guerrière* (9 August), the USS *Wasp* taking HMS *Frolic* (17 October), and the USS *United States* taking HMS *Macedonian* (October 26). At the end of the year, the USS *Constitution*, now under the command of Nathaniel Bainbridge, destroyed HMS *Java* (28 December).

The string of victories shocked the British out of their naval complacency and led them to concentrate their naval forces to avoid further humiliation at the hands of the American navy. At the end of 1812, the British proclaimed a blockade of the American coast from Chesapeake Bay to the Delaware River and throughout 1813 extended it to the principal ports and estuaries from the Mississippi to

Rhode Island. In late May, two British line-of-battle ships intercepted Commodore **Stephen Decatur** trying to get to sea with the USS *United States* and the *Macedonian* and forced his squadron to take refuge in New London, where they remained bottled up for the remainder of the war. Though the British navy had many more men-of-war, including more ships of the line than the U.S. Navy, concentrating their forces compromised their blockade and diminished the number of prizes they could retake from American **privateers**. That helped the USS *Essex* escape to the Pacific, where it cruised against British whaling vessels for a year before it was taken by two British frigates off Valpariso, Chile, in March 1814. But when Captain James Lawrence of the **USS *Chesapeake*** accepted the challenge of the commander of HMS *Shannon* to a naval duel off Boston on 1 June, he lost his ship and his life. Commodore **Oliver Perry**'s triumph on 10 September 1813 in the **Battle of Lake Erie** was the most significant naval engagement of that year.

Napoleon's abdication freed up Britain's navy and enabled it to extend its blockade to the entire American coastline in April 1814 and to immobilize what remained of the blue-water navy of the United States. With the exception of Commodore **Thomas Macdonough**'s victory in the **Battle of Lake Champlain**, most American naval resources during 1814 were devoted to defending American vessels against British attack while they remained in port. Authorities in Portsmouth, New Hampshire, and Boston, who were sympathetic to the **Federalist Party**, refused to cooperate in these defensive operations. Not until December 1814 did Decatur, now in the USS *President*, try to escape from **New York City**. Then he encountered a squadron of four men-of-war of comparable strength that forced him to surrender his ship. Thus, the naval war, begun on a surprisingly positive note on the high seas, concluded with a defeat.

WARREN, MERCY OTIS (25 September 1728–19 October 1814). Poet, dramatist, and historian, she was born in Barnstable, Massachusetts, into a politically influential family. Aside from sharing in the private classes her parents arranged for her brother, James Otis (who became a prominent revolutionary), she was largely self-taught. She married James Warren, a physician, who shared her brother's political commitments and who was a member of Massachusetts's revolutionary vanguard. **John Adams** and **Abigail Adams** also became her friends. As some aspects of the Revolution were organized in the Warren household, it was hardly surprising that Mercy undertook a contribution of her own in 1772, when she published a verse play titled *The Adulateur*. The work was never produced because her plays were meant to be read rather than acted, but it did contain a merciless attack on the province's royal governor, Thomas Hutchinson. In the course of the next few years, she produced several more verse satires of royal officials and Loyalists before turning her critical scrutiny against backsliding patriots. In 1781, the Warrens purchased former Governor Hutchinson's confiscated estate but were forced by financial pressures to sell it in 1788. That same year, she opposed ratification of the new federal constitution in an anonymous pamphlet attributed at the time to **Elbridge Gerry**. Experience eventually reconciled her to the new government, which she grew to see as the embodiment rather than a betrayal of **Republicanism**. Her three-volume history of the Revolution, which appeared in 1805, praised the work of the Philadelphia Convention. Unfortunately, it also had harsh things to say about John Adams's monarchical inclinations, which enlarged a rift that had already appeared between his Federalism and her Republicanism. But thanks to Gerry's skillful mediation, she and Adams were reconciled before her death. *See also* THEATER.

WARS OF THE FRENCH REVOLUTION. The European conflicts spawned by the **French Revolution** between 20 April 1792 and the Battle of Waterloo on 18 June 1815.

WASHINGTON BENEVOLENT SOCIETIES. Federalist Party criticism of the **republican societies** and **democratic societies** of the 1790s inhibited Federalists from publicly sponsoring such organizations until the crisis surrounding the **Embargo of 1807–1809** and its aftermath. Though there were several precursors dating back to **George Washington**'s death, the Washington Benevolent Society movement did not begin to gather momentum until 1809. In the years immediately preceding the **War of 1812**, Federalists in the areas where they had some strength—namely, the commercial centers, the Northeast, and isolated rural pockets of New York, New Jersey, and Maryland— founded Washington Benevolent Societies in an effort to recruit the younger generation to their cause. Though the societies claimed they were established for benevolent purposes, their chief function was political. At their peak, more than 200 such organizations busied themselves organizing political rallies on the occasion of Fourth of July celebrations, Washington's birthday, and even the anniversary of Washington's inauguration, 30 April. Under the guise of patriotism, the richer societies planned elaborate festivals the primary purpose of which was the perpetuation of Federalist principles. Though these were dressed up as loyalty to Washington's principles, the most important principle the societies embraced was opposition to the war against Britain. After the conflict was brought to a successful conclusion by the **Treaty of Ghent**, most of the Washington Benevolent Societies abruptly disappeared as the Federalist Party disbanded.

WASHINGTON, BURNING OF (24–25 August 1814). Once the British found themselves in command of the field at **Bladensburg**, Maryland, there was nothing to stop their advance on Washington. On the afternoon of 24 August, they marched to within a quarter mile of the Capitol before setting up camp. Detachments then deployed to burn the Capitol, the White House, and the War and Navy Departments. Private property was generally respected, and the residence of the French ambassador was spared since at the time Britain was officially at peace with France. But British Admiral Alexander Cockburn went out of his way to ensure that the office of the *National Intelligencer*, a **newspaper** regarded as the government's mouthpiece, was destroyed. After a thunderstorm during the night partially checked the flames, the British tried to reignite them. But the destruction of public property came to a halt around noon of the following day after another storm, described variously as a tornado or hurricane and an explosion in the Navy yard. Once the weather cleared, what was left of the British raiding force of 1,500 marched precipitously back to rendezvous with their fleet on Chesapeake Bay.

WASHINGTON, GEORGE (11 February 1732–14 December 1799). Commander of the Continental army during the Revolution and first president of the United States, he was born in Westmoreland County, Virginia. He began his career as a surveyor and a soldier, rising to the rank of lieutenant colonel by 1754 at the beginning of the French and Indian War. Emerging from that conflict a local hero, he was elected to the Virginia House of Burgesses in 1759. Thereafter, he played an influential role in Virginia's revolutionary movement and was a member of the first and second Continental Congresses before being chosen to command the Continental army.

Washington's genius was political rather than military, and his greatest achievement was to keep the army together throughout the war. Had it ever disbanded, the Revolution would have been lost. Sustaining it throughout a prolonged conflict brought Washington into contact with most of the nation's gentry leadership, many of whom he would later appoint to federal offices created by the **first Congress** as it put the new government into operation during 1789.

Though Washington is the only president to twice receive the unanimous endorsement of the **Electoral College**, he never took his political preeminence for granted. In the autumn of 1789, he toured the New England states to renew wartime associations. During the first years of his presidency, he experimented with the protocols governing the relationship between the executive and legislature branches. The experience of the war made establishing the credit of the new government as much a priority for him as it was for the secretary of the treasury, **Alexander Hamilton**. Washington supported Hamilton's ambitious **funding** proposal that involved the **assumption** of most of the state debts and resisted objections raised by his fellow Virginians against creating the **First Bank of the United States**. He also reluctantly agreed to a second term in order to consolidate the achievements of his first term, which seemed threatened by the emerging rivalry between Hamilton and Secretary of State **Thomas Jefferson**.

After war broke out between Britain and France in 1793, foreign policy took precedence over domestic concerns. Both belligerents had colonies in the New World proximate to the United States, which also had a strategic alliance with France. Recognizing the dangers in the situation, Washington issued his **Neutrality Proclamation** urging Americans to treat the belligerents impartially. But the Revolutionary War had left many Americans embittered against Britain. The French ambassador, **Edmund Genêt**, exploited this hostility in issuing commissions to Americans willing to take up arms against Britain in the

New World. Though a faction of what would become the **Federalist Party** managed to get Genêt recalled, that failed to stop Britain from treating the United States as if it were France's ally. Britain brought American vessels sailing to France into its own ports and seized an even greater number in the West Indies coming from the French islands. The American public responded angrily, and the emerging **republican societies** and **democratic societies** called for maintaining good relations with France whatever the consequences with Britain.

Washington appointed **John Jay** special envoy to Britain to defuse the crisis. Simultaneously, he confronted resistance to an excise tax on domestically distilled whiskey Congress had laid in 1792. Recognizing the adverse effect that the **Whiskey Rebellion** was likely to have on the British negotiation, Washington called on the **militias** of four states to crush the insurrection with a large army. The following autumn, he condemned the republican and democratic societies before Congress as "self-created." In the meantime, Jay negotiated a treaty that preserved the peace with Britain.

The **Jay Treaty** bought peace at the cost of some aspects of the **Franco-American alliance**, creating deep unease among leaders of the emerging **Republican Party** who felt the nation's security depended on maintaining good relations with France. Washington regarded the treaty with ambivalence. Though he submitted it to the Senate for their advice and consent, Secretary of State **Edmund Randolph** opposed promulgating it. A faction in Washington's cabinet then forced his hand by producing evidence that Randolph was under French influence. This convinced Washington he had to accept the treaty despite rising public hostility to it. He subsequently invoked executive privilege to deny the House access to correspondence bearing on the negotiation of the treaty when the House considered appropriating funds to implement it. Washington also recalled Ambassador **James Monroe**, who had been sent to France to reconcile its government to the Jay Treaty but instead had taken France's part against Washington's administration, and replaced him with **Charles C. Pinckney**.

Washington decided to retire in 1796 but saved his announcement until two months before the Electoral College was to vote in order to minimize domestic factionalism and foreign interference. The French ambassador, Pierre Adêt, announced that France would equalize the

Franco-American treaties by having French ships seize American vessels, hoping to influence the composition of the new Congress. Then he tried to sway the Electoral College by threatening to sever relations with the United States if Thomas Jefferson were not elected. His interventions proved futile partially because they illustrated the dangers Washington had pointed to in his **Farewell Address**. **John Adams** won the election and spent most of his presidency coping with France's wrath.

Washington retired to his home at Mount Vernon, Virginia, where he remained until he died of pneumonia in December 1799. He reemerged partially from private life when Adams asked him to assume command of the **provisional army** during the **Quasi-War**, but he insisted that Hamilton exercise actual command. Washington was the only substantial slaveholder among the founding fathers who made provision in his will for freeing the Africans belonging to him from **slavery**. His passing initiated a period of national mourning marked by countless public eulogies and ceremonies. Few Americans disputed that he had been first among his countrymen in leading and securing their republican revolution, but the Federalists would claim his legacy for their own far more aggressively than the Republicans did in the years to come.

WASHINGTON, MARTHA DANDRIDGE (2 June 1731–22 May 1802). Wife of **George Washington**, she was born Martha Dandridge in Virginia, the daughter of a prominent planter. In 1749, she married Daniel Parke Custes, one of the colony's wealthiest planters. They had four children, only two of whom were still living when her husband died in 1757. The property she brought with her marriage to Washington on 6 January 1759 elevated him to a prominence not previously enjoyed by members of the Washington family. The Washingtons had no children of their own, leaving Martha free, after raising her surviving son and daughter, to share in many of her husband's public burdens. During the Revolutionary War, she repeatedly joined him in the Continental army's winter encampments. And after Washington became the first president of the United States, as the nation's initial first lady, she helped lend style and dignity to the official entertainments they hosted. The evidence suggests that she regarded these responsibilities as a burden and that she was not a partner in

George Washington's final project of freeing his slaves. But the evidence is inconclusive because, on her husband's death, Martha destroyed most of their correspondence, thereby depriving future generations of access to the details about their personal life.

WEBSTER, DANIEL (18 January 1782–24 October 1852). Congressional leader and secretary of state, he was born in New Hampshire and attended Dartmouth College, graduating in 1801. Trained as a lawyer by prominent Massachusetts attorneys, he ran unsuccessfully for the New Hampshire legislature several times before the **War of 1812**. Soon after its beginning, he was elected a representative to the 13th Congress, where he took the lead in resisting the war measures of **James Madison**'s administration. As a freshman congressman, he proposed resolutions calling on the president to present Congress with whatever evidence he possessed that France had indeed acted as it had promised to in the **Cadore letter**. Since 1810, Madison's policy of confronting Britain had rested on the claim that France had repealed its decrees affecting U.S. **neutral commerce** despite evidence to the contrary. Though Webster's resolutions challenged the **Republican Party**'s ostensible justification for the war, many Republicans ending up voting for them to avoid the appearance of being involved in a cover-up. Secretary of State **James Monroe** then produced a lengthy report that defended the administration's war policy but failed to convince the Federalists that **Napoleon** had done what he had promised to do.

Webster privately approved of the **Hartford Convention** in 1814 but opposed **secession**, saving him from sharing in the disgrace that the convention's sponsors brought on themselves. Nonetheless, he chose to retire to private life at the end of the 14th Congress. In an age that valued rhetoric more than **literature**, Webster acquired fame with his orations celebrating the bicentenary of Plymouth Plantation, the 50th anniversary of the Battle of Bunker Hill, and the simultaneous deaths of **John Adams** and **Thomas Jefferson** on 4 July 1826. He also brought his elocutionary skills to bear in pleading important cases before the **Supreme Court**, including the **Dartmouth College Case**, ***McCullogh v. Maryland***, and ***Gibbons v. Ogden***.

Webster reentered Congress as a representative for Massachusetts in 1823 and proved influential in the House of Representatives' selection of **John Quincy Adams** as president in the **election of 1824**. After 1827, Webster emerged as a leader of the new **National Republican Party**, which evolved into the **Whig Party**, serving as secretary of state under President **William Henry Harrison** and John Tyler in the Whig's first administration and again during Millard Fillmore's presidency. His greatest diplomatic achievement was the Webster-Ashburton Treaty of 1842, which settled the northern boundary between the United States and Canada. Webster opposed the annexation of **Texas** and the Mexican-American War but supported the Compromise of 1850. He unsuccessfully sought the Whig presidential nomination in 1852 and died before the election of that year.

WEBSTER, NOAH (16 October 1758–28 May 1843). Pedagogue and lexicographer, he was born into a farm family of modest means in West Hartford, Connecticut. After graduating from Yale College in the class of 1778, he studied law with **Oliver Ellsworth** but failed to attract sufficient clients to sustain a practice. Teaching school instead, he quickly became aware of the absence of American pedagogical materials. Webster felt that independence required the new nation to create a national character distinct from Britain's. His *American Speller* (1783), *American Grammar* (1784), and *American Reader* (1785) were designed to imbue the next generation with distinctively American traditions expressed in an American language. Having virtually no competitors, his pedagogical works were an instant success, and before his death his *Speller* had sold over 24 million copies. Since the new nation lacked institutions for distributing his texts, Webster personally pedaled them in the early years. He was in Philadelphia when the Federal Convention completed its work in September 1787 and immediately wrote essays supporting its adoption.

In 1790, he moved to **New York City**, where he published a **newspaper**, the *Commercial Advertiser*, devoted to promoting the **Federalist Party**. Eventually, General **Alexander Hamilton** took offense at Webster's support of President **John Adams**'s peace initiative in 1799 and his bid for reelection in the **election of 1800**. In 1801, Hamilton helped establish the *New York Evening Post*, which inspired Webster to sell his *Commercial Advertiser*.

By now financially independent, he retired from the city to begin work on a dictionary, which he saw as a device for defining distinctive

American usages and making Americans more self-conscious about their culture. The American language Webster outlined included many words of non-English origin, among them **Indian** words used to describe the unique features of the American environment and words derived from French, German, and Dutch **immigrants**. The project was sufficiently complete by 1828 to justify the issuance of the first edition of Webster's *Dictionary*. He died while attempting a subsequent revision. But his enterprise was carried on by others who have continued to use his original title down to the present.

WEST, BENJAMIN (10 October 1738–11 March 1820). A painter, he began life in Pennsylvania. Though influenced by various local craftsmen, he was largely self-trained, starting to execute portraits around 1750 and attempting a history painting in 1756. West came to the attention of William Smith, the founder of the College of Philadelphia, who arranged for him to travel to Italy. After more than two years touring and studying there, West moved to London, where his American fiancée and his father joined him. There he remained for the rest of his life. West's success in Britain was ensured by his history painting, *Death of General Wolfe* (1770). George III was so impressed by it that he commissioned 60 paintings by West. Royal patronage elevated him among the circle of British artists who established the Royal Academy, over which West presided from 1792 to 1804. West's principal contribution to the development of American art was to train three generations of American painters, including **Charles Willson Peale**, **John Trumbull**, **Gilbert Stuart**, and **Washington Allston**.

WEST FLORIDA. Like **East Florida**, West Florida was the creation of the British Proclamation of 1763. But the northern boundary was extended in 1764 to a parallel running from the confluence of the Yazoo and the Mississippi to the Chattahoochee River. After Spain conquered Mobile from the British during the Revolutionary War, it claimed that West Florida's eastern boundary was the Flint River rather than the Chattahoochee, to its source, and then a line due north to the Hiwassee River. Spain's definition of West Florida's northern boundary followed the Hiwassee to the Tennessee, the Tennessee to the Ohio, and the Ohio to the Mississippi. Spain and the United States remained at odds over the definition of West Florida until Spain accepted a northern boundary of the 31st parallel in **Pinckney's Treaty** of 1795.

WESTWARD MOVEMENT. Access to western lands had been as much a source of the American Revolution as the fear of British taxation without representation. The fertility of American **women**, together with the penchant of colonial farm families for extensive **agriculture**, collided with the limits British authorities put on the expansion of European settlement to maintain peace with the American **Indians**. The revolutionaries assumed that one of the prizes of victory would be access to an enormous expanse of interior lands only thinly inhabited by an indigenous population that was as vulnerable to the superior military power of the Europeans as it was to the Europeans' diseases. White farmers needed access to these lands if they were to transmit to the next generation the family farming they had come to regard as traditional. Only by exchanging the improved land on which they had begun their families for less expensive, unimproved land in the West could they provide for their children and perpetuate the way of life they had known.

Under the Articles of Confederation, Congress had made considerable progress in organizing the **public domain** in the West, to which the Peace of Paris had given the nation title. But the westward movement failed to gain momentum until after the adoption of the new federal Constitution. The prosperity of the 1790s was the principal motor in driving the migration of families not only into the American West but southward toward **East Florida**, **West Florida**, **Louisiana**, and **Texas**. However, the initial migration into Kentucky, separated from Virginia and incorporated into the Union in 1792, followed in 1796 by Tennessee, was also a response to the declining fertility of eastern lands and the collapse of the demand for tobacco occasioned by the **French Revolution**. Early settlers on the eastern bank of the Mississippi still had no assurance that the crops they raised would have access to an international market until after **Pinckney's Treaty** in 1795. The invention of the **cotton gin**, together with the growing industrial demand for cotton, drove much of the westward movement after 1800. But the expansionist impulse predated the cotton boom, and the migration of families westward would have taken place anyway simply because American farm families, whether or not they were dependent on **slavery**, could achieve more of their goals through extensive agriculture than they could through intensive agriculture.

The **Louisiana Purchase**, in resolving any remaining uncertainties about the future of the West, gave an enormous impetus to the establishment of new settlements after 1803. Indian occupants remained in the way of unfettered access to new agricultural land, but the **War of 1812** soon severed the diplomatic and military alliance that had persisted between the British government and the Indians after 1783. This paved the way for the **removal** of the indigenous population to the western plains. The **Cherokees** offered the most effective resistance to being dispossessed of their lands, but even they could not establish a united front against white encroachments. **Sequoyah**, the inventor of the Cherokee syllabary, advocated acquiescence rather than resistance. Elsewhere, the advance of the European proceeded almost unimpeded, spurred on in the north by the completion in 1825 of the **Erie Canal**, which gave migrants access to cheap water transportation as far west as modern Minnesota. By this time, foreign **immigration** from northern and western Europe had resumed with the end of the **Napoleonic Wars**, providing additional buyers for improved lands in the East that financed the westward movement. Federal revenues, previously dependent on an **impost**, began to depend more and more on land sales, even as Congress progressively reduced the price of land. The unsettledness of so many lives fed a search for new connections that found religious expression in the continuing revivals of the **Second Great Awakening**. Those who participated in the westward movement thought they were preserving an agrarian Republic when in fact they were transforming it into a dynamic society very different from what the founders of the nation had taken such pains to establish.

WHIG PARTY. A nationwide political coalition that formed to oppose the **Democratic Party** after it succeeded in elevating **Andrew Jackson** to the presidency in the **election of 1828**. The Whig Party did not begin to form until the early years of the 1830s and initially posed as a continuation of **John Quincy Adams**'s **National Republican Party**. Former members of the **Republican Party** like **Henry Clay**, who was the Whig Party's nominee for president in 1832, provided the initial leadership for this coalition. But it also attracted former members of the **Federalist Party**, like **Daniel Webster** and, after 1832, those who had been active in the **anti-Masonic** movement. The rivalry between Whigs and Democrats would define a new national system of parties, usually referred to as the Second Party System, that persisted until the 1850s. Ideologically, the Whigs favored positive governmental initiatives like the **American system** and rechartering the **Second Bank of the United States**, while the Democrats celebrated a minimal, negative state that sheltered **slavery** from the threat of the national government's power. But the stability of this two-party system depended more on a nationwide competition to control the growing patronage at the disposal of the federal government than it did on ideological differences. When slavery eventually emerged as the dominant issue in national politics, the Second Party System quickly collapsed.

WHISKEY REBELLION. Secretary of the Treasury **Alexander Hamilton** persuaded Congress to levy a federal excise on whisky stills in 1792 to cover part of the deficit between the yields of the **impost** and the obligations incurred by his ambitious **funding** scheme. The western counties of Pennsylvania, already struggling under a state excise tax on stills, resisted this attempt at federal taxation by intimidating the officials responsible for its collection. They felt the tax to be unfair because the only way they could get their grain to market was to distill it into whiskey. When violence erupted against federal officials during 1794, President **George Washington** asked the governors of four states (New Jersey, Pennsylvania, Maryland, and Virginia) to call 12,900 **militia** into the field to suppress the insurrection. The force assembled at Carlisle, Pennsylvania, in September. After further negotiations proved futile, the army began its march over the mountains in mid-October. The insurgents melted away before such an overwhelming force, which ended up apprehending only 20 suspects. They were marched back to Philadelphia, where all but two were acquitted and the two convicted of treason were pardoned. Though from a modern perspective the episode resembles a farce—and has recently been portrayed as such by historians—Washington's overresponse can be explained by the crisis that had led him to dispatch **John Jay**

to London to head off a war with Britain shortly beforehand. Washington feared that Jay would not be taken seriously by the British government unless the U.S. government could demonstrate beyond the shadow of a doubt that it was master of its own house.

WHITNEY, ELI (8 December 1765–8 January 1825). Inventor and early industrialist, he was born into a farming family in Westboro, Massachusetts. He showed an early aptitude for making and repairing machinery. After earning enough by teaching school to put himself through Yale (class of 1792), he took a tutoring job in Georgia. There, Nathaniel Greene's widow, Caty Greene, suggested he invent a machine capable of separating the seeds from short staple cotton. Whitney had no trouble constructing a **cotton gin** that solved the problem, thus dramatically increasing the productivity of laborers processing raw cotton. But though he patented his device, he was unable to defend his invention against being pirated. Widespread copying opened the interior lands of the South to profitable cultivation and by the beginning of the 19th century had made cotton the nation's most valuable export. Later it would contribute to the expansion of northern textile manufacturing, but it also cemented the South's involvement with racial **slavery** until the Civil War.

In 1798, despairing of realizing further benefit from his gin, Whitney offered to contract with the U.S. government to produce 10,000 muskets. At the time, he had no prior experience with gun making, but the boldness of his proposal to use mechanical techniques in producing weapons attracted the attention of Secretary of the Treasury **Oliver Wolcott Jr.** and landed him the contract. Whitney bought land along a stream in New Haven, Connecticut, and built a factory at the site subsequently known as Whitneyville. During the first two years of its operation, he produced only 500 muskets. But in succeeding years, he managed to develop machine tools that harnessed water power to the manufacturing process. By 1807, he had completed the original contract largely with unskilled **labor**, demonstrating a capacity matched by no other arms producer in the United States. This laid the basis for a larger contract with the government for 15,000 muskets during the **War of 1812**. Controversy surrounds the claim that Whitney was the first either to conceive of or to apply the principle of interchangeable parts. But there can be no doubt that his technical innovations influenced how subsequent entrepreneurs mass-produced consumer goods like clocks and sewing machines. He was also a pioneer in the development of the mill town. He died a relatively wealthy man despite being deprived of most of the profits that he had hoped to reap from licensing the cotton gin. *See also* INDUSTRY; TECHNOLOGY.

WILKINSON, JAMES (? 1757–28 December 1825). Soldier, he was born in Maryland and apprenticed to a doctor. He was in the process of establishing a medical practice when the Revolutionary War began, and he abandoned his patients to join the army near Boston. After participating in Benedict Arnold's unsuccessful attempt to take Quebec, he joined Horatio Gates's staff but later quarreled and fought a **duel** with him. For the rest of the war, he served as clothier general until a discrepancy in his accounts led Congress to dismiss him in 1781.

After retiring from the army, he married a wealthy woman and moved to Kentucky, where he became prominent in the movement for statehood. He also spearheaded an attempt to break Spain's stranglehold on the navigation of the Mississippi. In this connection, he succeeded in convincing the Spanish governor in **New Orleans** that he favored bringing the western states into the Spanish Empire by swearing allegiance to the king. In turn, Wilkinson received a large annual pension from Spain.

Indian disturbances in the Northwest led him back into the army in 1791, where he served under General Anthony Wayne and distinguished himself at the **Battle of Fallen Timbers**. Wilkinson succeeded to Wayne's command after the latter's death in 1796 but not to his rank. In 1803, President **Thomas Jefferson** ordered Wilkinson to take charge of the territory acquired through the **Louisiana Purchase**, over which he served as its first governor. He encouraged **Zebulon Pike** to explore its western reaches at the same time he became involved in **Aaron Burr**'s intrigue with Spanish authorities to detach the western states from the Union. Wilkinson eventually exposed the Burr conspiracy to protect himself. Since neither was willing to testify against the other, Wilkinson escaped being called to account for his shady dealings, and the attempt to court-martial him in 1811 collapsed for lack of evidence.

At the beginning of the **War of 1812**, Wilkinson was promoted to major general and placed in charge of the invasion of Canada during the campaign of 1813. When that collapsed in a fiasco, he was relieved of his command. After the war, he moved to New Orleans, where he resided until 1822. Financial difficulties then led him to seek **Texas** lands from the government in Mexico City, where he died destitute.

WILLARD, EMMA HART (23 February 1787–15 April 1870). Pioneer in female **education**, she was born in Berlin, Connecticut. With her father's encouragement, she acquired the best schooling available in the new academies for **women** that were being established after the Revolution. At 19 she found herself temporarily in charge of the academy she had attended, and at 20 she struck out on her own to establish a female academy in Middlebury, Vermont. There she met John Willard, a widower considerably her senior; married him; and left teaching. But the failure of the Vermont State Bank, of which her husband was a director, soon forced her to resume teaching for financial reasons. In the interval, she had become aware from a nephew attending Middlebury College, who boarded with the family, of the difference between what men and women were being taught.

In 1814, she opened a female academy in her home. The academy's curriculum ignored the ancient languages and instead stressed mathematics, science, philosophy, and history while not entirely disregarding ornamental skills, such as sewing and music, that educated women were expected to possess. Though her academy was successful, she started looking for public support for female education at the college level. An appeal she published, addressed to **DeWitt Clinton**, brought her a charter from the New York legislature to establish a school in Waterford. But when the legislature proved unwilling to support her operating expenses, in 1821 she accepted the invitation of Troy, New York, to establish a school on premises provided by the town. Her academy was an immediate success, and before long a third of the student body were boarders. An unfortunate second marriage forced her in 1838 to leave the school in the hands of others, where it has prospered to this day. But she continued to write innovative textbooks on geography and history for women and to promote female education in public schools. The peace movement was the only **reform** outside of education that she supported. But many of her students would become prominent in the struggle to expand the rights of women.

WOLCOTT, OLIVER, JR. (11 January 1760–1 June 1833). Secretary of the treasury and governor of Connecticut, he was born in Litchfield, Connecticut. His father was a signer of the Declaration of Independence. The younger Wolcott graduated from Yale in the class of 1778 and then trained for the law. But his real talent was making sense of accounts. In 1782, the state appointed him to sort out its revolutionary finances, which were in chaos. In the postwar period, together with **Oliver Ellsworth**, Wolcott negotiated a settlement of Connecticut's accounts with the Confederation. When the new national government went into effect, he accepted appointment as the first auditor of the national treasury. In that capacity, he helped Secretary of the Treasury **Alexander Hamilton** implement his **funding** policy. Wolcott succeeded Hamilton at the Treasury Department in 1795, and President **John Adams** retained him in office throughout most of his administration despite Wolcott's having supplied Hamilton with some of the material he used in the pamphlet he wrote in order to persuade Federalist electors to favor **Charles C. Pinckney** in the **election of 1800**. When Wolcott finally resigned as secretary of the treasury on 31 December 1800, Adams appointed him a federal circuit judge in the expanded federal judiciary created by the **Judiciary Act of 1801**.

After the repeal of the Judiciary Act of 1801 deprived Wolcott of his judicial post, he settled in **New York City** and engaged in the China trade. As he prospered, he became increasingly involved in **banking**, first as president of the Merchant's Bank, then as a board member of the New York branch of the **First Bank of the United States**, and finally in 1812 as the founder of the Bank of America. Despite his prior association with the **Federalist Party**, he supported the **War of 1812**. After being forced out of the Bank of America in 1814, he returned to Connecticut in 1815 and headed a movement bent on giving the state a new constitution. He was elected governor of the state in 1817; in 1818, Connecticut got its first constitution, written by a popularly elected convention and ratified by the people. He continued as governor of Connecticut for a decade and retired during the last years of his life to New York.

WOMEN. The American Revolution was a masculine enterprise that liberated women far less than it liberated men. Men rather than women took credit for its heroic achievements, even though the men relied on women to perform many less glorious though essential tasks, such as making up for the absence of foreign imports through their household industry. The **Republicanism** of the Revolution gave rise to the notion of separate spheres in which women were assigned the function of producing the virtuous citizenry needed to perpetuate the Republic. This in turn led to greater emphasis on formal **education** for women and ensured that the vast majority, many of whom were already biblically literate, would be fully literate in the coming generation. It also opened up opportunities for women teachers that had not previously existed. **Emma Willard** even experimented with what today would be called higher education for women, though her school would be known as an academy rather than a college.

Separate spheres also led to a greater exclusion of women from public affairs, and it did little to expand women's marital rights. Instead, the legal doctrine of "coveture" denied a married women's legal existence independent of her husband. The male partner in a marriage could dispose of the property his wife brought to the marriage, subject only to a few inadequate restrictions. The postrevolutionary period also saw the closing of legal loopholes, like the one in the New Jersey constitution that had allowed some women to vote, as Republicanism also expanded the claims of patriarchy.

Nonetheless, the long-term implications of the Revolution proved liberating to women in two ways. First, during the **Second Great Awakening**, religious leaders borrowed from the revolutionary mobilization to enlist women, who were more likely to be full members of their churches than were men, in promoting piety through missionary and Bible societies and eventually in **reform** movements. Second, the new generation of fully literate women, at least in the North and the mid-Atlantic, provided an expanding market for the work of authors like **Lydia Maria Child**, **Sarah Josepha Buell Hale**, **Judith Murray**, **Susanna Rowson**, **Catherine Sedgwick**, and **Lydia Sigourney**, who addressed primarily a female audience.

Simultaneously, the gradual effect of the industrial revolution, coupled with the expansion of the market, increased the leisure of a growing body of "middle-class" women. This proved to be as important as the expansion of literacy in the cultural flowering of the early Republic and the progressive liberation of women from their traditional gender-defined roles. *See also* ROYALL, ANNE NEWPORT; WRIGHT, FRANCES.

WRIGHT, FRANCES (6 September 1795–13 December 1852). Author and reformer, she was the daughter of a Scottish linen merchant orphaned at the age of three. Along with her other siblings, Wright was brought up by relatives who saw to her **education** and allowed her access to the radical thought of the age. In 1818, she and her sister sailed for America. "Fanny" was immediately impressed with the United States, and after a sojourn in several eastern cities, where a play she had written as a youth was staged, she began to explore the interior. She published impressions of her travels as *Views of Society and Manners in America* (1821), which attracted a readership in both Europe and America. Her book won her recognition from such prominent individuals as Jeremy Bentham, the philosopher of utilitarianism, and the Marquis de **Lafayette**. Wright accompanied Lafayette on his triumphant tour of the United Sates in 1824, leading to speculation that the two were lovers. After a visit to Robert Owen's perfectionist experiment at **New Harmony**, Wright purchased a 640-acre section of land near modern Memphis, Tennessee, and established her own experimental community called "Nashoha." She hoped to demonstrate that African **slaves** could be transformed into free and productive citizens in five years if they were promised their freedom. But she alienated many who supported her experiment by also attacking organized **religion**. Nashoha soon collapsed amid lurid rumors of sexual license that Wright did little to counter. Nonetheless, she fulfilled her promise to the Africans involved by freeing them and personally escorting them to Haiti.

For a while, Wright helped Robert Dale Owen, Robert Owen's son, edit a **newspaper**, the *New Harmony Gazette*. This was the first collaboration of a woman with a male editor in America. She broke other conventions by addressing mixed audiences of men and women on a variety of subjects that included the evils of organized religion, free public education, and the benefits of birth control. Her public appearances sometimes provoked riots and earned her a notorious reputation that did not further the causes she embraced, such as the early Workingmen's

Party. After 1831, she spent much of her time in Europe, returning occasionally to the United States in the late 1830s and again in 1850. In 1831, she married a Frenchman by whom she had one child. But at the end of her life, she divorced him and died in Cincinnati.

– X –

XYZ DISPATCHES. The record of the diplomatic exchanges between the American commissioners **Charles C. Pinckney**, **John Marshall**, and **Elbridge Gerry** and **Talleyrand**'s three go-betweens that the French foreign minister used in making humiliating demands on the United States. The demands included an apology for statements made by President **John Adams** in his inaugural speech, a loan that would compromise American neutrality, and bribes. **John Trumbull** helped transmit the dispatches to the United States. Their release to the public in early April 1798 produced a spirited response from Americans that allowed the **Federalist Party** to capture full control of the fifth Congress and lead the nation into the **Quasi-War** with France.

– Y –

YAZOO LANDS. They were named for the Yazoo River, which flowed through them. After the Revolution, Congress invited the states to cede their claims to western lands. Georgia, whose boundaries stretched to the Mississippi River, initially declined to do so. Instead, the state tried to sell its immense domain to private land companies. In early January 1795, the state government conveyed 35 million acres to four land companies for $500,000 under questionable circumstances.

James Jackson, absent in Philadelphia as a U.S. senator, opposed the sale as a corrupt bargain and succeeded in getting the state legislature to revoke it in February 1796. But in the interim, title to much of this land had been conveyed to out-of-state purchasers. The largest parcel was acquired by northern investors in the New England Mississippi Company, centered in Boston and formed for the purpose of speculating in western lands. The northerners stood to lose from Georgia's repudiation of its initial Yazoo sale and over the ensuing 15 years lobbied for compensation. They did so largely by appealing to the federal government, which acquired title to the disputed lands in 1802.

Though the legal claim of the out-of-state investors was weak, President **Thomas Jefferson**, Secretary of the Treasury **Albert Gallatin**, and Secretary of State **James Madison** favored setting aside some of this land to compensate northerners for their losses. The New England Mississippi Company numbered as many prominent northern members of the **Republican Party** in its ranks as members of the **Federalist Party**, but in Congress the administration's plans ran afoul of Representative **John Randolph**, who objected to it on ideological grounds. He succeeded in blocking a legislative resolution of the issue until the northern claimants to Yazoo lands brought a suit designed to get the **Supreme Court** to decide some of the legal issues involved. In ***Fletcher v. Peck*** (1810), Chief Justice **John Marshall**, speaking for a unanimous Court, invalidated the act whereby Georgia rescinded the original land sale on the grounds that it was a contract whose sanctity was guaranteed under the Constitution. Congress did not get around to passing a bill compensating the Yazoo claimants until 31 March 1814. Under its provisions, $5 million of U.S. stock was set aside for this purpose to be administered by the secretary of the treasury and the attorney general. A total of $4,282,151 was eventually disbursed to northern investors.

YELLOW FEVER. Though hardly unknown during the colonial period, this tropical disease made more frequent appearances in northern ports during the early republican period because of the expansion of commercial contacts with the West Indies after the conclusion of the Revolutionary War. The mosquitoes that transmitted yellow fever were able to survive the two-week voyage on vessels that arrived in the late summer and early autumn. Philadelphia suffered an especially severe outbreak of yellow fever in 1793 in which it is thought that 5,000 perished. In subsequent years, the infection reappeared there and in **New York City** on several occasions. While the transmission of the disease was not understood until a century later, yellow fever epidemics stimulated efforts at improving public health in the nation's emerging cities. **Benjamin Rush** took the lead in promoting public health measures in Philadelphia, while New York embarked on an ambitious scheme to improve its water supply.

Appendix: Presidential Administrations of the Early Republic

WASHINGTON ADMINISTRATION, 1789–1797

President George Washington
Vice President John Adams
Secretary of State
  John Jay (acting 26 September 1789–22 March 1790)
  Thomas Jefferson 22 March 1790–31 December 1793
  Edmund Randolph 2 January 1794–19 August 1795
  Timothy Pickering (acting 20 August 1795–9 December 1795); from 10 December 1795 when confirmed
Secretary of the Treasury
  Alexander Hamilton 11 September 1789–1 January 1795
  Oliver Wolcott Jr. from 2 January 1795
Secretary of War
  Henry Knox 12 September 1789–1 January 1795
  Timothy Pickering (acting 2 January 1795–5 February 1796)
  James McHenry from 5 February 1796
Postmaster General
  Samuel Osgood 26 September 1789–summer 1791
  Timothy Pickering 12 August 1791–24 February 1795
  Joseph Habersham from 25 February 1795
Attorney General
  Edmund Randolph 26 September 1789–1 January 1794
  William Bradford 27 January 1794–23 August 1795
  Charles Lee from 10 December 1795

ADAMS ADMINISTRATION, 1797–1801

President John Adams
Vice President Thomas Jefferson
Secretary of State
Timothy Pickering until 12 May 1800
Charles Lee (acting 13 May 1800–6 June 1800)
John Marshall 6 June 1800–4 February 1801 and 3 March 1801
Secretary of the Treasury
Oliver Wolcott Jr. until December 31, 1800
Samuel Dexter from 1 January 1801
Secretary of War
James McHenry to 20 May 1800
Benjamin Stoddert 1 June 1800–12 June 1800
Samuel Dexter 1800; 1801 (acting 12 June 1800–31 December 1800)
Postmaster General
Joseph Habersham
Attorney General
Charles Lee
Secretary of the Navy
Benjamin Stoddert from 21 May 1798

JEFFERSON ADMINISTRATIONS, 1801–1809

President Thomas Jefferson
Vice President
Aaron Burr until 1805
George Clinton until 1809
Secretary of State
John Marshall (4 March 1801)
Levi Lincoln (acting 4 March 1801–5 May 1801)
James Madison from 5 May 1801
Secretary of the Treasury
Samuel Dexter to 6 May 1801
Albert Gallatin from 14 May 1801

Secretary of War
  Henry Dearborn 5 March 1801–16 February 1809
  John Smith (acting from 17 February 1809)
Postmaster General
  Joseph Habersham to 21 November 1801
  Gideon Granger from 21 November 1801
Attorney General
  Levi Lincoln 5 March 1801–31 December 1804
  John C. Breckinridge 7 August 1805–14 December 1806
  Caesar A. Rodney from 20 January 1807
Department of the Navy
  Benjamin Stoddert to 31 March 1801
  Henry Dearborn (acting 1 April 1801–26 July 1801)
  Robert Smith from 27 July 1801

MADISON ADMINISTRATIONS, 1809–1917

President James Madison
Vice President
  George Clinton to 20 April 1812
  Elbridge Gerry 14 March 1813–23 November 1814
Secretary of State
  Robert Smith 6 March 1809–2 April 1811
  James Monroe from 6 April 1811
Secretary of the Treasury
  Albert Gallatin to 21 April 1813
  William Jones 22 April 1813–9 February 1814
  George W. Campbell 9 February 1814–13 October 1814
  Alexander J. Dallas 14 October 1814–21 October 1816
  William H. Crawford from 22 October 1816
Secretary of War
  John Smith (acting to April 8, 1809)
  William Eustis 8 April 1809–31 December 1812
  James Monroe 1 January to 5 February 1813, (acting 30 August–1 October 1814); 1 October 1814–1 March 1815

John Armstrong 5 February 1813–30 August 1814
Alexander J. Dallas (acting 14 March 1815–8 August 1815)
William H. Crawford 8 August 1815–22 October 1816
George Graham (acting from 22 October 1816)
Postmaster General
Gideon Granger until 17 March 1814
Return J. Meigs Jr. from 11 April 1814
Attorney General
Caesar A. Rodney to 5 December 1811
William Pinkney 6 January 1812–10 February 1814
Richard Rush from 10 February 1814
Secretary of the Navy
Robert Smith to 7 March 1809
Charles W. Goldsborough (acting 8 March 1809–15 May 1809 and again 7 January 1813–18 January 1813)
Paul Hamilton 15 May 1809–31 December 1812
William Jones 19 January 1813–1 December 1814
Benjamin Homans (acting 2 December 1814–16 January 1815)
Benjamin W. Crowninshield from 16 January 1815

MONROE ADMINISTRATIONS, 1817–1825

President James Monroe
Vice President Daniel D. Tompkins
Secretary of State
John Graham (acting 4 March 1817)
Richard Rush (acting 10 March–21 September 1817)
John Quincy Adams from 22 September 1817
Secretary of the Treasury
William H. Crawford
Secretary of War
George Graham (acting 4 March–9 December 1817)
John C. Calhoun from 10 December 1817
Postmaster General
Return J. Meigs Jr. until 26 June 1823
John McLean from 1 July 1823

Attorney General
Richard Rush until 30 October 1817
William Wirt from 15 November 1817
Secretary of the Navy
Benjamin W. Crowninshield until 30 September 1818
John C. Calhoun (acting 1 October–31 December 1818)
Smith Thompson 1 January–31 August 1823
John Rogers (acting 1 September–15 September 1823)
Samuel Southard from 16 September 1823

JOHN QUINCY ADAMS ADMINISTRATION, 1825–1829

President John Quincy Adams
Vice President John C. Calhoun
Secretary of State
Daniel Brent (acting 4 March–6 March 1825)
Henry Clay from 7 March 1825
Secretary of the Treasury
Samuel L. Southard (acting 7 March–31 July 1825)
Richard Rush from 1 August 1825
Secretary of War
James Barbour 7 March 1825–25 May 1828
Samuel L. Southard (acting 26 May–20 June 1828)
Peter B. Porter from 21 June 1828
Postmaster General
John McLean
Attorney General
William Wirt
Secretary of the Navy
Samuel L. Southard

Bibliography

CONTENTS

I. INTRODUCTION

The history of the early Republic is rich in published primary sources. A good place to begin is with the *Documentary History of the First Federal Congress of the United States of America, March 4, 1789–March 3, 1791*, 14 vols. (1972–1997). The major speeches delivered in this and subsequent Congresses were published by Gales and Seaton between 1834 and 1856 as *The debates and proceedings in the Congress of the United States: with appendix, containing important state papers and public documents*. The series, commonly referred to as *Annals of Congress*, covered the first 17 Congresses and the first session of the 18th Congress through March 1823 and appeared after Gales and Seaton started issuing in 1825 their *Register of Debates in Congress*, which reprinted the proceedings of each Congress as quickly as possible. Volumes 1 through 5 of the new series (1825–1830) begins with the second session of the 18th Congress in December 1824 and continues to the end of the 20th Congress in March 1829. Gales and Seaton also issued *American State Papers: Documents, Legislative and Executive, of the Congress of the United States*, 38 vols. (Washington, D.C.: Gales and Seaton), between 1832 and 1861. In this series, volumes 1 to 6 are devoted to foreign relations, 7 to 8 to Indian affairs, 9 to 13 to finance, 14 to 15 to commerce and navigation, 16 to 22 to military affairs, 23 to 26 to naval affairs, 27 to the Post Office department, 28 to 35 to public lands, 36 to claims, and 37 to 38 to miscellaneous. Volumes 2 and 3 of *Treaties and Other International Acts of the United States of America*, Hunter Miller ed. (1931–1948), provide one with ready access to the texts of treaties between 1789 and 1829.

The funding provided in the 1950s by the *New York Times* and *Time* magazine to collect and publish the papers of Thomas Jefferson and John Adams set in motion similar projects for other prominent public figures involved in the nation's founding. Thanks to the continuing support of the National Historic Publications Commission and the National Endowment for the Humanities, the papers of most of the leaders of the early republican period are available in print. Preeminent among these series are the *Papers of George Washington*, William W. Abbot et al. eds., which, when completed will replace John C. Fitzpatrick, ed., *The Writings of George Washington*, 39 vols. (1931–1944). Those portions of the new series most relevant to the period covered by this volume are volumes 1 to 11 of the Presidential series up through January 1793; volumes 1 to 4 the Retirement series, which is now complete; and volumes 5 and 6 of the Diaries. Harold C. Syrett succeeded in completing the Hamilton Papers (27 vols.) in 1987, and volumes 5 to 27 bear most directly on the period covered by this work. *The Papers of Thomas Jefferson* are now available through May 1800 in 31 volumes, of which volumes 14 to 31 deal with the early republican period. *The Papers of James Madison* are complete to September 1812. The only portion of the published Adams papers relevant to this volume is volume 3 of the *Diary and Autobiography of John Adams* (1961). *The Papers of John Marshall* (1974–2002) are now complete in 11 volumes. In addition, the student can consult *The Papers of Andrew Jackson* (1980–2002), 6 vols. to date, covering up to 1828; *The Papers of John C. Calhoun* (1959–2003), volumes 1 to 11 being relevant to this period; volumes 1 to 8 of *The Papers of Henry Clay* (1959–1992); and *The Papers of Daniel Webster* (1974–1989). This last series is divided into seven volumes of correspondence, of which volumes 1 and 2 are relevant to the period 1789–1829, and four volumes of legal papers. Those interested in John Quincy Adams can consult Worthington C. Ford, ed., *Writings of John Quincy Adams*, 7 vols. (1913–1923), though this series extends only to June 1823. But the gaps in this and the other series that are still in process can be filled by consulting the manuscript records of those in question. For Washington, Jefferson, Madison, and James Monroe, the only president in the period for whom there is not a published series, the Library of Congress has the best collection, while the Massachusetts Historical Society has the most complete file of papers pertaining to both Adamses. Among the over nine million digitalized items currently available on the Library of Congress's American Memory website are its holdings of Washington, Jefferson, and Madison papers. These can be accessed and downloaded by going to http://memory.loc.gov/ammem/index.html, but when the digitalized documents are manuscripts, they are not always easy to read.

At the turn of the 20th century, Charles Evans began compiling a chronological list of everything published in the United States from the first imprint in 1639. The first 12 volumes of his *American Bibliography* (1903–1934) cover the period up to 1799, of which volumes 7 to 12 relate to the years treated in this dictionary. Clifford K. Shipton carried the work through 1800 in volume 13 (1959), and Roger P. Bristol supplied an index to the series (1961) together with two additional volumes of addenda with indexes (1970–1971). Beginning in 1964, Ralph R. Shaw and Richard H. Shoemaker extended Evans's project into the 19th century with 19 volumes covering the period up through 1819 (1958–1966). In 1964, Shoemaker began a new series cataloging publications of the 1820s that was completed by M. Frances Cooper in 1972 under the title *American Imprints*. In the 1950s and 1960s, the Readex Corporation, in association with the American Antiquarian Society, issued microcard editions of most of the items in the Evans and original Shaw–Shoemaker series. Subsequently, it issued a microfiche version of the same materials and more recently a digital version of the Evans texts that is available online to subscribers. The Readex Corporation is also filming as many early American newspapers as lend themselves to photoreproduction. Though stains on the surviving copies sometimes makes it difficult to use them, the project has done many newspapers up through the 1820s. Finally, the Readex Corporation recently began digitalizing the Shaw–Shoemaker texts, to which it is currently inviting subscriptions and is exploring digitalizing its newspaper series sometime in the future. The combined efforts of the Readex Corporation and the American Antiquarian Society have already made the basic sources for the early Republic widely available to those who do not have access to large research libraries and promises to extend these benefits even further in the years to come.

The founding of the Society for the Study of the Early Republic in 1977 and its sponsorship of the *Journal of the Early Republic* beginning in 1981 gave an enormous boost to scholarly investigations of the period. The fruits of that research have spilled over into the pages of the numerous historical journals specializing in American history. The bibliography that follows features secondary works produced in the past 20 years, many of which grew out of initial publications in these journals, supplemented by the works from the earlier period of special significance. The articles included are drawn from the *Journal of American History*, the *Journal of Economic History*, and the *William & Mary Quarterly*, which have a national focus, and two regional journals, the *New England Quarterly* and the

Journal of Southern History. Largely missing from this bibliography are articles that appeared in state historical journals, such as the *Pennsylvania Magazine of History and Biography*, the *Maryland Historical Magazine*, the *Virginia Magazine of History and Biography*, and the *North Carolina Historical Review*, to name some of the more prominent ones. Students pursuing research interests in these geographic areas should check the relevant historical journals of their area.

For background reference material on the Revolution, the early Republic, and the pre–Civil War periods in American history, the historical dictionaries published by Scarecrow Press are as good a place to begin as any. Those who want a thought-provoking synthesis of the early republican era would be well advised to start with Robert H. Wiebe, *The Opening of American Society: From the Adoption of the Constitution to the Eve of Disunion* (1984). Joseph J. Ellis, *Founding Brothers: The Revolutionary Generation* (2000), is more entertaining but tends to skirt around important issues. Those wishing to have the era's significance placed in the larger context of the American Revolution should consult Gordon S. Wood, *The Radicalism of the American Revolution* (1992). Those interested in a more radical perspective on the period can consult Alan Taylor, *Liberty Man and Great Proprietors: The Revolutionary Settlement on the Maine Frontier, 1760–1820* (1990) and *William Cooper's Town: Power and Persuasion on the Frontier of the Early American Republic* (1995) as well as Sean Wilentz, *Chants Democratic: New York City and the Rise of the American Working Class, 1788–1850* (1984).

The literature abounds with biographies of prominent figures in the age. Among the better ones apposite to the early Republic are Joseph J. Ellis, *American Sphinx: The Character of Thomas Jefferson* (1997); Drew McCoy, *The Last of the Fathers: James Madison and the Republican Legacy* (1989); David McCullough, *John Adams* (2001); Ron Chernow, *Alexander Hamilton* (2004); Henry Wiencek, *An Imperfect God: George Washington, His Slaves, and the Creation of America* (2003); and Joseph J. Ellis, *His Excellency* (2004).

For monographs on the First Party System, one should consult Stanley Elkins and Eric McKitrick, *The Federalist Era* (1993); Richard Hofstadter, *The Idea of a Party System: The Rise of Legitimate Opposition in the United States, 1780–1840* (1969); and Richard Buel Jr., *Securing the Revolution: Ideology in American Politics, 1789–1815* (1972) and *America at the Brink: Federalism during the Jeffersonian Ascendancy* (2005). For the diplomatic background of the War of 1812, Bradford Perkins, *Prologue to War: England and the United States 1805–1812* (1961), is especially useful. For the political context of the war, Henry Adams, *The History of the United States during the Administrations of James Madison*, first published in the late 19th century and reissued in 1986 with a copious index, has yet to be surpassed, though J. C. A. Stagg, *Mr. Madison's War: Politics, Diplomacy, and Warfare in the Early Republic, 1783–1830* (1983), comes close to doing so. For the postwar period, George Dangerfield, *The Era of Good Feelings* (1952), remains an enduring classic. For the beginnings of the

Second Party System, see Richard P. McCormick, *The Second American Party System: Party Formation in the Jacksonian Era* (1966).

The recent interest in slavery has produced a number of quality works on the subject that touch on but do not exclusively focus on the early republican period. They include David Brion Davis, *The Problem of Slavery in the Age of Revolution 1770–1823* (1975) and *Challenging the Boundaries of Slavery* (2003). Ira Berlin, *Many Thousands Gone: The First Two Centuries of Slavery in America* (1998), and Arthur Zilversmit, *First Emancipation: The Abolition of Slavery in the North* (1967), are worth comparing with each other.

For the economic history of the period, Douglass C. North, *The Economic Growth of the United States 1790–1860* (1961), remains authoritative. The other enduring classic in the field, George Rogers Taylor, *The Transportation Revolution 1815–1860* (1951), touches on developments before 1815 as well. Charles Sellers, *The Market Revolution: Jacksonian America 1815–1846* (1991), begins with a masterful summary of the nation's preindustrial economy before exploring the consequences of industrialization.

The most popular accounts of women's lives in the early Republic are Laurel Thatcher Ulrich, *A Midwife's Tale: The Life of Martha Ballard, Based on Her Diary, 1785–1812* (1990), and Nancy Cott, *The Bonds of Womanhood: "Women's Sphere" in New England, 1780–1835* (1977). They speak powerfully to contemporary aspirations. For a less present-oriented approach, see Joy D. and Richard Buel Jr., *The Way of Duty: A Woman and Her Family in Revolutionary America* (1984).

An interesting though problematic attempt to define the distinctive character of the early republican period can be found in Joyce Appleby, *Inheriting the Revolution: The First Generation of Americans* (2000).

II. BIBLIOGRAPHIES

Bibliographies of New England: Further Additions to 1994. Edited by Roger Parks. Hanover, N.H.: University Press of New England, 1995.

Brigham, Clarence S. *History and Bibliography of American Newspapers 1690–1820*. 2 vols. Worcester, Mass.: American Antiquarian Society, 1947.

Evans, Charles. *American Bibliography; A Chronological Dictionary of All Books, Pamphlets, and Periodical Publications Printed in the United States of America from the Genesis of Printing in 1639 Down to and Including the Year 1820. With Bibliographical and Biographical Notes*. 13 vols. Chicago: Privately printed for the author by the Blakely Press, 1903–1959.

Fredriksen, John C. *War of 1812 Eyewitness Accounts: An Annotated Bibliography*. Westport, Conn.: Greenwood Press, 1997.

Index of Printers, Publishers, and Booksellers Indicated by Charles Evans in His American Bibliography. Charlottesville: Bibliographical Society of the University of Virginia, 1961.

New England: A Bibliography of Its History. Edited by Roger Parks. Hanover, N.H.: University Press of New England, 1989.

Shaw, Ralph R., compiled with Richard H. Shoemaker. *American Bibliography: A Preliminary Checklist for 1801–1819*. 19 vols. New York: Scarecrow Press, 1958–1983.

Shoemaker, Richard H. *A Checklist of American Imprints for 1820–1829*. 10 vols. New York: Scarecrow Press, 1964–1971.

Supplement to Charles Evans' American Bibliography. Edited by Roger P. Bristol. Charlottesville: Published for the Bibliographical Society of America and the Bibliographical Society of the University of Virginia [by] the University Press of Virginia, 1970.

III. PUBLISHED PRIMARY SOURCES

A. Published State Papers and Public Records

American State Papers: Documents, Legislative and Executive, of the Congress of the United States. 38 vols. Washington, D.C.: Gales and Seaton, 1832–1861.

Circular Letters of Congressmen to Their Constituents, 1789–1829. Edited by Noble E. Cunningham Jr. 3 vols. Chapel Hill: University of North Carolina Press, 1978.

The Debates and Proceedings in the Congress of the United States: With Appendix, Containing Important State Papers and Public Documents. . . . 43 vols. Washington, D.C.: Gales and Seaton, 1834–1856.

Documentary History of the First Federal Congress of the United States. Edited by Kenneth R. Bolling et al. 17 vols. to date. Baltimore: The Johns Hopkins University Press, 1972–.

The Documentary History of the First Federal Elections, 1788–1790. Edited by Merrill Jensen et al. 4 vols. Madison: University of Wisconsin Press, 1976–1989.

The Documentary History of the Supreme Court of the United States, 1789–1800. Edited by Maeva Marcus et al. 6 vols. to date. New York: Columbia University Press, 1985–.

Naval Documents Related to the United States War with the Barbary Powers. . . . Naval Operations Including Diplomatic Background. . . . Published under Direction of the . . . Secretary of the Navy. Edited by Dudley W. Knox. 6 vols. Washington, D.C.: Department of the Navy, 1939–1944.

The Naval War of 1812: A Documentary History. Edited by William S. Dudley and Michael J. Crawford. 3 vols. Washington, D.C.: Department of the Navy, 1985–2002.

The Public Statutes at Large of the United States of America, from the Organization of the Government in 1789, to March 3, 1845. 8 vols. Boston: Little, Brown, 1845–1867.

Register of Debates in Congress . . . 14 vols. Washington, D.C.: Gales and Seaton, 1825–1837.

Treaties and Other International Acts of the United States of America. Edited by Hunter Miller. 8 vols. Washington, D.C.: U.S. Government Printing Office, 1931–1948.

White Slave, African Masters: An Anthology of American Barbary Captivity Narratives. Edited by Paul Baepter. Chicago: University of Chicago Press, 1999.

B. Papers of Public Figures

Diaries of George Washington. Edited by Donald Jackson. 6 vols. Charlottesville: University Press of Virginia, 1976–1979.

Diary and Autobiography of John Adams. Edited by Lyman H. Butterfield. 4 vols. Cambridge, Mass.: Harvard University Press, Belknap Press, 1961.

Ethan Allen and His Kin: Correspondence, 1772–1819. Edited by John F. Duffy et al. 2 vols. Hanover, N.H.: University Press of New England, 1998.

The Journals of the Lewis and Clark Expedition. Edited by Gary E. Moulton. 13 vols. to date. Lincoln: University of Nebraska Press, 1983–.

Letters of the Lewis and Clark Expedition, with Related Documents 1783–1854. Edited by Donald D. Jackson. Urbana: University of Illinois Press, 1962.

The Papers of Alexander Hamilton. Edited by Harold C. Syrett. 27 vols. New York: Columbia University Press, 1961–1987.

The Papers of Andrew Jackson. Edited by Sam B. Smith and Harriet Chappell Owsley. 6 vols. Knoxville: University of Tennessee Press, 1980–2002.

The Papers of Benjamin Henry Latrobe. Edited by Edward C. Carter II et al. 4 series. New Haven, Conn.: Yale University Press, 1977–1994.

The Papers of Daniel Webster: Correspondence. Edited by Charles M. Wiltse et al. 7 vols. Hanover, N.H.: University Press of New England, 1974–1986.

The Papers of Daniel Webster: Legal Papers. Edited by Alfred F. Konefsky and Andrew J. King. 4 vols. Hanover, N.H.: University Press of New England, 1982–1989.

The Papers of Daniel Webster: Speeches and Formal Writings. Edited by Charles M. Wiltse and Alan R. Berolzheimer. 2 vols. to date. Hanover, N.H.: University Press of New England, 1986–.

The Papers of George Washington. Edited by W. W. Abbot et al. 41 vols. to date in 5 series. Charlottesville: University Press of Virginia, 1983–.

The Papers of Henry Clay. Edited by James F. Hopkins. 11 vols. Lexington: University Press of Kentucky, 1959–1992.

The Papers of James Madison. Edited by William T. Hutchinson and William M. E Rachel et al. 10 vols. Chicago: University of Chicago Press, 1962–1977.

The Papers of James Madison. Edited by Robert R. Rutland. 7 vols. Charlottesville: University Press of Virginia, 1977–1991.

The Papers of James Madison: Presidential Series. Edited by Robert R. Rutland et al. 4 vols. to date. Charlottesville: University Press of Virginia, 1984–.

The Papers of James Madison: Secretary of State Series. Edited by Robert R. Rutland et al. 6 vols. Charlottesville: University Press of Virginia, 1986–2002.

The Papers of John C. Calhoun. Edited by Robert L. Meriwether et al. 11 vols. Columbia: University of South Carolina Press, 1959–2003.

The Papers of John Marshall. Edited by Herbert A. Johnson et al. 11 vols. Chapel Hill: University of North Carolina Press, 1974–2002.

The Papers of Thomas Jefferson. Edited by Julian P. Boyd et al. 30 vols. to date. Princeton, N.J.: Princeton University Press, 1950–.

The Papers of William Thornton. Edited by C. M. Harris and Daniel Preston. Charlottesville: University Press of Virginia, 1995.

Peter Porcupine in America: Pamphlets on Republicanism and Revolution. Edited by David A. Wilson. Ithaca, N.Y.: Cornell University Press, 1994.

Political Correspondence and Public Papers of Aaron Burr. Edited by Mary-Jo Kline and Joanne W. Ryan. 2 vols. Princeton, N.J.: Princeton University Press, 1983.

The Power of Her Sympathy: The Autobiography and Journal of Catherine Maria Sedgwick. Edited by Mary Kelley. Boston: Massachusetts Historical Society, 1993.

Selected Letters of Dolley Payne Madison. Edited by David B. Mattern and Holly C. Shulman. Charlottesville: University Press of Virginia, 2003.

The Selected Papers of Charles Willson Peale and His Family. Edited by Lillian B. Miller et al. 5 vols. to date. New Haven, Conn.: Yale University Press, 1983–.

Works of Fisher Ames, as Published by Seth Ames. Edited by W. B. Allen. 2 vols. Indianapolis: Liberty Fund, 1983.

The Writings of George Washington. Edited by John C. Fitzpatrick. 39 vols. Washington, D.C.: U.S. Government Printing Office, 1931–1944.

Writings of John Quincy Adams. Edited by Worthington Chauncey Ford. 7 vols. New York: Macmillan, 1913–1917.

C. Digital Editions of Primary Sources

The Dolley Madison Digital Edition. Edited by Holly Shulman. Charlottesville: University Press of Virginia, 2004.

Early American Imprints, Series I. Evans (1639–1800). Chester, Vt.: Archive of Americana, 2004.

Early American Imprints, Series II. Shaw–Shoemaker (1801–1819). Chester, Vt.: Archive of Americana, 2005–.

Early American Newspapers (1690–1876). Chester, Vt.: Archive of Americana, 2005–.

U.S. Congressional Serial Set (1817–1982) with *American State Papers (1789–1838)*. Chester, Vt.: Archive of Americana, 2003.

IV. SECONDARY WORKS

A. Standard Reference Works

American National Biography. Edited by John A. Garraty and Mark C. Carnes. 24 vols. New York: Oxford University Press, 1999.

Biographical Directory of the United States Congress 1774–1989. Bicentennial ed. Washington, D.C.: U.S. Government Printing Office, 1989.

Cappon, Lester J. *Atlas of Early American History: The Revolutionary Era 1760–1790*. Princeton, N.J.: Princeton University Press, 1976.

Dexter, Franklin Bowditch. *Biographical Sketches of the Graduates of Yale College with Annals of the College History* . . . 7 vols. New York: H. Holt, 1885–1913.

Dictionary of American Biography. Edited by Allen Johnson et al. 22 vols. New York: Charles Scribner's Sons, 1928–1958.

Dictionary of American History. Edited by Stanley I. Kutler. 3rd ed. 10 vols. New York: Charles Scribner's Sons, 2003.

Encyclopedia of the War of 1812. Edited by David S. Heidler and Jeanne T. Heidler. Santa Barbara, Calif.: ABC-CLIO, 1997.

Green, Rayna, and Melanie Fernandez. *The British Museum Encyclopedia of Native North America*. Bloomington: Indiana University Press, 1999.

Halloran, Peter C. *Historical Dictionary of New England*. Lanham, Md.: Scarecrow Press, 2003.

Malcomson, Robert. *Historical Dictionary of the War of 1812*. Lanham, Md.: Scarecrow Press, 2004.

Mays, Terry. *Historical Dictionary of Revolutionary America*. Lanham, Md.: Scarecrow Press, 2005.

McClelland, Peter D., and Richard T. Zeckhauser. *Demographic Dimensions of the New Republic: American Internal Migration, Vital Statistics, and Manumissions, 1800–1860*. Cambridge: Cambridge University Press, 1982.

New Historical Atlas of Religion in America. Edited by Edwin S. Gaustad and Philip L. Barlow. New York: Oxford University Press, 2001.

Oxford Companion to American Military History. Edited by John W. Chambers II. New York: Oxford University Press, 1999.

Oxford Companion to United States History. Edited by Paul S. Boyer. New York: Oxford University Press, 2001.

Paulin, Charles O. *Atlas of the Historical Geography of the United States*. Edited by John K. Wright. Baltimore: Carnegie Institute of Washington, 1932.

Population Abstract of the United States. Edited by Donna Androit. McLean, Va.: Documents Index, Inc., 1993.

Princetonians 1748–1794: A Biographical Dictionary. Edited and compiled by James McLachlan et al. 5 vols. to date. Princeton, N.J.: Princeton University Press, 1976–.

Richter, William L. *Historical Dictionary of the Old South*. Lanham, Md.: Scarecrow Press, 2004.

Sibley's Harvard Graduates: Biographical Sketches of Those Who Attended Harvard College . . . with Bibliographical and Other Notes. Compiled by John L. Sibley et al. 17 vols. to date. Boston and Cambridge: Massachusetts Historical Society and Harvard University Press, 1873–.

Wattenberg, Ben J. *The Statistical History of the United States from Colonial Times to the Present*. New York: Basic Books, 1976.

The West Point Atlas of American Wars. Edited by Vincent J. Esposito. 2 vols. New York: Frederick A. Praeger, 1959.

B. General Histories of the Period

Appleby, Joyce. *Inheriting the Revolution: The First Generation of Americans*. Cambridge, Mass.: Harvard University Press, 2000.

Cogliano, Francis D. *Revolutionary America, 1763–1815: A Political History*. New York: Routledge, 1999.

Ellis, Joseph J. *Founding Brothers: The Revolutionary Generation*. New York: Alfred A. Knopf, 2000.

Feller, Daniel. *The Jacksonian Promise: America, 1815–1840*. Baltimore: The Johns Hopkins University Press, 1995.

Ferguson, Robert A. *Reading the Early Republic*. Cambridge, Mass.: Harvard University Press, 2004.

Howe, Daniel Walker. *Making the American Self: Jonathan Edwards to Abraham Lincoln*. Cambridge, Mass.: Harvard University Press, 1997.

Wiebe, Robert H. *The Opening of American Society: From the Adoption of the Constitution to the Eve of Disunion*. New York: Alfred A. Knopf, 1984.

Wood, Gordon S. *The Radicalism of the American Revolution*. New York: Alfred A. Knopf, 1992.

———. "The Significance of the Early Republic." *Journal of the Early Republic* 8 (1988): 1–20.

C. Specialized Monographic Studies

1. Political History

a. Foundations

Anderson, Thornton. *Creating the Constitution: The Convention of 1787 and the First Congress*. University Park: Pennsylvania State University Press, 1994.

Bagnall, Norma H. *On Shaky Ground: The New Madrid Earthquakes of 1811–1812*. Columbia: University of Missouri Press, 1996.

The Bill of Rights: Government Proscribed. Edited by Ronald Hoffman and Peter J. Albert. Charlottesville: University Press of Virginia, 1997.

Bowling, Kenneth R. "'A Tub to the Whale': The Founding Fathers and the Adoption of the Federal Bill of Rights." *Journal of the Early Republic* 8 (1988): 223–51.

Boyd, Steven R. "The Contract Clause and the Evolution of American Federalism, 1789–1815." *William & Mary Quarterly* 44 (3rd ser., 1987): 529–49.

Casto, William R. *The Supreme Court in the Early Republic: The Chief Justiceships of John Jay and Oliver Ellsworth*. Columbia: University of South Carolina Press, 1995.

Clinton, Robert L. *Marbury v. Madison and Judicial Review*. Lawrence: University Press of Kansas, 1989.

Cohen, Patricia Cline. "Statistics and the State: Changing Social Thought and the Emergence of a Quantitative Mentality in America, 1790–1830." *William & Mary Quarterly* 38 (3rd ser., 1981): 35–55.

Coward, Joan Wells. *Kentucky in the New Republic: The Process of Constitution Making*. Lexington: University Press of Kentucky, 1979.

Cress, Lawrence D. "An Armed Community: The Origins and Meaning of the Right to Bear Arms." *Journal of American History* 71 (1984–1985): 22–42.

Currie, David P. *The Constitution in Congress: The Federalist Period, 1789–1801*. Chicago: University of Chicago Press, 1997.

Edling, Max, and Mark D. Kaplanoff. "Alexander Hamilton's Fiscal Reforms: Transforming the Structure of Taxation in the Early Republic." *William & Mary Quarterly* 61 (3rd ser., 2004): 713–44.

Hall, Mark D. *The Political and Legal Philosophy of James Wilson, 1742–1798*. New York: Columbia University Press, 1997.

Inventing Congress: Origins and Establishment of the First Federal Congress. Edited by Kenneth R. Bowling and Donald R. Kennon. Athens: Ohio University Press, 1999.

Kahn, Paul. *The Reign of Law: "Marbury v. Madison" and the Construction of America*. New Haven, Conn.: Yale University Press, 1997.

Keller, Claire W. "The Failure to Provide a Constitutional Guarantee on Representation." *Journal of the Early Republic* 13 (1993): 23–54.

Kennon, Donald R. *The Republic for the Ages: The United States Capitol and the Political Culture of the Early Republic*. Charlottesville: University Press of Virginia, 1999.

Keyssar, Alexander. *The Right to Vote: The Contested History of Democracy in the United States*. New York: Basic Books, 2000.

Klubes, Benjamin B. "The First Federal Congress and the First National Bank: A Case Study in Constitutional Interpretation." *Journal of the Early Republic* 11 (1991): 19–41.

Leiberger, Stuart. "James Madison and Amendments to the Constitution, 1787–1789: 'Parchment Barriers.'" *Journal of Southern History* 59 (1993): 441–68.

Lewis, Jan. "'Of Every Age Sex & Condition': The Representation of Women in the Constitution." *Journal of the Early Republic* 15 (1995): 259–387.

Lynch, Joseph M. *Negotiating the Constitution: The Earliest Debates over Original Intent*. Ithaca, N.Y.: Cornell University Press, 1999.

Maltz, Earl M. "The Idea of the Proslavery Constitution." *Journal of the Early Republic* 17 (1997): 37–59.

Nelson, William E. "Reason and Compromise in the Establishment of the Federal Constitution, 1787–1801." *William & Mary Quarterly* 44 (3rd ser., 1987): 458–84.

Origins of the Federal Judiciary: Essays on the Judiciary Act of 1789. Edited by Maeva Marcus. New York: Oxford University Press, 1992.

Perry, James R. "Supreme Court Appointments, 1789–1801: Criteria, Presidential Style, and the Press of Events." *Journal of the Early Republic* 6 (1986): 371–410.

"The Population of the United States, 1790: A Symposium." *William & Mary Quarterly* 41 (3rd ser., 1984): 85–135.

Rakove, Jack N. *Original Meanings: Politics and Ideas in the Making of the Constitution*. New York: Alfred A. Knopf, 1996.

Risjord, Norman K. "Partisanship and Power, House Committees and the Power of the Speaker, 1789–1801." *William & Mary Quarterly* 49 (3rd ser., 1992): 628–51.

Ritz, Wilfred J. *Rewriting the History of the Judiciary Act of 1789: Exposing Myths, Challenging Premises, and Using New Evidence*. Edited by Wythe Holt and L. H. LaRue. Norman: University of Oklahoma Press, 1990.

Seriatim: The Supreme Court before John Marshall. Edited by Scott D. Gerber. New York: New York University Press, 1998.

Shalhope, Robert E. "The Ideological Origins of the Second Amendment." *Journal of American History* 69 (1982–1983): 591–614.

Siemers, David J. *Ratifying the Republic: Antifederalists and Federalists in Constitutional Time*. Stanford, Calif.: Stanford University Press, 2002.

Slonim, Shlomo. "The Electoral College at Philadelphia: The Evolution of an Ad Hoc Congress for the Selection of a President." *Journal of American History* 73 (1986–1987): 35–58.

Stevens, Michael E. "Legislative Privilege in Post-Revolutionary South Carolina." *William & Mary Quarterly* 46 (3rd ser., 1989): 71–93.

Strum, Harvey. "Property Qualifications and Voting Behavior in New York, 1807–1816." *Journal of the Early Republic* 1 (1981): 347–71.

Swift, Elaine K. *The Making of an American Senate: Reconstitutive Change in Congress, 1787–1841*. Ann Arbor: University of Michigan Press, 1997.

Zagarri, Rosemary. "Representation and the Removal of State Capitals, 1776–1812." *Journal of American History* 74 (1988): 1239–56.

b. Political Culture

1. General Studies

Appleby, Joyce. *Capitalism and the New Social Order: The Republican Vision of the 1790s*. New York: New York University Press, 1984.

———. "Republicanism in Old and New Contexts." *William & Mary Quarterly* 43 (3rd ser., 1986): 20–34.

Banning, Lance. "Jeffersonian Ideology Revisited: Liberal and Classical Ideas in the New American Republic." *William & Mary Quarterly* 43 (3rd ser., 1986): 3–19.

Beyond the Founders: New Approaches to the Political History of the Early American Republic. Edited by Jeffrey L. Pasley, Andrew W. Robertson, and David Waldstreicher. Chapel Hill: University of North Carolina Press, 2004.

Brooke, John L. *The Heart of the Commonwealth: Society and Political Culture in Worcester County, Massachusetts, 1713–1861*. Cambridge: Cambridge University Press, 1990.

Burstein, Andrew. "The Political Character of Sympathy." *Journal of the Early Republic* 21 (2001): 601–32.

Bushman, Richard L. "A Poet, a Planter, and a Nation of Farmers." *Journal of the Early Republic* 19 (1999): 1–14.

Cogan, Jacob K. "The Reynolds Affair and the Politics of Character." *Journal of the Early Republic* 16 (1996): 289–417.

Crowley, John F. *The Privileges of Independence: Neomercantilism and the American Revolution*. Baltimore: The Johns Hopkins University Press, 1993.

"Deference or Defiance in Eighteenth-Century America?" Forum in *Journal of American History* 85 (1998): 13–97.

Durey, Michael. "Thomas Paine's Apostles: Radical Emigres and the Triumph of Jeffersonian Republicanism." *William & Mary Quarterly* 44 (3rd ser., 1987): 661–88.

Formisano, Ronald P. *The Transformation of Political Culture: Massachusetts Parties, 1790s–1840s*. New York: Oxford University Press, 1983.

Heale, M. J. *The Presidential Quest: Candidates and Images in American Political Culture, 1787–1852*. London: Longman, 1982.

Henderson, H. James. "Taxation and Political Culture: Massachusetts and Virginia, 1760–1800." *William & Mary Quarterly* 47 (3rd ser., 1990): 90–114.

Hoffer, Peter C. *Revolution and Regeneration: Life Cycle and the Vision of the Generation of 1776*. Athens: University of Georgia Press, 1983.

Hofstadter, Richard. *The Idea of a Party System: The Rise of Legitimate Opposition in the United States, 1780–1840*. Berkeley: University of California Press, 1969.

Huston, James L. "The American Revolutionaries, the Political Economy of Aristocracy, and the American Concept of the Distribution of Wealth, 1765–1900." *American Historical Review* 98 (1993): 1079–105.

Jordan, Daniel P. *Political Leadership in Jefferson's Virginia*. Charlottesville: University Press of Virginia, 1983.

Knouff, Gregory T. *The Soldiers' Revolution: Pennsylvanians in Arms and the Forging of Early American Identity*. University Park: Pennsylvania State University Press, 2004.

Kornfeld, Eve. "From Republicanism to Liberalism: The Intellectual Journey of David Ramsay." *Journal of the Early Republic* 9 (1989): 289–313.

McCormick, Richard P. *The Presidential Game: The Origins of American Presidential Politics*. New York: Oxford University Press, 1982.

Neither Separate nor Equal: Congress in the 1790s. Edited by Kenneth R. Bowling and Donald R. Kennon. Athens: Ohio University Press, 2000.

Newman, Simon P. "Principles or Men? George Washington and the Political Culture of National Leadership, 1776–1801." *Journal of the Early Republic* 12 (1992): 477–507.

Pasley, Jeffrey L. "A Journeyman, Either in Law or Politics": John Beckley and the Social Origins of Political Campaigning." *Journal of the Early Republic* 16 (1996): 533–69.

The Revolution of 1800: Democracy, Race, and the New Republic. Edited by James Horn, Jan E. Lewis, and Peter S. Onuf. Charlottesville: University Press of Virginia, 2002.

Robertson, Andrew W. "'Look at This Picture . . . and at This!' Nationalism, Localism, and Partisan Images of Otherness in the United States, 1787–1820." *American Historical Review* 106 (2001): 1263–80.

Samet, Elizabeth D. *Willing Obedience: Citizens, Soldiers, and the Progress of Consent in America, 1776–1898*. Stanford, Calif.: Stanford University Press, 2004.

Tise, Larry E. *The American Counter Revolution: The Retreat from Liberty, 1783–1800*. Mechanicsburg, Pa.: Stackpole Books, 1998.

Trees, Andrew S. *The Founding Fathers and the Politics of Character*. Princeton, N.J.: Princeton University Press, 2004.

Vanburkleo, Sandra F. "Honour, Justice, and Interest: John Jay's Republican Politics and Statesmanship on the Federal Bench." *Journal of the Early Republic* 4 (1984): 239–74.

Wood, Gordon S. "Conspiracy and the Paranoid Style: Causality and Deceit in the Eighteenth Century." *William & Mary Quarterly* 39 (3rd ser., 1982): 401–41.

Wright, Conrad. *Revolutionary Generation: Harvard Men and the Consequences of Independence*. Amherst: University of Massachusetts Press, 2005.

2. Communications and the Press

Brooke, John L. "To Be 'Read by the Whole People': Press, Party, and the Public Sphere in the United States, 1789–1840." *Proceedings of the American Antiquarian Society* 100 (2000): 41–118.

Brown, Richard D. *Knowledge Is Power: The Diffusion of Information in Early America, 1700–1865*. New York: Oxford University Press, 1989.

———. *The Strength of a People: The Idea of an Informed Citizenry in America, 1650–1870*. Chapel Hill: University of North Carolina Press, 1996.

The Conservative Press in Eighteenth- and Nineteenth-Century America. Edited by Ronald Lora and William H. Longton. Westport, Conn.: Greenwood Press, 1999.

Humphrey, Carol Sue. *The Press of the Young Republic, 1783–1833*. Westport, Conn.: Greenwood Press, 1996.

John, Richard R. *Spreading the News: The American Postal System from Franklin to Morse*. Cambridge, Mass.: Harvard University Press, 1996.

Kaplan, Catherine. "'He Summons Genius . . . to his Aid': Letters, Partnership, and the Making of the *Farmer's Weekly Museum*, 1775–1800." *Journal of the Early Republic* 23 (2003): 544–71.

Kielbowicz, Richard B. "The Press, Post Office, and Flow of News in the Early Republic." *Journal of the Early Republic* 3 (1983): 255–80.

Lewis, Benjamin M. *An Introduction to American Magazines, 1800–1810*. Ann Arbor: University of Michigan, Department of Library Sciences, 1961.

Pasley, Jeffrey L. *"The Tyranny of Printers": Newspaper Politics in the Early American Republic*. Charlottesville: University Press of Virginia, 2001.

Remer, Rosiland. *Printers and Men of Capital: Philadelphia Book Publishers in the New Republic*. Philadelphia: University of Pennsylvania Press, 1996.

Shalev, Eran. "Ancient Mask, American Fathers: Classical Pseudonyms during the American Revolution and the Early Republic." *Journal of the Early Republic* 23 (2003): 151–72.

Steffen, Charles G. "Newspapers for Free: The Economies of Newspaper Circulation in the Early Republic." *Journal of the Early Republic* 23 (2003): 381–419.

Tagg, James. *Benjamin Franklin Bache and the Philadelphia*. Aurora. Philadelphia: University of Pennsylvania Press, 1991.

Warner, Michael. *The Letters of the Republic: Publication and the Public Sphere in Eighteenth-Century America*. Cambridge, Mass.: Harvard University Press, 1990.

3. Dueling

Freeman, Joanne B. *Affairs of Honor: National Politics in the New Republic*. New Haven, Conn.: Yale University Press, 2001.

———. "Dueling as Politics: Reinterpreting the Burr-Hamilton Duel." *William & Mary Quarterly* 53 (3rd ser., 1996): 289–318.

Greenberg, Kenneth S. "The Nose, the Lie, and the Duel in the Antebellum South." *American Historical Review* 95 (1990): 57–74.

Rorabaugh, W. J. "The Political Duel in the Early Republic: Burr v. Hamilton." *Journal of the Early Republic* 15 (1995): 1–23.

Steward, Dick. *Duels and the Roots of Violence in Missouri*. Columbia: University of Missouri Press, 2000.

Williams, Jack K. *Dueling in the Old South: Vignettes of Social History*. College Station: Texas A&M University Press, 1980.

Wyatt-Brown, Bertram. *Southern Honor: Ethics and Behavior in the Old South*. New York: Oxford University Press, 1982.

4. Federalism

Arch, Stephen Carl. "Writing a Federalist Self: Alexander Craydon's *Memoirs of a Life*." *William & Mary Quarterly* 52 (3rd ser., 1995): 415–32.

Broussard, James. *The Southern Federalists*. Baton Rouge: Louisiana State University Press, 1978.

Crocker, Matthew H. *The Magic of Many: Josiah Quincy and the Rise of Mass Politics in Boston, 1800–1830*. Amherst: University of Massachusetts Press, 1999.

Federalism Reconsidered. Edited by Doron Ben-Atar and Barbara Oberg. Charlottesville: University Press of Virginia, 1998.

Foletta, Marshall. *Coming to Terms with Democracy: Federalist Intellectuals and the Shaping of American Culture*. Charlottesville: University Press of Virginia, 2001.

Gould, Philip. "New England Witch-Hunting and the Politics of Reason in the Early Republic." *New England Quarterly* 68 (1995): 58–82.

Kerber, Linda. *Federalism in Dissent: Imagery and Ideology in Jeffersonian America*. Ithaca, N.Y.: Cornell University Press, 1970.

Livermore, Shaw. *The Twilight of the Federalism: The Disintegration of the Federalist Party, 1815–1830*. Princeton, N.J.: Princeton University Press, 1962.

Taylor, Alan. "From Fathers to Friends of the People: Political Personas in the Early Republic." *Journal of the Early Republic* 11 (1991): 465–91.

——. *William Cooper's Town: Power and Persuasion on the Frontier of the Early American Republic*. New York: Alfred A. Knopf, 1995.

5. Foreign Relations

Demerritt, David. "Representing the 'True' St. Croix: Knowledge and Power in the Partition of the Northeast." *William & Mary Quarterly* 54 (3rd ser., 1997): 515–48.

Egan, Clifford L. *Neither Peace nor War: Franco-American Relations, 1803–1812*. Baton Rouge: Louisiana State University, 1983.

Fewster, Joseph. "The Jay Treaty and British Ship Seizures: The Martinique Cases." *William & Mary Quarterly* 45 (3rd ser., 1988): 426–52.

Goetzmann, William H. *When the Eagle Screamed: The Romantic Horizon in American Diplomacy, 1800–1860*. New York: John Wiley & Sons, 1966.

Graffagnino, J. Kevin. "'Twenty Thousand Muskets!!!': Ira Allen and the *Olive Branch* Affair, 1796–1800." *William & Mary Quarterly* 48 (3rd ser., 1991): 409–31.

Hickey, Donald R. "America's Response to the Slave Revolt in Haiti, 1791–1806," *Journal of the Early Republic* 2 (1982): 361–75.

——. "The Monroe-Pinkney Treaty of 1806: A Reappraisal." *William & Mary Quarterly* 44 (3rd ser., 1987): 65–88.

Hill, Peter P. *Napoleon's Troublesome Americans, 1804–1815*. Dulles, Va.: Potomac Books, 2005.

Irwin, Ray W. *The Diplomatic Relations of the United States and the Barbary Powers, 1771–1816*. New York: Russell & Russell, 1970.

Kaplan, Lawrence S. *"Entangling Alliances with None": American Foreign Policy in the Age of Jefferson*. Kent, Ohio: Kent State University Press, 1987.

Kitzen, Michael. "Money Bags or Cannon Balls: The Origins of the Tripolitan War, 1795–1801." *Journal of the Early Republic* 16 (1996): 601–24.

Lang, Daniel G. *Foreign Policy of the Early Republic: The Law of Nations and the Balance of Power*. Baton Rouge: Louisiana State University Press, 1985.

Lewis, James E. *The American Union and the Problem of Neighborhood: The United States and the Collapse of the Spanish Empire, 1783–1829*. Chapel Hill: University of North Carolina Press, 1998.

Matthewson, Tim. "Jefferson and Haiti." *Journal of Southern History* 61 (1995): 209–48.

——. *A Proslavery Foreign Policy: Haitian-American Relations during the Early Republic*. Westport, Conn.: Praeger, 2003.

Miller, Melanie Randolph. *Envoy to Terror: Gouverneur Morris and the French Revolution*. Dulles, Va.: Potomac Books, 2005.

Pappas, Paul C. *The United States and the Greek War for Independence, 1821–1828*. Boulder, Colo.: East European Monographs, 1984.

Parker, Richard B. *Uncle Sam in Barbary: A Diplomatic History*. Gainesville: University Press of Florida, 2004.

Perkins, Bradford. *The Cambridge History of American Foreign Relations. Vol. 1: The Creation of the Republican Empire, 1776–1865*. New York: Cambridge University Press, 1995.

Reuter, Frank T. *Trials and Triumphs: George Washington's Foreign Policy*. Fort Worth: Texas Christian University Press, 1983.

Rossignol, Marie-Jeanne. *The Nationalist Ferment: The Origins of American Foreign Policy, 1789–1812*. Translated by Lillian A. Parrott. Columbus: Ohio State University Press, 2004.

Silverstone, Scott A. *Divided Nation: The Politics of War in the Early American Republic*. Ithaca, N.Y.: Cornell University Press, 2004.

Smith, Robert W. *Ideology and Early American Diplomacy*. De Kalb: Northern Illinois University Press, 2004.

Wilson, Gary E. "American Hostages in Moslem Nations, 1784–1796: The Public Response." *Journal of the Early Republic* 2 (1982): 123–41.

6. Military Affairs

Beltman, Brian W. "Territorial Commands of the Army: The System Refined but Not Perfected, 1815–1821." *Journal of the Early Republic* 12 (1992): 185–218.

Cress, Lawrence D. *Citizens in Arms: The Army and Militia in American Society to the War of 1812*. Chapel Hill: University of North Carolina Press, 1982.

Gaff, Alan D. *Bayonets in the Wilderness: Anthony Wayne's Legion in the Old Northwest*. Norman: University of Oklahoma Press, 2004.

Higginbotham, Don. "The Federalized Militia Debate: A Neglected Aspect of Second Amendment Scholarship." *William & Mary Quarterly* 55 (3rd ser., 1998): 39–58.

Kohn, Richard. *Eagle and Sword: The Beginnings of the Military Establishment in America*. New York: Free Press, 1975.

Peskin, Allan. *Winfield Scott and the Profession of Arms*. Kent, Ohio: Kent State University Press, 2004.

Pitcavage, Mark. "Ropes of Sand: Territorial Militias, 1801–1812." *Journal of the Early Republic* 13 (1993): 481–500.

Silverstone, Scott A. *Divided Union: The Politics of War in the Early American Republic*. Ithaca, N.Y.: Cornell University Press, 2004.

Stuart, Reginald C. *War and American Thought: From the Revolution to the Monroe Doctrine*. Kent, Ohio: Kent State University Press, 1982.

Symonds, Craig L. *Navalists and Antinavalists: The Naval Policy Debate in the United States, 1785–1827*. Newark: University of Delaware Press, 1980.

7. Political Dissent and the Advent of Democracy

Bouton, Terry. "A Road Closed: Rural Insurgency in Post-Independence Pennsylvania." *Journal of American History* 87 (2000): 855–87.

Cornell, Saul. *Anti-Federalism and the Dissenting Tradition in America, 1788–1828*. Chapel Hill: University of North Carolina Press, 1999.

Gilje, Paul A. *The Road to Democracy: Popular Disorder in New York City, 1763–1834*. Chapel Hill: University of North Carolina Press, 1987.

Taylor, Alan. *Liberty Man and Great Proprietors: The Revolutionary Settlement on the Maine Frontier, 1760–1820*. Chapel Hill: University of North Carolina Press, 1990.

Wilentz, Sean. *Chants Democratic: New York City and the Rise of the American Working Class, 1788–1850*. New York: Oxford University Press, 1984.

8. Political Rhetoric

Grasso, Christopher. *A Speaking Aristocracy: Transforming Public Discourse in Eighteenth-Century Connecticut*. Chapel Hill: University of North Carolina Press, 1999.

Gustafson, Sandra. *Eloquence Is Power: Oratory and Performance in Early America*. Chapel Hill: University of North Carolina Press, 2000.

Howe, John R. "Republican Thought and the Political Violence of the 1790s." *American Quarterly* 19 (1967): 147–65.

Kann, Mark E. *A Republic of Men: The American Founders, Gendered Language, and Patriarchal Politics*. New York: New York University Press, 1998.

Smelser, Marshall. "The Federalist Period as Age of Passion." *American Quarterly* 10 (1958): 391–419.

9. Public Festivals

Burstein, Andrew. *America's Jubilee: How in 1826 a Generation Remembered Fifty Years of Independence*. New York: Alfred A. Knopf, 2001.

Cray, Robert E., Jr. "Commemorating the Prison Ship Dead: Revolutionary Memory and the Politics of the Sepulture in the Early Republic, 1776–1808." *William & Mary Quarterly* 56 (3rd ser., 1999): 565–90.

Davis, Susan G. *Parades and Power: Street Theater in Nineteenth-Century Philadelphia*. Philadelphia: Temple University Press, 1986.

Neely, Silvia. "The Politics of Liberty in the Old World and the New: Lafayette's Return to America in 1824." *Journal of the Early Republic* 6 (1986): 151–71.

Newman, Simon P. *Parades and the Politics of the Street: Festive Culture in the Early American Republic*. Philadelphia: University of Pennsylvania Press, 1997.

Purcell, Sarah J. *Sealed in Blood: War, Sacrifice, and Memory in Revolutionary America*. Philadelphia: University of Pennsylvania Press, 2002.

Travers, Len. *Celebrating the Fourth: Independence Day and the Rites of Nationalism*. Amherst: University of Massachusetts Press, 1997.

Waldstreicher, David. *In the Midst of Perpetual Fetes: The Making of American Nationalism, 1776–1820*. Chapel Hill: University of North Carolina Press, 1997.

10. Religion and Politics

Dickson, Charles Ellis. "Jeremiads in the New American Republic: The Case of Fasts in the John Adams Administration." *New England Quarterly* 60 (1987): 187–207.

Goodman, Paul. *Towards a Christian Republic: Antimasonry and the Great Transition in New England*. New York: Oxford University Press, 1988.

Saillant, John. "Lemuel Haynes's Black Republicanism and the American Republican Tradition, 1775–1820." *Journal of the Early Republic* 14 (1994): 295–324.

Snyder, K. Alan. "Foundation of Liberty: The Christian Republicanism of Timothy Dwight and Jedidiah Morse." *New England Quarterly* 56 (1983): 382–97.

11. Republicanism

The Key of Liberty: The Life and Democratic Writings of William Manning, "A Laborer," 1747–1811. Edited by Michael Miller and Sean Wilentz. Cambridge, Mass.: Harvard University Press, 1993.

Lenner, Andrew C. "John Taylor and the Origins of American Federalism." *Journal of the Early Republic* 17 (1997): 399–423.

McCoy, Drew. *The Elusive Republic: Political Economy in Jeffersonian America*. Chapel Hill: University of North Carolina Press, 1980.

Murrin, John M. "The Jeffersonian Triumph and American Exceptionalism." *Journal of the Early Republic* 20 (2000): 1–25.

Richards, Leonard L. *The Slave Power and Southern Domination, 1780–1860*. Baton Rouge: Louisiana State University Press, 2000.

Shalhope, Robert E. *John Taylor of Caroline: Pastoral Republican, 1785–1827*. New York: Columbia University Press, 1980.

Waldstreicher, David, and Stephen R. Grossbart. "Abraham Bishop's Vocation; or, the Mediation of Jeffersonian Politics." *Journal of the Early Republic* 18 (1998): 617–56.

Young, Alfred F. "George Robert Twelves Hewes (1742–1840): A Boston Shoemaker and the Memory of the American Revolution." *William & Mary Quarterly* 38 (3rd ser., 1981): 561–623.

c. First Party System

Banner, James M., Jr. *To the Hartford Convention: The Federalists and the Origin of Party Politics in Massachusetts, 1789–1815*. New York: Alfred A. Knopf, 1970.

Banning, Lance. *The Jeffersonian Persuasion: Evolution of a Party Ideology*. Ithaca, N.Y.: Cornell University Press, 1978.

Bogin, Ruth. "'Measures So Glaringly Unjust': A Response to Hamilton's Funding Plan by William Manning." *William & Mary Quarterly* 46 (3rd ser., 1989): 315–31.

Bowling, Kenneth R. *The Creation of Washington, D.C.: The Idea and Location of the American Capital*. Fairfax, Va.: George Washington University Press, 1991.

Buel, Richard, Jr. *Securing the Revolution: Ideology in American Politics, 1789–1815*. Ithaca, N.Y.: Cornell University Press, 1972.

Callahan, North. *Thanks, Mr. President: The Trail-Blazing Second Term of George Washington*. New York: Cornwall Books, 1991.

Cayton, Andrew R. L. *The Frontier Republic: Ideology and Politics in the Ohio Country, 1780–1825*. Kent, Ohio: Kent State University Press, 1986.

——. "Separate Interests and the Nation State: The Washington Administration and the Origins of Regionalism in the Trans-Appalachian West." *Journal of American History* 79 (1992): 39–67.

Clarfield, Gerard H. *Timothy Pickering and the American Republic*. Pittsburgh: University of Pittsburgh Press, 1980.

Dawson, Matthew Q. *Partisanship and the Birth of America's Second Party, 1796–1800: Stop the Wheels of Government*. Westport, Conn.: Greenwood Press, 2000.

Elkins, Stanley, and Eric McKitrick. *The Federalist Era*. New York: Oxford University Press, 1993.

Estes, Todd. "Shaping the Politics of Public Opinion: Federalists and the Jay Treaty Debate." *Journal of the Early Republic* 20 (2000): 393–422.

Fischer, David Hackett. *The Revolution of American Conservatism: The Federalist Party in the Era of Jeffersonian Democracy*. New York: Harper & Row, 1965.

Grant, C. L. "Senator Benjamin Hawkins: Federalist or Republican?" *Journal of the Early Republic* 1 (1981): 233–47.

Hoadley, John F. *Origins of American Political Parties, 1789–1803*. Lexington: University Press of Kentucky, 1986.

Kaminski, John P. *George Clinton: Yeoman Politician of the New Republic*. Madison, Wis.: Madison House, 1993.

Koschnik, Albrecht. "The Democratic Societies of Philadelphia and the Limits of the American Public Sphere, circa 1793–1795." *William & Mary Quarterly* 58 (3rd ser., 2001): 615–36.

Lamplugh, George R. "'Oh the Colossus! The Colossus!': James Jackson and the Jeffersonian Republican Party in Georgia, 1796–1806." *Journal of the Early Republic* 9 (1989): 315–34.

Launching the "Extended Republic: The Federalist Era. Edited by Ronald Hoffman and Peter J. Albert. Charlottesville: University Press of Virginia, 1996.

Lomask, Milton. *Aaron Burr: The Years from Princeton to Vice-President, 1756–1805*. New York: Farrar, Straus & Giroux, 1979.

Melton, Buckner F., Jr. *The First Impeachment: The Constitution's Framers and the Case of Senator William Blount*. Mercer, Ga.: Mercer University Press, 1998.

Peskin, Lawrence A. "How the Republicans Learned to Love Manufacturing: The First Parties and the 'New Economy.'" *Journal of the Early Republic* 22 (2002): 235–62.

Sassi, Jonathan D. "The First Party System and Southern New England's Public Christianity," *Journal of the Early Republic* 21 (2001): 261–99.

Schoenbachler, Matthew. "Republicanism in the Age of Democratic Revolution: The Democratic-Republican Societies of the 1790s." *Journal of the Early Republic* 18 (1998): 237–61.

Sharp, James Roger. *American Politics in the Early Republic: The New Nation in Crisis*. New Haven, Conn.: Yale University Press, 1993.

Sheridan, Eugene R. "Thomas Jefferson and the Giles Resolutions." *William & Mary Quarterly* 49 (3rd ser., 1992): 589–608.

Simon, James F. *What Kind of Nation: Thomas Jefferson, John Marshall, and the Epic Struggle to Create the United States*. New York: Simon & Schuster, 2002.

Slaughter, Thomas P. *The Whiskey Rebellion: Frontier Epilogue to the American Revolution*. New York: Oxford University Press, 1986.

Tachau, Mary K. Bonsteel. "George Washington and the Reputation of Edmund Randolph." *Journal of American History* 73 (1986–1987): 15–34.

———. "The Whiskey Rebellion in Kentucky: A Forgotten Episode of Civil Disobedience." *Journal of the Early Republic* 2 (1982): 239–59.

The Whiskey Rebellion: Past and Present Perspectives. Edited by Stephen R. Boyd. Westport, Conn.: Greenwood Press, 1985.

d. Quasi-War and Its Repercussions

Austin, Aleine. *Matthew Lyon: "New Man" of the Democratic Revolution, 1749–1822*. University Park: Pennsylvania State University Press, 1981.

DeConde, Alexander. *The Quasi-War: The Politics and Diplomacy of the Undeclared War with France 1797–1801*. New York: Charles Scribner's Sons, 1966.

Dunn, Susan. *Jefferson's Second Revolution: The Election Crisis of 1800 and the Triumph of Republicanism*. New York: Houghton Mifflin, 2004.

Ferling, John. *Adams vs. Jefferson: The Tumultuous Election of 1800*. New York: Oxford University Press, 2004.

Freeman, Joanne B. "Explaining the Unexplainable: The Cultural Context of the Sedition Act." In *The Democratic Experiment: New Directions in American Political History*, edited by Meg Jacobs, William J. Novak, and Julian E. Zelizer. Princeton, N.J.: Princeton University Press, 2003, 20–49.

Gough, Robert. "Officering the American Army, 1798." *William & Mary Quarterly* 43 (3rd ser., 1986): 460–71.

Gutzman, Kevin R. "A Troublesome Legacy: James Madison and 'The Principles of '98.'" *Journal of the Early Republic* 15 (1995): 569–89.

———. "The Virginia and Kentucky Resolutions Reconsidered: 'An Appeal to the *Real Laws* of Our Country.'" *Journal of Southern History* 61 (2000): 473–96.

Leiner, Frederick C. *Millions for Defense: The Subscription Warships of 1798*. Annapolis, Md.: United States Naval Institute Press, 1999.

Lendler, Marc. "'Equally Proper at All Times and at All Times Necessary': Civility, Bad Tendency, and the Sedition Act." *Journal of the Early Republic* 24 (2004): 419–44.

Newman, Paul D. *Fries's Rebellion: The Enduring Struggle for the American Revolution*. Philadelphia: University of Pennsylvania Press, 2004.

Palmer, Michael A. *Stoddert's War: Naval Operations during the Quasi-War with France, 1798–1801*. New York: Columbia University Press, 1987.

Ray, Thomas M. "'Not One Cent for Tribute': The Public Addresses and American Popular Reaction to the XYZ Affair, 1798–1799." *Journal of the Early Republic* 3 (1983): 389–412.

Smith, James Morton. *Freedom's Fetters: The Alien and Sedition Laws and American Civil Liberties*. Ithaca, N.Y.: Cornell University Press, 1956.

Stinchcombe, William. "Talleyrand and the American Negotiation of 1797–1798." *Journal of American History* 62 (1975–1976): 575–90.

Watkins, William J., Jr. *Reclaiming the American Revolution: The Kentucky and Virginia Resolutions and Their Legacy*. New York: Palgrave Macmillan, 2004.

Weisberger, Bernard A. *America Afire: Jefferson, Adams, and the Revolutionary Election of 1800*. New York: William Morrow, 2000.

e. Jeffersonian Ascendancy

Adams, Henry. *History of the United States during the Administrations of Thomas Jefferson*. Reprint, New York: Library of America, 1986.

Allison, Robert J. *The Crescent Obscured: The United States and the Muslim World, 1776–1815*. New York: Oxford University Press, 1995.

Armstrong, Thom M. *Politics, Diplomacy and Intrigue in the Early Republic: The Cabinet Career of Robert Smith, 1801–1811*. Dubuque, Iowa: Kendall/Hunt, 1991.

Brown, Jeffrey P. "The Ohio Federalists, 1803–1815." *Journal of the Early Republic* 2 (1982): 261–82.

Brown, Stephen W. *Voice of the New West: John G. Jackson, His Life and Times*. Macon, Ga.: Mercer University Press, 1985.

Browne, Howard. *Jefferson's Call for Nationhood: The First Inaugural Address*. College Station: Texas A&M University Press, 2003.

Crackel, Theodore J. *Mr. Jefferson's Army: Political and Social Reform of the Military Establishment, 1801–1809*. New York: New York University Press, 1987.

Cunningham, Noble E. *The Process of Government under Jefferson*. Princeton, N.J.: Princeton University Press, 1978.

Ellis, Richard E. *The Jeffersonian Crisis: Courts and Politics in the Young Republic*. New York: Oxford University Press, 1971.

Establishing Congress: The Removal to Washington, D.C. and the Election of 1800. Edited by Kenneth R. Bolling and Donald R. Kennon. Athens: Ohio University Press, 2005.

Fleming Thomas. *Duel: Alexander Hamilton, Aaron Burr and the Future of America*. New York: Basic Books, 1999.

——. *The Louisiana Purchase*. New York: John Wiley & Sons, 2003.

Gannon, Kevin M. "Escaping 'Mr. Jefferson's Plan of Destruction': New England Federalists and the Idea of a Northern Confederacy, 1803–1804." *Journal of the Early Republic* 21 (2001): 413–43.

Haw, James, Francis F. Beirne, R. Rosemond, and R. Samuel Jett. *Stormy Patriot: The Life of Samuel Chase*. Baltimore: Maryland Historical Society, 1980.

Magrath, C. Peter. *Yazoo: Law and Politics in the New Republic: The Case of Fletcher v. Peck*. Providence, R.I.: Brown University Press, 1966.

Malone, Kathryn R. "The Fate of Revolutionary Republicanism in Early National Virginia." *Journal of the Early Republic* 7 (1987): 27–51.

Nash, Howard P. *The Forgotten Wars: The Role of the U.S. Navy in the Quasi War with France and the Barbary Wars, 1799–1805*. South Brunswick, N.J.: A. S. Barnes, 1968.

Oberg, Barbara B. "A New Republican Order, Letter by Letter." *Journal of the Early Republic* 25 (2005): 1–20.

Opal, J. M. "The Politics of 'Industry': Federalism in Concord and Exeter, New Hampshire, 1790–1805." *Journal of the Early Republic* 20 (2000): 637–71.

Ratcliffe, Donald J. "Voter Turnout in Early Ohio." *Journal of the Early Republic* 7 (1987): 223–51.

The Revolution of 1800: Democracy, Race, and the New Republic. Edited by James Horn, Jan Ellen Lewis, and Peter Onuf. Charlottesville: University Press of Virginia, 2002.

Risjord, Norman K. *The Old Republicans: Southern Conservatism in the Age of Jefferson*. New York: Columbia University Press, 1965.

Rogow, Arnold A. *A Fatal Friendship: Alexander Hamilton and Aaron Burr*. New York: Hill & Wang, 1998.

Shankman, Andrew. *Crucible of American Democracy: The Struggle to Fuse Egalitarianism and Capitalism in Jeffersonian Pennsylvania*. Lawrence: University Press of Kansas, 2004.

——. "Malcontents and Tertium Quids: The Battle to Define Democracy in Jeffersonian Philadelphia." *Journal of the Early Republic* 19 (1999): 43–72.

——. "'A New Thing on Earth': Alexander Hamilton, Pro-Manufacturing Republicans, and the Democratization of American Political Economy." *Journal of the Early Republic* 23 (2003): 323–52.

Tucker, Robert W., and David C. Hendrickson. *Empire of Liberty: The Statecraft of Thomas Jefferson*. New York: Oxford University Press, 1990.

f. Politics of the War of 1812

Adams, Henry. *The History of the United States during the Administrations of James Madison.* Reprint, New York: Library of America, 1986.

Brown, Roger. *The Republic in Peril: 1812*. New York: Columbia University Press, 1964.

Buel, Richard, Jr. *America on the Brink: How the Political Struggle over the War of 1812 Almost Destroyed the Young Republic*. New York: Palgrave Macmillan, 2005.

Cress, Lawrence D. "'Cool and Serious Reflection': Federalist Attitudes towards the War of 1812." *Journal of the Early Republic* 7 (1987): 123–45.

Feldman, Jay. *When the Mississippi Ran Backwards: Empire, Intrigue, Murder, and the New Madrid Earthquake*. New York: Free Press, 2005.

Hatzenbuehler, Ronald L. *Congress Declares War: Rhetoric, Leadership, and Partisanship in the Early Republic*. Kent, Ohio: Kent State University Press, 1983.

Hickey, Donald R. "Trade Restrictions during the War of 1812." *Journal of American History* 68 (1981–1982): 517–38.

Mason, Matthew. "'Nothing Is Better Calculated to Excite Division': Federalist Agitation against Slave Representation during the War of 1812." *New England Quarterly* 75 (2002): 531–61.

Masterson, William H. *Tories and Democrats: British Diplomats in Pre-Jacksonian America*. College Station: Texas A&M University Press, 1985.

McCaughey, Robert A. *Josiah Quincy 1772–1864: The Last Federalist*. Cambridge, Mass.: Harvard University Press, 1974.

McKee, Christopher. "Foreign Seamen in the United States Navy: A Census of 1808." *William & Mary Quarterly* 42 (3rd ser., 1985): 383–93.

Perkins, Bradford. *Prologue to War: England and the United States 1805–1812*. Berkeley: University of California Press, 1961.

Prentiss, Hervey Putnam. *Timothy Pickering as the Leader of New England Federalism, 1800–1815*. New York: De Capo Press, 1972.

Quincy, Edmund. *Life of Josiah Quincy: By His Son*. Boston: Little, Brown, 1891.

Siry, Steven E. "The Sectional Politics of 'Practical Republicanism': De Witt Clinton's Presidential Bid, 1810–1812." *Journal of the Early Republic* 5 (1985): 441–62.

Spivak, Burton. *Jefferson's English Crisis: Commerce, Embargo, and the Republican Revolution* Charlottesville: University Press of Virginia, 1979.

Stagg, J. C. A. "Between Black Rock and a Hard Place: Peter B. Porter's Plan for an Invasion of Canada in 1812." *Journal of the Early Republic* 19 (1999): 385–422.

——. "James Madison and the Coercion of Great Britain: Canada, the West Indies, and the War of 1812." *William & Mary Quarterly* 38 (3rd ser., 1981): 3–34.

——. *Mr. Madison's War: Politics, Diplomacy, and Warfare in the Early Republic, 1783–1830*. Princeton, N.J.: Princeton University Press, 1983.

Tucker, Spencer C., and Frank T. Reuter. *Injured Honor: The Chesapeake-Leopard Affair, June 22, 1807*. Annapolis, Md.: United States Naval Institute Press, 1996.

Watts, Steven. *The Republic Reborn: War and the Making of Liberal America, 1790–1820*. Baltimore: The Johns Hopkins University Press, 1987.

g. Military Dimensions of the War of 1812

Berton, Pierre. *Flames across the Border: The Canadian American Tragedy, 1813–1814*. Boston: Little, Brown, 1982.

——. *The Invasion of Canada, 1812–1813*. Boston: Little, Brown, 1980.

Borneman, Walter. *1812: The War That Forged a Nation*. New York: HarperCollins, 2004.

Brodine, Charles E., Michael J. Crawford, and Christine F. Hughes. *Against All Odds: U.S. Sailors in the War of 1812*. Washington, D.C.: Naval Historical Center, 2004.

Crisman, Kevin J. *The* Eagle: *An American Brig on Lake Champlain during the War of 1812*. Shelburne, Vt.: New England Press, 1987.

Cusick, James G. *The Other War of 1812: The Patriot War and the American Invasion of East Florida*. Gainesville: University Press of Florida, 2003.

deKay, James Tertius. *The Battle of Stonington: Torpedoes, Submarines, and Rockets in the War of 1812*. Annapolis, Md.: United States Naval Institute Press, 1990.

——. *Chronicles of the Frigate Macedonian, 1809–1922*. New York: W. W. Norton, 1995.

Dudley, Wade G. *Splintering the Wooden Wall: The British Blockade of the United States, 1812–1815*. Annapolis, Md.: United States Naval Institute Press, 2003.

Duffy, Stephen W. H. *Captain Blakely and the Wasp: The Cruise of 1814*. Annapolis, Md.: United States Naval Institute Press, 2001.

Everett, Allan S. *The War of 1812 in the Champlain Valley*. Syracuse, N.Y.: Syracuse University Press, 1981.

Fabel, Robin F. A. "Self-Help in Dartmoor: Black and White Prisoners in the War of 1812." *Journal of the Early Republic* 9 (1989): 165–90.

Fowler, William M., Jr. *Jack Tars and Commodores: The American Navy, 1783–1815*. Boston: Houghton Mifflin, 1984.

Friedman, Lawrence J., and David C. Skaggs. "Jesse Duncan Elliott and the Battle of Lake Erie: The Issue of Mental Stability." *Journal of the Early Republic* 11 (1991): 493–516.

Graves, Donald E. *The Battle of Lundy's Lane: On the Niagara in 1814*. Baltimore: Nautical & Aviation Publishing, 1993.

Hickey, Donald R. *The War of 1812: A Forgotten Conflict*. Urbana: University of Illinois Press, 1989.

Hiedler, David S., and Jeanne T. Hiedler. *Old Hickory's War: Andrew Jackson and the Quest for Empire*. Mechanicsburg, Pa.: Stackpole Books, 1996.

Horsman, Reginald. "Nantucket's Peace Treaty with England in 1814." *New England Quarterly* 54 (1981): 180–98.

Long, David F. *Sailor-Diplomat: A Biography of Commodore James Biddle, 1783–1848*. Boston: Northeastern University Press, 1983.

Malcomson, Robert, and Thomas Malcomson. *HMS* Detroit*: The Battle for Lake Erie*. Annapolis, Md.: United States Naval Institute Press, 1990.

Morris, John D. *Sword of the Border: Major General Jacob Jennings Brown, 1775–1828*. Kent, Ohio: Kent State University Press, 2000.

Norton, Louis Arthur. *Joshua Barney: Hero of the Revolution and 1812*. Annapolis, Md.: United States Naval Institute Press, 2000.

Owsley, Frank L., Jr. *Struggle for the Gulf Borderlands: The Creek War and the Battle of New Orleans, 1812–1815*. Gainesville: University Press of Florida, 1981.

Pitch, Anthony S. *The Burning of Washington: The British Invasion of 1814*. Annapolis, Md.: United States Naval Institute Press, 1998.

Sheppard, George. *Plunder, Profit, and Paroles: A Social History of the War of 1812 in Upper Canada*. Montreal: McGill-Queen's University Press, 1994.

Skaggs, David C., and Gerar T. Altoff. *A Signal Victory: The Lake Erie Campaign, 1812–1813*. Annapolis, Md.: United States Naval Institute Press, 1997.

Skeen, C. Edward. *Citizen Soldiers in the War of 1812*. Lexington: University Press of Kentucky, 1999.

——. *John Armstrong, Jr., 1758–1843: A Biography*. Syracuse, N.Y.: Syracuse University Press, 1981.

Skelton, William B. "High Army Leadership in the Era of the War of 1812: The Making and Remaking of the Officer Corps. *William & Mary Quarterly* 51 (1994): 253–74.

Stagg, J. C. A. "Enlisted Men in the United States Army, 1812–1815: A Preliminary Survey." *William & Mary Quarterly* 43 (3rd ser., 1986): 615–45.

———. "The Madison Administration and Mexico: Reinterpreting the Gutiérrez-Magee Raid of 1812–1813." *William & Mary Quarterly* 59 (3rd ser., 2002): 449–80.

———. "Soldiers in Peace and War: Comparative Perspectives on the Recruitment of the United States Army, 1802–1815." *William & Mary Quarterly* 58 (3rd ser., 2001): 79–120.

Sugden, John. *Tecumseh's Last Stand*. Norman: University of Oklahoma Press, 1985.

Tucker, Spencer C. *The Jeffersonian Gunboat Navy*. Columbia: University of South Carolina Press, 1993.

Whitehorne, Joseph. *While Washington Burned: The Battle for Fort Erie, 1814*. Baltimore: Nautical & Aviation Publishing, 1992.

h. Era of Good Feelings

Cunningham, Noble E., Jr. *The Presidency of James Monroe*. Lawrence: University Press of Kansas, 1996.

Dangerfield, George. *The Era of Good Feelings*. New York: Harcourt, Brace, 1952.

Heidler, David S. "The Politics of National Aggression: Congress and the First Seminole War." *Journal of the Early Republic* 13 (1993): 501–30.

Maine in the Early Republic. Edited by Charles E. Clark, James S. Leamon, and Karen Bowden. Hanover, N.H.: University Press of New England, 1988.

Owsley, Frank L. "Ambister and Arbuthnot: Adventurers or Martyrs for British Honor?" *Journal of the Early Republic* 5 (1985): 289–308.

Resch, John. *Suffering Soldiers: Revolutionary War Veterans, Moral Sentiment, and Political Culture in the Early Republic*. Amherst: University of Massachusetts Press, 1999.

Sheidley, Harlow W. *Sectional Nationalism: Massachusetts Conservative Leaders and the Transformation of America, 1815–1836*. Boston: Northeastern University Press, 1999.

Skeen, C. Edward. *1816: America Rising*. Lexington: University Press of Kentucky, 2003.

———. "'Vox Populi, Vox Dei': The Compensation Act and the Rise of Popular Politics." *Journal of the Early Republic* 6 (1986): 253–74.

Vipperman, Carl J. *William Lowndes and the Transition of Southern Politics, 1782–1822*. Chapel Hill: University of North Carolina Press, 1989.

i. Emergence of the Second Party System

Baker, Pamela L. "The Washington National Road and the Struggle to Adopt a Federal System of Internal Improvements." *Journal of the Early Republic* 22 (2002): 437–64.

Cole, Donald B. *A Jackson Man: Amos Kendall and the Rise of American Democracy*. Baton Rouge: Louisiana State University Press, 2004.

Huston, James L. "Virtue Besieged: Virtue, Equality, and the General Welfare in the Tariff Debates of the 1820s." *Journal of the Early Republic* 14 (1994): 523–47.

John, Richard R. "Affairs of Office: The Executive Departments, the Election of 1828, and the Making of the Democratic Party." In *The Democratic Experiment: New Directions in American Political History*, edited by Meg Jacobs, William J. Novak, and Julian E. Zelizer. Princeton, N.J.: Princeton University Press, 2003, 50–84.

Kruman, Marc W. "The Second American Party System and the Transformation of Revolutionary Republicanism." *Journal of the Early Republic* 12 (1992): 509–37.

Kutolowski, Kathleen Smith. "Antimasonry Reexamined: Social Bases of the Grass Roots Party." *Journal of American History* 71 (1984): 269–93.

McCormick, Richard P. *The Second American Party System: Party Formation in the Jacksonian Era*. Chapel Hill: University of North Carolina Press, 1966.

Mushkat, Jerome, and Joseph G. Rayback. *Martin Van Buren: Law, Politics, and the Shaping of Republican Ideology*. De Kalb: Northern Illinois University Press, 1997.

Pincus, Jonathan J. *Pressure Groups: Politics in Antebellum Tariffs*. New York: Columbia University Press, 1977.

Pocock, Emil. "Popular Roots of Jacksonian Democracy: The Case of Dayton, Ohio, 1815–1830." *Journal of the Early Republic* 9 (1989): 489–515.

Ratcliffe, Donald J. *The Politics of Long Division: The Birth of the Second Party System in Ohio, 1818–1828*. Columbus: Ohio State University Press, 2000.

Roth, Randolph. "The Other Masonic Outrage: The Death and Transfiguration of Joseph Burnham." *Journal of the Early Republic* 14 (1994): 35–69.

Schoen, Brian. "Calculating the Price of Union: Republican Economic Nationalism and the Origins of Southern Sectionalism." *Journal of the Early Republic* 23 (2003):173–206.

Sellers, Charles. *The Market Revolution: Jacksonian America 1815–1846*. New York: Oxford University Press, 1991.

Sibley, Joel H. *Martin Van Buren and the Emergence of American Popular Politics*. Lanham, Md.: Rowman & Littlefield, 2002.

Tinkler, Robert. *James Hamilton of South Carolina*. Baton Rouge: Louisiana State University Press, 2004.

Tregle, Joseph G., Jr. "Andrew Jackson and the Continuing Battle of New Orleans." *Journal of the Early Republic* 1 (1981): 373–93.

Van Atta, John R. "Western Lands and the Political Economy of Henry Clay's American System." *Journal of the Early Republic* 21 (2001): 633–65.

Wallace, Michael. "Changing Concepts of Party in the United States: New York 1815–1828." *American Historical Review* 74 (1968): 453–91.

Watson, Harry L. *Liberty and Power: The Politics of Jacksonian America*. New York: Hill & Wang, 1990.

2. *Social History*

a. Community and Association

Beeman, Richard R. *The Evolution of the Southern Backcountry: A Case Study of Lunenburg County, Virginia, 1746–1832*. Philadelphia: University of Pennsylvania Press, 1984.

Botscharow-Kamau, Lucy J. "Neighbors: Harmony and Conflict on the Indiana Frontier." *Journal of the Early Republic* 11 (1991): 507–29.

Bullock, Steven C. *Revolutionary Brotherhood: Freemasonry and the Transformation of the American Social Order, 1730–1840*. Chapel Hill: University of North Carolina Press, 1996.

Faragher, John M. *Sugar Creek: Life on the Illinois Prairie*. New Haven, Conn.: Yale University Press, 1986.

Holmes, Richard. *Communities in Transition: Bedford and Lincoln Massachusetts, 1729–1850*. Ann Arbor: University of Michigan Research Press, 1980.

Laver, Harry S. "Rethinking the Social Role of the Militia: Community Building in Antebellum Kentucky." *Journal of Southern History* 68 (2002): 777–816.

Tolbert, Lisa C. *Constructing Townscapes: Space and Society in Antebellum Tennessee*. Chapel Hill: University of North Carolina Press, 1999.

Watkinson, James D. "'Fit Objects of Charity': Community, Race, Faith, and Antebellum Lancaster County, Virginia, 1817–1860." *Journal of the Early Republic* 21 (2001): 41–70.

b. Crime and Punishment

Brown, Irene Quenzler, and Richard D. Brown. *The Hanging of Ephraim Wheeler: A Story of Rape, Incest, and Justice in Early America*. Cambridge, Mass.: Harvard University Press, 2003.

Cohen, Daniel A. "Social Justice, Sexual Violence, Spiritual Transcendence: Constructions of Interracial Rape in Early American Crime Literature, 1767–1817." *William & Mary Quarterly* 56 (3rd ser., 1999): 481–526.

Cohen, Patricia Cline. *The Murder of Helen Jewett: The Life and Death of a Prostitute in Nineteenth-Century New York*. New York: Alfred A. Knopf, 1998.

Hirsch, Adam J. *The Rise of the Penitentiary: Prisons and Punishment in Early America*. New Haven, Conn.: Yale University Press, 1992.

Lee, Deborah A., and Warren R. Hofstra. "Race, Memory, and the Death of Robert Berkeley: 'A Murder . . . of . . . Horrible and Savage Barbarity.'" *Journal of Southern History* 65 (1999): 41–76.

Masur, Louis P. *Rites of Execution: Capital Punishment and the Transformation of American Culture, 1776–1865*. New York: Oxford University Press, 1989.

McFarland, Gerald. *The Counterfeit Man: The True Story of the Boorn-Colvin Murder Case*. New York: Pantheon Books, 1990.

Meranze, Michael. *Laboratories of Virtue: Punishment, Revolution, and Authority in Philadelphia, 1760–1835*. Chapel Hill: University of North Carolina Press, 1996.

Merrill, Boynton. *Jefferson's Nephews: A Frontier Tragedy*. Princeton, N.J.: Princeton University Press, 1976.

Rice, Jim. "'This Province, So Meanly and Thinly Inhabited': Punishing Maryland's Criminals, 1681–1850." *Journal of the Early Republic* 19 (1999): 15–42.

Rothman, David J. *The Discovery of the Asylum: Social Order and Disorder in the New Republic*. Boston: Little, Brown, 1971.

Steinberg, Allen. *The Transformation of Criminal Justice: Philadelphia, 1800–1880*. Chapel Hill: University of North Carolina Press, 1989.

c. Dependency (Insanity and Poverty)

Alexander, John K. *Render Them Submissive: Responses to Poverty in Philadelphia, 1760–1800*. Amherst: University of Massachusetts Press, 1980.

Blackmar, Elizabeth. *Manhattan for Rent, 1785–1850*. Ithaca, N.Y.: Cornell University Press, 1989.

Clement, Priscilla F. *Welfare and the Poor in the Nineteenth-Century City: Philadelphia, 1800–1854*. Rutherford, N.J.: Fairleigh Dickinson University Press, 1985.

Cray, Robert E., Jr. *Paupers and Poor Relief in New York City and Its Rural Environs, 1700–1830*. Philadelphia: Temple University Press, 1988.

Down and Out in Early America. Edited by Billy G. Smith. University Park: Pennsylvania State University Press, 2004.

Grigg, Susan. *The Dependent Poor of Newburyport: Studies in Social History, 1800–1830*. Ann Arbor: University of Michigan Press, 1984.

Newman, Simon P. *Embodied History: The Lives of the Poor in Early Philadelphia*. Philadelphia: University of Pennsylvania Press, 2003.

Soltow, Lee. *Distribution of Wealth and Income in the United States in 1798*. Pittsburgh: University of Pittsburgh Press, 1990.

d. Education

Addis, Cameron. *Jefferson's Vision for Education: 1760–1845*. New York: Peter Lang, 2003.

The American College in the Nineteenth Century. Edited by Roger L. Geiger. Nashville: Vanderbilt University Press, 2000.

Barlow, William, and David O. Powell. "A Dedicated Medical Student: Solomon Mordecai, 1891–1822." *Journal of the Early Republic* 7 (1987): 377–97.

Boylan, Anne M. *Sunday School: The Formation of an American Institution, 1790–1880*. New Haven, Conn.: Yale University Press, 1989.

Calhoun, Daniel H. "Eye for the Jacksonian World: William C. Woodbridge and Emma Willard." *Journal of the Early Republic* 4 (1984): 1–26.

——. *Professional Lives in America: Structure and Aspiration, 1750–1850*. Cambridge, Mass.: Harvard University Press, 1965.

Cremin, Lawrence A. *American Education: The National Experience 1783–1876*. New York: Harper & Row, 1980.

Durrill, Wayne K. "The Power of Ancient Words: Classical Teaching and Social Change at South Carolina College, 1804–1860." *Journal of Southern History* 65 (1999): 469–98.

Gilmore, William J. *Elementary Literacy on the Eve of the Industrial Revolution: Trends in Rural New England*. Worcester, Mass.: American Antiquarian Society, 1982.

Glover, Lorri. "An Education in Southern Masculinity: The Ball Family of South Carolina in the Early Republic." *Journal of Southern History* 69 (2003): 39–70.

Hellenbrand, Harold. *The Unfinished Revolution: Education and Politics in the Thought of Thomas Jefferson*. Newark: University of Delaware Press, 1990.

Jabour, Anya. "'Grown Girls, Highly Cultivated': Female Education in an Antebellum Southern Family." *Journal of Southern History* 64 (1998): 23–64.

Johnson, Eldon L. "The Dartmouth College Case: The Neglected Educational Meaning." *Journal of the Early Republic* 39 (1983): 45–67.

Kaestle, Carl F. *Pillars of the Republic: Common Schools and American Society, 1780–1860*. New York: Hill & Wang, 1983.

Katz, Michael B. *Reconstructing American Education*. Cambridge, Mass.: Harvard University Press, 1987.

Kilbride, Daniel. "Southern Medical Students in Philadelphia, 1800–1861: Science and Sociability in the Republic of Medicine." *Journal of Southern History* 65 (1999): 697–732.

Lucas, Christopher J. *American Higher Education: A History*. New York: St. Martin's Press, 1994.

Monaghan, E. Jennifer. *A Common Heritage: Noah Webster's Blue-Book Speller*. Hamden, Conn.: Archon Books, 1983.

Murray, Gail S. "Rational Thought and Republican Virtues: Children's Literature, 1789–1820." *Journal of the Early Republic* 8 (1988): 159–77.

Murray, John E. "Family, Literacy, and Skill Training in the Antebellum South: Historical-Longitudinal Evidence from Charleston." *Journal of Economic History* 64 (2004): 773–99.

Noll, Mark A. *Princeton and the Republic, 1768–1822*. Princeton, N.J.: Princeton University Press, 1989.

Opal, J. M. "Exciting Emulation: Academies and the Transformation of the Rural North, 1780s–1820s." *Journal of American History* 91 (2004): 445–70.

Pickering, Samuel F., Jr. *Moral Instruction and Fiction for Children, 1749–1820*. Athens: University of Georgia Press, 1993.

Prangle, Lorraine S., and Thomas L. Prangle. *The Learning of Liberty: The Educational Ideas of the American Founders*. Lawrence: University Press of Kansas, 1993.

Rollins, Richard M. *The Long Journey of Noah Webster*. Philadelphia: University of Pennsylvania Press, 1980.

Rudolph, Lloyd. *The American College and University: A History*. New York: Alfred A. Knopf, 1962.

Snyder, K. Alan. *Defining Noah Webster: Mind and Morals in the Early Republic*. Lanham, Md.: University Press of America, 1990.

Thomas Jefferson's Military Academy: Founding West Point. Edited by Robert M. S. McDonald. Charlottesville: University Press of Virginia, 2004.

Vinovskis, Maris A. *Education, Society, and Economic Opportunity: A Historical Perspective on Persistent Issues*. New Haven, Conn.: Yale University Press, 1995.

Whitescarver, Keith. "Creating Citizens for the Republic: Education in Georgia, 1776–1810." *Journal of the Early Republic* 13 (1993): 455–79.

e. Ethnicity

1. Europeans

Chartier, Armand B. *Histoire des Franco-Américains de la Nouvelle-Angleterre, 1775–1990*. Sillery, Quebec: Les éditions du Septentrion, 1991.

Gleason, David T. *The Irish of the South, 1815–1877*. Chapel Hill: University of North Carolina Press, 2001.

Nolt, Steven M. "Becoming Ethnic Americans in the Early Republic: Pennsylvania German Reaction to Evangelical Protestant Reformism." *Journal of the Early Republic* 20 (2000): 423–46.

———. *Strangers in Their Own Land: Pennsylvania Germans in the Early Republic*. University Park: Pennsylvania State University Press, 2002.

Roby, Yves. *Les Franco-Américains de la Nouvelle-Angleterre, 1776–1930*. Sillery, Quebec: Les editions du Septentrion, 1991.

2. African American Experience

a. Slavery: General Treatments

Berlin, Ira. *Many Thousands Gone: The First Two Centuries of Slavery in America*. Cambridge, Mass.: Harvard University Press, Belknap Press, 1998.

"Crossing Slavery's Boundaries." Forum in *American Historical Review* 105 (2000): 451–84.

Davis, David Brion. *Challenging the Boundaries of Slavery*. Cambridge, Mass.: Harvard University Press, 2003.

——. *The Problem of Slavery in the Age of Revolution 1770–1823*. Ithaca, N.Y.: Cornell University Press, 1975.

Diouf, Sylviane. A. *Servants of Allah: African Muslims Enslaved in the Americas*. New York: New York University Press, 1988.

Finkelman, Paul. *Slavery and the Founders: Race and Liberty in the Age of Jefferson*. Armonk, N.Y.: M. E. Sharpe, 1996.

Gomez, Michael L. *Exchanging Our Country Marks: The Transformation of African Identities in the Colonial and Antebellum South*. Chapel Hill: University of North Carolina Press, 1998.

Kolchin, Peter. *American Slavery, 1619–1877*. New York: Hill & Wang, 1993.

The Meaning of Slavery in the North. Edited by David Roediger and Martin H. Blatt. New York: Garland Publishing, 1998.

Nash, Gary B. *Race and Revolution*. Madison, Wis.: Madison House, 1990.

Wilson, Carol. *Freedom at Risk: The Kidnapping of Free Blacks in America, 1780–1865*. Lexington: University Press of Kentucky, 1994.

Wyatt-Brown, Bertram. "The Mask of Obedience: Male Slave Psychology in the Old South." *American Historical Review* 93 (1988): 1228–52.

b. Slavery: Specialized Studies

1. Defenses of Slavery

Ambrose, Douglas. "Proslavery Christianity in Early National Virginia." In *Religion and the Antebellum Debate over Slavery*, edited by John R. McKivigan and Mitchell Snay. Athens: University of Georgia Press, 1998, 36–67.

Balancing Evils Judiciously: The Proslavery Writings of Zephaniah Kingsley. Edited by Daniel W. Stowell. Gainesville: University Press of Florida, 2000.

Newman, Richard S. "Prelude to the Gag Rule: Southern Reaction to the Antislavery Petitions in the First Federal Congress." *Journal of the Early Republic* 16 (1996): 571–99.

Tise, Larry E. *Proslavery: A History of the Defense of Slavery in America, 1701–1840*. Athens: University of Georgia Press, 1988.

Young, Robert. *Domesticating Slavery: The Master Class in Georgia and South Carolina, 1670–1837*. Chapel Hill: University of North Carolina Press, 1999.

2. Expansion

Finkelman, Paul. "Slavery and the Northwest Ordinance: A Study in Ambiguity." *Journal of the Early Republic* 6 (1986): 343–70.

Hammond, John Craig. "'They Are Very Much Interested in Obtaining an Unlimited Slavery': Rethinking the Expansion of Slavery in the Louisiana Purchase Territories, 1803–1805." *Journal of the Early Republic* 23 (2003): 353–80.

Kennedy, Roger G. *Mr. Jefferson's Lost Cause: Lands, Farmers, Slavery and the Louisiana Purchase*. New York: Oxford University Press, 2003.

Rothman, Adam. *Slave Country: American Expansion and the Origins of the Deep South*. Cambridge, Mass.: Harvard University Press, 2005.

Simeone, James. *Democracy and Slavery in Frontier Illinois: The Bottomland Republic*. De Kalb: Northern Illinois University Press, 2000.

3. Insurrections and Runaways

Designs against Charleston: The Trial Record of the Denmark Vesey Slave Conspiracy of 1822. Edited by Edward A. Pearson. Chapel Hill: University of North Carolina Press, 1999.

Egerton, Douglas R. *Gabriel's Rebellion: The Virginia Slave Conspiracies of 1800 and 1802*. Chapel Hill: University of North Carolina Press, 1993.

———. *He Shall Go Forth Free: The Lives of Denmark Vesey*. Madison, Wis.: Madison House, 1999.

Finkelman, Paul. "The Kidnapping of John Davis and the Adoption of the Fugitive Slave Law of 1793." *Journal of Southern History* 56 (1990): 397–422.

Hadden, Sarah E. *Slave Patrols: Law and Violence in Virginia and the Carolinas*. Cambridge, Mass.: Harvard University Press, 2001.

Hinks, Peter P. *To Awaken My Afflicted Brethren: David Walker and the Problem of Antebellum Slave Resistance*. University Park: Pennsylvania State University Press, 1997.

Johnson, Michael P. "Runaway Slaves and Slave Communities in South Carolina, 1799 to 1830." *William & Mary Quarterly* 38 (3rd ser., 1981): 418–41.

"The Making of a Slave Conspiracy." (Denmark Vesey's) Forum in *William & Mary Quarterly* 58 (3rd ser., pt. 1, 2001): 913–76; 59 (3rd ser., pt. 2, 2002): 138–202.

Meaders, Daniel, ed. *Advertisements for Runaway Slaves in Virginia, 1801–1820*. New York: Garland Publishing, 1997.

Robertson, David. *Denmark Vesey*. New York: Alfred A. Knopf, 1999.

Sidbury, James. *Ploughshares into Swords: Race, Rebellion, and Identity in Gabriel's Virginia, 1730–1810*. New York: Cambridge University Press, 1997.

———. "Saint Domingue in Virginia: Ideology, Local Meanings, and Resistance to Slavery, 1790–1800." *Journal of Southern History* 63 (1997): 531–52.

4. Plantation Slavery

Blassingame, John W. *The Slave Community: Plantation Life in the Antebellum South*. New York: Oxford University Press, 1972.

Chaplin, Joyce E. "Tidal Rice Cultivation and the Problem of Slavery in South Carolina and Georgia, 1760–1815." *William & Mary Quarterly* 49 (3rd ser., 1992): 26–61.

Genovese, Eugene D. *Roll, Jordan, Roll: The World the Slaves Made*. New York: Pantheon, 1974.

Hamilton, Phillip. "Revolutionary Principles and Family Loyalties: Slavery's Transformation in the St. George Tucker Household of Early National Virginia." *William & Mary Quarterly* 55 (3rd ser., 1998): 531–56.

Heath, Barbara J. *Hidden Lives: Archeology of Slave Life at Thomas Jefferson's Poplar Forest*. Charlottesville: University Press of Virginia, 1999.

Morgan, Philip D. "Work and Culture: The Task System and the World of Lowcountry Blacks, 1700 to 1880." *William & Mary Quarterly* 39 (3rd ser., 1982): 563–99.

Smith, Mark M. *Mastered by the Clock: Time, Slavery, and Freedom in the American South*. Chapel Hill: University of North Carolina Press, 1997.

Stampp, Kenneth M. *The Peculiar Institution: Slavery in the Ante-Bellum South*. New York: Alfred A. Knopf, 1956.

5. Slave Trade

Deyle, Steven. "The Irony of Liberty: Origins of the Domestic Slave Trade." *Journal of the Early Republic* 12 (1992): 37–62.

Gudmestad, Robert H. *A Troublesome Commerce: The Transformation of the Interstate Slave Trade*. Baton Rouge: Louisiana State University Press, 2003.

Johnson, Walter. *Soul by Soul: Life inside the Antebellum Slave Market*. Cambridge, Mass.: Harvard University Press, 1999.

Lightner, David L. "The Founders and the Interstate Slave Trade." *Journal of the Early Republic* 22 (2002): 25–51.

Mason, Matthew E. "Slavery Overshadowed: Congress Debates Prohibiting the Atlantic Slave Trade to the United States, 1806–1807." *Journal of the Early Republic* 20 (2000): 59–81.

McMillin, James A. *The Final Victims: Foreign Slave Trade to North America, 1783–1810*. Columbia: University of South Carolina Press, 2004.

Shugerman, Jed Handelsman. "The Louisiana Purchase and South Carolina's Reopening of the Slave Trade in 1803." *Journal of the Early Republic* 22 (2002): 263–90.

6. Urban Slavery

Ingersoll, Thomas N. *Mammon and Manon in Early New Orleans: The First Slave Society in the Deep South*. Knoxville: University of Tennessee Press, 1999.

Swan, Robert J. "John Teasman: African-American Educator and the Emergence of Community in Early Black New York, 1787–1815." *Journal of the Early Republic* 12 (1992): 331–56.

Takagi, Midori. *"Rearing Wolves to our own Destruction": Slavery in Richmond, Virginia, 1782–1865*. Charlottesville: University Press of Virginia, 1999.

c. Emancipation

1. Pressures for Freedom

Antislavery Violence: Sectional, Racial, and Cultural Conflict in Antebellum America. Edited by John R. McKivigan and Stanley Harrold. Knoxville: University of Tennessee Press, 1999.

Barker, Andrew J. *Captain Charles Stuart: Anglo-American Abolitionist*. Baton Rouge: Louisiana State University Press, 1986.

Blight, David W. "Perceptions of Southern Intransigence and the Rise of Radical Antislavery Thought, 1816–1830." *Journal of the Early Republic* 3 (1983): 139–63.

Crothers, A. Glen. "Quaker Merchants and Slavery in Early National Alexandria, Virginia." *Journal of the Early Republic* 25 (2005): 47–77.

diGiamcomantonio, William C. "'For the Gratification of a Volunteering Society': Antislavery Pressure and Pressure Group Politics in the First Congress." *Journal of the Early Republic* 15 (1995): 171–97.

Essig, James D. *The Bonds of Wickedness: American Evangelicals against Slavery, 1770–1808*. Philadelphia: Temple University Press, 1982.

Forbes, Robert. "Slavery and the Evangelical Enlightenment." In *Religion and the Antebellum Debate over Slavery*, edited by John R. McKivigan and Mitchell Snay. Athens: University of Georgia Press, 1998, 68–106.

Gellman, David N. "Race, the Public Sphere, and Abolition in Late Eighteenth-Century New York." *Journal of the Early Republic* 20 (2000): 607–36.

Glaude, Edie S., Jr. *Exodus! Religion, Race, and Slavery in Early Nineteenth-Century Black America*. Chicago: University of Chicago Press, 2000.

Huston, James L. "The Experiential Basis of the Northern Antislavery Impulse." *Journal of Southern History* 56 (1990): 609–40.

Landers, Jane. "Black Community and the Culture in the Southeastern Borderlands." *Journal of the Early Republic* 18 (1998): 117–34.

Mason, Matthew. "The Battle of the Slaveholding Liberators: Great Britain, the United States, and Slavery in the Early Nineteenth Century." *William & Mary Quarterly* 59 (3rd ser., 2002): 665–96.

Melish, Joanne Pope. "The 'Condition' Debate and Racial Discourse in the Antebellum North." *Journal of the Early Republic* 19 (1999): 651–72.

White, Shane. *Somewhat More Independent: The End of Slavery in New York City, 1770–1810*. Athens: University of Georgia Press, 1991.

Zeitz, Joshua M. "The Missouri Compromise Reconsidered: Antislavery Rhetoric and the Emergence of the Free Labor Synthesis." *Journal of the Early Republic* 20 (2000): 447–85.

Zilversmit, Arthur. *First Emancipation: The Abolition of Slavery in the North*. Chicago: University of Chicago Press, 1967.

2. Fruits of Emancipation

Beyan, Amos J. *The American Colonization Society and the Creation of the Liberian State: A Historical Perspective, 1822–1900*. Lanham, Md.: University Press of America, 1991.

Bolster, W. Jeffrey. *Black Jack: African American Seamen in the Age of Sail*. Cambridge, Mass.: Harvard University Press, 1997.

Cashin, Joan E. "Black Families in the Old Northwest." *Journal of the Early Republic* 15 (1995): 449–75.

Clegg, Claude A. *The Price of Liberty: African-Americans and the Making of Liberia*. Chapel Hill: University of North Caroline Press, 2004.

Curry, Leonard P. *The Free Black in Urban America, 1800–1850: The Shadow of the Dream*. Chicago: University of Chicago Press, 1981.

Davis, Hugh. "Northern Colonization and Free Blacks, 1823–1837: A Case Study of Leonard Bacon." *Journal of the Early Republic* 17 (1997): 651–75.

Desroches, Robert E., Jr. "'Not Fade Away': The Narrative of Venture Smith, an African American in the Early Republic." *Journal of American History* 84 (1997): 40–66.

Egerton, Douglas R. "'Its Origin Is Not a Little Strange': A New Look at the American Colonization Society." *Journal of the Early Republic* 5 (1985): 463–80.

Gilje, Paul A., and Howard B. Rock. "'Sweep O! Sweep O!': African-American Chimney Sweeps and Citizenship in the New Nation." *William & Mary Quarterly* 51 (3rd ser., 1994): 507–38.

Hanger, Kimberly S. *Bounded Lives, Bounded Places: Free Black Society in Colonial New Orleans, 1769–1803*. Durham, N.C.: Duke University Press, 1997.

Harris, Katherine. *African and American Values: Liberia and West Africa*. Lanham, Md.: University Press of America, 1985.

Horton, James O., and Lois E. Horton. *In Hope of Liberty: Culture, Community and Protest among Northern Free Blacks, 1700–1860*. New York: Oxford University Press, 1997.

Johnson, Whittington B. *The Promising Years, 1750–1830: The Emergence of Black Labor and Business*. New York: Garland Publishing, 1993.

Lebsock, Suzanne. *Free Women of Petersburg: Status and Culture in a Southern Town, 1784–1860*. New York: W. W. Norton, 1984.

Litwack, Leon. *North of Slavery: The Negro in the Free States, 1790–1860*. Chicago: University of Chicago Press, 1961.

Levesque, George A. *Black Boston: African American Life and Culture in Urban America, 1750–1860*. New York: Garland Publishing, 1994.

Nash, Gary B. *Forging Freedom: The Formation of Philadelphia's Black Community, 1720–1840*. Cambridge, Mass.: Harvard University Press, 1988.

Stewart, James Brewer. "'Modernizing 'Difference': The Political Meanings of Color in the Free States, 1776–1840." *Journal of the Early Republic* 19 (1999): 691–712.

Sweet, John Wood. *Bodies Politic: Negotiating Race in the American North, 1730–1830*. Baltimore: The Johns Hopkins University Press, 2003.

Thomas, Lamont D. *Rise to Be a Free People: A Biography of Paul Cuffee*. Urbana: University of Illinois Press, 1986.

White, Shane. *Stories of Freedom in Black New York*. Cambridge, Mass.: Harvard University Press, 2002.

——. "'We Dwell in Safety and Pursue Honest Callings': Free Blacks in New York City, 1783–1810." *Journal of American History* 75 (1978–1979): 445–70.

Winch, Julie. *Philadelphia's Black Elite: Activism, Accommodation, and the Struggle for Autonomy, 1787–1848*. Philadelphia: Temple University Press, 1988.

3. Religion

Black Itinerants of the Gospel: The Narratives of John Jea and George White. Edited by Graham R. Hodges. Madison, Wis.: Madison House, 1993.

Cornelius, Janet D. *Slave Missions and the Black Church in the Antebellum South*. Columbia: University of South Carolina Press, 1999.

Smith, Edward D. *Climbing Jacob's Ladder: The Rise of Black Churches in Eastern American Cities, 1740–1877*. Washington, D.C.: Smithsonian Institution Press, 1988.

3. Native Americans

a. General Histories

Baron, Donna K., Edward J. Hood, and Holly V. Izard. "They Were Here All Along: The Native American Presence in Lower-Central New England in the Eighteenth and Nineteenth Centuries." *William & Mary Quarterly* 53 (3rd ser., 1996): 561–86.

Dowd, Gregory Evans. *A Spirited Resistance: The North American Indian Struggle for Unity, 1745–1815*. Baltimore: The Johns Hopkins University Press, 1992.

Kornfeld, Eve. "'Encountering "the Other"': American Intellectuals and Indians in the 1790s." *William & Mary Quarterly* 52 (3rd ser., 1995): 287–314.

Mancall, Peter C. *Deadly Medicine: Indians and Alcohol in Early America*. Ithaca, N.Y.: Cornell University Press, 1995.

Native Americans and the Early Republic. Edited by Frederick E. Hoxie, Ronald Hoffman, and Peter J. Albert. Charlottesville: University Press of Virginia, 1999.

White, Richard. *The Middle Ground: Indians, Empires, and Republics in the Great Lakes Region, 1650–1815*. New York: Cambridge University Press, 1991.

b. Displacements and Removals

Andrew, John A., III. *From Revivals to Removal: Jeremiah Evarts, the Cherokee Nation, and the Search for the Soul of America*. Athens: University of Georgia Press, 1992.

Benn, Carl. *The Iroquois in the War of 1812*. Toronto: University of Toronto Press, 1998.

Hauptman, Laurence M. *Conspiracy of Interests: Iroquois Dispossession and the Rise of New York State*. Syracuse, N.Y.: Syracuse University Press, 1999.

Jones, Dorothy V. *License for Empire: Colonialism by Treaty in Early America*. Chicago: University of Chicago Press, 1982.

The Oneida Journey: From New York to Wisconsin, 1784–1860. Edited by Laurence M. Hauptman and L. Gordon McLester III. Madison: University of Wisconsin Press, 1999.

Owens, Robert M. "Jeffersonian Benevolence on the Ground: The Indian Land Cession Treaties of William Henry Harrison." *Journal of the Early Republic* 22 (2002): 405–35.

Prucha, Francis P. *American Indian Policy in the Formative Years: The Indian Trade and Intercourse Acts, 1780–1834*. Cambridge, Mass.: Harvard University Press, 1962.

Ronda, James P. "'We Have a Country': Race, Geography, and the Invention of Indian Territory." *Journal of the Early Republic* 19 (1999): 739–55.

c. Tribal Studies

Braund, Kathryn E. Holland. "The Creek Indians, Blacks, and Slavery." *Journal of Southern History* 57 (1991): 601–36.

Carson, James T. *Searching for the Bright Path: The Mississippi Choctaws from Prehistory to Removal*. Lincoln: University of Nebraska Press, 1999.

The Choctows before the Removal. Edited by Carolyn K. Reeves. Jackson: University Press of Mississippi, 1985.

Conley, Robert J. *The Cherokee Nation: A History*. Albuquerque: University of New Mexico Press, 2005.

Covington, James W. *The Seminoles of Florida*. Gainesville: University Press of Florida, 1993.

Ethridge, Robbie. *Creek Country: The Creek Indians and Their World*. Chapel Hill: University of North Carolina Press, 2003.

McLoughlin, William G. *Cherokees and Christianity, 1789–1830: Essays on Acculturation and Cultural Persistence*. Athens: University of Georgia Press, 1994.

———. *Cherokee Renaissance in the New Republic*. Princeton, N.J.: Princeton University Press, 1986.

O'Brien, Greg. *Choctows in a Revolutionary Age, 1750–1830*. Lincoln: University of Nebraska Press, 2002.

Perdue, Theda. *Cherokee Women: Gender and Cultural Change, 1700–1835*. Lincoln: University of Nebraska Press, 1998.

Saunt, Claudio. *A New Order of Things: Property, Power, and the Transformation of the Creek Indians, 1733–1816*. New York: Cambridge University Press, 1999.

White, Richard. "The Winning of the West: The Expansion of the Western Sioux in the Eighteenth and Nineteenth Centuries." *Journal of American History* 65 (1978–1979): 319–43.

Wishart, David M. "Evidence of Surplus Production in the Cherokee Nation Prior to Removal." *Journal of Economic History* 55 (1995): 120–38.

Wright, J. Leitch. *Creeks and Seminoles: Destruction and Regeneration of the Muscogulge People*. Lincoln: University of Nebraska Press, 1986.

d. Individuals

Carter, Harvey Lewis. *The Life of Little Turtle: First Sagamore of the Wabash*. Urbana: University of Illinois Press, 1987.

Cave, Alfred A. "The Shawnee Prophet, Tecumseh, and Tippecanoe: A Case Study of Historical Myth-Making." *Journal of the Early Republic* 22 (2002): 636–73.

Desmore, Christopher. *Red Jacket: Iroquois Diplomat and Orator*. Syracuse, N.Y.: Syracuse University Press, 1999.

Edmunds, R. David. *The Shawnee Prophet*. Lincoln: University of Nebraska Press, 1983.

———. *Tecumseh and the Quest for Indian Leadership*. Boston: Little, Brown, 1984.

Griffith, Benjamin W., Jr. *McIntosh and Weatherford, Creek Leaders*. Tuscaloosa: University of Alabama Press, 1988.

Kelsay, Isabel T. *Joseph Brant, 1743–1807: Man of Two Worlds*. Syracuse, N.Y.: Syracuse University Press, 1984.

Sudgen, John. *Tecumseh: A Life*. New York: Henry Holt, 1997.

e. Political and Cultural Interactions between Indians and Others

Braund, Kathryn E. *Deerskins and Duffels: The Creek Indian Trade with Anglo-America, 1685–1815*. Lincoln: University of Nebraska Press, 1993.

Calloway, Colin. *Crown and Calumet: British-Indian Relations, 1783–1815*. Norman: University of Oklahoma Press, 1987.

The Collected Works of Benjamin Hawkins, 1796–1810. Edited by Thomas Foster. Tuscaloosa: University of Alabama Press, 2003.

Contact Points: American Frontiers from the Mohawk Valley to the Mississippi, 1750–1830. Edited by Andrew R. L. Cayton and Fredrika J. Teute. Chapel Hill: University of North Carolina Press, 1998.

Cumfer, Cynthia. "Local Origins of National Indian Policy: Cherokees and Tennessean Ideas about Sovereignty and Nationhood, 1790–1811." *Journal of the Early Republic* 23 (2003): 21–46.

Davis, Karl. "'Remember Fort Mims': Reinterpreting the Origins of the Creek War." *Journal of the Early Republic* 22 (2002): 611–36.

Henri, Florette. *The Southern Indians and Benjamin Hawkins, 1796–1816*. Norman: University of Oklahoma Press, 1986.

Hurt, R. Douglas. *The Indian Frontier, 1763–1846*. Albuquerque: University of New Mexico Press, 2002.

Mandell, Daniel R. "'The Indian's Pedigree' (1794): Indians, Folklore, and Race in Southern New England." *William & Mary Quarterly* 61 (3rd ser., 2004): 521–38.

——. "Shifting Boundaries of Race and Ethnicity: Indian-Black Intermarriage in Southern New England, 1760–1880." *Journal of American History* 85 (1998): 466–501.

McLoughlin, William G. *Cherokees and Missionaries, 1789–1839*. New Haven, Conn.: Yale University Press, 1984.

Nelson, Larry L. *A Man of Distinction among Them: Alexander McKee and the Ohio Country Frontier, 1754–1799*. Kent, Ohio: Kent State University Press, 1999.

Perdue, Theda. *"Mixed Blood" Indians: Racial Reconstruction in the Early South*. Athens: University of Georgia Press, 2002.

Richter, Daniel K. "'Believing That Many of the Red People Suffer Much for the Want of Food': Hunting, Agriculture, and a Quaker Construction of Indianness in the Early Republic." *Journal of the Early Republic* 19 (1999): 6012–28.

Taylor, Alan. "The Divided Ground: Upper Canada, New York, and the Iroquois Six Nations, 1783–1815." *Journal of the Early Republic* 22 (2002): 55–75.

Unser, Daniel H. "American Indians on the Cotton Frontier: Changing Economic Relations with Citizens and Slaves in the Mississippi Territory." *Journal of American History* 72 (1985–1986): 297–317.

Vibert, Elizabeth. *Traders' Tales: Narratives of Cultural Encounters in the Columbia Plateau, 1807–1846*. Norman: University of Oklahoma Press, 1997.

Wallace, Anthony F. C. *Jefferson and the Indians: The Tragic Fate of the First Americans*. Cambridge, Mass.: Harvard University Press, Belknap Press, 1999.

f. Family

Cashin, Joan E. "The Structure of Antebellum Planter Families: 'The Ties That Bound Us Was Strong.'" *Journal of Southern History* 56 (1990): 55–70.

Dicken-Garcia, Hazel. *In the Western Woods: The Breckinridge Family Moves to Kentucky in 1793*. Rutherford, N.J.: Fairleigh-Dickinson University Press, 1991.

Ditz, Toby L. *Property and Kinship: Inheritance in Early Connecticut, 1750–1820*. Princeton, N.J.: Princeton University Press, 1986.

Doyle, Christopher L. "The Randolph Scandal in Early National Virginia, 1792–1815: New Voices in the 'Court of Honour.'" *Journal of Southern History* 69 (2003): 283–318.

Gutman, Herbert G. *The Black Family in Slavery and Freedom, 1750–1925*. New York: Pantheon, 1976.

Hessinger, Rodney. *Seduced, Abandoned, and Reborn: Visions of Youth in Middle Class America, 1780–1850*. Philadelphia: University of Pennsylvania Press, 2005.

Jabour, Anya. *Marriage in the Early Republic: Elizabeth and William Wirt and the Companionate Ideal*. Baltimore: The Johns Hopkins University Press, 1998.

Johansen, Shawn. *Family Men: Middle Class Fatherhood in Early Industrializing America*. New York: Routledge, 2001.

Keiner, Cynthia A. "'The Dark and Dense Cloud Perpetually Lowering over Us': Gender and the Decline of the Gentry in Postrevolutionary Virginia." *Journal of the Early Republic* 20 (2000): 185–217.

Kett, Joseph F. *Rites of Passage: Adolescence in America 1790 to the Present*. New York: Basic Books, 1977.

Kilbride, Daniel. "Cultivation, Conservatism, and the Early National Gentry: The Manigault Family and their Circle." *Journal of the Early Republic* 19 (1999): 221–56.

Lewis, Charlene W. Boyer. *Ladies and Gentlemen on Display: Planter Society at the Virginia Springs, 1790–1860*. Charlottesville: University Press of Virginia, 2001.

Lewis, Jan. *The Pursuit of Happiness: Family Life and Values in Jeffersonian Virginia*. New York: Cambridge University Press, 1983.

Reimer, Jacqueline S. "Rearing the Republican Child: Attitudes and Practices in Post-Revolutionary Philadelphia." *William & Mary Quarterly* 39 (3rd ser., 1982): 150–63.

Robbins, Karen. "Power among the Powerless: Domestic Resistance by Free and Slave Women in the McHenry Family of the Early Republic." *Journal of the Early Republic* 23 (2003): 47–68.

Rothman, Joshua D. "'Notorious in the Neighborhood': An Interracial Family in Early National and Antebellum Virginia." *Journal of Southern History* 67 (2001): 37–72.

Ryan, Mary P. *The Cradle of the Middle Class: The Family in Oneida County, New York, 1790–1865*. New York: Cambridge University Press, 1981.

Sievens, Mary Beth. "'The Wicked Agency of Others': Community, Law, and Marital Conflict in Vermont, 1790–1830." *Journal of the Early Republic* 21 (2001): 19–39.

A Yankee Jeffersonian: Selections from the Diary and Letters of William Lee of Massachusetts. Edited by Mary Lee Mann. Cambridge, Mass.: Harvard University Press, 1958.

g. Immigration

Durey, Michael. *Transatlantic Radicals and the Early Republic*. Lawrence: University Press of Kansas, 1997.

Grubb, Farley. "The End of European Immigrant Servitude in the United States: An Economic Analysis of Market Collapse, 1772–1835." *Journal of Economic History* 54 (1994): 794–824.

Kennedy, Roger G. *Orders from France: The Americans and the French in a Revolutionary World*. New York: Alfred A. Knopf, 1989.

h. Reform and Improvement

Bernard, Paul R. "Irreconcilable Opinions: The Social and Educational Theories of Robert Owen and William Maclure." *Journal of the Early Republic* 8 (1988): 21–44.

Bestor, Arthur E., Jr. *Backwoods Utopias: The Sectarian and Owenite Phases of Communitarian Socialism in America, 1663–1829*. Philadelphia: University of Pennsylvania Press, 1950.

——. *Education and Reform at New Harmony: Correspondence of William MacClure and Marie Duclos Fretagot, 1820–1833*. Indianapolis: Indianapolis Historical Society, 1948.

Bushman, Richard L. "The Early History of Cleanliness in America." *Journal of American History* 74 (1987–1988): 1213–38.

A Documentary History of the Indiana Decade of the Harmony Society, 1814–1824. Edited by Karl J. R. Arndt. 2 vols. Indianapolis: Indiana Historical Society, 1975.

Durey, Michael. "John Lithgow's Lithconia: The Making and Meaning of America's First 'Utopian Socialist' Tract." *William & Mary Quarterly* 49 (3rd ser., 1992): 675–94.

Eckhardt, Celia M. *Fanny Wright: Rebel in America*. Cambridge, Mass.: Harvard University Press, 1984.

Hampel, Robert L. *Temperance and Prohibition in Massachusetts, 1813–1852*. Ann Arbor: University of Michigan Research Press, 1982.

Hemphill, C. Dallett. *Bowing to Necessities: A History of Manners in America, 1620–1860*. New York: Oxford University Press, 1999.

Hood, Fred J. *Reformed America, 1783–1837*. Tuscaloosa: University of Alabama Press, 1980.

John, Richard R. "Taking Sabbatarianism Seriously: The Postal System, the Sabbath, and the Transformation of American Political Culture." *Journal of the Early Republic* 11 (1991): 517–67.

Kolmerten, Carol A. *Women in Utopia: The Ideology of Gender in the American Owenite Communities*. Bloomington: Indiana University Press, 1990.

McCarthy, Kathleen D. *American Creed: Philanthropy and the Rise of Civil Society, 1700–1865*. Chicago: University of Chicago Press, 2003.

McMahon, Sarah F. "A Comfortable Subsistence: The Changing Composition of Diet in Rural New England, 1620–1840." *William & Mary Quarterly* 42 (3rd ser., 1985): 26–65.

Quist, John W. "Slaveholding Operatives of the Benevolent Empire: Bible, Tract, and Sunday School Societies in Antebellum Tuscaloosa County, Alabama." *Journal of Southern History* 62 (1996): 481–526.

Rorabaugh, W. J. *The Alcoholic Republic: An American Tradition*. New York: Oxford University Press, 1979.

Tyrell, Ian R. *Sobering Up: From Temperance to Prohibition in Antebellum America, 1800–1860*. Westport, Conn.: Greenwood Press, 1979.

Wright, Conrad. *Transformation of Charity in Post Revolutionary New England*. Boston: Northeastern University Press, 1992.

i. Regionalism

George Washington's South. Edited by Tamara Harvey and Greg O'Brien. Gainesville: University Press of Florida, 2004.

Merchant, Carolyn. *Ecological Revolution: Nature, Gender, and Science in New England*. Chapel Hill: University of North Carolina Press, 1989.

Nylander, Jance C. *Our Own Snug Fireside: Images of the New England Home, 1760–1860*. New York: Alfred A. Knopf, 1993.

Smith, Daniel Scott. "All in Some Way Related to Each Other: A Demographic and Comparative Resolution of the Anomaly of New England Kinship." *American Historical Review* 94 (1989): 44–79.

Varg, Paul A. *New England and Foreign Relations, 1789–1850*. Hanover, N.H.: University Press of New England, 1983.

j. Urban History

Burrows, Edwin G., and Mike Wallace. *Gotham: A History of New York City to 1898*. New York: Oxford University Press, 1999.

Carr, Jacqueline B. "A Change 'as Remarkable as the Revolution Itself': Boston Demographics, 1780–1800." *New England Quarterly* 73 (2000): 583–602.

Heale, M. J. "From City Fathers to Social Critics: Humanitarianism and Government in New York, 1790–1860." *Journal of American History* 63 (1976–1977): 21–41.

Miller, Roberta B. *City and Hinterland: A Case Study of Urban Growth and Regional Development*. Westport, Conn.: Greenwood Press, 1979.

k. Women's History

1. Life Experiences

"Beyond Roles, Beyond Spheres: Thinking about Gender in the Early Republic." Forum in *William & Mary Quarterly* 46 (3rd ser., 1989): 565–85.

Buel, Joy D., and Richard Buel Jr. *The Way of Duty: A Woman and Her Family in Revolutionary America*. New York: W. W. Norton, 1984.

Bye, Nancy Schron, and Daniel Blake Smith. "Mother Love and Infant Death, 1750–1920." *Journal of American History* 73 (1986–1987): 339–53.

Cott, Nancy F. *The Bonds of Womanhood: "Women's Sphere" in New England, 1780–1835*. New Haven, Conn.: Yale University Press, 1977.

Gelles, Edith B. *Portia: The World of Abigail Adams*. Bloomington: Indiana University Press, 1992.

Gillespie, Joanna Bowen. "'The Clear Leanings of Providence': Pious Memoirs and the Problem of Self-Realization for Women of the Early Nineteenth Century." *Journal of the Early Republic* 5 (1985): 197–221.

———. *The Life and Times of Martha Laurens Ramsay, 1759–1811*. Columbia: University of South Carolina Press, 2001.

Hoffert, Sylvia D. *Private Matters: American Attitudes toward Childbearing and Infant Nurture in the Urban North, 1800–1860*. Urbana: University of Illinois Press, 1989.

Jabour, Anya. "'It Will Never Do to Be Married': The Life of Laura Wirt Randall, 1803–1833." *Journal of the Early Republic* 17 (1997): 193–236.

Jensen, Joan M. *Loosening the Bonds: Mid-Atlantic Farm Women, 1750–1850*. New Haven, Conn.: Yale University Press, 1986.

Kelly, Mary. "Beyond the Boundaries." *Journal of the Early Republic* 21 (2001): 73–78.

Kierner, Cynthia A. *Beyond the Household: Women's Place in the Early South 1700–1835*. Ithaca, N.Y.: Cornell University Press, 1998.

Klepp, Susan E. "Revolutionary Bodies: Women and the Fertility Transition in the Mid-Atlantic Region, 1760–1820." *Journal of American History* 85 (1998–1999): 466–501.

Miller, Marla R. "'My Part Alone': The World of Rebecca Dickinson, 1787–1802." *New England Quarterly* 71 (1998): 341–77.

Nagel, Paul C. *The Adams Women: Abigail and Louisa Adams, Their Sisters and Daughters*. New York: Oxford University Press, 1987.

Norling, Lisa. *Captain Ahab Had a Wife: New England Women and the Whalefishery, 1720–1870*. Chapel Hill: University of North Carolina Press, 2000.

Skemp, Sheila. *Judith Sargent Murray: A Brief Biography with Documents*. Boston: Bedford Books, 1998.

Stansell, Christine. *City of Women: Sex and Class in New York, 1789–1860*. New York: Alfred A. Knopf, 1986.

To Read My Heart: The Journal of Rachel Van Dyke, 1810–1811. Edited by Lucia McMahon and Deborah Schriver. Philadelphia: University of Pennsylvania Press, 2000.

Ulrich, Laurel Thatcher. "'The Living Mother of a Living Child': Midwifery and Mortality in Post-Revolutionary New England." *William & Mary Quarterly* 46 (3rd ser., 1989): 27–48.

———. *A Midwife's Tale: The Life of Martha Ballard, Based on Her Diary, 1785–1812*. New York: Alfred A. Knopf, 1990.

Wilson, Lisa. *Life after Death: Widows in Pennsylvania, 1750–1850*. Philadelphia: Temple University Press, 1992.

Withey, Lynn. *Dearest Friend*. New York: Free Press, 1981.

Wood, Betty. *Gender, Race, and Rank in a Revolutionary Age: The Georgia Lowcountry, 1750–1820*. Athens: University of Georgia Press, 2000.

2. Economic Role

Blewett, Mary H. "Women Shoemakers and Domestic Ideology: Rural Outwork in Early Nineteenth-Century Essex County." *New England Quarterly* 60 (1987): 403–28.

Branson, Susan. "Women and the Family Economy in the Early Republic: The Case of Elizabeth Meredith." *Journal of the Early Republic* 16 (1996): 47–71.

Dublin, Thomas Lewis. "Rural Putting-Out Work in Early Nineteenth-Century New England: Women and the Transition to Capitalism in the Countryside." *New England Quarterly* 64 (1991): 531–73.

———. *Transforming Women's Work: New England Lives in the Industrial Revolution*. Ithaca, N.Y.: Cornell University Press, 1994.

Ulrich, Laurel Thatcher. *The Age of Homespun: Objects and Stories in the Creation of an American Myth*. New York: Knopf, Random House, 2001.

———. "Wheels, Looms, and the Gender Division of Labor in Eighteenth-Century New England." *William & Mary Quarterly* 55 (3rd ser., 1998): 3–38.

Waciega, Lisa W. "A 'Man of Business': The Widow of Means in Southeastern Pennsylvania, 1750–1850." *William & Mary Quarterly* 44 (3rd ser., 1987): 40–64.

3. Legal Status

Boyle, Susan C. "Did She Generally Decide? Women in Ste. Genevieve, 1750–1805." *William & Mary Quarterly* 44 (3rd ser., 1987): 775–89.

Riley, Glenda. "Legislative Divorce in Virginia, 1803–1850." *Journal of the Early Republic* 11 (1991): 51–67.

Salmon, Marylynn. *Women and the Law of Property in Early America*. Chapel Hill: University of North Carolina Press, 1986.

Zagarri, Rosemarie. "The Rights of Man and Women in Post-Revolutionary America." *William & Mary Quarterly* 55 (3rd ser., 1998): 203–36.

4. Education and Reform

Boylan, Anne M. "Women in Groups: An Analysis of Women's Benevolent Organizations in New York and Boston, 1793–1840." *Journal of American History* 71 (1984–1985): 497–523.

Haviland, Margaret M. "Beyond Women's Sphere: Young Quaker Women and the Veil of Charity in Philadelphia, 1790–1810." *William & Mary Quarterly* 51 (3rd ser., 1994): 419–46.

Meckel, Richard A. "Educating a Ministry of Mothers: Evangelical Maternal Associations, 1815–1860." *Journal of the Early Republic* 2 (1982): 403–23.

Nash, Margaret A. "Rethinking Republican Motherhood: Benjamin Rush and the Young Ladies' Academy of Philadelphia." *Journal of the Early Republic* 17 (1997): 171–91.

Perlmann, Joel, and Dennis Shirley. "When Did New England Women Acquire Literacy?" *William & Mary Quarterly* 48 (3rd ser., 1991): 50–67.

Robbins, Sarah. "'The Future Good and Great of Our Land': Republican Mothers, Female Authors, and Domesticated Literacy in Antebellum New England." *New England Quarterly* 75 (2002): 562–91.

5. Female Religious Leaders

Braude, Ann. *Radical Spirits: Spiritualism and Women's Rights in Nineteenth-Century America*. Boston: Beacon Press, 1989.

Brekus, Catherine A. *Strangers and Pilgrims: Female Preaching in America, 1740–1845*. Chapel Hill: University of North Carolina Press, 1998.

Juster, Susan. *Disorderly Women: Sexual Politics and Evangelicalism in Revolutionary New England*. Ithaca, N.Y.: Cornell University Press, 1994.

Juster, Susan, and Ellen Hartigan-O'Connor. "The 'Angel Delusion' of 1806–1811: Frustration and Fantasy in Northern New England." *Journal of the Early Republic* 22 (2002): 375–404.

Westerkamp, Marilyn J. *Women and Religion in Early America, 1600–1850: The Puritan and Evangelical Traditions*. New York: Routledge, 1999.

6. Relationship to Politics

Allgor, Catherine. *Parlor Politics: In Which the Ladies of Washington Helped Build a City and a Government*. Charlottesville: University Press of Virginia, 2000.

Baker, Paula. "The Domestication of Politics: Women and American Political Society, 1780–1820." *American Historical Review* 89 (1984): 620–47.

Blackwell, Marilyn S. "The Republican Vision of Mary Palmer Blackwell." *Journal of the Early Republic* 12 (1992): 11–35.

Boylan, Anne M. "Women and Politics in the Era before Seneca Falls." *Journal of the Early Republic* 10 (1990): 363–82.

Branson, Susan. *These Fiery Frenchified Dames: Women and Political Culture in Early National Philadelphia*. Philadelphia: University of Pennsylvania Press, 2001.

Kann, Mark E. *The Gendering of American Politics: Founding Mothers, Founding Fathers, and Political Patriarchy*. Westport, Conn.: Greenwood Press, 1999.

Kerber, Linda K. "The Paradox of Women's Citizenship in the Early Republic: The Case of *Martin vs. Massachusetts*, 1805." *American Historical Review* 97 (1992): 349–78.

Klinghoffer, Judith A., and Lois Elkis. "'The Petticoat Electors': Women's Suffrage in New Jersey, 1776–1807." *Journal of the Early Republic* 12 (1992): 159–93.

Roberts, Cokie. *Founding Mothers: The Women Who Raised Our Nation*. New York: William Morrow, 2004.

7. Symbols of Virtue and Vice

Brown, Chandos. "Mary Wollstonecraft, or, the Female Illuminati: The Campaign against Women and 'Modern Philosophy' in the Early Republic." *Journal of the Early Republic* 15 (1995): 391–424.

Clapp, Elizabeth J. "'A Virago-Errant in Enchanted Armor'? Anne Royall's 1829 Trial as a Common Scold." *Journal of the Early Republic* 23 (2003): 207–32.

Kierner, Cynthia A. *Scandal at Bizarre: Rumor and Reputation in Jefferson's Virginia*. New York: Palgrave Macmillan, 2004.

Lewis, Jan. "The Republican Wife: Virtue and Seduction in the Early Republic." *William & Mary Quarterly* 44 (3rd ser., 1987): 689–721.

3. Economic History

a. Macroeconomic Perspectives

Henretta, James A. "'The 'Market' in the Early Republic." *Journal of the Early Republic* 18 (1998): 289–304.

Isenberg, Andrew C. "The Market Revolution in the Borderlands: George Champlin Sibley in Missouri and New Mexico, 1808–1826." *Journal of the Early Republic* 21 (2001): 445–65.

Matson, Cathy D. "Capitalizing Hope: Economic Thought and the Early National Economy." *Journal of the Early Republic* 16 (1996): 273–91.

North, Douglass C. *The Economic Growth of the United States 1790–1860*. Englewood Cliffs, N.J.: Prentice Hall, 1961.

Taylor, George Rogers. *The Transportation Revolution 1815–1860*. New York: Rinehart & Company, 1951.

Vickers, Daniel. "Competency and Competition: Economic Culture in Early America." *William & Mary Quarterly* 47 (3rd ser., 1990): 3–29.

b. Culture of Capitalism

Appleby, Joyce O. "The Vexed Story of Capitalism Told by American Historians." *Journal of the Early Republic* 21 (2001): 1–18.

Clark, Christopher. *The Roots of Rural Capitalism: Western Massachusetts, 1780–1860*. Ithaca, N.Y.: Cornell University Press, 1990.

German, James D. "The Social Utility of Wicked Self-Love: Calvinism, Capitalism, and Public Policy in Revolutionary New England." *Journal of American History* 82 (1995–1996): 965–98.

Johnson, Paul E. "The Modernization of Mayo Greenleaf Patch: Land, Family, and Marginality in New England, 1766–1815." *New England Quarterly* 55 (1982): 488–516.

Kulikoff, Allan. *The Agrarian Origins of American Capitalism*. Charlottesville: University Press of Virginia, 1993.

———. "The Transition to Capitalism in Rural America." *William & Mary Quarterly* 46 (3rd ser., 1989): 120–44.

Lamoreaux, Naomi. "Rethinking the Transition to Capitalism in the Early American Northeast." *Journal of American History* 90 (2003–2004): 437–67.

Lubov, Lisa B. "From Carpenter to Capitalist: The Business of Building in Postrevolutionary Boston." In *Entrepreneurs: The Boston Business Community, 1700–1850*, edited by Conrad E. Wright and Katheryn P. Viens. Boston: Northeastern University Press, 1997, 191–209.

Nobles, Gregory H. "Commerce and Community: A Case Study in the Rural Broommaking Business in Antebellum Massachusetts." *Journal of the Early Republic* 4 (1984): 287–308.

Royster Charles. *The Fabulous History of the Dismal Swamp Company: A Story of George Washington's Times*. New York: Alfred A. Knopf, 1999.

Wood, Gordon S. "The Enemy Is Us: Democratic Capitalism in the Early Republic." *Journal of the Early Republic* 16 (1996): 293–308.

c. Agriculture

Appleby, Joyce. "Commercial Farming and the 'Agrarian Myth' in the Early Republic." *Journal of American History* 68 (1981–1982): 833–49.

Chaplin, Joyce E. *An Anxious Pursuit: Agricultural Innovation and Modernity in the Lower South, 1730–1815*. Chapel Hill: University of North Carolina Press, 1993.

———. "Creating a Cotton South in Georgia and South Carolina, 1860–1815." *Journal of Southern History* 57 (1991): 171–200.

Craig, Lee A. *To Sow One Acre More: Childbearing and Farm Productivity in the Antebellum North*. Baltimore: The Johns Hopkins University Press, 1993.

Dupre, Daniel S. *Transforming the Cotton Frontier: Madison County, Alabama, 1800–1840*. Baton Rouge: Louisiana State University Press, 1997.

Egerton, Douglas R. "Markets without a Market Revolution: Southern Planters and Capitalism." *Journal of the Early Republic* 16 (1996): 207–21.

Grettler, David J. "Environmental Change and Conflict in Early Nineteenth-Century Delaware." *Journal of the Early Republic* 19 (1999): 197–220.

Moore, John Hebron. *The Emergence of the Cotton Kingdom in the Old Southwest: Mississippi, 1770–1860*. Baton Rouge: Louisiana State University Press, 1988.

Shalhope, Robert E. *A Tale of New England: The Diaries of Hiram Harwood, Vermont Farmer, 1810–1837*. Baltimore: The Johns Hopkins University Press, 2003.

Skeen, C. Edward. "The Year without a Summer: A Historical View." *Journal of the Early Republic* 7 (1987): 51–67.

Steffen, Charles E. "In Search of a Good Overseer: The Failure of the Agricultural Reform Movement in Low Country South Carolina, 1827–1834." *Journal of Southern History* 63 (1997): 753–807.

Thornton, Tamara P. "Between Generations: Boston Agricultural Reform and the Aging of New England, 1815–1830." *New England Quarterly* 59 (1986): 189–211.

d. Commerce and the Expansion of the Market

Bruegel, Martin. *Farm, Shop, Landing: The Rise of a Market Society in the Hudson Valley, 1780–1860*. Durham, N.C.: Duke University Press, 2002.

——. "Unrest: Manorial Society and the Market in the Hudson Valley, 1780–1850." *Journal of American History* 82 (1995–1996): 1393–424.

Fowler, William. "Marine Insurance in Boston: The Early Years of the Boston Marine Insurance Company, 1799–1807." In *Entrepreneurs: The Boston Business Community, 1700–1850*, edited by Conrad E. Wright and Katheryn P. Viens. Boston: Northeastern University Press, 1997, 151–79.

Friend, Craig T. "Merchants and Markethouses: Reflections on Moral Economy in Early Kentucky." *Journal of the Early Republic* 17 (1997): 553–74.

Gibson, James R. *Otter Skins, Boston Ships, and China Goods: The Maritime Fur Trade of the Northwest Coast, 1785–1841*. Montreal: McGill-Queen's University Press, 1992.

Jaffee, David. "Peddlers of Progress and the Transformation of the Rural North, 1760–1860." *Journal of American History* 78 (1991–1992): 511–35.

Jones, Daniel P. *The Economic and Social Transformation of Rural Rhode Island, 1780–1850*. Boston: Northeastern University Press, 1992.

Labaree, Benjamin. "The Making of an Empire: Boston and Essex County, 1740–1850." In *Entrepreneurs: The Boston Business Community, 1700–1850*, edited by Conrad E. Wright and Katheryn P. Viens. Boston: Northeastern University Press, 1997, 343–63.

Larkin, Jack. *The Reshaping of Everyday Life, 1790–1840*. New York: Harper & Row, 1988.

Lockley, Timothy J. "Trading Encounters between Non-Elite Whites and African Americans in Savannah, 1790–1860." *Journal of Southern History* 66 (2000): 25–48.

Perkins, Elizabeth H. "The Consumer Frontier: Household Consumption in Early Kentucky." *Journal of American History* 78 (1991–1992): 486–510.

Rothenberg, Winifred B. *From Market-Places to a Market Economy: The Transformation of Rural Massachusetts, 1750–1850*. Chicago: University of Chicago Press, 1992.

Sellers, Charles. *The Market Revolution: Jacksonian America 1815–1846*. New York: Oxford University Press, 1991.

"A Symposium on Charles Sellers, *The Market Revolution: Jacksonian America 1815–1846*." *Journal of the Early Republic* 12 (1992): 445–76.

e. Communication and Transportation

Foley, Michael S. "A Mission Fulfilled: The Post Office and the Distribution of Information in Rural New England, 1821–1835." *Journal of the Early Republic* 17 (1997): 611–50.

McCall, Edith. *Conquering the Rivers: Henry Miller Shreve and the Navigation of America's Inland Waterways*. Baton Rouge: Louisiana State University Press, 1984.

Shaw, Ronald E. *Canals for a Nation: The Canal Era in the United States, 1790–1860*. Lexington: University Press of Kentucky, 1991.

Sheriff, Carol. *The Artificial River: The Erie Canal and the Paradox of Progress*. New York: Hill & Wang, 1996.

f. Finance

Bodenhorn, Howard. *A History of Banking in Antebellum America: Financial Markets and Economic Development in an Era of Nation Building*. New York: Cambridge University Press, 2000.

———. "Making the Little Guy Pay: Payments System Networks, Cross-Subsidization, and the Collapse of the Suffolk System." *Journal of Economic History* 62 (2002): 147–69.

———. *State Banking in Early America: A New Economic History*. New York: Oxford University Press, 2002.

Haeger, John Dennis. *John Jacob Astor: Business and Finance in the Early Republic*. Detroit: Wayne State University Press, 1991.

Jennings, Robert, Donald F. Swanson, and Andrew P. Trout. "Alexander Hamilton's Tontine Proposal." *William & Mary Quarterly* 45 (3rd ser., 1988): 107–15.

Kaplan, Edward. *The Bank of the United States and the American Economy*. Westport, Conn.: Greenwood Press, 1999.

Lane, Carl. "For 'A Positive Profit': The Federal Investment in the First Bank of the United States, 1792–1802." *William & Mary Quarterly* 54 (3rd ser., 1997): 601–12.

Perkins, Edwin J. *American Public Finance and Financial Services, 1700–1815*. Columbus: Ohio State University Press, 1994.

Riley, James C. "Foreign Credit and Fiscal Stability: Dutch Investment in the United States, 1781–1794." *Journal of American History* 65 (1978–1979): 654–78.

Ruwell, Mary E. *Eighteenth-Century Capitalism: The Formation of American Marine Insurance Companies*. New York: Garland Publishing, 1993.

Swanson, Donald F., and Andrew P. Trout. "Alexander Hamilton, 'the Celebrated Mr. Neckar,' and Public Credit." *William & Mary Quarterly* 47 (3rd ser., 1990): 422–30.

——. "Alexander Hamilton's Hidden Sinking Fund." *William & Mary Quarterly* 49 (3rd ser., 1992): 108–19.

Van Fenstermaker, J. *The Development of American Commercial Banking: 1782–1837*. Kent, Ohio: Kent State University Press, 1965.

Wright, Robert E. *Hamilton Unbound: Finance and the Creation of the American Republic*. Westport, Conn.: Greenwood Press, 2002.

——. *The Origins of Commercial Banking in America, 1750–1800*. Lanham, Md.: Rowman & Littlefield, 2001.

——. *The Wealth of Nations Rediscovered: Integration and Expansion in American Financial Markets, 1780–1850*. Cambridge: Cambridge University Press, 2002.

g. Industry and Manufacturing

Bezis-Selfa, John. *Forging America: Ironworkers, Adventurers, and the Industrious Revolution*. Ithaca, N.Y.: Cornell University Press, 2004.

Faler, Paul G. *Mechanics and Manufacturers in the Early Industrial Revolution: Lynn, Massachusetts, 1780–1860*. Albany: State University of New York Press, 1981.

Hoke, Donald R. *The Rise of the American System of Manufactures in the Private Sector*. New York: Columbia University Press, 1990.

Hindle, Brooke, and Steven Lubar. *Engines of Social Change: The American Industrial Revolution, 1790–1860*. Washington, D.C.: Smithsonian Institution Press, 1986.

Irwin, Douglas A. "The Aftermath of Hamilton's 'Report on Manufactures.'" *Journal of Economic History* 64 (2004): 806–21.

Meyer, David R. *The Roots of American Industrialization*. Baltimore: The Johns Hopkins University Press, 2003.

Martello, Robert. "Paul Revere's Last Ride: The Road to Rolling Copper." *Journal of the Early Republic* 20 (2000): 219–39.

Mohanty, Gail F. "Putting Up with Putting-Out: Power-Loom Diffusion and Outwork for Rhode Island Mills, 1821–1829." *Journal of the Early Republic* 9 (1989): 191–216.

Nelson, John R., Jr. "Alexander Hamilton and American Manufacturing: A Re-Examination." *Journal of American History* 65 (1978–1979): 931–95.

Paskoff, Paul F. *Industrial Evolution: Organization, Structure, and Growth of the Pennsylvania Iron Industry, 1750–1860*. Baltimore: The Johns Hopkins University Press, 1984.

Peskin, Lawrence A. *Manufacturing Revolution: The Intellectual Origins of Early American Industry*. Baltimore: The Johns Hopkins University Press, 2003.

Prude, Jonathan. "Capitalism, Industrialization, and the Factory in Post-Revolutionary America." *Journal of the Early Republic* 16 (1996): 237–55.

——. *The Coming of Industrial Order: Town and Factory Life in Rural Massachusetts, 1810–1860*. Cambridge: Cambridge University Press, 1983.

Shelton, Cynthia J. *The Mills of Manayunk: Industrialization and Social Conflict in the Philadelphia Region, 1787–1837*. Baltimore: The Johns Hopkins University Press, 1986.

Tucker, Barbara M. *Samuel Slater and the Origins of the American Textile Industry, 1790–1860*. Ithaca, N.Y.: Cornell University Press, 1985.

Weil, François. "Capitalism and Industrialization in New England, 1815–1845." *Journal of American History* 84 (1997–1998): 1334–54.

Young, Otis E., Jr. "Origins of the American Copper Industry." *Journal of the Early Republic* 3 (1983): 117–37.

h. Internal Improvements

Bernstein, Peter L. *Wedding of the Waters*. New York: W. W. Norton, 2005.

Harrison, Joseph H., Jr. "'Sic Et Non': Thomas Jefferson and Internal Improvements." *Journal of the Early Republic* 7 (1987): 335–49.

Larson, John L. "Bind the Republic Together: The National Union and the Struggle for a System of Internal Improvements." *Journal of American History* 74 (1987): 363–87.

——. "A Bridge, a Dam, a River: Liberty and Innovation in the Early Republic." *Journal of the Early Republic* 7 (1987): 337–75.

——. *Internal Improvement: National Public Works and the Promise of Popular Government in the United States*. Chapel Hill: University of North Carolina Press, 2001.

Malone, Laurence J. *Opening the West: Federal Internal Improvements before 1860*. Westport, Conn.: Greenwood Press, 1998.

Sunderland, Henry deLeon, and Jerry E. Brown. *The Federal Road through Georgia, the Creek Nation, and Alabama*. Tuscaloosa: University of Alabama Press, 1989.

i. Labor

Bezis-Selfa, John. "A Tale of Two Ironworks: Slavery, Free Labor, Work, and Resistance in the Early Republic." *William & Mary Quarterly* 56 (3rd ser., 1999): 677–700.

Blewett, Mary H. *Men, Women, and Work: Class, Gender, and Protest in the*

Early New England Shoe Industry, 1789–1910. Urbana: University of Illinois Press, 1988.

Boyston, Jeanne. *Home and Work: Housework, Wages, and the Ideology of Labor in the Early Republic*. New York: Oxford University Press, 1990.

———. "The Woman Who Wasn't There: Women's Labor and the Transition to Capitalism in the United States." *Journal of the Early Republic* 16 (1996): 183–206.

Dawley, Alan. *Class and Community: The Industrial Revolution in Lynn*. Cambridge, Mass.: Harvard University Press, 1976.

Doerflinger, Thomas M. "Rural Capitalism in Iron Country: Staffing a Forest Factory, 1808–1815." *William & Mary Quarterly* 59 (3rd ser., 2002): 3–38.

Gilje, Paul A. *Liberty on the Waterfront: American Maritime Culture in the Age of Revolution*. Philadelphia: University of Pennsylvania Press, 2004.

Hirsch, Susan E. *Roots of the American Working Class: The Industrialization of Crafts in Newark, 1800–1860*. Philadelphia: University of Pennsylvania Press, 1978.

Kahana, Jeffrey S. "Master and Servant in the Early Republic, 1780–1830." *Journal of the Early Republic* 20 (2000): 27–57.

Kornblith, Gary J. "The Artisanal Response to Capitalist Transformation." *Journal of the Early Republic* 10 (1990): 315–21.

———. "'Cementing the Mechanic Interest': Origins of the Providence Association of Mechanics and Manufacturers." *Journal of the Early Republic* 8 (1988): 355–87.

Lause, Mark A. *Some Degree of Power: From Hired Hand to Union Craftsman in the Preindustrial American Printing Trade, 1778–1815*. Fayetteville: University of Arkansas Press, 1991.

Newman, Simon P. "Reading the Bodies of Early American Seafarers." *William & Mary Quarterly* 55 (3rd ser., 1998): 59–82.

Rock, Howard. *The New York City Artisan, 1789–1825*. Albany: State University of New York Press, 1989.

Rorabaugh, W. J. *The Craft Apprentice from Franklin to the Machine Age in America*. New York: Oxford University Press, 1986.

Salinger, Sharon V. "Artisans, Journeymen, and the Transformation of Labor in Late Eighteenth-Century Philadelphia." *William & Mary Quarterly* 40 (3rd ser., 1983): 62–84.

Skelton, Cynthia. "The Role of Labor in Early Industrialization: Philadelphia, 1787–1837." *Journal of the Early Republic* 4 (1984): 365–94.

Smith, Billy G. *The "Lower Sort": Philadelphia's Laboring People, 1750–1800*. Ithaca, N.Y.: Cornell University Press, 1990.

———. "The Material Lives of Laboring Philadelphians, 1750–1800." *William*

& Mary Quarterly 38 (3rd ser., 1981): 163–202.

Steffer, Charles G. *The Mechanics of Baltimore: Workers and Politics in the Age of Revolution, 1763–1812*. Urbana: University of Illinois Press, 1984.

Stott, Richard. "Artisans and Capitalist Development." *Journal of the Early Republic* 16 (1996): 257–71.

Vickers, Daniel. *Farmers and Fishermen: Two Centuries of Work in Essex County, Massachusetts, 1630–1850*. Chapel Hill: University of North Carolina Press, 1994.

———. "Nantucket Whalemen in the Deep-Sea Fishery: The Changing Anatomy of an Early American Labor Force." *Journal of American History* 72 (1985–1986): 277–96.

Vickers, Daniel, with Vince Walsh. *Young Men and the Sea: Maritime Society in Salem Massachusetts, 1630–1850*. New Haven, Conn.: Yale University Press, 2005.

Way, Peter. *Common Labour: Workers and the Digging of North American Canals, 1780–1860*. New York: Cambridge University Press, 1993.

———. "Evil Humors and Ardent Spirits: The Rough Culture of Canal Construction Laborers." *Journal of American History* 79 (1993): 1397–428.

j. Legal System

Banner, Stuart. *Legal Systems in Conflict: Property and Sovereignty in Missouri, 1750–1860*. Norman: University of Oklahoma Press, 2000.

Cain, Narvin R. "Claims, Contracts and Custom: Public Accountability and a Department of Law, 1789–1849." *Journal of the Early Republic* 4 (1984): 27–45.

Dargo, George. *Law in the New Republic: Private Law and the Public Estate*. New York: Alfred A. Knopf, 1983.

Horwitz, Morton J. *The Transformation of American Law, 1780–1860*. Cambridge, Mass.: Harvard University Press, 1977.

Huebner, Timothy S. *The Southern Judicial Tradition: State Judges and Sectional Distinctiveness, 1790–1890*. Athens: University of Georgia Press, 1999.

A Law unto Itself?: Essays in the New Louisiana Legal History. Edited by Warren M. Billings and Mark F. Fernandez. Baton Rouge: Louisiana State University Press, 2001.

Mann, Bruce H. *Republic of Debtors: Bankruptcy in the Age of American Independence*. Cambridge, Mass.: Harvard University Press, 2002.

———. "'Tales form the Crypt': Prison, Legal Authority, and the Debtors' Constitution in the Early Republic." *William & Mary Quarterly* 51 (3rd ser., 1994): 183–202.

Reid, John Philip. *Controlling the Law: Legal Politics in Early National New Hampshire*. De Kalb: Northern Illinois University Press, 2004.

k. Panic of 1819

Blackson, Robert M. "Pennsylvania Banks and the Panic of 1819: A Reinterpretation." *Journal of the Early Republic* 9 (1989): 335–58.

Cayton, Andrew R. L. "The Fragmentation of 'A Great Family': The Panic of 1819 and the Rise of the Middling Interest in Boston, 1818–1822." *Journal of the Early Republic* 2 (1982): 143–67.

Haulman, Clyde. "Virginia Commodity Prices during the Panic of 1819." *Journal of the Early Republic* 22 (2002): 675–88.

Rothbard, Murray N. *The Panic of 1819: Reactions and Policies*. New York: Columbia University Press, 1962.

l. Public Policy

Handlin, Oscar, and Mary Flug. *Commonwealth: A Study of the Role of Government in the American Economy: Massachusetts 1774–1861*. New York: Oxford University Press, 1947.

Hartz, Louis. *Economic Policy and Democratic Thought: Pennsylvania, 1776–1860*. Cambridge, Mass.: Harvard University Press, 1948.

Nelson, John R., Jr. *Liberty and Property: Political Economy and Policy Making in the New Republic, 1789–1812*. Baltimore: The Johns Hopkins University Press, 1987.

Prince, Carl E., and Seth Taylor. "Daniel Webster, the Boston Associates, and the U.S. Government's Role in the Industrializing Process, 1815–1830." *Journal of the Early Republic* 2 (1982): 283–99.

m. Science and Technology

Ben-Atar, Doron S. *Trade Secrets: Intellectual Property and the Origins of American Industrial Power*. New Haven, Conn.: Yale University Press, 2004.

Brown, Chandos. *Benjamin Silliman: A Life in the Young Republic*. Princeton, N.J.: Princeton University Press, 1990.

Cassedy, James H. *American Medicine and Statistical Thinking, 1800–1860*. Cambridge, Mass.: Harvard University Press, 1984.

———. *Medicine in America: A Short History*. Baltimore: The Johns Hopkins University Press, 1991.

Delbourgo, James. "Common Sense, Useful Knowledge, and Matter of Fact in the Late Enlightenment: The Transatlantic Career of Perkins's Tractors." *William & Mary Quarterly* 61 (3rd ser., 2004): 643–84.

Greene, John C. *American Science in the Age of Jefferson*. Ames: Iowa State University Press, 1984.

Hart-Davis, Duff. *Audubon's Elephant: America's Greatest Naturalist and the Making of "The Birds of America."* London: Weidenfeld & Nicolson, 2003.

Hindle, Brooke. *Emulation and Invention*. New York: New York University Press, 1981.

Hutcheon, Wallace S. *Robert Fulton: Pioneer of Undersea Warfare*. Annapolis,

Md.: United States Naval Institute Press, 1981.
Jeremy, David J. *Transatlantic Industrial Revolutions: The Diffusion of Textile Technologies between Britain and America, 1790–1830s*. Cambridge: Cambridge University Press, 1981.
Leavitt, Judith W. "Science Enters the Birthing Room: Obstetrics in America since the Eighteenth Century." *Journal of American History* 70 (1983–1984): 281–304.
McGraw, Judith A. *Early American Technology: Making and Doing Things from the Colonial Era to 1850*. Chapel Hill: University of North Carolina Press, 1994.
Preston, Daniel. "The Administration and Reform of the U.S. Patent Office, 1790–1836." *Journal of the Early Republic* 5 (1985): 331–53.
Rhodes, Richard. *John James Audubon: The Making of an American*. New York: Alfred A. Knopf, 2004.
Shallat, Todd. *Structures in the Stream: Water, Science, and the Rise of the U.S. Army Corps of Engineers*. Austin: University of Texas Press, 1994.
Souder, William. *Under the Wild Sky: John James Audubon and the Making of "The Birds of America."* New York: North Point Press, 2004.
Stroud, Patricia T. *Thomas Say: New World Naturalist*. Philadelphia: University of Pennsylvania Press, 1992.
Sutcliffe, Andrea J. *Steam: The Untold Story of America's First Great Invention*. New York: Palgrave Macmillan, 2004.

n. Resource Extraction and the Expansion of Settlement

Adler, Jeffrey S. *Yankee Merchants and the Making of the Urban West: The Rise and Fall of Antebellum St. Louis*. Cambridge: Cambridge University Press, 1991.
Aron, Stephen. *How the West Was Lost: The Transformation of Kentucky from Daniel Boone to Henry Clay*. Baltimore: The Johns Hopkins University Press, 1996.
Bolton, S. Charles. *Territorial Ambition: Land and Society in Arkansas, 1800–1840*. Fayetteville: University of Arkansas Press, 1993.
Cashin, Joan E. *Men and Women on the Southwestern Frontier*. New York: Oxford University Press, 1991.
Cayton, Andrew R. L. "The Contours of Power in a Frontier Town: Marietta, Ohio, 1788–1803." *Journal of the Early Republic* 6 (1986): 103–26.
The Center of a Great Empire: The Ohio Country in the Early Republic. Edited by Andrew R. L. Cayton and Stuart D. Hobbs. Athens: Ohio University Press, 2005.
Davis, James E. *Frontier Illinois: A History of the Trans-Appalachian Frontier*. Bloomington: Indiana University Press, 1998.
Dupre, Daniel. "Ambivalent Capitalists on the Cotton Frontier: Settlement and

Development in the Tennessee Valley of Alabama." *Journal of Southern History* 56 (1990): 215–40.

Fischer, David H., and James C. Kelly. *Bound Away: Virginia and the Westward Movement*. Charlottesville: University Press of Virginia, 2000.

Flores, Dan. "Bison Ecology and Bison Diplomacy: The Southern Plains from 1800–1850." *Journal of American History* 78 (1991–1992): 465–85.

Harrison, Lowell H. *Kentucky's Road to Statehood*. Lexington: University Press of Kentucky, 1992.

Kastor, Peter J. "Motives of Peculiar Urgency: Local Diplomacy in Louisiana, 1803–1821." *William & Mary Quarterly* 58 (3rd ser., 2001): 819–48.

McCormick, Virginia E., and Robert W. McCormick. *New Englanders on the Ohio Frontier: Migration and Settlement of Worthington, Ohio*. Kent, Ohio: Kent State University Press, 1998.

Moore, John Hebron. "The Cypress Lumber Industry of the Old Southwest and the Public Land Laws, 1803–1850." *Journal of Southern History* 49 (1983): 203–22.

Nelson, Paul David. "General Charles Scott, the Kentucky Mounted Militia, and the Northwest Indian Wars, 1784–1794." *Journal of the Early Republic* 6 (1986): 219–51.

Onuf, Peter S. *Statehood and Union: A History of the Northwest Ordinance*. Bloomington: Indiana University Press, 1987.

The Reminiscences of George Strother Gaines, 1805–1843. Edited by James P. Tate. Tuscaloosa: University of Alabama Press, 1998.

Shannon, Timothy J. "The Ohio Company and the Meaning of Opportunity in the American West, 1786–1795." *New England Quarterly* 64 (1991): 393–413.

Steward, Dick. *Frontier Swashbuckler: The Life and Legend of John Smith T*. Columbia: University of Missouri Press, 2000.

Sword, Wiley. *President Washington's Indian War: The Struggle for the Old Northwest, 1790–1795*. Norman: University of Oklahoma Press, 1985.

Taylor, Alan. "'A Kind of War': The Contest for Land on the Northeastern Frontier, 1750–1820." *William & Mary Quarterly* 46 (3rd ser., 1989): 3–26.

Van Alstyne, Richard W. *The Rising American Empire*. New York: Oxford University Press, 1960.

Weeks, William E. *Building the Continental Empire: American Expansion from the Revolution to the Civil War*. Chicago: Ivan R. Dee, 1996.

Weiman, David A. "Peopling the Land by Lottery? The Market in Public Lands and the Regional Differentiation of Territory on the Georgia Frontier." *Journal of Economic History* 51 (1991): 835–60.

Wyckoff, William. *The Developer's Frontier: The Making of the Western New York Landscape*. New Haven, Conn.: Yale University Press, 1988.

o. Exploration and the Fur Trade

Across the Continent: Jefferson, Lewis and Clark, and the Making of America. Edited by Douglas Seefeldt, Jeffrey L. Hantman, and Peter S. Onuf. Charlottesville: University Press of Virginia, 2005.

Ambrose, Stephen E. *Undaunted Courage: Meriwether Lewis, Thomas Jefferson, and the Opening of the American West.* New York: Simon & Schuster, 1996.

The First Description of Cincinnati and Other Ohio Settlements: The Travel Report of Johann Heckwelder (1792). Edited by Don H. Tolzmann. Lanham, Md.: University Press of America, 1988.

From Pittsburgh to the Rocky Mountains: Major Stephen Long's Expedition, 1819–1820. Edited by Maxine Benson. Golden, Colo.: Fulcrum, 1988.

Furtwangler, Albert. *Acts of Discovery: Visions of America in the Lewis and Clark Journals.* Urbana: University of Illinois Press, 1993.

Goodman, George J., and Cheryl A. Lawson. *Retracing Major Stephen H. Long's Expedition: The Itinerary and Botany.* Norman: University of Oklahoma Press, 1995.

Jones, Robert F., ed. *Astorian Adventure: The Journal of Alfred Seton, 1811–1815.* New York: Fordham University Press, 1993.

Lawson, Russell M. *The Land between the Rivers: Thomas Nuttall's Ascent of the Arkansas, 1819.* Ann Arbor: University of Michigan Press, 2004.

Reid, John Phillip. *Contested Empire: Peter Skene Ogden and the Snake River Expeditions.* Norman: University of Oklahoma Press, 2002.

Ronda, James P. *Astoria and Empire.* Lincoln: University of Nebraska Press, 1990.

———. "Dreams and Discoveries: Exploring the American West, 1760–1815." *William & Mary Quarterly* 46 (3rd ser., 1989): 145–64.

———. *Finding the West: Explorations with Lewis and Clark.* Albuquerque: University of New Mexico Press, 2001.

Slaughter, Thomas P. *Exploring Lewis and Clark: Reflections on Men and Wilderness.* New York: Alfred A. Knopf, 2003.

Weber, David J. *The Californios versus Jedediah Smith, 1826–1827.* Spokane, Wash.: Arthur A. Clark, 1990.

Wood, W. Raymond. *Prologue to Lewis and Clark: The Mackay and Evans Expedition.* Norman: University of Oklahoma Press, 2003.

4. Religious History

a. General Studies

Ahlstrom, Sydney E. *A Religious History of the American People.* New Haven, Conn.: Yale University Press, 1972.

Butler, Jon. *Awash in a Sea of Faith: Christianizing the American People.* Cambridge, Mass.: Harvard University Press, 1990.

Hatch, Nathan O. *The Democratization of American Christianity*. New Haven, Conn.: Yale University Press, 1989.

Heyrman, Christine L. *Southern Cross: The Beginnings of the Bible Belt*. New York: Alfred A. Knopf, 1998.

Religion in a Revolutionary Age. Edited by Ronald Hoffman and Peter J. Albert. Charlottesville: University Press of Virginia, 1994.

b. Church and State

Driesbach, Daniel L. *Thomas Jefferson and the Wall between Church and State*. New York: New York University Press, 2002.

Gerardi, Donald F. "Zephaniel Swift and Connecticut's Standing Order: Sceptism, Conservatism, and Religious Liberty in the Early Republic." *New England Quarterly* 67 (1994): 234–53.

McLoughlin, William G. *New England Dissent, 1630–1833: The Baptists and the Separation of Church and State*. Cambridge, Mass.: Harvard University Press, 1971.

c. Revivals and Reactions to Revivals

Bilhartz, Terry D. *Urban Religion and the Second Great Awakening: Church and Society in Early National Baltimore*. Rutherford, N.J.: Fairleigh Dickinson University Press, 1986.

Carwardine, Richard. *Transatlantic Revivalism: Popular Evangelicalism in Britain and America, 1790–1865*. Westport, Conn.: Greenwood Press, 1978.

Conkin, Paul. *Cane Ridge: America's Pentecost*. Madison: University of Wisconsin Press, 1990.

Eslinger, Ellen. *Citizens of Zion: The Social Origins of Camp Meeting Revivalism*. Knoxville: University of Tennessee Press, 1999.

Grasso, Christopher. "Skepticism and American Faith: Infidels, Converts, and Religious Doubt in the Early Nineteenth Century." *Journal of the Early Republic* 22 (2002): 465–508.

Hambrick-Stowe, Charles E. *Charles G. Finney and the Spirit of American Evangelicalism*. Grand Rapids, Mich.: W. B. Eerdmans, 1996.

Johnson, Curtis D. *Islands of Holiness: Rural Religion in Upstate New York, 1790–1860*. Ithaca, N.Y.: Cornell University Press, 1989.

Johnson, Paul E. *A Shopkeeper's Millennium: Society and Revivals in Rochester, New York, 1815–1837*. New York: Hill & Wang, 1978.

Johnson, Paul E., and Sean Wilentz. *The Kingdom of Matthias*. New York: Oxford University Press, 1994.

Juster, Susan. *Doomsayers: Anglo-American Prophecy in the Age of Revolution*. Philadelphia: University of Pennsylvania Press, 2003.

Kling, David W. *A Field of Divine Wonders: The New Divinity and Village Revivals in Northwestern Connecticut, 1792–1822*. University Park: Pennsylvania State University Press, 1993.

McLoughlin, William G. *Revivals, Awakenings, and Social Change in America, 1607–1977*. Chicago: University of Chicago Press, 1978.

Moorhead, James H. "Between Progress and Apocalypse: A Reassessment of Millennialism in American Religious Thought, 1800–1880." *Journal of American History* 71 (1984–1985): 524–42.

Potash, P. Jeffrey. *Vermont's Burned-Over District: Patterns of Community Development and Religious Activity, 1751–1850*. Brooklyn, N.Y.: Carlson Publishing, 1991.

Shiels, Richard D. "The Scope of the Second Great Awakening: Andover Massachusetts, as a Case Study." *Journal of the Early Republic* 5 (1985): 223–46.

d. Social Implications of Protestant Piety

Howe, Daniel Walker. "Church, State, and Education in the Young American Republic." *Journal of the Early Republic* 22 (2002): 1–24.

McCrossen, Alexis. *Holy Day, Holiday: The American Sunday*. Ithaca, N.Y.: Cornell University Press, 2000.

Rohrer, S. Scott. "Evangelism and Acculturation in the Backcountry: The Case of Wachovia, North Carolina, 1753–1830." *Journal of the Early Republic* 21 (2001): 199–229.

Schantz, Mark S. *Piety in Providence: Class Dimensions of Religious Experience in Antebellum Rhode Island*. Ithaca, N.Y.: Cornell University Press, 2000.

Shain, Barry A. *The Myth of American Individualism: The Protestant Origins of American Political Thought*. Princeton, N.J.: Princeton University Press, 1994.

West, John G., Jr. *The Politics of Revelation: Religion and Civic Life in the New Nation*. Lawrence: University Press of Kansas, 1996.

1. Evangelicalism and Missions

Berlin, George L. "Joseph S. C. F. Frey, the Jews, and Early Nineteenth-Century Millenarianism." *Journal of the Early Republic* 1 (1981): 27–49.

Bloch, Ruth H. *Visionary Republic: Millennial Themes in American Thought, 1756–1800*. Cambridge: Cambridge University Press, 1985.

Brown, Candy Gunther. *The Word in the World: Evangelical Writing, Publishing, and Reading in America, 1789–1880*. Chapel Hill: University of North Carolina Press, 2004.

Carter, Michael D. *Converting the Wasteplaces of Zion: The Maine Missionary Society (1807–1862)*. Wolfboro, N.H.: Longwood Academic, 1990.

Comforti, Joseph. "David Brainerd and the Nineteenth-Century Missionary Movement." *Journal of the Early Republic* 5 (1985): 309–29.

Grimshaw, Patricia. *Paths of Duty: American Missionary Wives in Nineteenth-Century Hawaii*. Honolulu: University of Hawaii Press, 1989.

Zwiep, Mary. *Pilgrim Path: The First Company of Women Missionaries to Hawaii*. Madison: University of Wisconsin Press, 1991.

2. Reform and Resistance to Reform

Abzug, Robert H. *Crumbling Cosmos: American Reform and the Religious Imagination*. New York: Oxford University Press, 1994.

Bailey, David T. *Shadow of the Church: Southwestern Evangelical Religion and the Issue of Slavery, 1783–1860*. Ithaca, N.Y.: Cornell University Press, 1985.

e. Theology

Bradbury, M. L. "British Apologetics in Evangelical Garb: Samuel Stanhope Smith's 'Lectures on the Evidences of the Christian Religion.'" *Journal of the Early Republic* 5 (1985): 177–195.

Guelzo, Allen C. "An Heir or Rebel? Charles Grandison Finney and the New England Theology." *Journal of the Early Republic* 17 (1997): 61–94.

Hatch, Nathan O. "The Christian Movement and the Demand for a Theology of the People." *Journal of American History* 67 (1980–1981): 546–67.

Noll, Mark A. *America's God: From Jonathan Edwards to Abraham Lincoln*. New York: Oxford University Press, 2002.

———. "The Irony of the Enlightenment for Presbyterians in the Early Republic." *Journal of the Early Republic* 5 (1985): 149–75.

Saillant, John. "Slavery and Divine Providence in New England Calvinism: The New Divinity and a Black Protest, 1775–1895." *New England Quarterly* 68 (1995): 584–608.

Sweeney, Douglas A. *Nathaniel Taylor, New Haven Theology, and the Legacy of Jonathan Edwards*. New York: Oxford University Press, 2003.

f. Deism

Walters, Kerry S. *Elihu Palmer's "Principles of Nature": Text and Commentary*. Wolfboro, N.H.: Longwood Academic, 1990.

———. *Rational Infidels: The American Deists*. Durango, Colo.: Longwood Academic, 1992.

g. Protestant Sects

1. Baptists

Buckley, Thomas E. "Evangelical Triumphant: The Baptists' Assault on the Virginia Glebes, 1780–1801." *William & Mary Quarterly* 45 (3rd ser., 1988): 33–69.

McLoughlin, William G. *Soul Liberty: The Baptist Struggle in New England, 1630–1833*. Hanover, N.H.: University Press of New England for Brown University Press, 1991.

2. Congregationalism

Field, Peter S. *The Crisis in the Standing Order: Clerical Intellectuals and Cultural Authority in Massachusetts, 1780–1833*. Amherst: University of Massachusetts Press, 1998.

Grossbart, Stephen R. "Seeking Divine Favor: Conversion and Church Admission in Eastern Connecticut, 1711–1832." *William & Mary Quarterly* 46 (3rd ser., 1989): 696–740.

Phillips, Joseph W. *Jedidiah Morse and New England Congregationalism*. New Brunswick, N.J.: Rutgers University Press, 1983.

Rabinowitz, Richard. *The Spiritual Self in Everyday Life: The Transformation of Personal Religious Experience in Nineteenth-Century New England*. Boston: Northeastern University Press, 1989.

Rohrer, James R. *Keepers of the Covenant: Frontier Missions and the Decline of Congregationalism, 1774–1818*. New York: Oxford University Press, 1995.

Sassi, Jonathan D. *A Republic of Righteousness: The Public Christianity of the Post-Revolutionary New England Clergy*. New York: Oxford University Press, 2001.

3. Methodism

Andrews, Dee E. *The Methodists and Revolutionary America: The Shaping of an Evangelical Culture*. Princeton, N.J.: Princeton University Press, 2000.

Hempton, David. *Methodism: Empire of the Spirit*. New Haven, Conn.: Yale University Press, 2005.

Lyerly, Cynthia L. *Methodism and the Southern Mind, 1770–1810*. New York: Oxford University Press, 1998.

Richey, Russell E. *Early American Methodism*. Bloomington: Indiana University Press, 1991.

Wigger, John H. *Taking Heaven by Storm: Methodism and the Rise of Popular Christianity in America*. New York: Oxford University Press, 1998.

Williams, William H. *The Garden of American Methodism: The Delmarva Peninsula, 1769–1820*. Wilmington, Del.: Scholarly Resources, 1984.

4. Quakers

Ingle, H. Larry. *Quakers in Conflict; The Hicksite Reformation*. Knoxville: University of Tennessee Press, 1986.

5. Shakers

Burns, Deborah E. *Shaker Cities of Peace, Love, and Union: A History of the Hancock Bishopric*. Hanover, N.H.: University Press of New England, 1993.

Sasson, Diane. *The Shaker Spiritual Narrative*. Knoxville: University of Tennessee Press, 1985.

6. Unitarianism

Arkin, Marc M. "The Force of Ancient Manners: Federalist Politics and the Unitarian Controversy Revisited." *Journal of the Early Republic* 22 (2002): 575–610.

Goodheart, Lawrence B., Richard O. Curry, and Elizur Wright Jr. "The Trinitarian Indictment of Unitarianism: The Letters of Elizur Wright Jr., 1826–1827." *Journal of the Early Republic* 3 (1983): 281–96.

Howe, Daniel Walker. *The Unitarian Conscience: Harvard Moral Philosophy, 1805–1861*. Cambridge, Mass.: Harvard University Press, 1970.

Wright, Conrad. *The Liberal Christians: Essays on American Unitarian History*. Boston: Beacon Press, 1970.

h. Catholicism

Clark, Emily, and Virginia M. Gould. "The Feminine Face of Afro-Catholicism in New Orleans, 1727–1852." *William & Mary Quarterly* 59 (3rd ser., 2002): 409–48.

Corey, Patrick W. "Republicanism within American Catholicism, 1785–1860." *Journal of the Early Republic* 3 (1983): 413–37.

Saunders, R. Frank, Jr. "Bishop John England of Charleston: Catholic Spokesman and Southern Intellectual, 1820–1842." *Journal of the Early Republic* 13 (1993): 301–22.

i. Judaism

"Jews and Protestants in Early America." Forum in *William & Mary Quarterly* 58 (3rd ser., 2001): 849–912.

Pencak, William. *Jews and Gentiles in Early America*. Ann Arbor: University of Michigan Press, 2005.

j. Islam

Gomez, Michael A. "Muslims in Early America." *Journal of Southern History* 60 (1994): 671–710.

k. Individual Religious Leaders

Berk, Stephen E. *Calvinism versus Democracy: Timothy Dwight and the Origins of American Evangelical Orthodoxy*. Hamden, Conn.: Archon, 1974.

Brown, Richard D. "'Not Only Extreme Poverty, but the Worst Kind of Orphanage': Lemuel Haynes and the Boundaries of Racial Tolerance on the Yankee Frontier, 1770–1820." *New England Quarterly* 61 (1988): 502–618.

Fitzmier, John. *New England's Moral Legislator: Timothy Dwight, 1752–1817*. Bloomington: Indiana University Press, 1998.

Haynes, Lemuel. *Black Preacher to White America: The Collected Writings of Lemuel Haynes, 1774–1833*. Edited by Richard Newman. Brooklyn, N.Y.: Carlson Publishing, 1990.

Imholt, Robert S. "Timothy Dwight, Federalist Pope of Connecticut." *New England Quarterly* 73 (2000): 386–411.

Kenny, Michael G. *The Perfect Law of Liberty: Elias Smith and the Providential History of America*. Washington, D.C.: Smithsonian Institution Press, 1994.

McLoughlin, William G. *Isaac Backus and the American Pietistic Tradition*. Boston: Little, Brown, 1967.

Moss, Richard J. *The Life of Jedidiah Morse: A Station of Peculiar Exposure*. Knoxville: University of Tennessee Press, 1995.

Peterson, Owen. *A Divine Discontent: The Life of Nathan S. S. Benan*. Macon, Ga.: Mercer University Press, 1986.

Rogers, James A. *Richard Furman: Life and Legacy*. Macon, Ga.: Mercer University Press, 1985.

Silverman, Kenneth. *Timothy Dwight*. New York: Twayne Publishers, 1969.

5. Cultural History

a. General Studies

Baatz, Simon. "Philadelphia Patronage: The Institutional Structure of Natural History in the New Republic, 1800–1833." *Journal of the Early Republic* 8 (1988): 111–38.

Garvan, Beatrice B. *Federal Philadelphia, 1785–1825: The Athens of the Western World*. Philadelphia: University of Pennsylvania Press, 1987.

The Italian Presence in American Art, 1769–1860. Edited by Irma B. Jaffe. New York: Fordham University Press; Rome: Istituto Della Enciclopedia Italiana, 1989.

Jaffee, David. "The Village Enlightenment in New England 1760–1820." *William and Mary Quarterly* 47 (3rd ser., 1990): 327–46.

Johnson, Paul E. *Sam Patch, the Famous Jumper*. New York: Hill & Wang, 2003.

Kett, Joseph F., and Patricia A. McClurg. *Book Culture in Post-Revolutionary Virginia*. Worcester, Mass.: American Antiquarian Society, 1984.

Rigal, Laura. *The American Manufactory: Art, Labor, and the World of Things in the Early Republic*. Princeton, N.J.: Princeton University Press, 1998.

Schofield, Robert E. *The Enlightened Joseph Priestley: A Study of His Life and Work from 1773–1804*. University Park: Pennsylvania State University Press, 2004.

Winterer, Caroline. "From Royal to Republican: The Classical Image in Early America." *Journal of American History* 91 (2005): 1264–90.

Zakim, Michael. *Ready-Made Democracy: A History of Men's Dress in the American Republic, 1760–1860*. Chicago: University of Chicago Press, 2003.

b. Architecture and City Planning

Arnebeck, Bob. *Through a Fiery Trial: Building Washington, 1790–1800*. Lanham, Md.: Madison Books, 1991.

Bibber, Joyce K. *A Home for Everyone: The Greek Revival and Maine Domestic Architecture*. Lanham, Md.: University Publishing Associates for the

American Association for State and Local History and Greater Portland Landmarks, 1998.

Buggeln, Gretchen. *Temples of Grace: The Material Transformation of Connecticut Churches, 1790–1840*. Hanover, N.H.: University Press of New England, 2003.

Bushman, Richard L. *The Refinement of America: Persons, Houses, Cities*. New York: Alfred A. Knopf, 1993.

Cohen, Jeffrey A., and Charles E. Brownell. *The Papers of Benjamin Henry Latrobe, Series II: The Architectural and Engineering Drawings*. New Haven, Conn.: Yale University Press, 1994.

Harris, C. M. "Washington's Gamble, L'Enfant: Dreams, Politics, Design, and the Founding of the Nation's Capital." *William & Mary Quarterly* 56 (3rd ser., 1999): 527–64.

Hutslar, Donald A. *The Architecture of Migration: Log Construction in the Ohio Country, 1750–1850*. Athens: Ohio University Press, 1986.

Lanier, Gabrielle M. *The Delaware Valley in the Early Republic: Architecture, Landscape, and Regional Identity*. Baltimore: The Johns Hopkins University Press, 2004.

Reps, John W. *Washington on View: The Nation's Capitol since 1790*. Chapel Hill: University of North Carolina Press, 1991.

Small, Nora Pat. *Beauty and Convenience: Architecture and Order in the New Republic*. Knoxville: University of Tennessee Press, 2003.

———. "The Search for a New Rural Order: Farmhouses in Sutton, Massachusetts, 1790–1830." *William & Mary Quarterly* 53 (3rd ser., 1996): 67–86.

Sutton, Robert K. *Americans Interpret the Parthenon: The Progression of Greek Revival Architecture from the East Coast to Oregon, 1800–1860*. Niwot: University Press of Colorado, 1992.

c. Arts (Painting, Engraving, and Sculpture)

Calvert, Karen. "Children in America: Family Portraiture, 1670–1810." *William & Mary Quarterly* 39 (3rd ser., 1982): 87–113.

Harding, Annelise. *John Lewis Krimmel: Genre Artist of the Early Republic*. Winterthur, Del.: Winterthur Publications, 1994.

Kornhauser, Elizabeth M. *Ralph Earl: The Face of the Young Republic*. New Haven, Conn.: Yale University Press, 1991.

Lawson, Karol Ann Reard. "An Inexhaustible Abundance: The National Landscape Depicted in American Magazines, 1780–1820." *Journal of the Early Republic* 12 (1992): 303–30.

Lovell, Margaretta M. *Art in a Season of Revolution: Painters, Artisans, and Patrons in Early America*. Philadelphia: University of Pennsylvania Press, 2004.

Lyons, Maura. *William Dunlap and the Construction of an American Art History*. Amherst: University of Massachusetts Press, 2005.

Miller, Lillian B. *In Pursuit of Fame: Rembrandt Peale, 1778–1860*. Washington, D.C.: National Portrait Gallery; Seattle: University of Washington Press, 1993.

Raher, Susan. "Benjamin West's Professional Endgame and the Historical Conundrum of William Williams." *William & Mary Quarterly* 59 (3rd ser., 2002): 821–64.

Richardson, Edgar P., Brooke Hindle, and Lillian B. Miller. *Charles Willson Peale and His World*. New York: Henry N. Abrams, 1983.

Rosand, David. *The Invention of Painting in America*. New York: Columbia University Press, 2004.

Sloat, Caroline F., ed. *Meet Your Neighbors: New England Portraits, Painters and Society, 1790–1850*. Sturbridge, Mass.: Old Sturbridge Village, 1992.

Staiti, Paul J. *Samuel F. B. Morse*. Cambridge: Cambridge University Press, 1989.

d. Letters

Arner, Robert D. *Dobson's Encyclopedia: The Publisher, Text, and Publication of America's First Britannica, 1789–1803*. Philadelphia: University of Pennsylvania Press, 1991.

Bennett, Maurice J. "A Portrait of the Artist in Eighteenth-Century America: Charles Brockden Brown's Memoirs of Stephen Calvert." *William & Mary Quarterly* 39 (3rd ser., 1982): 492–507.

Berthold, Dennis. "Charles Brockden Brown, *Edgar Huntly*, and the Origins of the American Picturesque." *William & Mary Quarterly* 41 (3rd ser., 1984): 67–84.

Buell, Lawrence. *New England Literary Culture: From the Revolution through the Renaissance*. New York: Cambridge University Press, 1986.

Cohen, Daniel A. "Arthur Mervyn and His Elders: The Ambivalence of Youth in the Early Republic." *William & Mary Quarterly* 43 (3rd ser., 1986): 361–80.

Conger, Danielle G. "Toward a Native American Nationalism: Joel Barlow's *The Vision of Columbus*." *New England Quarterly* 72 (1999): 558–76.

Crain, Patricia. *The Story of A: The Alphabetization of America from* The New England Primer *to* The Scarlet Letter. Stanford, Calif.: Stanford University Press, 2000.

Davidson, Cathy N. *Revolution and the Word: The Rise of the Novel in America*. New York: Oxford University Press, 2004.

Dowling, William C. *Literary Federalism in the Age of Jefferson: Joseph Dennie and the* Port Folio, *1801–1811*. Columbia: University of South Carolina Press, 1999.

———. *Poetry and Ideology in Revolutionary Connecticut*. Athens: University of Georgia Press, 1990.

Gardner, Jared. *Master Plots: Race and the Founding of an American Literature, 1787–1845*. Baton Rouge: Louisiana State University Press, 1998.

Giles, Paul. *Transatlantic Insurrections: British Culture in the Formation of American Literature, 1730–1860*. Philadelphia: University of Pennsylvania Press, 2001.

Gilmore, William J. *Reading Becomes a Necessity of Life: Material and Cultural Life in Rural New England, 1780–1835*. Knoxville: University of Tennessee Press, 1989.

Herman, Daniel J. "The Other Daniel Boone: The Nascence of a Middle-Class Hunter Hero, 1784–1860." *Journal of the Early Republic* 18 (1998): 429–57.

Kafer, Peter. *Charles Brockden Brown's Revolution and the Birth of the American Gothic*. Philadelphia: University of Pennsylvania Press, 2004.

Kelley, Mary. "Negotiating a Self: The Autobiography and Journals of Catharine Maria Sedgwick." *New England Quarterly* 66 (1993): 366–98.

Kirsch, George B. "Jeremy Belknap: Man of Letters in the Young Republic." *New England Quarterly* 54 (1981): 33–53.

Lawson, Russell M. *The American Plutarch: Jeremy Belknap and the Historian's Dialogue with the Past*. Westport, Conn.: Greenwood Press, 1998.

Lepore, Jill. *A Is for America: Letters and Other Characters in the Newly United States*. New York: Alfred A. Knopf, 2002.

Martin, Scott. *Killing Time: Leisure and Culture in Southeastern Pennsylvania, 1800–1850*. Pittsburgh: University of Pittsburgh Press, 1995.

Morris, Colin Jeffrey. "To 'Shut Out the World': Political Alienation and the Privatized Self in the Early Life and Works of Charles Brockden Brown, 1776–1794." *Journal of the Early Republic* 24 (2004): 609–39.

Mott, Frank Luther. *A History of American Magazines*. Vol. 1. Cambridge, Mass.: Harvard University Press, 1930.

Rice, Grantland S. *The Transformation of Authorship in America*. Chicago: University of Chicago Press, 1997.

Roth, Sara N. "The Mind of a Child: Images of African Americans in Early Juvenile Fiction." *Journal of the Early Republic* 25 (2005): 79–109.

Scheckel, Susan. *The Insistence of the Indian: Race and Nationalism in Nineteenth-Century American Culture*. Princeton, N.J.: Princeton University Press, 1997.

Wallace, James D. *Early Cooper and His Audiences*. New York: Columbia University Press, 1986.

Watts, Edward. *Writing and Postcolonialism in the Early Republic*. Charlottesville: University Press of Virginia, 1997.

Watts, Steven. "Masks, Morals, and the Market: American Literature and Early Capitalist Culture, 1780–1820." *Journal of the Early Republic* 6 (1986): 127–50.

——. *The Romance of Real Life: Charles Brockden Brown and the Origins of American Culture*. Baltimore: The Johns Hopkins University Press, 1995.

Zagarri, Rosemarie. *David Humphreys's "Life of Washington" with George Washington's "Remarks."* Athens: University of Georgia Press, 1991.

Ziff, Lazar. *Writing in the New Nation: Prose, Print, and Politics in the Early United States*. New Haven, Conn.: Yale University Press, 1991.

e. Museums

Hart, Sidney, and Ward, David C. "The Waning of the Enlightenment Ideal: Charles Willson Peale's Philadelphia Museum, 1790–1820." In *New Perspectives on Charles Willson Peale: A 250th Anniversary Celebration*, edited by Lillian B. Miller and David C. Ward. Pittsburgh: University of Pittsburgh Press, 1991, 219–35.

Orosz, Joel J. *Curators and Culture: The Museum Movement in America, 1740–1870*. Tuscaloosa: University of Alabama Press, 1990.

f. Music

Broyles, Michael. *"Music of the Highest Class": Elitism and Populism in Antebellum Boston*. New Haven, Conn.: Yale University Press, 1992.

The Complete Works of William Billings. Edited by Karl Kroeger. 4 vols. Boston: American Musicological Society and Colonial Society of Massachusetts, 1977–1990.

DeJong, Mary G. "'Both Pleasure and Profit': William Billings and the Uses of Music." *William & Mary Quarterly* 42 (3rd ser., 1985): 104–16.

Porter, Susan L. *With an Air Debonair: Musical Theatre in America, 1785–1815*. Washington, D.C.: Smithsonian Institution Press, 1991.

g. Theater

Dudden, Faye E. *Women in the American Theater: Actresses and Audiences, 1790–1870*. New Haven, Conn.: Yale University Press, 1994.

Hughes, Glenn. *A History of American Theatre 1700–1950*. New York: Samuel French, 1951.

V. BIOGRAPHICAL STUDIES

A. Multiple Biographies and Autobiographies

Cunningham, Noble E., Jr. *Jefferson vs. Hamilton: Confrontations That Shaped a Nation*. Boston: St. Martin's Press, 2000.

Higginbotham, Don. "Virginia's Trinity of Immortals: Washington, Jefferson, and Henry, and the Story of Their Fractured Relationships." *Journal of the Early Republic* 23 (2003): 521–43.

Kennedy, Roger G. *Burr, Hamilton, and Jefferson: A Study in Character*. New York: Oxford University Press, 2000.

Leibiger, Stuart. *Founding Friendship: George Washington, James Madison, and the Creation of the American Republic*. Charlottesville: University Press of Virginia, 1999.

The Noblest Minds: Fame, Honor, and the American Founding. Edited by Peter McNamarra. Lanham, Md.: Rowan & Littlefield, 1999.

Read, James H. *Madison, Hamilton, Wilson, and Jefferson*. Charlottesville: University Press of Virginia, 2000.

Recollections of the Early Republic: Selected Autobiographies. Edited by Joyce Appleby. Boston: Northeastern University Press, 1997.

Watson, Harry L. *Andrew Jackson vs. Henry Clay: Democracy and Development in Antebellum America*. Boston: Bedford/St. Martin's, 1998.

B. Major Public Figures

1. John Adams

Ellis, Joseph J. *Passionate Sage: The Character and Legacy of John Adams*. New York: W. W. Norton, 1993.

Ferling, John. *John Adams: A Life*. Knoxville: University of Tennessee Press, 1992.

Ferling, John, and Lewis E. Braverman. "John Adams's Health Reconsidered." *William & Mary Quarterly* 55 (3rd ser., 1998): 83–104.

Grant, James. *John Adam: Party of One*. New York: Farrar, Straus & Giroux, 2005.

John Adams and the Founding of the Republic. Edited by Richard A. Ryerson. Boston: Northeastern University Press, 2001.

Thompson, C. Bradley. *John Adams and the Spirit of Liberty*. Lawrence: University Press of Kansas, 1998.

Trees, Andrew S. "John Adams and the Problem of Virtue." *Journal of the Early Republic* 21 (2001): 393–412.

2. John Quincy Adams

Lewis, James E., Jr. *John Quincy Adams: Policy Maker for the Union*. Wilmington, Del.: Scholarly Resources, 2001.

Nagel, Paul C. *John Quincy Adams: A Public Life, a Private Life*. New York: Alfred A. Knopf, 1997.

Parsons, Lynn Hudson. *John Quincy Adams*. Madison, Wis.: Madison House, 1998.

Thompson, Robert R. "John Quincy Adams, Apostate: From 'Outrageous Federalist' to 'Republican in Exile,' 1801–1809." *Journal of the Early Republic* 12 (1992): 161–83.

Weeks, William E. *John Quincy Adams and American Global Empire*. Lexington: University Press of Kentucky, 1992.

3. John C. Calhoun

Bancroft, Frederic. *Calhoun and the South Carolina Nullification Movement*. Baltimore: The Johns Hopkins University Press, 1928.

Bartlett, Irving H. *John C. Calhoun: A Biography*. New York: W. W. Norton, 1993.

Niven, John. *John C. Calhoun and the Price of Union: A Biography*. Baton Rouge: Louisiana State University Press, 1988.

4. Henry Clay

Baxter, Maurice G. *Henry Clay and the American System*. Lexington: University Press of Kentucky, 1995.

Baxter, Maurice G. *Henry Clay the Lawyer*. Lexington: University Press of Kentucky, 2000.

Shankman, Kimberly C. *Compromise and Constitution: The Political Thought of Henry Clay*. Lanham, Md.: Lexington Books, 1999.

5. DeWitt Clinton

Cornog, Evan. *The Birth of Empire and the American Experience, 1769–1828*. New York: Oxford University Press, 1998.

Hanyan, Craig, and Mary L. Hanyan. *DeWitt Clinton and the Rise of the People's Men*. Montreal: McGill-Queen's University Press, 1996.

Siry, Steven E. *DeWitt Clinton and the American Political Economy: Sectionalism, Politics, and Republican Ideology, 1787–1828*. New York: Peter Lang, 1990.

6. Alexander Hamilton

Brookhiser, Richard. *Alexander Hamilton, American*. New York: Free Press, 1999.

Chernow, Ron. *Alexander Hamilton*. New York: Penguin, 2004.

Cooke, Jacob E. *Alexander Hamilton*. New York: Charles Scribner's Sons, 1982.

Flamenhaft, Harvey. *The Effective Republic: Administration and Constitution in the Thought of Alexander Hamilton*. Durham, N.C.: Duke University Press, 1992.

Hendrickson, Robert A. *The Rise and Fall of Alexander Hamilton*. New York: Van Nostrand Reinhold, 1981.

Kaplan, Lawrence S. *Alexander Hamilton: Ambivalent Anglophile*. Wilmington, Del.: SR Books, 2002.

Martin, Robert W. T. "Reforming Republicanism: Alexander Hamilton's Theory of Republican Citizenship and Press Liberty." *Journal of the Early Republic* 25 (2005): 21–46.

7. Andrew Jackson

Remini, Robert V. *The Life of Andrew Jackson*. New York: Harper & Row, 1988.

Wyatt-Brown, Betram. "Andrew Jackson's Honor." *Journal of the Early Republic* 17 (1997): 1–36.

8. John Jay

Stahr, Walter. *John Jay: Founding Father*. New York: Palgrave Macmillan, 2005.

9. Thomas Jefferson

Bedini, Silvio A. *Thomas Jefferson: Statesman of Science*. New York: Macmillan, 1990.

Bernstein, R. R. *Thomas Jefferson*. New York: Oxford University Press, 2003.

Burstein, Andrew. *The Inner Jefferson: Portrait of a Grieving Optimist*. Charlottesville: University Press of Virginia, 1995.

——. *Jefferson's Secrets: Death and Desire at Monticello*. New York: Perseus, 2005.

Cunningham, Noble E., Jr. *In Pursuit of Reason: The Life of Thomas Jefferson*. Baton Rouge: Louisiana State University Press, 1987.

Dorsey, Frank L. *Thomas Jefferson: Lawyer*. Charlottesville: University Press of Virginia, 1986.

Ellis, Joseph J. *American Sphinx: The Character of Thomas Jefferson*. New York: Alfred A. Knopf, 1997.

Gordon-Reed, Annette. *Thomas Jefferson and Sally Hemings: An American Controversy*. Charlottesville: University Press of Virginia, 1997.

Helo, Ari, and Peter S. Onuf. "Jefferson, Morality, and the Problem of Slavery." *William & Mary Quarterly* 61 (3rd ser., 2004): 583–614.

Kaplan, Lawrence S. *Thomas Jefferson: Westward the Course of Empire*. Wilmington, Del.: Scholarly Resources, 1998.

Kelsall, Malcolm. *Jefferson and the Iconography of Romanticism: Folk, Land, Culture and the Romantic Nation*. New York: St. Martin's Press, 1999.

Leiberger, Stuart. "Thomas Jefferson and the Missouri Crisis: An Alternative Interpretation." *Journal of the Early Republic* 17 (1997): 121–30.

Malone, Dumas. *Jefferson and His Time*. 6 vols. Boston: Little, Brown, 1948–1981.

Matthews, Richard K. *The Radical Politics of Thomas Jefferson: A Revisionist View*. Lawrence: University Press of Kansas, 1985.

Mayer, David N. *The Constitutional Thought of Thomas Jefferson*. Charlottesville: University Press of Virginia, 1994.

McDonald, Robert M. S. "Thomas Jefferson's Changing Reputation as Author of the Declaration of Independence: The First Fifty Years." *Journal of the Early Republic* 19 (1999): 169–95.

O'Brien, Connor C. *The Long Affair: Thomas Jefferson and the French Revolution, 1785–1800*. Chicago: University of Chicago Press, 1996.

Onuf, Peter S. "'To Declare Them a Free and Independent People': Race, Slavery, and National Identity in Jefferson's Thought." *Journal of the Early Republic* 18 (1998): 3–46.

——. *Jefferson's Empire: The Language of American Nationhood*. Charlottesville: University Press of Virginia, 2000.

Peterson, Merrill D. *Thomas Jefferson and the New Nation: A Biography*. New York: Oxford University Press, 1970.

——. *Thomas Jefferson: A Reference Biography*. New York: Charles Scribner's Sons, 1986.

Quimby, Lee. "Thomas Jefferson: The Virtue of Aesthetics and the Aesthetics of Virtue." *American Historical Review* 87 (1982): 337–56.

Risjord, Norman K. *Thomas Jefferson*. Madison, Wis.: Madison House, 1994.

Sally Hemings and Thomas Jefferson: History, Memory, and Civic Culture. Edited by Jan E. Lewis and Peter S. Onuf. Charlottesville: University Press of Virginia, 1999.

Sears, Louis Martin. *Jefferson and the Embargo*. Durham, N.C.: Duke University Press, 1927.

Sloan, Herbert E. *Principle and Interest: Thomas Jefferson and the Problem of Debt*. New York: Oxford University Press, 1995.

Smith, Daniel Scott. "Population and Political Ethics: Thomas Jefferson's Demography of Generations." *William & Mary Quarterly* 56 (3rd ser., 1999): 591–612.

Thomas Jefferson and the Education of a Citizen. Edited by James Gilreath. Hanover, N.H.: University Press of New England, 1999.

"Thomas Jefferson and Sally Hemings Redux." Forum in *William & Mary Quarterly* 58 (3rd ser., 2001): 121–210.

Tucker, Robert W., and David C. Hendrickson. *Empire of Liberty: The Statecraft of Thomas Jefferson*. New York: Oxford University Press, 1990.

Wilson, Douglas L. "Jefferson vs. Hume." *William & Mary Quarterly* 46 (3rd ser., 1989): 49–70.

10. James Madison

Banning, Lance. *The Sacred Fire of Liberty: James Madison and the Founding of the Federal Republic*. Ithaca, N.Y.: Cornell University Press, 1995.

James Madison and the American Nation 1751–1836: An Encyclopedia. Edited by Robert A. Rutland. New York: Simon & Schuster, 1994.

"The Madison Moment." Forum in *William & Mary Quarterly* 59 (3rd ser., 2002): 865–956.

Matthews, Richard K. *If Men Were Angels: James Madison and the Heartless Empire of Reason*. Lawrence: University Press of Kansas, 1995.

McCoy, Drew R. *The Last of the Fathers: James Madison and the Republican Legacy*. Cambridge: Cambridge University Press, 1989.

Rakove, Jack N. *James Madison and the Creation of the American Republic*. Glenview, Ill.: Scott, Foresman/Little, Brown Higher Education, 1990.

Rutland, Robert A. *The Presidency of James Madison*. Lawrence: University Press of Kansas, 1990.

Sheldon, Garrett Ward. *The Political Philosophy of James Madison*. Baltimore: The Johns Hopkins University Press, 2000.

11. John Marshall

Hobson, Charles F. *The Great Chief Justice: John Marshall and the Rule of Law*. Lawrence: University Press of Kansas, 1996.

Johnson, Herbert A. *The Chief Justiceship of John Marshall, 1801–1835*. New York: Columbia University Press, 1997.

Stites, Francis. *John Marshall: Defender of the Constitution*. Boston: Little, Brown, 1981.

12. Gouverneur Morris

Adams, William Howard. *Gouverneur Morris: An Independent Life*. New Haven, Conn.: Yale University Press, 2003.

Brookhiser, Richard. *Gentleman Revolutionary. Gouverneur Morris: The Rake Who Wrote the Constitution*. New York: Free Press, 2003.

Miller, Melanie Randolph. *Envoy to the Terror: Gouverneur Morris and the French Revolution*. Dulles, Va.: Potomac Books, 2005.

13. George Washington

Alden, John R. *George Washington: A Biography*. Baton Rouge: Louisiana State University Press, 1984.

Burns, James M., and Susan Dunn. *George Washington*. New York: Times Books, 2004.

Brookhiser, Richard. *Founding Father: Rediscovering George Washington*. New York: Free Press, 1996.

Dalzell, Robert F., Jr., and Lee Baldwin. *George Washington's Mount Vernon: At Home in Revolutionary America*. New York: Oxford University Press, 1998.

Ellis, Joseph J. *His Excellency*. New York: Alfred A. Knopf, 2004.

Ferling, John E. *The First of Men: A Life of George Washington*. Knoxville: University of Tennessee Press, 1988.

Higginbotham, Don. *George Washington: Uniting a Nation*. Lanham, Md.: Rowman & Littlefield, 2002.

Rasmussen, William M. S., and Robert S. Tilton. *George Washington: The Man behind the Myths*. Charlottesville: University Press of Virginia, 1999.

Smith, Richard Norton. *Patriarch: George Washington and the New American Nation*. Boston: Houghton Mifflin, 1993.

Wiencek, Henry. *An Imperfect God: George Washington, His Slaves, and the Creation of America*. New York: Farrar, Straus & Giroux, 2003.

Wills, Garry. *Cincinnatus: George Washington and the Enlightenment: Images of Power in Early America*. Garden City, N.Y.: Doubleday, 1984.

14. Daniel Webster

Fuess, Claude Moore. *Daniel Webster*. 2 vols. Boston: Little, Brown, 1930.

Remini, Robert V. *Daniel Webster: The Man and His Times*. New York: W. W. Norton, 1997.

VI. DIGITAL SECONDARY SOURCES

The best way to seek secondary materials on the Web is to go to a search engine and type in the subject you wish to learn about. The two leading search engines are google.com for basic information of the sort one would seek in an encyclopedia and scholar.google.com for more in-depth explorations of a subject. Google has announced that it is embarking on an ambitious program to digitalize the collections of some of the larger libraries in the country. When this project is completed, most of the secondary works pertaining to the early Republic will be available online. In addition, the American Council of Learned Societies has launched a History E-Book Project designed to make roughly 800 scholarly monographs available online. Though reading a book online requires adjustment for those used to printed books, electronic searching is much easier and quicker than consulting an index and then finding the appropriate entry on a printed page.

To date, most digital publishing of books has been confined to scanning works already in print. With the establishment of JSTOR in the mid-1990s, the leading scholarly journals have started publishing online at the same time they appear in hard copy, making themselves simultaneously available in both formats to library and individual subscribers. Many libraries have also acquired digital versions of the back files of the journals carried by JSTOR. For the purposes of exploring the history of the early Republic, the most significant journals available online to subscribing libraries are the *Journal of the Early Republic*, the *American Historical Review*, the *Journal of American History*, the *William & Mary Quarterly* (3rd ser.), the *New England Quarterly*, and the *Journal of Southern History*.

To date, relatively little material has been published exclusively in electronic format. The American Memory website of the Library of Congress does contain some secondary commentary on the American presidents whose papers it has digitalized. And several years ago, the American Historical Association with Columbia University Press launched the Gutenberg-E Project to bring out prize-winning dissertations electronically. But to date, only 11 have appeared, and none deal with the early republican period. It is possible that the digital publication of original materials will expand with time, but as of this writing that moment still seems to be on the distant horizon. Those wishing to stay abreast of online resources in the field would be well advised to monitor the postings on H-SHEAR@H-NET.MSU.EDU.

About the Author

Richard Buel Jr. was educated at Amherst College (B.A., 1955) and Harvard University (Ph.D., 1962). He taught early American history at Wesleyan University, Middletown, Connecticut, for 40 years prior to his retirement in 2002. For 21 years between 1970 and 1991, he was an associate editor of *History and Theory*. He is the author of five books on revolutionary America and the early Republic: *Securing the Revolution: Ideology in American Politics, 1789–1815* (1972); *Dear Liberty: Connecticut's Mobilization for the Revolutionary War*, with Joy Day Buel (1980); *The Way of Duty: A Woman and Her Family in Revolutionary America* (1984); *In Irons: Britain's Naval Supremacy and the American Revolutionary Economy* (1998); and *America on the Brink: How the Political Struggle over the War of 1812 Almost Destroyed the Young Republic* (2005). Fellowships awarded by the American Council of Learned Societies, the National Endowment for the Humanities, and the John S. Guggenheim Memorial Foundation, along with the generous sabbatical leave policy of Wesleyan University, supported the research and writing of his books. He is a past president of the New England Historical Association and is the recipient of an emeritus faculty fellowship awarded by the Andrew W. Mellon Foundation.